top
WATER

top WATER

FLY-FISHING ALASKA, THE LAST FRONTIER

TROY LETHERMAN

and

TONY WEAVER

THE COUNTRYMAN PRESS
WOODSTOCK, VERMONT

Library of Congress Cataloging-in-Publication Data
Letherman, Troy.
  Top water : fly fishing Alaska, the last frontier / Troy Letherman
  and Tony Weaver.— 1st ed.
    p. cm.
  ISBN 0-88150-616-8
  1. Fly fishing—Alaska. 2. Fishes—Alaska. I. Weaver, Tony.
  II. Title.
SH467.L46 2004
799.12'4'09798—dc22   2004045534

Book and jacket design by Eugenie S. Delaney
Maps by Paul Woodward, © The Countryman Press
Fly photos in Appendix © Richard F. Johnson
Illustrations by Tony Weaver and Dave Laymon
Front jacket photograph: Jake Jordan, a well-respected guide,
    fishing on the Tsiu River in Southeast Alaska; © Tony Weaver
Rear jacket photograph: A steelheader fishes a run in a tea-colored
    southeast stream (detail); © Brian O'Keefe

Published by The Countryman Press, P.O. Box 748, Woodstock,
Vermont 05091

Distributed by W. W. Norton & Company, Inc., 500 Fifth Avenue,
New York, NY 10010

Printed in Spain

10 9 8 7 6 5 4 3 2 1

contents

acknowledgments

THANKING EVERYONE that played a part in the completion of *TopWater* would inevitably stretch this binding even farther. Suffice to say that the authors owe considerable thanks to Kermit Hummel, Jennifer Thompson, and the rest of the folks at The Countryman Press for their support and their tireless efforts on our behalf.

Also particularly worthy of thanks are the talented photographers, authors, and other professionals who directly contributed their time, work, or valued opinions to the project. We feel extremely fortunate to feature Brian O'Keefe's incomparable images on many of the following pages, as well as the fly photography of Alaska's own Rich Johnson, the illustrations of David Laymon, and additional photography from Daryl Pederson, E. Donnall Thomas Jr., Tyson O'Connell, René Limeres, Greg Syverson, Tom Cappiello, and Jim Teeny. Jake Jordan, Jim Repine, and Greg Thomas are also on the list of those whom we owe more than can probably ever be repaid, both for their friendship and the fly-fishing wisdom they are so willing to impart. Lastly, René Limeres, Greg Thomas, and Marcus Weiner deserve special mention for taking the time to read and comment on portions of the manuscript.

The professionals at the Alaska Department of Fish and Game (ADF&G) provided a good deal of technical information and recent research to the authors, often going far out of their way to help. To Barry Stratton, Jason Dye, Fred DeCicco, John Burr, Len Schwarz, and Tom Brookover—all of whom are fishermen as well as fisheries biologists—we'd like to express our sincere gratitude for their assistance, and for the work they do to keep Alaska's fisheries wild and thriving.

Doug's Bugs and Umpqua Feather Merchants deserve recognition as well, as the great majority of the flies presented in the appendix to this work are available commercially and were provided for Rich Johnson's photographic work. John Staser at Mountain View Sports in Anchorage also provided a handful of local patterns from his shop's fly bins.

Obviously, none of this would have been possible without having access to Alaska's wonderful remote fisheries, and for that, we're heavily indebted to the host of lodge owners, air taxi operators, and guides who've always made sure we found fish. Some of the many who offered their services as well as additional information gleaned from their vast experience were Doug Brewer of Alaska West Air, George Davis, Mark Glassmaker, Laurence John at the Great Alaska Adventure Lodge, Brian Kraft at the Alaska Sportsman's Lodge, Tony Sarp at Katmai Lodge, Curt Trout, Kirk Wilson, Jim Young, John Wilson at Lake Marie Lodge, and the folks at Saltery Lake Lodge on Kodiak Island.

We'd certainly like to recognize the innumerable fly-fishers, fly-tiers, and authors who came before us as well,

BRIAN O'KEEFE

Sockeye doubles.

Setting the hook on a milling coho salmon.

though the sheer length of that list precludes listing them individually. Almost all knowledge is cumulative, especially in matters of science, art, and fly-fishing, and without their commitment, innovation, and the works they published, there would have been little for us to write.

Also, both authors owe considerable debts to their families. Tony Weaver would like to thank his father for always taking him fishing and his mother for always encouraging him to follow his dreams. Troy Letherman owes his sons—Cody, Bailey, and Conor—and his wife, Sally, far more than he'd care to admit for their never-ending support. He'd also like to thank Joe and Jennifer Anderson and Dave and Alison Doucet for their friend-

ship and for providing the excuse to occasionally escape the office, and last but definitely not least Skip Wittey, who was more than willing to make the long drive to the Anchor and back to accommodate a quick steelhead getaway.

The list could go on, but in the interest of at least a little brevity, we'll leave it at that. Suffice to say some were left off this list at their own request, probably for fear the publicity would cause the downfall of their secret fishing holes, and others were undoubtedly forgotten. To the latter, we both apologize and thank you. To the former, we pity—and completely understand—you.

introduction

Fly-Fishing the Last Frontier

AT FIRST DESCRIPTION, much of Alaska seems as far-fetched as any realm sprung from the pen of Jonathan Swift. Only instead of Lilliput, there's the tea-colored water, the overwhelming old growth, and the misty coastlines of Southeast. Glaciers the size of states sprawl across the landscape, snowcapped peaks look down on the emerald carpet of coastal forests, and pristine rivers flow as veins of life in an environment humans can only marvel at. There's no Brobdingnag but there are the fjordlike incisions of the Wood-Tikchik Lake system, the wild and desolate Lost Coast, the towering mountains and massive ice sheets of the Alaska, Wrangell–St. Elias, and Aleutian Ranges.

Wariness to words is understandable, perhaps even advisable, in this hyperbole-driven age, where *oversell* seems to be the marketing mantra. But what you've heard of the grandeur and sheer magnificence of this vast state is more than true. There are few places in the world where you might find such enormity unchecked by what some insist on calling progress; and nowhere else will you find civilization and the wild in such proximity.

Unfortunately, some would have fly-fishers believe Alaska is fished out, that there is nowhere left to discover new or uncrowded water. No other statement about the state could be quite so ludicrous. This sort of thing is usually uttered by those trying to sell high-dollar expeditions to Kamchatka or those whose annual Alaska angling has never extended beyond the Brooks River, the Kenai, or Lower Talarik Creek. No one with much experience in the Last Frontier would ever commit such verbal incontinence. Three million lakes, three thousand rivers, and innumerable small streams: Water is not in short supply in the Great Land. Nor are game fish. Nearly all of those fresh waters are filled with fish. Five species of Pacific salmon return to the state in strong, healthy

Sunset over a Prince of Wales Island estuary.

DARYL PEDERSON

BRIAN O'KEEFE

TOP: *Sockeye jumpers.*

ABOVE: *Fly boxes ready for both Alaska's trout and salmon.*

RIGHT: *Iceberg.*

populations. Wild rainbow trout have staked out their most critical and productive North American habitats. Steelhead return widely—to more than two thousand streams in Southeast alone and who knows how many on the desolate Alaska Peninsula or the still-unexplored Lost Coast. Dolly Varden, Arctic char, lake trout, grayling, northern pike, and even the exotic sheefish call Alaska waters home. Fly-fishing deserves such a home.

Planning a foray into this wilderness can be taxing, and even the most well-traveled anglers can make mistakes, something the Last Frontier often doesn't forgive. Still, this book is not intended to be a guidebook. There are already a few of those (we recommend René Limeres's *Alaska Fishing: The Complete Guide to Hundreds of Prime Fishing Spots on Rivers, Lakes, and the Coast*). Instead,

this book is the fly-fisher's guide—to the state, to the sport, to the state's sport fish. Some may think the chapters are a little too slanted toward the biology and life history of the individual species of game fish. We believe, however, that anglers should come to know their quarry as intimately as possible. The most successful always do. And if you truly understand a fish—its habits and tendencies, its likes and dislikes, its needs—there's no reason for a guidebook. The best fly-anglers can go anywhere, be placed on any piece of water, and find fish.

Thus, what we've strived for is balance.

No one likes to be told how to fish—and no one should expect to be. Where something may be particular to Alaska, we've mentioned the techniques and angling tactics that have worked well in the past.

DARYL PEDERSON

Where an application used to success in the Lower Forty-eight has significance here, we've mentioned that.

We've given a few suggestions on good flies for each of the state's game fish—both in how to design successful patterns and some specific flies that can be purchased. Lastly, we've handed out a few hints, and sometimes, much more than that, on some of the best places in the state where good fishing for a species can be found, always mindful of the fly-fisher's penchant for choosing quality of experience over quantity of fish. And unless noted otherwise, all the fish we mention here are wild. Alaska does have a thriving hatchery program—for salmon, obviously, but also for rainbow trout, Arctic char, and others. While this creates much public opportunity, usually near population centers, we won't pretend anyone would ever want to undertake the expense of an Alaska trip to fish for hatchery trout—not when the state is one of the planet's last great strongholds for wild fish.

In the end, fly-fishing the Last Frontier can come wrapped in simplicity enough to make Thoreau proud. It can also involve long flights by floatplane or helicopter, weeklong float trips, and other extensive logistical necessities. Once on the stream, however, fly-fishing never changes, rewarding persistence above all else. Perhaps that's the beauty of our sport, that we can travel anywhere in the world—to the sprawling wilderness of little-visited Northwest Alaska, to the myriad coastal streams of the Aleutian chain, to the boreal forests of the isle-dotted Southeast—and find what we are looking for. That it might in the end not be fish after all should remain our little secret.

LEFT: *Casting to staging silvers in the salt.*

ABOVE: *On a mother ship voyage through Southeast Alaska's Inside Passage, fly-anglers are often afforded a little taste of the good life.*

Fighting a Southeast
Alaska steelhead.

RIGHT: A wild steelhead.

steelhead

THERE IS SOMETHING UNIQUE, something primal, maybe even something cathartic about a first steelhead. No one ever forgets the experience. Just listen to a devout steelheader speak of his or her true religion and you'll soon hear sheer reverence spilling forth: The quest for one of fresh water's greatest game fish will undoubtedly turn epic in nature. That first tug on the line, surprising in its suddenness. The rod alive, dancing to an imperceptible tune. And at the end, after all the aerial acrobatics and the line-burning runs, the ultimate prize awaits, a sea-run beauty cradled in the most appreciative of hands, a fly hanging from the corner of its mouth.

This first streamside rendezvous between angler and steelhead makes deep tracks in the memory. Coal-black spots shimmer beneath a brilliant silver flank. Clinging sea lice and translucent fins confirm a recent freshwater return, while the

5

musculature at the base of the caudal fin tells of the power to roam seas, ascend streams, and smoke titanium reels. The compounding effects are numbing, much more so than the rain or late-autumn cold. One last look prompts thoughts of the transoceanic wanderings that preceded this moment. Then, with a thrash of its tail, the steelhead is gone and an angler's life is forever altered, every nuance of that first meeting to return one day like the yearning for a long-lost love. As the first-timer will soon discover, every steelhead is like the first. Every one is recorded, fawned over, and released to the same thrill and with the same sense of spiritual harmony. Shipwrecked on these shores of sea-run chrome, fly-fishers are powerless to prevent the fever that inevitably grips their minds. Anglers remember their first fish. Steelhead anglers remember their one hundred and their first. These are fish that offer no middle ground.

The great steelhead rivers, engendering considerable mystique on their own, tend to be as captivating as the fish themselves. In fact, all throughout the Pacific Northwest, the two are as indelibly linked as moms, baseball, and apple pie are in the rest of the country. What began with cane rods and silk lines on the Eel in the 1890s is exactly what led Zane Grey to immortalize "the cool green forests, the dark shade, the thundering rapids, and the wonderful steelhead trout of the Rogue." That same power, manifest in both river and fish, sent Joe Brooks deep into the legendary Skeena system. And it propels anglers into lonely locales they know only by names like Kispiox, Dean, Nass, or Thompson, chasing fish that, for reasons the high seas neglect to share, might not even be there. Soaked through by autumn rains, chilled to the bone, rich in some ways and probably nearing bankruptcy in others, they knock the ice from their guides and promise themselves just one more cast.

In the end, it may not be Homer, but the steelhead anglers of today continue on this odyssey of equal,

DARYL PEDERSON

The Steelhead Trout
(Oncorhynchus mykiss)

Of all the rainbow trout roaming fresh waters from the southern drainages of Alaska's Kuskokwim River to the Sierra Madre Occidental in Mexico, anadromous forms occur in only two subspecies: the coastal rainbow (*Oncorhynchus mykiss irideus*) and the redband trout (*Oncorhynchus mykiss gairdneri*) of the Columbia River basin. Alaska's rainbows, both stream-resident and sea-run, are of the coastal rainbow subspecies, which scientists generally consider the most evolutionarily advanced of the group.

But how to differentiate between anadromous and entirely freshwater-dwelling coastal rainbows? After all, it's never easy to explain to the uninformed the precise characteristics that make a steelhead a steelhead. The standard reply? *A steelhead is a rainbow trout that spends part of its life in the sea.* Yet while this is taxonomically correct, there can also be differences in shape, color, and overall appearance between the two, differences that are dictated both by diet and by the divergent nature of their lifestyles.

First, though, are the numerous similarities. Unlike the species of Pacific salmon, also members of the genus *Oncorhynchus*, both stream-resident and anadromous coastal rainbows are heavily spotted above and below the lateral line. Spots are small and irregularly scattered over the body, head, and on the dorsal and caudal fins, the latter of which is squarish and often shows only a slight fork. In most, the black coloration of the spots fades over the lateral line to a silver-white coloration, blending more to white on the stomach. Coastal rainbows also have white leading edges on the anal, pectoral, and pelvic fins, and the color of their backs can range from blue-green to olive. The signature band of color along the lateral line and on the cheek can vary from pink to dark

if not mythical stature. Like their forebears, Alaska steelheaders can still stumble across wild fish in undiscovered water. Of course, there are famous Last Frontier destinations, too. The Anchor, the Situk, and Kodiak's Karluk River immediately come to mind, each synonymous with the species in the forty-ninth state, and for good reason. Still to be fully realized, however, are the many runs returning to the wild and desolate Lost Coast area south of Cordova, to the tea-stained coastal rivers of Southeast, and to the Alaska Peninsula's myriad streams. Bears, bald eagles, and black-tailed deer, timbered valleys, volcanoes, and glaciers the size of states shape this heroic landscape. Here, not only do the fish remain large, aggressive, and wild, but they're also found among a setting without blemish and in waters still pristine. As any maven of sea-run rainbows will tell you, it is a milieu worthy of the steelhead.

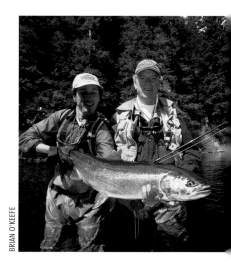

BRIAN O'KEEFE

A Southeast Alaska spring steelhead.

red, though, unlike cutthroat trout, coastal rainbows lack a red slash on the underjaw. While most resident rainbows display the rosy tint throughout their adult lives, steelhead begin to exhibit a similar stripe only with the onset of the spawning condition. With reproductive duties completed, the blush of pink-and-red coloration that adorns a spawning steelhead gradually returns to the more characteristic chrome the fish display during their ocean sojourn.

For the most part, though, the differences between sea-run and resident rainbows are such that they can be easily discerned with an attentive eye. Basically, steelhead are sleek and streamlined in shape, more so than most resident rainbows. Also, the dominant color of steelhead is silver. The colors and spots expected of a rainbow are there, only they appear to be emanating from beneath an overriding sheen. This silver gradually fades as the steelhead spend more time in fresh water and the spawning period approaches a period in which they become difficult to distinguish from resident rainbows. Nevertheless, some rainbows from the big lakes, particularly drainages of the Iliamna and Naknek systems, are very similar to their oceangoing cousins and display the same shimmering bright sides.

The steelhead diet, like that of resident rainbow trout, consists primarily of aquatic and terrestrial invertebrates, salmon eggs, fish, and, for the oceangoing steelhead, squid. Returning steelhead are believed to feed rarely or very little, though spawning steelhead have been documented with food in their stomachs, indicating that feeding does continue to some degree after the fish enter fresh water. The size of the species varies among populations and depends on a variety of factors, including length of time at sea and the type and availability of food. Genetics must play at least some part, too. For example, the steelhead of the Skeena system in British Columbia are noted for their massive proportions and are generally considered to be the largest of the species, while other drainages regularly produce fish of much smaller dimensions. In Alaska, the Situk River near Yakutat is home to seven of the state's ten largest sport-caught steelhead on record and produces fish over 36 inches in length every year.

LIFE HISTORY

Alaska's steelhead trout lead a life that's anything but mundane. While resident rainbows might never leave a small section of flowing water and coastal cutthroats take only short journeys into the salt to feed, steelhead can spend half their lives or more at sea, far from any shore, roaming thousands of miles in the open waters of the North Pacific. There they must evade any number of large marine predators, including seals, sea lions, sharks, and killer whales, before eventually reaching sexual maturity and returning to their natal fresh waters to spawn.

Different steelhead populations vary in the number of years juveniles spend in fresh water before smolting and going to sea, the number of years then spent in the ocean before sexual maturation, the time when spawning runs from the ocean into rivers are initiated, and the time of spawning itself. Also, some populations of steelhead travel great distances from salt water into the upper reaches of freshwater drainages to spawn, while others move only a few miles upstream. And the way they do it differs as well. Witness the steelhead within the Hanagita River in the upper Copper River drainage. They migrate from the Gulf of Alaska, through the Copper River delta and up the river of the same name, continuing on to the Chitina then Tebay Rivers and finally to their spawning locations on the Hanagita—all by early fall. This is unlike other documented Copper River tributary stocks that might have similar distances to travel, such as Tazlina and Gulkana steelhead; as those fish in spring continue to migrate significant distances to spawning areas after overwintering in fresh water.

The example of Hanagita steelhead and such close neighbors as the Gulkana stock raises the hypothesis that these sea-run rainbow trout have developed their differing migration patterns through basic evolutionary realities. In all likelihood, the timing of the Hanagita run is late summer or early fall based upon the nature of the final migration: Between the confluence of the Tebay and Chitina Rivers and Hanagita Lake, pre-spawning steelhead gain nearly 2,000 feet of elevation while traveling a mere 20 miles. Along this stretch of heavy whitewater, the stream gradient may be as steep as 375 feet per mile of river. It is possible and perhaps even probable that Hanagita-bound steelhead thus take advantage of lower flows in late summer and fall to ascend the river, rather than making their final migration to the spawning beds in the spring when snow and glacial melt combine to produce significantly higher water flows.

While there are undeniable differences from one population to the next, Alaska's steelhead are also connected by certain similarities in life history. For instance, each spring thousands of 6-inch steelhead smolt begin their journeys to the ocean. Of every hundred that depart for the salt, less than ten will return to spawn. And regardless of when they enter fresh water, Alaska's steelhead all spawn at the same time of year. In fact, every species of wild rainbow trout has a hereditary basis for spawning in the spring when water temperatures are rising. The time of spawning is usually initiated when the daily temperature exceeds 42 to 44 degrees, regardless of geographic area. In Alaska, that means spawning usually commences from about mid-April through May and June.

Steelhead return to spawn at sizes ranging from about 24 inches and 5 pounds to 40 inches or more, and during the spawning period a robust buck may spawn with sev-

BRIAN O'KEEFE

eral females. Steelhead are trout, which means that they can survive the reproductive cycle to spawn again. In fact, most steelhead over 28 inches in length are repeat spawners, though survival to second spawning in most populations is less than 10 percent. A host of natural factors can affect post-spawning mortality, like weather patterns and the amount of predation. However, many of Alaska's steelhead stocks return for subsequent spawnings at a higher rate than their southern cousins. According to samples taken intermittently since 1954 by the ADF&G on Anchor River stocks, the estimated number of repeat spawners for the drainage has varied from 3.5 to 33 percent for any given year, averaging 18.8 percent since 1954. In the spring of 1996, an ADF&G mark-recapture experiment on the Karluk River estimated that spawning survival for that drainage was 36 percent, while in 1994 repeat spawners accounted for 59 percent of a Situk River sample population.

After the mating rituals are complete, steelhead kelts

Returning to the mother ship after a day of searching for steelhead in the estuaries and unnamed streams of Southeast Alaska.

will slowly begin to migrate downstream toward the enriching saltwater environment, where they will replenish bodies ragged from the trials of the spawning beds. Lost fats are restored, energy is returned, and adult specimens migrate to the feeding regions of their first ocean migrations. While the spawning wounds are healing in the adults, the eggs that were deposited deep in the gravel during spring quickly develop into alevins or "sac-fry." These tiny fish gradually absorb the yolk sac and work their way to the surface. By midsummer, fry emerge from the gravel, minus the yolk sac, and seek refuge along stream margins and in other protected areas. Tremendous numbers of eggs and fry are killed or washed from the stream each year, but by autumn, 2- to 3-inch steelhead populate habitat that hopefully will carry them through the first winter. Generally, the juvenile steelhead will remain in the parent stream for about three years before out-migrating to salt water. In warmer climates like the coastal rivers of California, fry may begin the saltwater migration as early as in their first or second year; however, the colder climate and slower growth rates found in Alaska's steelhead environs typically yield fry that are bound to the stream for a longer stretch of time, some as long as four years.

Within a one-, two-, or sometimes three-year period at sea, Alaska steelhead will have moved hundreds of miles or more from the parent stream. Some fish can spend up to five years roaming the vast migration corridors of the open ocean, but most steelhead return within three years. There is actually very little information on the ocean migration of Alaska steelhead. However, large numbers of steelhead are intercepted in high-seas fisheries and caught in net fisheries off the coast of Japan, and undoubtedly many are of Alaska origin. Also, the tracking of marked fish has shown that steelhead roam up to thousands of miles in the Pacific Ocean before returning to their natal streams to spawn.

During their life at sea, steelhead eat a variety of foods, including squid, other fish, and crustaceans (amphipods). They grow quickly because of both the abundance of food and the unrestricted habitat. Studies show that smolts entering salt water grow 1 inch in length per month and can continue at this rate for the 15 to 30 months until they return to fresh water.

Most steelhead have an average life span of between four and seven years, with nine being the oldest known specimen. The life span of Alaska steelhead may be extended somewhat beyond the species' average due to the state's cold water and short growing season, which combine to keep the annual metabolic energy expenditure of the fish low.

If all steelhead left the stream at the same age, returned after the same length of time in the ocean, and died after spawning, the adults in a given stream would be of similar size and age. They don't. Add to this the complications of summer-, spring-, and fall-run fish spawning at the same time and in the same stream and a rather complicated situation has developed. Perhaps nature has conspired to make steelhead life history complicated so that a severe flood, such as was experienced on the Kenai Peninsula in the fall of 2002, a volcanic eruption, extraordinary high-seas attrition, or a harsh winter or drought doesn't destroy all of a given population. Multiyear spawnings coupled with returns in three seasons creates a perfect scenario for the propagation of the species.

Fly-Fishing for Alaska's Steelhead

As a group, the steelhead-afflicted tend to make Rocky Mountain trout bums look like Ward Cleaver. No other self-respecting, even halfway-responsible citizen would drop everything—spouse, job, 401(k)—to chase an anadromous fish species around the globe. Nonetheless, these metalheads (as author Greg Thomas has dubbed them, speaking first and foremost about himself) would sell everything but their last rod and a handful of flies for just ten more casts at a likely-looking lie.

It's a vexing business, this chasing of steelhead. As if sensing their power over us, the fish plan their return for the least inviting times of year. Still we come. They feed capriciously or not at all, and still we spend days deliberating over the flies we carry. Steelhead fishing is full of long, wet, cold hours of toil, often punctuated by crushing moments of the darkest despair. More than once, fly-fishers must face the reality that they may cast ten thousand more times without experiencing so much as a tug ever again.

But then, as both the readers of T.S. Eliot's *Ulysses* and dedicated steelheaders know, the most difficult pleasures are the best kind. For sometimes when we come, the stream is as welcoming as a pub on St. Patrick's Day. The water is gin-clear, the river's banks are deserted, and dime-bright steelhead are gathered thick, all willing to rise and devastate a well-presented fly. It's these rarest of moments that bring steelheaders back to their streams, braving the worst that Mother Nature can throw their way, rods in hand, flies selected, responsibilities miles away.

RUN TIMING

For the steelhead stocks of the Kenai and Alaska Peninsulas, the Copper River drainage, and Kodiak Island, most returns occur in the fall. In Southeast Alaska, however, the majority of the runs occur in the spring. This region also receives fair numbers of autumn—and even a very few summer—steelhead returns, though neither are nearly as prevalent as the spring-returning fish. On Prince of Wales Island, for example, the ADF&G has determined that approximately fourteen streams receive runs of fall fish, about one for every five or six steelhead streams on the island. Department biologists also believe that the fall runs in Southeast tend to be smaller than spring returns, but as yet there is very little definite stock-assessment information to support the supposition.

Spring steelhead in Southeast typically begin to arrive in mid- to late March and continue entering their natal drainages right up until spawning, with runs stretching across the months of April, May, and even early June. The fall fish, which are much more common to other areas of the state, arrive at their freshwater destinations in August, September, October, and throughout the winter

TONY WEAVER

LEFT: *Running the Sandy River, Alaska Peninsula.*

The Lost Coast: the Katalla River from the air.

eggs, providing anglers an opportune occasion to drift Glo-Bugs or other egg patterns through the best steelhead lies.

GEAR FOR STEELHEAD

Unfortunately, there is no such as thing as a "normal" setup for fishing steelhead. The conditions you will inevitably encounter in fishing for the species are varied enough to make manned space flight look steady and reassuring. Alaska's steelhead can be found in everything from the pocket water of short, shallow coastal streams to the deep runs of a larger river like some found on the windswept Alaska Peninsula. An angler might only need a 6-weight rod and floating line one day, while the next rising water levels might require stepping up to a rod more capable of casting heavy sinking lines.

months. In some rivers, like the Situk, the Karluk, and the Thorne, anglers fishing during the early months of the year will find mixed stocks of overwintered fall and dime-bright spring fish.

In general, steelhead that return in the fall are bound for river systems with headwater lakes. There are few exceptions, as only large streams with plenty of pools and water deep enough to ensure survival throughout the winter can host fall-returning fish. Whether a return occurs during the spring or fall really shouldn't matter to an angler trying to locate steelhead, though; both seasons can be found holding in the same type of water during the run. Nonetheless, some believe fall steelhead are more willing and more aggressive biters. If this is indeed true, it might have something to do with there being generally higher water temperatures in the fall, after a summer of increased daylight hours. Or perhaps fall fish have evolved with a more prominent freshwater feeding impulse, since it's necessary for them to feed at least some to survive the winter. The only certain thing, however, is that Alaska's fall returnees will hold at the heads of pools and runs and pick off drifting salmon

If there's any common trait to steelhead gear, it's that anglers will want a fast-action rod with a stiff butt section. No matter the line weight it's designed to cast, a rod with a faster action will allow anglers to throw tighter loops; such a rod aids not only in casting for distance, but also when forced to deliver a fly through driving wind. Rich Culver, a Juneau-based steelhead guide who's been chasing sea-run rainbows from Northern California to the misty islands of Southeast Alaska for over a decade, reiterates the need for versatility in a steelhead rod. "I'm looking for a steelhead rod that not only can cast a fly through wind with pinpoint precision," Culver says, "but also excels in all phases of line control, from simple flip mends to complex aerial mends and everything in between." To get something near that level of performance, most anglers today prefer the new generation of graphite fly rods common among the high-end rod manufacturers. Nine- to 10-foot lengths are generally the most frequent choice for Alaska steelheaders. The longer rods, especially 10-foot models, allow anglers to roll-cast, mend, and pick up line easier and faster.

Longer rods are also more versatile. An angler fishing a 10-foot, 7-weight fly rod can "high-stick" and use a Leisenring Lift technique to probe good holding water on the Situk with a floating line, and then use that same rod when loading up with sinking lines to swing streamers on the Karluk River in a 20-knot wind.

For specific rod weights, a 6 is probably the lightest all-purpose steelhead rod an angler will want to use in Alaska. A 9½- or 10-foot 7-weight may be the ideal steelhead fly rod for the state, though anglers needing to toss big, bushy flies in all but gale-force winds will want an 8-weight. Unless steelhead over 15 pounds are expected, which is rare in Alaska, the size of the fish should actually play little part in rod choice, since a 6-weight will still allow an angler to completely control a 10-pound steelhead. In some conditions, however, an 8- or 9-weight rod can come in handy, especially if forced to toss the heaviest of sinking lines.

A relatively recent sight on many of Alaska's bigger rivers is the two-handed or Spey rod. These are quite popular with the anglers of the Pacific Northwest, who need such long, powerful rods for fishing big-water rivers like the Deschutes, Thompson, or Skagit. Most of Alaska's steelhead streams aren't large enough to require the use of a two-handed rod, although when the water is up during the fall both the Karluk and the Sandy are notable exceptions. Seven- and 8-weight (11½- to 13-foot-long) rods are sufficient for most of the state's bigger steelhead water, including the Sandy, Karluk, and Thorne Rivers during fall fisheries. The larger, 15-foot 8- and 9-weight rods will probably be overkill on Alaska's steelhead streams.

With steelhead lines, again, versatility is the key. Where fish are holding in the water column depends on a number of factors, including water temperature and conditions, fishing pressure, and the time of day. To consistently make the most desirable presentations, anglers

TONY WEAVER

must be prepared to deliver a fly at the proper water level under any possible circumstances. Toward this end, a full range of lines from a weight-forward floating line to sinking tips and fast, full-sinking lines may be needed. The most experienced anglers will know what line they need to deliver the fly before making even a single cast.

Today's anglers have a number of choices they can

Fighting a Southeast Alaska steelhead.

Fishing a large steelhead flat on the Alaska Peninsula.

make in regard to floating lines: Many of the most popular fly-line companies have begun manufacturing tapers intended to maximize results under specialized circumstances. Many of these lines are tailored to the steelheader, and all will remain supple in the cold-water environments most early-spring and fall anglers will encounter. Steelhead tapers and similar weight-forward lines can be a great asset if fishing large, wind-resistant streamers. Specialty nymph lines with short heads can also be handy for the small-stream steelheader, as they're designed to load quickly. Most of the new steelhead tapers and nymph lines also allow for more precise and efficient mending. A third type of specialty weight-forward floating line is designed for big-water fishing. These lines frequently have longer heads for increased

distance casting and extended-rear tapers, which facilitate long-distance mends and line pickup. For subsurface presentations, a selection from Type III sinking tips to the newer and much quicker sinking Type VI lines will suffice for almost any occasion, as will a range of Teeny Tip Taper or T-Series sinking lines in 130 to 400 grains. Short 5- to 7-foot sinking tips can be ideal for fishing less water or softer flows.

Perhaps the first requirement to consider in constructing steelhead leaders is the wariness of the fish. Even on their best days, steelhead are cagey; in low- or clearwater situations, they can be downright skittish. Fluorocarbon leaders enjoy low refraction indexes and allow anglers to retain greater line strengths without compromising stealth. The material does not absorb water and has less stretch than monofilament, perhaps increasing sensitivity. Either level leaders or those constructed in step-down tapers can be used. When using fluorocarbon, however, knots should be tied carefully, well lubricated, and pulled down incrementally to ensure they're completely seated.

If fishing sinking tips or full-sinking lines, nothing longer than 6 feet is necessary. Leaders longer than this will inevitably rise even while the line sinks, repeatedly causing the fly to drift out of the zone. In situations where the water carries a high rate of turbidity, or when fishing heavy riffles or otherwise broken water, long leaders again become less important. However, on rivers with low flows where the steelhead are holding in deeper pools, extending leader length is the prudent choice. In shallow water, a short leader will put the fly line on the water much too near holding fish, usually spooking them from their lie and guaranteeing a bump-free drift. Longer leaders in these situations will make for a decidedly better presentation, keeping the fly line—and its shadow—away from holding fish. A good general starting point is a leader of 9 feet. By closely monitoring their drift, anglers can then shorten or lengthen the leader as the situation dictates, always keeping the fly working at the proper level in the water column.

FLIES FOR STEELHEAD

Steelhead and Atlantic salmon share a common heritage, similar life histories, and passionate followings, as both provoke fanaticism of every sort in the angling community. Until 1989, the two were even joined in the same genus, *Salmo*.

Fly-fishing for the species is also very much alike, because the tactics used for one are usually successful with the other. The bond between the two prized sport fish extends further, though—right down to the knot at the end of the tippet, in fact, because the very first steel-

head flies were traditional Atlantic salmon patterns like the Lady Caroline and the Carron Fly. And even though the advent of lead-core shooting heads in the 1950s changed much of the thinking about steelhead fly design, the two remain connected, with many of today's most widespread steelhead enticers retaining at least some influence from their birth as Spey- and Dee-type patterns. Many are actually direct descendants from Atlantic salmon patterns of the past and would probably work just as well on the Miramichi as they do on the Kispiox.

Generally speaking, there are five important groups of steelhead flies, Spey patterns being the first. Many popular Northwest patterns like the Freight Train, Skykomish Sunrise, and Green Butt Skunk can be tied in a variety of ways, one of which is the Spey style. The second group contains waking flies such as bombers and sliders, none of them very common on Alaska streams. Faithful imitations of various nymphs make up another class of steelhead flies, and patterns from this troupe are seen a bit more regularly on Last Frontier steelhead waters. The next collection comprises more realistic shrimp and prawn imitations. First introduced to North American steelheaders in the winter fisheries of British Columbia, this group is embodied by the oft-imitated General Practitioner. The last of the five contains the marabou flies ordinarily tied in the style of the Alaskabou series. In Alaska, especially in the areas where fall returns occur, there should probably be a sixth group added: flies representing salmon eggs. Glo-Bugs, Babine Specials, and the

Looking for the perfect steelhead fly in Southeast Alaska.

A Royal Coachman amid volcanic rock.

choosing pinks, oranges, yellow, and fluorescent green. A good percentage of anglers follow the *bright day, bright fly—dark day, dark fly* mantra, but color theory should also take into account proximity to salt water. A lot of times anglers fishing the tides or near river mouths will find that patterns displaying the same intense colors as those exhibited by favored steelhead food sources—prawns, shrimp, squid—are the most successful.

ANGLING STRATEGIES

The steelhead is an angler's fish. The lightning-quick runs, a penchant for going airborne, bulldozer power, and limitless amounts of heart all come easily to mind. However, steelhead can be considered an angler's fish for another reason as well, and that's the number of different techniques fly-fishers must harbor within their repertoires if anything close to consistent success is ever to be approached. Because of where the fish hold—sometimes spread along the bottom of deep, slow-moving pools; other times in the solitary troughs and cutouts of pocket water—steelhead tactics must be adjusted throughout the day. In Alaska, where the terrain is so diverse, adaptation may in fact be the only real hallmark of the steelheader's trade.

In the early spring, when steelhead are beginning to return to a few of the rivers on Kodiak Island, the Alaska Peninsula, and most of the streams of Southeast, fly-fishers familiar with other, more southern-lying drainages might be surprised by the temperature of the water. Again in the late fall, temperatures will drop swiftly enough from their summer highs to make an angler contemplate returning the old neoprenes to action. And even though fresh fish continue into many systems throughout the winter, the severe temperatures of the water in December and January preclude much angling for the species. Yes, Alaska steelhead waters are cold, most hovering around the 40-degree mark for

ubiquitous Egg-Sucking Leech would have to go here.

Even with the wide range of patterns available, most anglers would agree that size and presentation remain the most important details in choosing a steelhead fly. And size considerations are primarily connected to water clarity and depth. When the water is exceedingly clear, a small, sparse fly (down to a size 8) will almost always produce the most consistent results, regardless of color. If the water is turbid, a large fly will often be the best choice. Drab colors (purple and black) are also the way to go when fishing deep, dark, or off-color water; in those situations, steelhead probably won't see much color variation anyway. Hence a big profile is the key. Good sizes for these times can range all the way up to 1/0. Colors for high-water situations usually range toward the brighter end of the scale, with many anglers much of the season. In much of British Columbia and the Lower Forty-eight, sub-40-degree waters would bring the fishing to a standstill. Usually if water temperatures drop much below this, Alaska's steelhead, too, become ingrained in their lethargic, bottom-hugging mode. However, warmer flows blowing in from the Gulf of Alaska, a little ambient light, and a rise in water temperature of even a degree or two will activate the fish.

Still, fly-fishers hoping for 50-degree water and the chance of taking fish on top will quickly learn that this is not the place. Except in very rare instances, Alaska's steelhead will be found deep, and an angler might have to literally drop a fly on the fish's nose to trigger a response. Thus, hoping to give a fish ample time to react to the fly, most will abide by the axiom *low and slow* when making a presentation.

First, though, fly-fishers must determine the portions of the stream that most likely are holding fish. Typically found in holding water with a depth of 4 feet or more, depending some on the clarity of the stream, steelhead seem to prefer moderate current rather than fast flows or the slack water that many species of Pacific salmon opt for. They're especially fond of the transition water formed where a point or group of rocks diverts a stream's primary current. These seams can be short or extend for hundreds of yards downstream, with a fish possibly holding anywhere throughout. A good pool can also hold several prime lies. Many of Alaska's smaller steelhead streams can offer anglers plenty of pocket water to fish as well, where large rocks, ledges, and downed logs obstruct the stream's flow and create pools of good holding water. Much of Southeast is like this, with anglers quickly working from pool to pool. On the larger streams, tailouts can be fished with success as well. Here, where silt and gravel pile up at the end of a pool or seam, flows are generally comfortable for steelhead, though the shallow nature of most tailouts will

make these fish tense and warier than usual. A steelhead angler should not overlook any possible mainstem lies, either. Often a patch of darker water color will indicate a slot that's been carved into the substrate, a prime lie for resting steelhead.

For fishing all of these scenarios, the steelhead fly-fisher should employ two principal methods: the traditional wet-fly swing, which will work best where longer casts are required or where more water needs to be covered, and deep nymphing tactics, tops for fishing pocket water, narrow migration lanes, and the slots or bucket-shaped troughs in a stretch of broken water. Nymphing tactics can also be successful in Alaska's cold waters, where sluggish steelhead may be reluctant to move to a swinging fly. By dead-drifting the fly in a steady, controlled manner, directly in line with holding fish, anglers will increase their chances of hooking up.

To swing for steelhead, it's best to employ a sinking-tip line suited for the pace and depth of the water. Cast at a 45-degree angle downstream, and then, if needed,

Anglers prepare for a day of steelheading on a misty Southeast Alaska morning.

BRIAN O'KEEFE

Floaters arrive at the Karluk weir, Kodiak.

proceed to mend the line to let the fly swing at the proper speed. Controlling the rate at which the fly moves across the river is the very essence of the wet-fly swing. In stronger flows, merely casting across the stream and letting the drift proceed untended will give the fly too much speed for finicky steelhead. Remember, *low and slow*. Here an angler fishing a floating line (with a weighted fly) can utilize a series of upstream mends to keep the current from dragging the fly at too great a pace. This isn't as simple when using sinking lines: Once the line sinks, it can no longer be mended. When fishing a sinking line in faster current, a large upstream mend should be thrown into the line the moment the cast is completed. Keeping an extra few feet of line off the reel for shooting with the mend will aid immeasurably in the process. Conversely, when fishing in slower flows, anglers may have to shoot extra line into a downstream mend, putting more line on the water to help speed up the fly and attain a better swing.

While a swinging fly will do a good job of prospecting wide swaths of water or substantial pools where holding fish may be scattered—a long, slow bend in the stream, for instance—the technique is less profitable on small streams or in pocket water, two situations widely encountered by Alaska steelheaders. Here, then, anglers will need to adjust their tackle and employ nymphing techniques for the best results.

Most Alaska nymph setups for steelhead consist of a weight-forward floating line and tapered leaders of at least 9 feet in length (8- to 12-pound tippet). For fishing short lines and small streams, overlining by a line size or two will help load the rod. Hybrid lines can be used—10- or 11-weight bellies married or spliced to thinner running lines. Most major line manufacturers market specialty nymph tapers that can also be an asset for this type of fishing. In addition, a good number of steelhead fly-fishers will use a strike indicator placed on the butt end of their leader. Commercially sold Corkies, yarn indicators, and homemade indicators made of braided polyester macramé cord seem to be the most popular and effective at both controlling the drift of the fly and telegraphing the slightest of strikes. To aid in getting the fly to the proper depth, split shot can be added to a short dropper made from the tippet knot's tag end, but casting this setup is awkward. The split shot or a heavily weighted fly will bounce or shock the line when traditional casting mechanics are used. Open loops and circle or Belgian casts can be used in this instance to maintain constant tension with the end of the fly line. A Belgian cast combined with tuck casts and aerial mends will get flies to the proper depth quickly.

To begin, cast upstream of the lie, then stack-mend line behind the indicator (if employing one) to let the fly sink faster. Casts are usually short, as anything more than about 30 feet of line will become difficult to manage when using this technique. Treat the drifting indicator as

Casting.

a dry fly, mending to maintain a drag-free presentation and managing the slack carefully in case of a sudden strike.

Large, deep pools, which can be magnets for resting steelhead, are nearly unfishable for fly-anglers in many cases. By casting heavy-density sinking lines nearly straight downstream, however, anglers will be able to "hover" the fly in front of holding fish. Casting at a steep angle is often overlooked, because it seems to limit the length of the arc the fly travels. But when fishing sinking lines on the wet-fly swing, the amount of time a fly is in front of a fish is actually minuscule. With this hover technique, though, time in the hang-down position is extended and steelhead can sometimes be prompted to move a few feet to intercept, even in colder waters. Flies that have animation work better with this technique, including marabou, hackled, and rabbit strip creations, all of which will breathe and dance in the current.

For the two other techniques, the choice of fly generally boils down to the angler's preference. Some, obviously, hold fast to color theory for steelhead, insisting that color and no other element is the most important aspect of a steelhead fly. Still, to be effective, the proper presentation, namely speed and depth, must be made before anything about the fly really matters. Perhaps this can best be illustrated by the success of the Jim Teeny system for steelhead, which is almost entirely predicated on depth control and color theory. Teeny has perfected his ability to totally control the speed and depth of his delivery first. He then simply substitutes colors (of his general-profile flies) until he finds a combination steelhead are willing to chase.

There are occasions in Alaska when water temperatures do reach the 45-degree-and-warmer plateau, and at these times steelhead will normally move a little farther to a fly. In even more rare circumstances, some greased-line or dry-fly fishing is possible. When water temperatures are up, anglers looking to entice a steelhead to the surface should seek out flows of clear water, 3 to 6 feet deep, with a medium-paced current. Chances for taking steelhead on top are also greatly increased if the fish are well rested and haven't seen a lot of recent pressure. Dead-drifted flies will occasionally find success, but waking flies, which employ a much stronger trigger, will undoubtedly stimulate a greater response rate.

For topwater prospects in Alaska, the streams south of Port Moller on the Alaska Peninsula are probably an angler's best bet. During the spring months, low, clear flows combine with the remote, unmolested nature of these streams to open small windows of opportunity for dry-fly fishers. Fall is out of the question, though, when much higher water levels keep the steelhead spread out and hugging the bottom. In the short coastal streams of Southeast Alaska, there isn't as much opportunity for topwater angling, mainly due to the tannic tint of the waters.

For steelheading in general, it is important to remember that the low-light hours of the early morning and late in the evening are almost always the best time of the day to fish. In the mornings especially, fish might be tucked close to banks. Many anglers wade right through these fish, or cast directly over them without ever realizing they're present. Anglers can also spook fish by allowing their profile to cross the horizon in view of the fish. During the height of day, it's important to keep track of shadows. Steelhead are cautious fish and plenty difficult to catch without anglers further stacking the deck against themselves by making obnoxious approaches and sloppy presentations.

Steelhead in Alaska

Anyone who's ever been near a stream understands anglers' desire to keep for themselves the sweetest seams and the most prolific holding water. In Alaska, the landscape is vast, with lots of secluded lakes and remote rivers for fly-fishers to ply their trade minus interruption from the masses. But when it comes to the state's salmon fishing, there's also Ship Creek and the Russian/Kenai confluence and Ninilchik on Memorial Day and a host of other scenes traumatic enough to induce nightmares in the hardiest of minds. Steelhead anglers, especially, understand and fear all this.

Thus, penning much of anything substantial on the most productive steelhead destinations is a tricky business. In nearly any conversation about the fish, almost never will words of real detail creep out, even among the best of friends. A regional hint or perhaps the whisper of a watershed is the best that can be expected. In very rare cases, the name of a river itself may surface—as starkly out of place as chinook sipping midges—but only if it is already deemed well known, or perhaps if uttered as a kind of wild goose for you to chase. In Alaska, we've all heard the common names before—the Situk, the Thorne, the Karluk, the Anchor. Steelhead return to a good number of the streams of the state's southern coast, however, from Dixon Entrance north along the panhandle and throughout the islands of the Inside Passage. They return to the rivers of the Gulf of Alaska shoreline as far north as Cordova and to a few Kenai Peninsula streams. Steelhead runs occur on Kodiak Island and the Afognak Archipelago and in many of the short coastal watersheds of the Alaska Peninsula. But while the well-known steelhead streams in the state entertain fairly substantial runs, the great majority of the rest are small and proportionately fragile. In Southeast Alaska, where the ADF&G conservatively estimates 331 streams host steelhead populations, returns of more than a few hundred fish are actually quite rare.

Consequently, the ancient Sicilian code of *omertà* lives on, not only with the famously reticent mafioso of Mario Puzo's fiction but also among steelheaders who congregate in fly shops, coffeehouses, and streamside campgrounds across the Last Frontier. It's a wall of silence that's perfectly understandable for Alaska, where the fish remain wild and the rivers run silently through the hurried terrain, the best of them doubly blessed with fish of crimson and chrome and the peace of an unknown name.

SOUTHEAST ALASKA

The temperate rain forests of Southeast Alaska provide a stunning backdrop to some of the state's finest steelhead fishing. It's precious country, more J. R. R. Tolkien than twenty-first-century North America, with innumerable coastal streams winding through thick, twisted timber

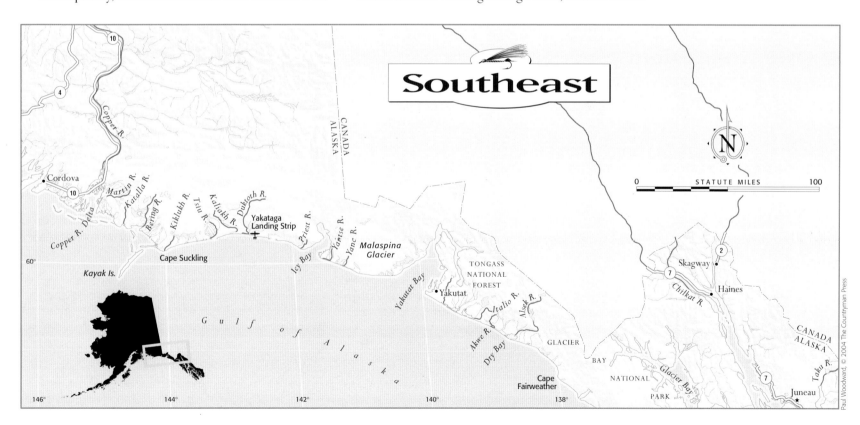

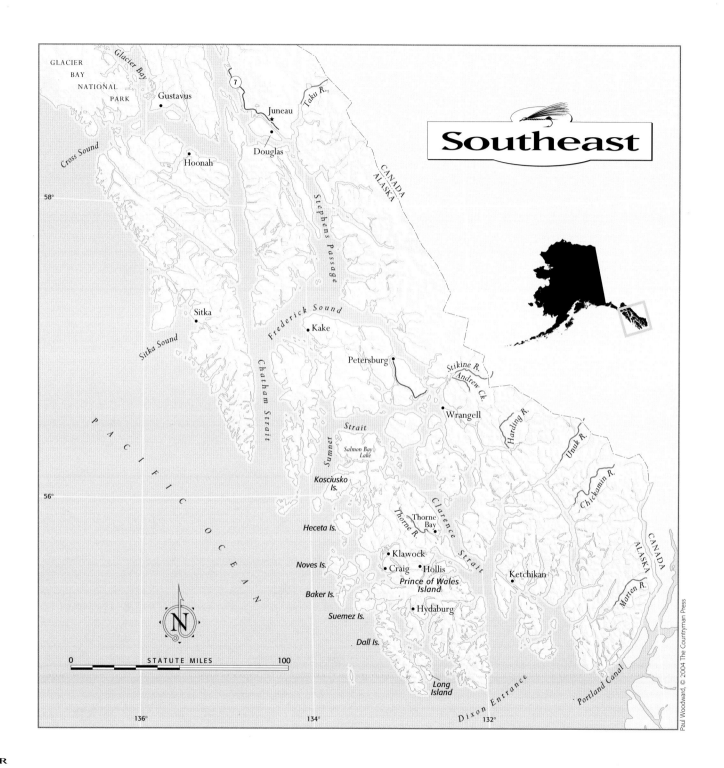

GLACIER
BAY
NATIONAL
PARK

Glacier Bay

Gustavus

Juneau ★

Douglas

Hoonah

Cross Sound

7

Taku R.

CANADA
ALASKA

Southeast

58°

Stephens Passage

Sitka

Sitka Sound

Frederick Sound

Kake

Petersburg

Stikine R.

Andrew Ck.

Wrangell

Harding R.

Unuk R.

Chatham Strait

Sumner

Strait

Salmon Bay
Lake

Kosciusko
Is.

PACIFIC

56°

Clarence Strait

Chickamin R.

Heceta Is.

Thorne
Bay

Thorne R.

Klawock

Noyes Is.

Craig

Hollis

Ketchikan

CANADA
ALASKA

OCEAN

Baker Is.

Prince of Wales
Island

Suemez Is.

Hydaburg

N

Dall Is.

Marten R.

Long
Island

Portland Canal

Dixon Entrance

136°

134°

132°

0   STATUTE MILES   100

Paul Woodward, © 2004 The Countryman Press

that begins right at river's edge, massive old-growth trees lording over the water, dark green moss blanketing their limbs. Almost all of Southeast is contained within 17-million-acre Tongass National Forest, an ecological theme park filled with dense spruce-hemlock forests, rolling muskeg meadows, and towering mountain ranges. By utilizing one of more than 150 U.S. Forest Service cabins available in the region, anglers can escape to a world where glaciers span entire valleys and tea-colored streams carve dark avenues through the landscape, most of which promise a springtime dance with the prince of sport fish.

To get there, however, takes some moxie. Despite the region's potential, very little guided effort for steelhead takes place. Most of the area's lodges and charters are either strongly oriented toward the bountiful saltwater fisheries or not open during the steelhead runs. Do-it-yourself anglers must be savvy, piloting 15-foot skiffs through fog and otherwise inclement weather, navigating amid a maze of channels and narrow straits between islands. Tidal currents can be treacherous, while mistiming an outgoing tide can leave a person stranded on the mudflats for days. Even when everything else goes right, it's not easy country to fish. In much of the area, there are no defined trails, only pathways beaten down by grizzly bears traveling the river corridors in search of food. Clambering over fallen tree trunks the size of small cars and sliding down slippery, high-walled banks, clinging to devil's club and the stalks of exposed root systems for support, anglers must struggle to reach the solitary pools and boulder-filled runs that hold fresh steelhead.

Then again, once there, the stream could be blown out, as these short coastal waters are prone to being after prolonged periods of rainfall. Or the fish might not be in at all, instead still roaming the migration and feeding lanes of the open ocean. If timing is off by even a day or two, they could be gone, too, having already moved on to

Wading to the steelhead among the old growth of Southeast's Tongass National Forest.

headwater lakes or upriver spawning beds. This hit-or-miss crapshoot nature of steelheading in much of Southeast is simply a by-product of fishing small runs of fish in streams nobody knows much about. But when everything goes right—welcoming tides, the fish big and bold, the weather glorious—the steelhead-smitten will be convinced they've found the last best place on earth.

The major steelhead fisheries in Southeast Alaska occur on the few larger systems within the area, like the Naha, Karta, Thorne, and Situk Rivers. The rest (and bulk) of the steelhead stocks return to less sizable streams, most of them small, many still waiting to be discovered. Hubs for the region's steelhead fishing are the major communities—Ketchikan, Wrangell, Petersburg, Sitka, Juneau, and Yakutat. From any one of these small towns, anglers can board a floatplane or boat and in under an hour be stalking steelhead on a deserted stream. In the case of Ketchikan, steelhead actually return within walking distance of the airport.

Locals and travelers with a few hours to spare expend most fishing effort on Ketchikan Creek, working the incoming tides where the short, swift stream empties into Tongass Narrows. There are also limited number of steelhead returning to the streams of Gravina Island, just minutes away by boat. A few miles north of town, another Revillagigedo Island drainage can be reached with little effort. The Ward Lake system, accessible by

car on the Ketchikan road system, offers a few good opportunities for steelhead. Farther northwest lies one of Southeast's larger steelhead streams, the 17-mile-long Naha River, which encompasses eight small lakes and offers fly-fishers fine chances for success near outlets and the mouths of tributary streams. At the end of Yes Bay on the southern mainland, the McDonald Lake system (especially Wolverine Creek) provides yet another known opportunity for steelhead anglers, this healthy run of steelhead returning from mid-April through early May.

A short jaunt west from Ketchikan lies Prince of Wales Island, the third largest island in North America and home to a concentration of quality-fishing streams unlike anywhere else in Alaska. The island hosts two of the state's most popular and best-known steelhead fisheries on the Thorne and Karta Rivers, though, all told, over seventy streams on Prince of Wales support wild stocks. Some of the less publicized but still productive steelhead locations are the Klawock and Harris Rivers and Kegan, Staney, Salmon Bay, and Steelhead Creeks. The communities of Craig, Klawock, and Hollis serve as jumping-off points for anglers, who can further access the many small streams and isolated drainages by making use of Forest Service cabins and the more than 700 miles of old logging roads that crisscross the island. Daily air service and a ferry shuttle prospective anglers from Ketchikan.

Steelhead anglers fishing from Wrangell are most likely to begin on the Thoms or Anan Creek systems, though the Stikine River, a heavily silted, braided river, is by far the largest system in the area. Due to the turbidity of the water, however, fly-anglers are limited to fishing the mouths of tributary streams, of which Andrew Creek is best known for steelhead. A little farther to the northwest lie Kupreanof Island and the community of Petersburg. There are numerous other islands in the area, most with very short coastal streams that attract at least a few returning steelhead. Either of these communities can serve as an excellent starting point for skiff excursions through the Wrangell Narrows or Duncan Canal to both proven producers and little-known coastal streams alike. Petersburg Creek, just across the narrows from Petersburg, garners one of the most consistently productive steelhead returns to Kupreanof Island, though Duncan Saltchuck Creek and the Kah Sheets River each provide good to excellent fly-fishing for the species.

Situated on the western coast of sprawling Baranof Island, the community of Sitka is another great hub city for adventurous steelheaders, though the island it sits on actually offers fewer steelhead opportunities than its two closest neighbors, Chichagof and Admiralty Islands. Sitkoh Creek, just 35 miles northeast of Sitka on Chichagof Island, has one of the larger steelhead runs in Southeast, with over a thousand fish returning in good years. There are several lodges in the area, and angler, can also gain access by floatplane or boat from Sitka. Admiralty Island—*Xootsnoowu*, or "fortress of the bears," to the area's Tlingit Indians—is probably more renowned for the sheer splendor of its environs than for sea-run rainbow trout, even though quality populations occur in several of the area's coastal streams, especially in the Mitchell Bay system, a complex of lakes and streams that eventually empty in Chatham Strait. Besides the steelhead, the island hosts the greatest known concentration of nesting bald eagles in the world, averaging more than one nest per mile of coastline in Seymour Canal. Approximately one grizzly bear for every two eagles also calls the area home. Perhaps that's why the first Russian name for the island was *Ostrov Kutsnoi*—"fear island."

Just across Stephens Passage from Admiralty Island lies Alaska's capital city, Juneau, which sits within an hour's flight from at least a dozen quality steelhead streams. A few are on the road system surrounding the town, while the remainder, like most of the streams in Southeast, take a little more effort—and usually a plane or boat ride—to locate. The Taku River produces well, with the best fishing in or near the mouths of tributary creeks, while Cowee and Montana Creeks, both accessible by car from Juneau, sustain limited returns.

Nothing written on steelhead fishing in Alaska could be complete without mentioning the Situk River near Yakutat, which has long been regarded as one of the state's premier steelhead destinations. Despite its diminutive size, the Situk carries a large reputation, mostly due to the fact that it has the largest known run of steelhead in Alaska, sometimes stretching to more than nine thousand fish per year. The relatively simple logistics of fishing the Situk have also aided its popularity.

There is daily commercial jet service from Anchorage and Seattle to Yakutat, and once there, anglers can either choose from a number of lodges, guides, and outfitters or simply do it all themselves. The flats near the Situk's mouth occasionally offer a chance to watch steelhead come in on the tides, and when the timing's right, anglers can engage in some truly exciting fishing. On the river itself, fly-fishers will see some of Alaska's largest steelhead resting in crystal-clear waters, frequently holding under deadfall logs and other snags. Fish over 20 pounds are caught yearly, with most of the angling pressure occurring between mid-April and the first week of May. Still, if a single attribute beyond the numbers and size of the fish could define the Situk, it

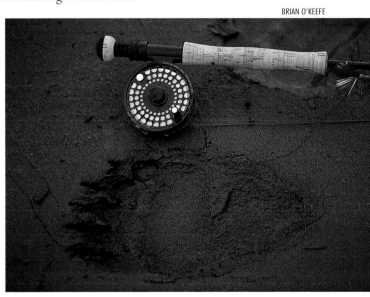

BRIAN O'KEEFE

Grizzly tracks.

Playing a steelhead on the Anchor River in Southcentral Alaska.

might be the river's trim characteristics. At just 22 miles in length, the Situk narrowly winds through the dense terrain from Situk Lake to reach the sea. Most steelheaders float and fish, while others use a network of trails that borders the river and hike to favorable holding water.

Heading up the coast from Yakutat toward Cordova, the rain forest ends and the number of small streams dwindles. This the rugged Lost Coast, which runs from Icy Bay to Cordova and is home to the Tsiu, Katalla, Kiklukh, Tashalich, and a number of other rivers and streams that host steelhead. Most are of a short, coastal nature, and trips must be timed just right to intersect with the travels of returning steelhead. Many of these streams are not listed as steelhead waters by the ADF&G, primarily because the fantastically remote nature of the fisheries has prevented much study. Outside of the larger systems nearer Cordova, very few anglers have fished this area; fewer still have tried for steelhead. Raw, unpredictable weather dominates this section of the Gulf of Alaska coastline, and there are very few lakes large enough to support air access. Thus, entry into the area is largely limited to beach landings, and during the times of year steelhead favor, these can be a little uncertain to say the least. People who have ventured very far into the region's watersheds, however, insist the sky's the limit, hinting that there's more than a few quality steelhead streams just waiting to be discovered.

SOUTHCENTRAL ALASKA

The Anchor River of Southcentral Alaska is one of those places so familiar to Alaska steelheaders that only the name of a particular lie need be mentioned to evoke the setting for a tale. Dudas, Slide, or Grassy Holes and many others conjure memories of fish hooked and landed, and spark dreams of the chrome-bright steelhead to come.

These are one of Alaska's most famous wild runs of steelhead. As the river sits just a four-hour drive from Anchorage, they draw strong contingents of weekend warriors and steelhead diehards alike. Still, a kind of tranquility falls on the community of Anchor Point in late autumn, when the oppressive crowds of weekend salmon anglers have gone and the river's left to the returning steelhead and the anglers who pursue them.

Part of the Anchor's allure is its intimate nature. Primarily a pocket fishery, the stream nevertheless offers a surprising amount of varied water. Almost every corner will have a different flavor than the previous. For example, anglers might be able to find a boulder garden, a seemingly bottomless pool, and a long, medium-depth riffle within a few hundred yards of each other, all holding fresh steelhead. It's a very easy river to fish as well, unlike many of the oversized, rambling waters Pacific Northwest steelheaders may be accustomed to. The Anchor usually heats up in mid- to late September, though a good proportion of the run usually doesn't enter the river until after October 1. The Anchor River did come precariously close to losing its steelhead in the 1980s, but changes in management and the adoption of a catch-and-release policy for steelhead have enabled the wild brood to endure. Thankfully, Anchor steelhead can now be found in numbers reminiscent of the early years.

Home base on the river is the Anchor Angler, owned by Stan Harrington, where sage advice and current conditions can be had with a phone call. Other local features to remember are the inexpensive rooms at the Anchor River Inn, and the hot showers that come with them, both of which will seem like luxuries after wading in forty-degree water all day. The Anchor can also serve as a staging area for adventuresome anglers in search of other

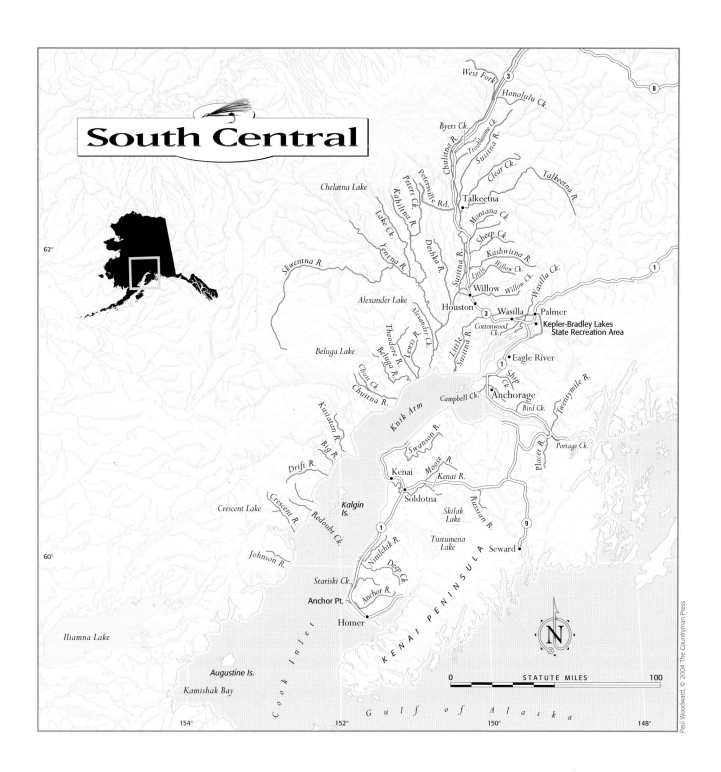

South Central

West Fork

Honolulu Ck.

Byers Ck.

Troublesome Ck.

Clear Ck.

Talkeetna R.

Chelatna Lake

Petersville Rd.

Peters Ck.

Kahiltna R.

Chulitna R.

Susitna R.

Talkeetna

Montana Ck.

Sheep Ck.

Lake Ck.

Yentna R.

Deshka R.

Susitna R.

Kashwitna R.

Willow Ck.

Little Willow Ck.

Willow

Wasilla Ck.

Skwentna R.

Alexander Lake

Houston

Wasilla

Palmer

Alexander Ck.

Lewis R.

Little Susitna R.

Cottonwood Ck.

Kepler-Bradley Lakes
State Recreation Area

Theodore R.

Beluga Lake

Beluga R.

Eagle River

Chuit Ck.

Chuitna R.

Knik Arm

Campbell Ck.

Ship Ck.

Anchorage

Bird Ck.

Twentymile R.

Kustatan R.

Big R.

Swanson R.

Moose R.

Placer R.

Portage Ck.

Drift R.

Kenai

Kenai R.

Crescent Lake

Crescent R.

Redoubt Ck.

Kalgin Is.

Soldotna

Skilak Lake

Russian R.

Johnson R.

Tustumena Lake

Seward

Stariski Ck.

Ninilchik R.

Deep Ck.

Anchor R.

KENAI PENINSULA

Anchor Pt.

Homer

Iliamna Lake

Augustine Is.

Kamishak Bay

Cook Inlet

Gulf of Alaska

N

STATUTE MILES

0   100

62°

60°

154°   152°   150°   148°

Paul Woodward, © 2004 The Countryman Press

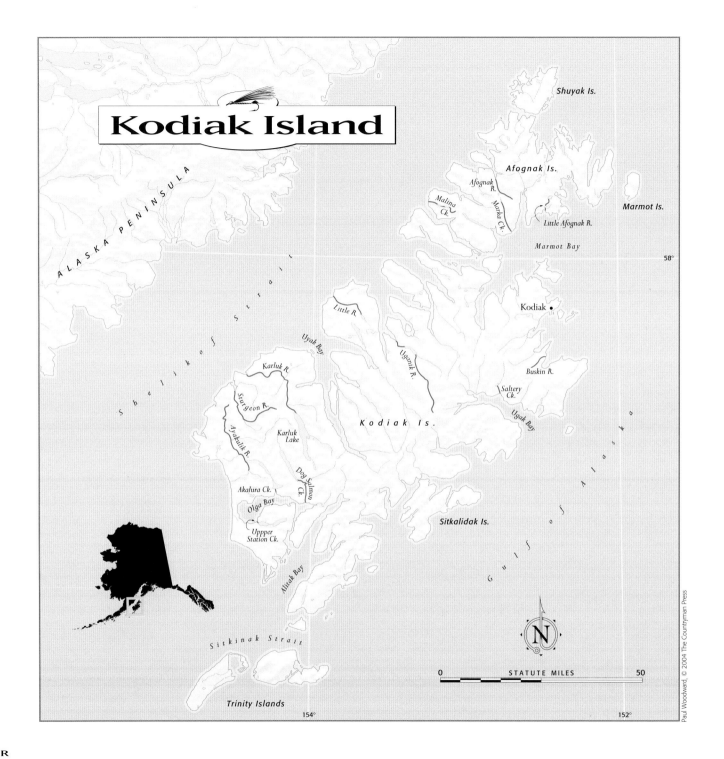

Kodiak Island

Shuyak Is.

Afognak Is.

Afognak R.

Malina Ck.

Marka Ck.

Little Afognak R.

Marmot Is.

ALASKA PENINSULA

Marmot Bay

58°

Little R.

Kodiak •

Uyak Bay

Karluk R.

Uganik R.

Buskin R.

Sturgeon R.

Saltery Ck.

Ayakulik R.

Karluk Lake

Kodiak Is.

Ugak Bay

Akalura Ck.

Dog Salmon Ck.

Olga Bay

Sitkalidak Is.

Uppper Station Ck.

Alitak Bay

Gulf of Alaska

Sitkinak Strait

N

STATUTE MILES

0   50

Trinity Islands

154°   152°

Paul Woodward, © 2004 The Countryman Press

stocks of the Kenai Peninsula steelhead. Deep Creek, the Ninilchik River, and Stariski Creek also support runs, and all are within short driving distance of Anchor Point. Farther north is an old standby, the perhaps long-forgotten Kasilof River, where past hatchery progeny still prowl Crooked Creek in the fall and a few wild descendants appear during a small spring fishery. None of these streams supports as significant a return as the Anchor does. They usually receive lighter effort, though, and impeccable timing can result in some great fall fishing.

KODIAK ISLAND

The meandering Karluk River contains the largest population of steelhead on Kodiak Island, with runs averaging between four and eight thousand fish. In Alaska, only the Situk River has a higher annual return. The Ayakulik, Uganik, Saltery, and Litnik Rivers also support populations, as do Dog Salmon and Pauls Creeks, with each averaging between a few hundred and fifteen hundred returning steelhead each year. The steelhead in both the Karluk and Ayakulik Rivers are fall fish, entering fresh water in mid-August and continuing throughout the winter months. There is rumored to be a small spring run in the Karluk River as well, but the peak of the runs on Kodiak normally occur in October, with fish averaging 6 to 7 pounds and occasional trophies up to 15 pounds being taken. A spring catch-and-release fishery has recently been opened for both the Karluk and Ayakulik Rivers, however, and the next few years should shed much greater light on the strength of the early-season returns.

The Karluk, flowing just over 20 miles from its source at Karluk Lake to a terminus at Karluk Lagoon and Shelikof Strait, can be exceedingly skinny water. There are few places for steelhead to hold throughout the stream, with the exception of a handful of areas near the

TONY WEAVER

Portage where fish can be found in concentrated numbers. Otherwise the Karluk's steelhead are moving, stopping to rest occasionally in the little holding water available, which usually amounts to small divots in the streambed and small cuts next to banks. Anglers might locate a handful of steelhead in a stretch of river, only to find the next half mile isn't more than 10 inches deep. Steelhead will blow through these areas, not stopping until they find acceptable cover.

Viable populations of steelhead are also known to inhabit the Afognak Archipelago and the streams that empty into Raspberry Strait. René Limeres, an Alaska outfitter who fishes Afognak regularly, explains that fishing this area may take a little more planning than some other Alaska steelhead locales. "Most of the Afognak rivers are short," Limeres says, "and hitting them just right requires a little due diligence." That being said, some great fishing can be had when anglers do stumble on the right conditions. "Plan around big fall tides to bring the fish," Limeres adds. Unfortunately, some of the

Much of the time, Alaska's best fishing doesn't coincide with its best weather.

fall tides occur during the night, which makes fishing them virtually impossible. Plus, these short Afognak rivers often have very little holding water, and most of the fish will travel to headwaters near or into the source lake, sometimes completing the entire journey in under a couple of hours' time.

In all, sixteen river systems on Kodiak and Afognak Islands support populations of steelhead, and this is actually quite common for many of them. Some, like the Litnik River and Saltery and Malina Creeks are no more than about 3 miles long. Fishing any of this type of stream for steelhead, and finding success, is heavily dependent on the tides, when tidewater areas and whatever holding water is available in the streams themselves can provide phenomenal action. However, as Limeres notes, within a few hours of the tide having come in, all the fish may be gone. "Finding fish, especially fast-moving steelhead, in streams that have limited holding water can be problematic," Limeres continues. "But the overall ambience of the experience and the vast solitude that can be found on Afognak keep the mystique of the island alive."

Most travel on Kodiak is accomplished by boat or plane, and several charter businesses and local air carriers are based on the island. Major air carriers also service Kodiak on a daily basis. Once on the island, a good number of lodges cater to late-season steelheaders, who will inevitably be sharing camp with deer and brown bear hunters. Air taxis and local outfitters are also available in the communities of Kodiak, Larsen Bay, and Old Harbor.

THE ALASKA PENINSULA

Wild, esoteric stretches of virgin land dominate much of North America's most remote western holdings, where the weather in both the early spring and late fall—the peaks of the Aleutian steelhead runs—is fickle and notoriously nasty. That only makes the logistics of planning for this already challenging destination more daunting.

The rewards are ample, however, as here, at the root of the arm that forms the Aleutian chain, some of Alaska's greatest steelhead rivers lie almost unnoticed.

Most of the Aleutian coastal streams are relatively short. Born in the foothills on the back side of the Pacific Ring of Fire, these rivers often find their origins through aquifers in the ground and are birthed from cauldrons welling up clear artesian water. Although mostly stable in temperature, high water sometimes makes the streams unfishable for days at a time. There is also a benefit to shorter rivers, though, and that is the rebound effect—shorter rivers mean quicker clearing. Despite the wicked weather, the coastal rivers of the Aleutians are seldom blown out for extended periods of time.

Beyond the scenery and the unrivaled sense of adventure, why should an angler venture to this end-of-the-earth locale? Steelhead, of course, with some of these streams boasting trophy fish of 20 pounds and more. One such producer is the Sandy River, which is backdropped by volcanic Mount Veniaminof and home to the largest known run of Alaska Peninsula steelhead. The pea-gravel-bottomed stream features some classic steelhead water, almost like a mini Skagit with its long riffles, big, deep flats, and ample holding water. There is a proliferation of gravel bars on the river, and casting room is endless. In the fall, the Sandy is one of the few Alaska steelhead streams where a two-handed rod can be used to good effect, though it's certainly not mandatory Spey water like many of the more famous Pacific Northwest and British Columbia steelhead rivers.

Most of the other steelhead possibilities in this isolated region of the Last Frontier are located in the zone between Port Heiden and Cold Bay. The Bear and Nelson Rivers are two, though at least a dozen more verified steelhead streams bisect the rugged, barren-tundra coastline. Farther north on the Alaska Peninsula are a few more, including the Cinder River. Not much is known

The Gulkana is a clear runoff stream that begins above the timberline at Gunn Creek, a tributary to Summit Lake, and flows south out of the Alaska Range, running approximately 100 miles before reaching the Copper River near Glennallen. The mainstem Gulkana has two major tributaries of its own, the West Fork and the Middle Fork, both of which require access by plane or combinations of canoeing and overland portaging. Steelhead primarily use the Middle Fork downstream of Dickey Lake and within Hungry Hollow Creek for spawning.

The Hanagita River is also a clear runoff stream. Originating on the northern flanks of the Chugach Range in a series of three lakes (Upper, Middle, and Lower Hanagita Lakes), the river flows swiftly to its confluence with the Tebay River, averaging only 3 to 4 feet deep. Above Lower Hanagita Lake, the river gradually descends from Upper and Middle Hanagita Lakes through an open valley comprising wet-muskeg tundra. ADF&G studies have shown that this is the area the Hanagita steelhead use for overwintering and then spawning, which usually commences near the last week of May. Some light fishing does occur for steelhead on both drainages, but run sizes are small enough and fish so difficult to intercept that the crowds stay away. In the case of the Upper Hanagita especially, difficult access also helps keep the number of prospective anglers down.

about any of these streams; the Sandy draws the majority of what little angling pressure exists. Access to most of the waters of the area can be obtained from local air carriers based in King Salmon or Cold Bay, and a few lodges and rustic tent camps are available.

INTERIOR ALASKA

The northernmost wild steelhead population in North America returns each year to the sprawling Copper River drainage in interior Alaska. It's a small population that receives very little directed angling effort and primarily consists of two separate stocks, one heading to the Middle Fork Gulkana River and the other the Hanagita River stock.

Kenai Peninsula

BRIAN O'KEEFE

CHAPTER TWO

chinook salmon

WHAT SHAKESPEARE REFERRED TO as the sweet of the year springs upon the Great Land in a matter of moments, not weeks or days. Seemingly overnight, several feet of lingering ice vanishes from the state's lakes and streams, the banks of which trade cloaks of winter white for at least a dozen different shades of green. Ever-lengthening days soon render months of dark into mere memory. And the most famous residents of the Last Frontier—its boundless fish and wildlife—are found marking the occasion with increasing vigor.

For angling aesthetes, the dawn of this new season is a matter of mercy. Legions of snow-stymied fly-fishers step back from their tying tables, wave farewell to their families, and emerge with the kind of bounce in their step only a well-spent hibernation can provide. Promises to fish less are returned to storage with the other halfhearted and ill-conceived vows society forces upon the restless angler. Lines have been cleaned, reels oiled,

Chinook salmon.

BRIAN O'KEEFE

and every fly box filled. It is time to stop dreaming and start fishing.

For many, the first harbinger of this newfound clemency is the return of Alaska's most popular game fish—the chinook salmon. Anglers are drawn from points across the globe, hoping their travels intersect with those of the year's first returnees from the Pacific. Comfortable in deep, swift waters and canny to the point of being considered reticent by some, the species is not easily fished. But that in no way diminishes the effect these seagoing missiles have on the devoted angler. Chinook are capable of reaching tremendous sizes and are favored with almost unspeakable power, especially bright, fresh-from-the-sea specimens. Once initiated into their world, a fly-angler has little choice but to return again and again, addicted to the thrill of hooking into one of North America's brawniest freshwater fish. Fittingly, in Alaska they are known by only one name, king salmon.

The Chinook Salmon
(Oncorhynchus tshawytscha)

The chinook is the least abundant of North America's five species of Pacific salmon. It's also the largest. Individual fish routinely exceed 30 pounds and can grow much larger. In 1949, a 126-pound king was captured in a commercial fish trap near Petersburg, while unverified reports of fish up to 135 pounds have filtered down from Cook Inlet's commercial fleet. The all-tackle world record, a 97.4-pound early-run chinook, was hauled from Southcentral Alaska's Kenai River, where a 50-pounder isn't even considered a trophy catch.

Historically, king salmon in North America ranged from Point Hope to the Ventura River in southern California. Today, however, no populations of wild chinook are believed to occur south of the Sacramento River basin. In Alaska, their native range begins near

Point Hope just north of Kotzebue Sound and stretches south to the Islands of the Four Mountains in the Aleutian chain and from there west across the Gulf of Alaska to Dixon Entrance. The species is most abundant from the southeastern panhandle north to the Yukon River, with major populations returning to the state's great watersheds, namely the Yukon, Kuskokwim, Nushagak, Susitna, and Copper River systems. Important runs also occur in many other Alaska rivers, among them the Alagnak, Karluk, Kenai, Naknek, Togiak, and a few of the larger transboundary streams in Southeast. At the northern end of the species' range, strays have been reported in several streams of the Arctic Coast.

While still in fresh water, juvenile chinook are difficult to differentiate from other small salmon, trout, and char, but they can be recognized by their well-developed and usually wider parr marks, which are bisected by the lateral line. Adult king salmon, on the other hand, are much easier to distinguish from their salmonid cousins.

Mature kings are robust, full-bodied fish, with a broad and moderately forked tail and teeth of pronounced development (an attribute that's even more manifest in breeding males). A signature characteristic of the adult chinook is the erratic black spotting along its back, dorsal fins, and on both lobes of the caudal fin. These spots—highly irregular in size and shape—only occur above the lateral line. When in marine waters, the chinook displays the bright silver tint typical of anadromous species. But after entering fresh water, the salmon undergo a rapid transformation; soon their body colors range from copper to red to an almost purplish black, depending on location and the degree of sexual maturation. Males generally exhibit deeper hues than females and can also be distinguished by their hooked nose or kype. These changes may appear significant, but chinook undergo less pronounced alterations in coloration and body morphology than do pink, chum, and sockeye salmon.

LIFE HISTORY

Because they're segregated at the time of spawning, individual chinook salmon stocks are adapted to very specific parts of a drainage. Fisheries scientists have thus determined that life history, not variations in things like the number of gill rakers or vertebrae, can present the most important delineation between various populations.

Across their North American range, chinook can mostly be separated by the age at which the young leave fresh water for the sea. In the southern part of the species' range, the fry often depart for the ocean during the first year of life, sometimes after spending as few as

Where the power comes from—the caudal fin of a chinook.

three months in their natal streams. Although some Yukon River fish don't abandon fresh water for the salt until year three, most of Alaska's juvenile king salmon smolt up during the spring of their second year of life, losing their parr marks and migrating en masse to the bays and estuaries where their streams of origin terminate. Here they usually feed for a short time until they're large enough to risk the open ocean.

Upon entering salt water, the majority of chinook salmon stocks undertake extensive migrations, roaming over thousands of miles in the North Pacific and Bering Sea, while others, particularly some of the Southeast Alaska populations, remain in inshore waters for the duration of their saltwater existence. These so-called

Underwater chinook.

feeder kings can provide year-round fisheries. While at sea, king salmon experience rapid growth, often averaging a pound per month. As the chinook continue to grow, they can feed upon larger and larger forage fish, with oceangoing kings primarily preying upon sand lance, pilchards, herring, smelt, sand fish, sticklebacks, and anchovies, as well as walleye pollack, Pacific cod, tomcod, rockfish, squid, euphausiids, amphipods, and crab larvae. However, feeding habits inevitably vary from year to year and in different areas.

Chinook are the longest lived of the Pacific salmon and reach sexual maturity at anywhere from two to nine years of age, which can result in great size variances among the fish of a single year's return. Most Alaska fish return from three to five years after leaving fresh water, with females tending to be older than the males at maturity. This return to the streams of their birth usually begins during the winter, with the first fish positioned near river mouths by spring. As a general rule, the fish entering fresh water earliest will travel the farthest upstream to spawn. However, the distances that separate stocks travel will vary widely. The most obvious example can be found in some of the Yukon River populations bound for the river's headwaters in Canada. These fish undertake the longest-known freshwater spawning migration of any anadromous species—from 1,500 to 2,000 miles—to reach their spawning beds. In Alaska, most streams receive a single run of king salmon in the period from May through late July.

Once in fresh water, chinook, like all Pacific salmon, cease feeding, and their stomachs atrophy. This creates the room needed for eggs in females and milt in males. During this time, the salmon employ stored body materials for both the energy needed to continue their migrations and that required for the development of reproductive products. Spawning for Alaska kings usually occurs in July and August and then mostly in larger streams and rivers, as chinook seem to be able to manage the larger substrate and greater stream flows of main channels better than other Pacific salmon. While references to populations spawning in mainstem, glacial rivers are sparse, a few Alaska stocks known to do just that, most notably kings of the Kenai, Tonsina, and Klutina Rivers. Though glacial in origin, each of those rivers is buffered by a large lake (or two in the Kenai's case) that reduces the turbidity and the extreme summer flows occurring in the main channels.

Fly-Fishing for Alaska's Chinook

Nearly every statement made about fly-fishing, and fly-fishing for Pacific salmon in particular, needs qualifying. In fact, if anything is categorically true, it's that the words *never* and *always* belong nowhere near an angling discussion. What works once may not ever work again. Swinging a fuchsia bunny fly through a deep pocket of holding water on an overcast day might produce strike after vicious strike, while trying the same technique with the exact same fly in similar conditions a day or even an hour later can leave an angler with no fish and less hope.

Basically, when fly-fishing fresh water for chinook salmon, anglers are attempting to entice a fish that is not feeding to strike at their offering. Not an easy proposition under even the best of circumstances. Not easy—but not impossible, either.

RUN TIMING

As when fishing any anadromous species, timing is probably the most critical ingredient to successful chinook salmon angling. A group of fish can come in on a tide and shoot straight upriver, not holding and presenting anglers with many opportunities to make a presentation. An incoming tide can also be completely void of fish, while

Free-jumping chinook.

the next might bring hundreds of sea-lice-toting chromers in from the sea. Or in some cases, fish can enter a river on the incoming tide, mill around during the slack period, then decide there's something about the conditions they don't like and retreat to salt water again on the outgoing tide. Rarer yet but still possible, the salmon just might not return in any kind of numbers in a particular year. Whether high rates of interception, poor ocean survival, a change in environmental conditions, or low fecundity in brood stock is to blame can never be fully known.

Making matters even more chaotic for anglers, salmon run times are not static events, even when populations are healthy and booming. The peak of a run can change from year to year, sometimes differing by as much as two weeks from previous years' returns, especially when a season coincides with drastically altered environmental conditions such as unseasonably warm

chinook salmon | **37**

weather or flooding. In the end, close study of the historical run-timing data for a drainage should put an angler close to a return's peak dates, but unfortunately an element of luck plays at least a small part in even the best-planned trips.

In Southcentral Alaska, chinook runs usually occur from late May through late July. The Cook Inlet area generally begins to see the first kings in about mid-May, with scattered reports of fish begin taken from the lower reaches of the Little Susitna River, the Kenai, and the hatchery-enhanced Kasilof River during the month. Most runs peak in mid- to late June in the region, continuing into July. The second and larger return of Kenai River chinook typically reaches its peak in late July.

For Southwest Alaska, the first kings are customarily seen in early to mid-June, with the run picking up steam by the first two weeks of July and then tapering off by the end of the month. Most years, for instance, the height of the large chinook run on the Nushagak River occurs in the last week of June or first week of July. The returns to the Karluk and Ayakulik Rivers on Kodiak Island usually show peaks from mid-June through early July and in the first half of June, respectively.

In the Northwest region of the state, and the northernmost extent of the chinook's range, runs begin in mid-June and continue through mid-July, typically peaking somewhere near July 1. In the Interior, kings enter the Yukon River in June and reach the Canadian border by mid- to late July. The tributaries of the Copper River see their best chinook angling from early to late July.

King salmon in catchable numbers can be had in the saltwater intercept fishery of Southeast Alaska from mid- to late April through mid-July, with the months of May and June representing the prime fishing times. Where chinook salmon fishing is permitted in fresh water, namely the Gulf Coast streams near Yakutat, peak times usually occur during the month of June.

GEAR FOR KINGS

Stout, high-quality gear becomes a necessity whenever the largest of all Pacific salmon is the intended target. Anglers can occasionally get away with fishing a heavy 9-weight, or even an 8 at times, but a 9-foot 10-weight is the rod of choice for most Alaska king salmon anglers. For fast, powerful fish in big water, you might even consider stepping up to an 11- or 12-weight outfit. A backup rod is often a good thing to have along, too, for many an outing has ended early with an angler holding nothing but pieces of splintered graphite.

Another possibility for chinook anglers to consider are Spey or two-handed rods, which are sighted with growing frequency on some of Alaska's bigger salmon streams. Two-handed rods provide anglers the ability to cover more water and mend more line with greater ease. Sizes for Spey rods will vary, with 9- through 12-weights in 14- and 15-foot lengths the most popular. Deciding between European and traditional Spey actions is a personal choice.

For taking on deep-water chinook in the open ocean, fast-action rods designed to handle heavy lines are required. G. Loomis, Sage, Scott, and a few others all make excellent fast-action saltwater fly rods. These are not the traditional 10- and 12-weights, but specialized tools often used for large warm-water pelagic species, which frequently run deep or sound, forcing the angler to fight and lift them straight over the gunnels. The blue-water rods designed for tuna or dorado, with heavy butts and quick, flexible tips for casting, are ideal tools for saltwater king salmon; conventional fly-rod tapers might cast well, but their lifting power is usually compromised. If targeting inshore chinook, those feeding at shallower depths in estuaries and river mouths, traditional 10- through 12-weight rods will work well. If there's a chance salt- and freshwater fishing may be combined, and you can make only one choice, most prudent anglers

TONY WEAVER

will split the difference and go with a fast-action 11-weight. Heavy freshwater or light saltwater reels capable of holding at least 250 yards of 30-pound backing are highly recommended for freshwater chinook salmon angling. Quality drag systems are a must as well; reels with old-style click drags or those that have been ill maintained offer an angler very little assistance when hooked up with a 50-pound bruiser. In the salt, machined reels with a minimum capacity of 300 yards of Dacron backing are needed. Of course, backing capacities can also be increased by utilizing gel-spun or Spectra low-stretch products. The newer top-of-the-line reels with carbon or other synthetic drag systems are a good universal choice, as they are impervious to the elements, which can be especially harsh in the saltwater environment. As an added bonus, they are virtually maintenance-free. Abel, Charlton, Loop, Tibor, Billy Pate, and Ross all manufacture reels that are sound and reliable.

For a floating line, weight-forward tapers with short heads (designed for quick, powerful casts) are ideal for almost all chinook salmon applications and where big, bushy flies are the norm. Pike and bass specialty tapers often fit this bill, as do most lines designed for casting

*Imitating the local baitfish is
rule number one for saltwater
fly-anglers.*

larger streamers or baitfish patterns. In the great majority of freshwater king salmon scenarios, however, the
action is going to be taking place below the surface. And
as the old maxim states, most fish are caught long before
ever putting a fly in the water. Anglers looking to fish
more efficiently—and more successfully—should carry
an assortment of heads or sinking tips between 100 and
750 grains. (A floating line with interchangeable tips will
work as well, if you don't mind the loop-to-loop connections.) Study the water, determining depth and current
speed, and then adjust your tackle to suit. Having the
right line for the water and technique to be fished
negates the need to load up with split shot and also
allows anglers to utilize more animated, less heavily
weighted flies. Being able to consistently select the right
line will ultimately result in more hookups, and while
the denser lines may seem like overkill, they are the only
ones that will get the job done in some situations (for
example, when fishing the hover technique, described
below). For leaders, short is the standard for sinking-line
presentations, allowing anglers to maintain better control of the fly. As chinook generally aren't leader-shy, 4
to 6 feet of 15- to 25-pound test is sufficient. Longer, 8-
to 10-foot leaders are needed for floating line or some
sinking-tip presentations. In these situations, anglers are
advised to begin building their leaders with a butt section
that's approximately 65 percent of the diameter of the
fly line, then taper the leader via a series of blood knots
to 15- or 12-pound tippet. A standard formula could be
3 feet of 40-pound test to 2 feet of 25, 3 feet of 20, and
the 1-foot tippet. Fluorocarbon should be used in ultra-
clearwater situations. Otherwise, leaders should be constructed with abrasion-resistant monofilament. Mason,
Hard, Rio Saltwater, and Maxima Clear are all Alaska staples. Extruded leaders can be used, but properly built
tapered leaders perform immeasurably better when casting the large, bulky flies often used for chinook.

FLIES FOR ALASKA'S CHINOOK

The only time patterns imitating an actual food source
are effective for king salmon is when fishing for the
species in the saltwater environment, when they're still
actively feeding. Both generalist baitfish patterns that
don't exactly imitate anything in nature—like Lefty's
Deceiver—and more complicated designs will work in a
variety of circumstances. Examples of the latter category
would include patterns like Trey Combs's Sea Habits and
the family of epoxy-headed flies originated by Bob
Popovics. Rich Culver, a Southeast Alaska guide, prefers
sparsely tied ALF (Anchovy Looking Fly) patterns for
intercepting ocean-feeding chinook along their outer
Chichagof Island migration routes. Culver ties his ALF
patterns in a variety of sizes ranging from 1/0 to 4, with
the most common colors being green or blue for backs
and white for the body.

Anglers designing their own Alaska baitfish patterns
should mind a few common elements. For most imitative
patterns, the inclusion of eyes, gills, and some translucence in the body of the fly can be critical. Creating flies
of the correct size can also be key, as is maintaining a
decent amount of animation. If fishing for deep-running
kings, the incorporation of some white or phosphorescent materials is usually necessary to aid in making the
fly more visible at lower light levels.

The vast majority of chinook salmon angling in
Alaska, however, occurs once the fish have vacated salt
water for their natal rivers and streams. But as has been
noted previously, king salmon are no longer actively
feeding once they enter fresh water. Thus, the challenge
in successfully fly-fishing for the species in rivers and
streams is to design patterns that will either elicit a territorial response from the fish or flies so harmless—or
realistic—looking that they will be picked up almost
reflexively. Personal preference is the most significant
criterion of design, but if there is one certainty when it

comes to king salmon flies, it's that effective colors and patterns can change from day to day and week to week, or even if the sun retreats behind a layer of clouds. Expect streamside experimentation.

Most Alaska chinook patterns are large, full-bodied creations tied on heavy-wire salmon hooks in sizes ranging from 4 to 3/0. Many call for barbell or bead-chain eyes and underbody wraps of lead. It is wise to keep in mind that generally speaking, the lighter the fly, the more lifelike it will appear. Often, a lot of weight serves only to dampen a pattern's animation. A better strategy would be to use a minimum number of wraps or none at all and instead employ sinking lines to get the offering down. As far as effective colors, theories abound. That salmon can be taken consistently on a plain black fly has been proven many times over. Still, when it comes to tying attractor patterns for Alaska's chinook, most anglers prefer vibrant hues, with red, hot pink, and chartreuse leading the way. Mixing colors, especially black and the more garish tints, will often help evenly distribute the tonal values of a fly, making it appear more lifelike. The last and probably most important thing to keep in mind is that a making a successful presentation is almost always furthered when you feel good about your fly. Patterns that don't inspire confidence shouldn't even be tied on the end of the tippet, as it's doubtful they'll ever be fished with the kind of methodical, sustained endeavor necessary to encounter success with chinook salmon.

ANGLING STRATEGIES

Anglers hoping to hook a king can maximize their chances long before making that first cast by choosing the right fishery. Although dense with anadromous fish, Alaska's great rivers (like the Yukon, Nushagak, Susitna, Copper, Kenai, and Kuskokwim) are also large and intimidating. Often much of the sport fishing for chinook

BRIAN O'KEEFE

on these rivers takes place in lower, tidally influenced sections of slow-moving water, which should be anathema to fly-fishers. Many of the largest of these salmon highways, like the Yukon, Kuskokwim, Copper, and Susitna, also carry heavy silt loads and are unfishable in their mainstems. If targeting chinook in one of these rivers is the only option available, the fly-angler's only recourse is to prospect feeder streams, pockets of holding water, and accessible upriver seams.

Salmon streamers for every occasion.

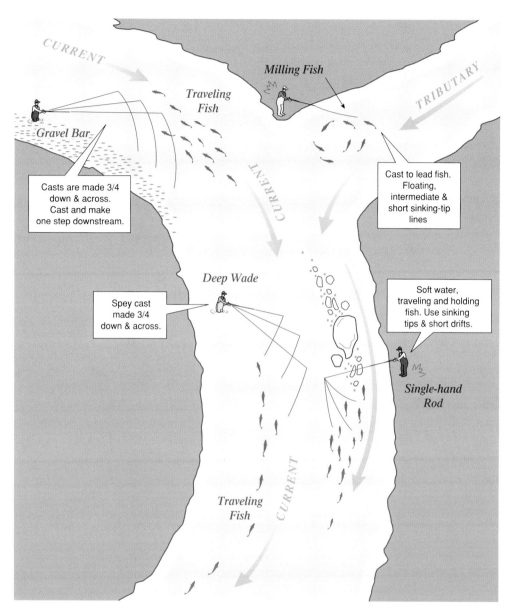

CURRENT

Milling Fish

TRIBUTARY

Traveling Fish

Gravel Bar

Casts are made 3/4 down & across. Cast and make one step downstream.

CURRENT

Cast to lead fish. Floating, intermediate & short sinking-tip lines

Deep Wade

Spey cast made 3/4 down & across.

Soft water, traveling and holding fish. Use sinking tips & short drifts.

Single-hand Rod

Traveling Fish

CURRENT

Ideally, anglers can choose a productive salmon stream with clear water, where sight-fishing is possible, since it usually takes fairly precise presentations—within a few feet, depending on conditions—to entice a chinook to strike. Selected water should be neither too

shallow for big-bodied kings to hold nor too deep to effectively present a fly. Most chinook anglers also like to fish areas closer to the sea if possible, as the fish are generally brighter and more aggressive when fresh from the salt. If the water is occluded or conditions are otherwise averse to sight-fishing, it's wise to look for signs of fish before committing. Much good angling time is wasted when blind-fishing dead water. Like other Pacific salmon species, chinook in fresh water will often roll and allow anglers an easy opportunity to isolate their position. Still, if good numbers of fish aren't visible in the water or showing themselves on the surface, there are a few other characteristics typical of quality salmon haunts to look for.

Understanding migration corridors and the staging and resting points favored by chinook will pay dividends to the angler. For the most part, kings will be found moving and holding in the main channels of rivers, so begin there, especially if fishing a smaller, more "user-friendly" stream. Shallow, choppy runs with moderate current and consistent gravel bottoms can be perfect for fly-fishing salmon in lower rivers. Chinook will be found at greater depths than other salmon; cutbanks or river bends where the channel is deeper are often premium lies. Deep, slow pools are also magnets for holding fish, which use these areas to rest and recuperate from the rigors of their migration. Tailouts, ledge pools, eddies, the edges of sloughs, and the current seams created by large boulders and islands provide additional chinook water. Areas near a confluence with a tributary stream are usually another sure bet, as salmon will hold among the cleaner, more oxygenated flows of the creek mouth. Upriver, kings will also hold beneath a tributary stream in which they intend to spawn, ostensibly waiting for the conditions to be just right or for their eggs and milt to ripen before commencing upon the final leg of their freshwater journey.

In any of these situations, chinook salmon holding in a specific area are precisely what the angler should be seeking, as these are usually rested and more territorial than moving fish, making them much more willing to strike. With holding fish, anglers are also offered more opportunities to present their fly. And king salmon do frequently hold in one place for varying lengths of time, sometimes weeks, during their in-river migrations. ADF&G radio telemetry studies in the Kenai River have done much to illuminate the milling nature of king

salmon. Here, radio-tagged chinook frequently held in the upper intertidal stretches of the lower river for anywhere from one to several weeks before moving the final few miles to a spawning site. One fish milled in a single location for thirty-four days until moving only 3 more miles upstream to spawn. Similar behavior has been observed for chinook of the Susitna River, including fish that overshot their target streams and then returned later to enter and spawn. Anglers can reasonably assume that migrating chinook across their Alaska range behave much the same as these populations.

For big-water rivers, like the giants mentioned previously, the lack of noticeable structure can be daunting. Seams are visible in rivers like the Nushagak or Kenai and are often pathways for fish, but they can run a quarter mile in length. Bank fishing in these areas is notoriously difficult. One of the profitable techniques applied in such situations is to fish two-handed rods from a boat. If the conditions warrant, the boat can be anchored or kept under power by a skilled operator while casts are made quartered downstream. This technique can also be employed from driftboats or jet sleds on small and medium-sized streams.

As explained above, the clearwater pullouts that feeder streams provide to big-water chinook can also be fantastic locations for fly-anglers to ply their trade. After traveling through silt-laden, colder flows of a main channel, freshly arrived fish are regularly seen rolling and flushing sediment from their gills in the warmer, cleaner flows. They seem to become much more energetic, and because these water intersections are often stacked with fish, casting to the well-rested and territorial kings can be exciting. In general, floating lines and lighter heads work best under these circumstances.

Tactics are quite different for fishing Alaska's smaller rivers, of course, though the term "smaller" is relative in the state. Quality king salmon streams, like the Karluk,

ABOVE: *Chrome-bright chinook.*

LEFT: *Chinook salmon.*

Ayakulik, Aniak, or Kanektok, are much smaller than big-water drainages like the Yukon or Copper Rivers, but it's doubtful many Lower Forty-eight anglers would consider the Karluk a "small" river. Often tributaries to the great systems, these smaller waters are home to much of the state's classic fly water. Narrow braids and deep pools are frequently congested with rested fish, which can be targeted with floating lines and, on rare occasions, fished with topwater flies. In addition, spotting, casting, and delivering the fly to shallow-holding fish can be thrilling.

When fishing some of the smaller chinook streams, the lack of good holding water is a benefit: Anglers can more easily find fish. Kodiak's Karluk River, very similar in appearance to the Madison River in Montana, is the archetypal example of such a sprawling, rock-bottomed Alaska river, with very little holding water available except in small channels and the pools beneath undercut banks. A prime lie on the Karluk may be nothing more than a 20-foot seam trailing from behind a large rock. Chinook in rivers like this are primarily travelers, rarely stopping until they find a decent place to hold for an extended period of time. Moving kings are very easy to see in shallow water, though they don't exhibit the same sort of territorial disposition as fish schooled in deep pools. Casts must be made expediently and flies fished as deep as possible, because the tendency is for thin-water kings to hug the bottom. Strikes are often reflexive, with hard grabs the exception, not the rule. However, king salmon hooked in shallow water are more likely to sprint away from the angler rather than simply sit down and sulk in deep water like big-river fish. Chasing a running chinook downstream over boulders while into your backing is a daunting challenge. Trying to land green fish on short lines in heavy, shallow currents is a recipe for disaster.

Small water doesn't necessarily have to mean shallow,

though; some other smaller Alaska rivers, like the Situk River and Willow, Montana, and Sheep Creeks, flow deep and clear. Fishing the deep flows on these diminutive chinook streams presents its own trials. Floating lines with split shot or heavily weighted flies are cumbersome to cast and require the angler to rely on short, inefficient drifts to keep from fouling in the numerous deadfalls and snags typical of these waters. Sinking-tip lines could help in this regard, of course, but they're not as effective when fished in close quarters.

As far as the best specific fishing conditions—beyond the water—the early and late hours on overcast or windy days are hard to beat, for king salmon are very sensitive to light and seem to prefer bad weather and the quiet hours of the day for most of their activity. That is why so much more surface rolling is seen very early in the morning and during the lingering hours of Alaska's midnight sun. When the water has been selected and it's time to finally make that initial presentation, anglers would do well to remember the importance of first getting deep and then staying there. While chinook will occasionally move a few feet for a fly, they almost never move up to take. Precision is everything at this stage: The fly must approach a fish at a controlled speed and depth, usually passing within inches of its face. The most common approach is to employ the standard wet-fly swing. Here an angler will make an across-stream or down-and-across cast and then point the rod at the fly to follow it downstream. It's important to remain in a good (tip-down) position to set the hook during the drift when swinging a fly through salmon water, as even the slightest hesitation in the line's progress can signal a chinook strike.

While the standard swing is often the most productive manner, there is merit in sometimes combining a short, sharp retrieve with the drift. Also, it can pay to hesitate at the end of the swing and then strip the fly back in a few feet before lifting the line to cast again. A profitable

BRIAN O'KEEFE

Chinook silhouette.

fast-water tactic is to cast at a 45-degree angle upstream and then strip the fly in front of holding salmon. When chinook are found in still- or frog-water locations, however, the best bet is to employ a mini tip or other short sinking-tip line or an intermediate sinking line with a longer (9-foot) leader. Once a school's orientation has been determined, you can cast ahead of the group, count down to give the fly a chance to sink, and then strip it back directly in front of the milling salmon. If a group of kings suddenly goes into lockjaw, refusing any and all offerings, try moving upstream and casting directly at the fish. Let the fly drift through them and then strip it up

from behind. Sometimes the sudden appearance of a fly arriving from the rear will trigger vicious strikes from previously tight-lipped chinook.

For small, deep-water streams like Willow Creek, an excellent tactic to employ is one that's very similar to the methods used by anglers back-trolling deep plugs in the big rivers of the Pacific Northwest. Fly-fishers can use the same technique by casting heavier-grain lines at steep downstream angles. The fly in this scenario virtually hovers in front of holding fish during the short swing. Since the drift is much shorter, though, it's even more important to get down quickly—and, in these often heavier waters, to stay down. The lines you'd consider normal when looking at this type of water from a wet-fly-swing perspective—say, 200- to 400-grain sinking lines—simply will not be effective. Anglers, like Jim Teeny, who perfected the tactic for Alaska's kings, commonly use upward of 600-grain lines and have found great success in this hover technique.

A properly fished fly can instigate a wide variety of strike responses, both vicious and otherwise. Much probably depends on the temperament of the individual fish; takes can range from violent, teeth-jarring crashes to an almost imperceptible bump, when a salmon will simply stop the fly momentarily before spitting it back out. Specifically, observation points to at least five different varieties of takes. These responses are similar for other anadromous fish, especially the four remaining members of North America's Pacific salmon fleet, with divergence probably manifest only in the frequency a particular response is encountered.

First is a take borne of feeding habits that returned with the fish from the sea. However, such a take is rarely vigorous. The second type is without a doubt the chinook response most popular with anglers—aggression. Here a fish will display an instantaneous and apparently reflexive reaction to a fly that suddenly appears within its territory. Violence is the hallmark of this take, and reels are usually singing before the angler even has a chance to move. Next is the induced response, which can seem very similar to the more habitual feeding just mentioned. In this circumstance, salmon are most likely reacting to something that appears to be getting away, often taking as the fly begins to rise at the very end of the swing. The fourth possibility is predicated upon simple inquisitiveness. No aggression is apparent; there is no chasing after escaping prey. Rather these fish just stop, inhale, or even nudge a fly traveling directly in their path. Last is the aggravated response. Comparable to the aggression take,

a chinook salmon in this instance crunches a fly it has simply had enough of. These are usually fish that have refused previous offerings but suddenly attack on the third or fourth pass. There is no mistaking this fish. No matter what kind of take is displayed, set the hook immediately and with authority, for chinook salmon have notoriously hard mouths. The strip-strike, a popular technique among saltwater fly-anglers, is a good alternative for kings. After the hook is set, hold on.

FLY-FISHING AT NIGHT

When fishing many of the chinook rivers in Alaska, anglers can be quite surprised by the lackluster bite that often takes place during the height of the day in the months of June and July. Water temperatures in some areas of the state can reach seventy degrees and higher at this time of year, especially in tannin-influenced rivers of low gradient, which literally become heat sinks under the hot summer sun. Chinook traveling in these waters will rest in the deepest holes and spend very little time moving in daylight, hot-sun conditions. At these times, a different approach is needed.

TONY WEAVER

RIGHT: *Night can often be the best time to fish for chinook.*

If floating during the doldrums of an Alaska summer—especially in smaller streams like Alexander Creek or the Deshka River, which drain muskeg-covered lowlands and flow with little impetus—it wouldn't be out of the ordinary for king salmon anglers to think they'd stumbled upon water completely devoid of fish. Even when chinook can be seen in such a setting, they're not willing biters during the middle of the day. Summer nights, however, are an entirely different matter. The evenings of June and July often bring all kinds of excitement to the Alaska wilds, as bears and other animals come out and roam the river corridors for food. Salmon are also on the move, having rested through the heat of the day, and the shallow riffles and other transition water that seemed vacant just a few hours earlier will be alive with large, aggressive chinook. Now the deep pools serve not as locations for extended recuperation but as pit stops where the fish can pull over and rest before moving on to the next pool.

This increase in activity offers great opportunity to the fly-angler. Besides the fact that these energized fish are incalculably more likely to strike, the constant movement will keep a single pool filled with fresh fish for hours, as new arrivals continue to push into the prime lies and force holding fish upriver. Approaches to water are typically not critical for night fishing chinook; nor is it usually profitable to get too caught up in selecting the right fly. Large-profile, noisy flies, like many deer hair creations, will work just fine when drifted through pools or even riffled transition water, since the amplified energy level of the fish and their increased penchant to defend against territorial intrusions incite chinook to new levels of aggression. The best angling will take place during the hours of lowest light, which, in Alaska's extended daytime, is closer to dusk than real darkness. This nocturnal window of peak fishing usually occurs from about 10 PM to 5 AM. Pay attention to current regulations, though—some rivers are closed to fishing at night.

TOPWATER CHINOOK

Coho salmon are well known for their propensity to rise and attack patterns skated across the surface. Under the right circumstances, both chum and pink salmon will also come up for a waking fly. Much less susceptible to topwater enticements are chinook salmon.

Normally the deepest-running of the Pacific salmon, the king prefers the power water in most streams and rivers where they can only be reached by deploying sinking lines. Still, there are times when the well-presented offering will tempt chinook to raid the uppermost layers of water.

Disregarding the occasional reckless, totally random take, attracting king salmon to the surface requires a great deal of patience most of the time, with anglers averaging hundreds of casts per hookup. Maybe that's why so few fly-fishers even carry a topwater chinook pattern in their box.

Success also requires nearly perfect conditions . . . in just the right location. When searching for the latter, the mouths of clearwater rivers are the best place to start. An angler fishing one of Alaska's many small coastal drainages can almost always find a few pockets of fairly shallow holding water near a stream's terminus. Chinook will stack in the pools as they move in from the sea. These are aggressive fish that likely harbor at least some feeding reflexes held over from their years in the ocean's great feeding lanes. Fly-anglers already know this, of

TONY WEAVER

Chinook attractors.

course, as sea-lice-toting kings are ready takers of most subsurface offerings. What many don't know, however, is that this same scenario can also offer outstanding possibilities for making a topwater presentation. This is especially true during peak tides when large groups of fresh fish will move in and stack on top of each other in the first available buckets of deeper water.

George Davis, an Alaska fly-fishing guide known for his pursuit of salmon on top, says that when looking for surface action he almost always targets chinook within a quarter mile of the salt. In the early 1990s, Davis and a few others regularly fishing the coastal streams south of Yakutat soon noticed that the freshest kings would aggressively chase Deceivers and other baitfish patterns when fished on a floating line just beneath the surface. Occasionally, a fish would even swirl on an offering before it had a chance to sink completely. Shortly there-

after, Davis began experimenting with topwater designs. The first patterns used were flies that skittered through the surface film. Fish would take these patterns less frequently than they would a subsurface fly, but action increased noticeably as pressure from additional fish pushing into the lower river reaches intensified.

Coastal streams aren't the only environments where chinook will rise for a fly, though. Slower upriver pools where migrating fish tend to hold often contain salmon similarly inclined. The upper portions of the Susitna and Yentna River drainages, for example, offer a good number of small clearwater feeder streams where chinook will stack like cordwood. John Wilson, owner of the area's Lake Marie Lodge, says these kings will occasionally move up for a surface offering. Wilson adds that in his experience, alpha males seem most susceptible to a topwater fly, sometimes following one all the way across a pool before finally crunching it. In clear water, anglers patient enough to sit and study the milling fish for a moment can easily see which of a particular group are the most aggressive. Success rates are obviously heightened by singling out and casting toward these "chasers" first.

For topwater chinook offerings, Wilson prefers a fly that pops and has developed a number of his own patterns, including the Lake Marie Popper, a cork-bodied fly that's tied with Krystal Flash and a marabou tail. Pink is the most common color for the LMP, though the same fly in chartreuse can be effective under certain circumstances. Good results can be had when fishing the pattern with a distinctive strip-pop-stop action. Surface patterns like pencil poppers and other slim-profile flies work well with brighter fish closer to the ocean. Davis looks for his topwater chinook patterns to ride in the surface film and push water. To accomplish this, he favors a foam-bodied slider that can be either fished on the swing as a waking fly or stripped with a high rod tip, producing a skittering effect.

FAR RIGHT: *In Southeast Alaska, fishing in the salt is often the only option for a chinook angler.*

BELOW: *Lake Marie Poppers.*

Although chinook returns are widespread in Alaska, only a few areas of the state present prime water for taking kings on the surface. For coastal chinook, finding a combination of shallow (less than 3 feet), sandy-bottomed pools and strong numbers of fresh fish is the key. The area between Port Moller and Cold Bay on the southern Alaska Peninsula may be one of the best locations; many of this region's short, crystal-clear streams host quality runs of chinook and receive little pressure. The coastal rivers south of Yakutat, including the Situk, also offer reliable potential for topwater angling. In larger inland systems like those of the Susitna, Nushagak, and Kuskokwim Rivers, possibilities are primarily limited to clearwater pools near tributary mouths when significant numbers of fish can be found. Even then, fishing for king salmon on the surface is never a sure thing, and anglers should be prepared for refusals to greatly outnumber takes.

THE SALTWATER CHINOOK

While kings can be readily found in freshwater environs, their propensity for deep feeding and otherwise elusive nature make them tough quarry in the open ocean. In some areas of the Gulf of Alaska and the Bering Sea, these fish are known to feed at depths greater than 200 feet. Yet there are also places where sea-roaming king salmon can be found cruising well within reach. Fly-fishing for open ocean chinook may be one of the most difficult challenges an angler will ever undertake, but by understanding some of the variables found in the saltwater environment, and by applying a few proven techniques, it can be done.

First, it is absolutely critical to gain an understanding of the tides and what they mean to the angler. In Alaska, tides are extreme, with water differentials between high and low tide sometimes exceeding 30 feet. This is especially true in the Cook Inlet area, which has some of the

BRIAN O'KEEFE

largest tidal changes in the world. In any region, on any size of tide, the greatest movement of water occurs around the peak of the flood tide, with about an hour and a half before this high and another hour and a half into the ebb tide being very productive: The greater the water movement, the greater the activity of baitfish, crustaceans, and, yes, salmon. However, while inshore waters are worth taking a look at, most areas of open ocean are virtually impossible to fly-fish during large tide changes. Only the brief slack period will likely yield decent opportunities.

Tides with slighter water differentials between high and low tide often have less baitfish activity, but they are much more conducive to fly-fishing. There is considerably less current during these tides, and more time to fish. In Alaska waters, a 5- to 8-foot water differential is a good place to start. Anglers can also attempt to intercept salmon migrating from one area to another during tidal changes. Tide books will give detailed tide information for different areas, which can be used to help pinpoint locations and times with peak fishing possibilities.

Of course, saltwater fly-fishers should remain mindful of the wind as well, which can profoundly affect angling possibilities. In Prince William Sound, a southerly wind can bring treacherous swells rolling in from the Gulf of Alaska, while a northern wind in Resurrection Bay will turn shallow bays into a frothy chop. Wind blowing in the same direction as an incoming tide can increase the depth and movement of water, further reducing fly-fishing opportunities, just as a wind that shears a tide's course can nullify much of the uppermost current. Keeping a few secret bays, coves, or lee points in reserve for times of the worst conditions will often provide alternatives when none seem to exist.

Even on a perfectly still day, with a favorable tide, finding success in the salt is far from a foregone conclusion. Concentrations of chinook are hard to locate, and fish pass through their migration zones randomly at best. Plus, there's always the depth factor. Heavily used feeding grounds near kelp beds and inshore points, coves, and bays found close to streams of salmon origin usually yield more consistent results than large areas of open water. During peak run times, the salt- and freshwater mix near the mouths of rivers will hold staging chinook. They are easier to fish as well, since they tend to be shallower, with higher concentrations of fish. In fact, in some areas, sight-fishing to kings milling near these river entrances is a distinct possibility. However, spotting fish fairly easily usually means the sun is out. Overcast, slightly windy days will bring feeding chinook closer to the surface and improve the angler's odds.

Deep fish require the use of specialized equipment. Heavy sinking lines and heads (750 grains and more) are the norm for saltwater chinook angling, with casts being made upcurrent and the line allowed to drift down to the proper depth. Lines can be marked for accurate, depth-controlled fishing, particularly if a school of feeding fish has been located by the boat's electronics. This technique is very similar to the big-water technique used when fishing from boats in Alaska's largest rivers. Only on the open ocean, instead of a horizontal swing at the end of a three-quartered down-and-across cast, lines will sweep vertically until they reach their maximum depth. At the hang-down position, anglers can employ a short jigging motion before retrieving the line to make another cast.

However, even along a known migration route, fishing can be very slow, punctuated by periods of intense action as fresh schools pass through. Some of Alaska's better potential intercept areas for saltwater chinook are Montague Strait in Prince William Sound, the inshore areas from Anchor Point to Deep Creek, bays and coves near Kodiak Island, the coastal waters from Yakutat to Icy Bay, and the waters near Sitka and Chichagof and Prince of Wales Islands in Southeast.

Chinook Salmon in Alaska

Although the chinook accounts for only about 5 percent of the total commercial catch of all Pacific salmon, it has historically been, and remains, a fish of great importance to Native Alaskans. Sport anglers, too, regard the chinook with the highest esteem; it's probably the most prized game fish in the state, and easily accessible streams with even moderately decent returns draw large crowds of anglers. The annual sport harvest has recently reached one hundred thousand or more fish, with Cook Inlet and adjacent watersheds contributing over half the catch. When added to Alaska's commercial catch of better than half a million chinook, a subsistence take of ninety thousand fish or more per year, and increasing reports detailing the decline of the country's wild fisheries, it might appear that Alaska's native king salmon populations are headed for trouble. However, unlike the Endangered Species Act–protected stocks of the Pacific Northwest, the chinook's status in Alaska has for the most part remained remarkably stable.

In fact healthy and, in a lot of places, thriving returns of wild chinook occur along most of the southern and western coasts of Alaska, from Dixon Entrance to Point Hope. The most popular fisheries are undoubtedly those found along the road system in the Southcentral region of the state. The Kenai River, paralleled by the Sterling Highway for much of its length, receives by far the most angling pressure of any king salmon river in Alaska; trophy hunters from all over the world annually flock to its charming blue-green waters. The tributaries of the Susitna River, most of which intersect the Parks Highway north of Anchorage, also garner significant angling interest. And despite the occasional crowds, anglers willing to get off the beaten path can still find fantastic angling mixed with a true wilderness setting on many of these clearwater streams.

LEFT: *A short stream drains a large Prince William Sound ice field.*

For the devoted fly-angler who might be looking to package what are undoubtedly the world's best king salmon fly-fishing opportunities with some of the most remote, awe-inspiring settings in the Last Frontier, the clear-flowing rivers of Southwest Alaska must appear to be a little slice of heaven right here on earth. The renowned streams of the Bristol Bay region and of the raw, untamed Alaska Peninsula, as well as the many tributaries of the lower and middle Kuskokwim River, present more abundant fly-fishing prospects than just about anywhere else in the state. The Karluk and Ayakulik Rivers of Kodiak Island can also offer nearly unequaled king salmon angling, along with the chance to soak up some of the splendor of Alaska's own Emerald Isle.

Though king salmon fishing is restricted in much of the freshwater angling environment in Southeast, the coastal streams near Yakutat are home to a few good to excellent returns. In the Interior, king salmon can be found in and below just about every clearwater confluence of the Yukon. The Gulkana, the Klutina, and most of the other tributaries of the Copper River also host significant chinook fisheries. And finally, near the northern end of the chinook's range, a few noteworthy returns can be found in drainages spilling into either Kotzebue or Norton Sounds.

All of these regions are of colossal size on their own, and each plays host to several quality king salmon returns. Some of these rivers, such as the Kenai, the Situk, and the Alagnak, were long ago made famous by the earliest-returning Pacific salmon of the year. Others, because of location or logistics, have managed to escape much of the crowding that can define chinook angling in many Alaska streams. Others have yet to be discovered.

SOUTHEAST ALASKA

For an area as well known a sport-fishing destination as Southeast Alaska, it may seem strange to find but a few

opportunities available for taking king salmon on a fly rod. This is because most of the panhandle—from Dixon Entrance south of Ketchikan to Cape Fairweather, which sits along the Gulf of Alaska Coast between the community of Yakutat and Cross Sound—is restricted to fishing for the species in fresh water. Plainly put, a substantial majority of the chinook angling (which can be outstanding, by the way) that takes place each year in the region is accomplished in saltwater fisheries. This Southeast Alaska saltwater harvest—both commercial and sport—is known to be composed of stocks originating from the Yakutat area to the southern coast of Oregon. The principal contributing non-Alaska populations include several of British Columbia's large wild stocks (such as king salmon from the Nass, Skeena, and Fraser Rivers), hatchery stocks from the west coast of Vancouver Island and Georgia Strait, the native Upriver Bright stock from the Columbia River, and wild chinook from various Oregon and Washington coastal rivers.

There are several drainages within Southeast that receive decent to strong returns of chinook. However, in the mid-1970s it became apparent that many of these local stocks had fallen from their historical levels of production. A fisheries management program was implemented to rebuild the stocks in eleven key streams: the transboundary (streams that eventually flow into Southeast Alaska coastal waters but have origins in Canada) Taku, Stikine, Alsek, Unuk, Chickamin, and Chilkat Rivers, and the nontransboundary Blossom, Keta, Situk, and King Salmon Rivers, along with Andrew Creek. Of the eleven, only two, the Situk and Alsek, are outside the Cape Fairweather to Dixon Entrance freshwater closure. This rebuilding program has since been incorporated into the U.S./Canada Pacific Salmon Treaty, and as of 2003, ten of the eleven stocks are judged to be healthy. In fact, many of these streams have recently seen a return to record chinook salmon outputs.

LEFT: *Outside Anchorage.*

The 2001 Stikine River escapement of about sixty-three thousand large spawners was the highest on record since estimation began in 1973. Also in 2001, another of the eleven index streams, Andrew Creek, witnessed its highest escapement on record—2,260 chinook. The Taku River, a large glacial system that originates in the high plateau country of northwestern British Columbia and discharges its flow into the Pacific just east of Juneau, has experienced a threefold increase in its chinook salmon escapements in the three decades since the new regulations have been in effect. The Taku, which produces the largest local population of chinook salmon on average in Southeast Alaska, has seen the rebuilding process raise its average number of returning kings from an estimated 19,500 large spawners in the 1970s to an estimated average of 62,750 throughout the 1990s.

There is but one chance for freshwater anglers to chase chinook salmon in the area south of Cape Fairweather, and it occurs only when the ADF&G opens—by emergency-order authority—a few small freshwater areas to the harvest of hatchery king salmon. Some of the typical openings include small systems like the Juneau roadside streams, Pullen Creek near Skagway, Blind Slough near Petersburg, and Sawmill Creek near Sitka. Often these fisheries are small, but local residents take advantage of the opportunities, with some systems receiving more interest recently.

The area from Cape Fairweather northwest to Cape Suckling, which includes the Yakutat Forelands, is another story entirely. There, sport fishing for king salmon is open in fresh water, and several clearwater systems—the Situk, East, Italio, and Akwe Rivers being most the prominent—not only produce king salmon but also provide anglers reasonable chances of success with a fly.

The Situk River, a small but disproportionately productive drainage located just a few miles east of Yakutat, is classified by the ADF&G as a medium-producing

chinook salmon system, with annual total returns estimated to be from fifteen hundred to ten thousand adult fish (most runs are in the two- to five-thousand-fish range). Situk River kings appear to be an outside rearing stock, migrating west and north into the Gulf of Alaska for the duration of their saltwater existence. They return in the spring, with adults migrating into the lower Situk River from late May through the end of July (run peaks usually occur from mid-June through early July). Most Situk chinook anglers concentrate their efforts from Nine Mile Bridge to the flats near the river's mouth.

At least part of the reason for the Situk's king salmon productivity is that the number of adults produced per spawner in this drainage is greater than for most other Southeast Alaska chinook stocks. The majority—anywhere from 60 to 95 percent—of the smolt are subyearling fish that emigrate to the sea the year after spawning. This early (by Alaska standards) out-migration enables juvenile Situk chinook to bypass mortality that would occur for most other king salmon stocks during the year spent in fresh water as fry. Other Yakutat Forelands stocks, like chinook from the Akwe and Italio, also produce a high percentage of subyearling smolt. The most likely hypothesis for the peculiarity of these stocks is based upon the lagoons available for rearing in these systems. The only other locations where subyearling smolt have been observed in Southeast Alaska are the Keta and Blossom Rivers, two clearwater rivers far to the south.

Of the other Yakutat Forelands streams known to receive runs of king salmon, the East Alsek River is probably the best known, and the fly-angler's best bet. Smaller even than the Situk, the East Alsek (or East) River is a fishery on the rise. Located along the Gulf Coast about 60 miles southeast of Yakutat and only a few miles south of the glacial Alsek River, the East Alsek is accessible via wheel planes, which can land either at the

BRIAN O'KEEFE

airstrip located near the river's middle section or a few miles farther downriver on the gravel beaches near the mouth. The chinook run is short but intense, providing steady to fantastic action when anglers hit it just right. The run usually peaks around the first two weeks of June.

There is one more area of Southeast that enterprising chinook anglers should take note of, and that's the region stretching from Yakutat north to Cordova, the wild and virtually untapped Lost Coast. Backdropped by a spectacular collection of mountains and glaciers, a plethora of short, tidally influenced streams bisect the coastline, only a few of which have even begun to be explored. The status or even location of chinook stocks in this region are unknown to all but a tight-lipped few, and because the logistics of getting in remain daunting, it looks to stay that way for a while to come. For fly-rodders looking to do a little exploring, however, there are a few operators who will make a foray into the area, which primarily involves flying out from either Cordova or Yakutat. Perhaps most intriguing in the area for the pursuit of king salmon on a fly are the deserted beaches of the Icy Bay coastline, where a handful of rivers meander toward one of the most fabulously productive saltwater environments anywhere in the world. This rugged stretch of the North Gulf Coast may truly be one of the last few sanctuaries for those with the spirit for adventure fly-fishing.

SOUTHCENTRAL ALASKA

Home to Alaska's largest city, its most extensive road system, and more than half the state's total population, Southcentral predictably garners the vast majority of the angling pressure. And with chinook salmon in this part of the state, there is plenty of pressure to go around.

On the southern end of the Kenai Peninsula, between the communities of Soldotna and Homer, a triad of clearwater streams cross the Sterling Highway en route to Cook Inlet. Each stream supports a returning population

TONY WEAVER

of king salmon and can provide excellent opportunities for fly-anglers. The two southernmost streams, the Anchor River and Deep Creek, support native stocks, while the king salmon returning to the Ninilchik River are a mixture of wild and hatchery fish (the chinook stocking program has been in effect on the Ninilchik since 1988). The majority of the salmon angling on these streams takes place in lower stretches, below the Sterling Highway bridges, and each area is primarily restricted to weekend-only openings; the most productive king fishing takes place during the first half of June.

Traveling north toward Soldotna, the next chinook salmon fishery encountered after the Ninilchik is the glacial Kasilof River, which also supports a mixture of hatchery and wild fish. The bulk of the Kasilof kings typically return in early June, though a second run occurs in late July, with numbers of fish greatly reduced but average size being larger. Because of its turbid nature, the Kasilof is a difficult proposition for fly-rodders, with the

Unloading the gear. Helicopter fishing on the west side of Cook Inlet.

best possibility for success offered near the stream's confluence with tannic Crooked Creek. Just a few more miles up the Sterling Highway, however, lies one of the world's most famous king salmon streams—the mighty Kenai.

Another large, glacial runoff system, the Kenai issues from the outlet at Kenai Lake and flows some 80 miles to its rendezvous with Cook Inlet. Chinook salmon returning to the Kenai River support one of the largest and most intensively managed recreational fisheries in Alaska. Kenai kings are among the largest in the world and have sustained in excess of one hundred thousand angler-days of fishing effort annually. The fishery has been politically explosive over the years, primarily due to allocation quarrels among commercial, subsistence, personal-use, and sport concerns. Recently, the river has also spawned a growing conflict between residents and the guide–sport angler contingent.

Chinook salmon returning to the Kenai River are managed as two distinct runs, early and late, which typically peak around the second week of June and again in late July. Most early-run fish are tributary spawners, 80 percent or more, while almost all late-run fish spawn in the mainstem Kenai. Five-ocean fish are rather familiar to the river, unlike almost every other system in the state, and the all-tackle world-record king was a six-ocean fish. Counting other species as well, more current International Game Fish Association world records have been pulled from the Kenai's turquoise waters than from any other river in the world. But while the river's monster reputation fools many, this in no way should be considered a high-numbers chinook fishery. In fact, ADF&G escapement goals for Kenai kings are only 9,000 and 22,300 fish for the early and late runs, respectively. Department studies have estimated that it takes an average of twenty-nine hours of angling for every king landed on the Kenai.

The vast majority of the chinook angling takes place in the river's far lower reaches, below the Sterling Highway bridge in Soldotna. However, this fishery is nearly impossible for the fly-angler to crack, with hundreds of guide and private boats drifting, boondogging, and back-bouncing through all the celebrated king holes. Probably the best chance for success with a fly—and one of the very few places on the entire river where a modicum of opportunity awaits the bank angler—is near the Kenai's confluence with the Moose River in Sterling, along a private bank owned by the Great Alaska Adventure Lodge. Several large, potential world-fly-rod-record brutes have been taken from this bank over the years, with every hookup possibly another 50-plus-pound Kenai king.

While the crowds continue to flock to the Kenai Peninsula every year to do battle with each other, and occasionally a chrome-bright chinook, directly across Cook Inlet exist a few small, sparsely visited coastal watersheds that can offer excellent opportunities to entice ocean-fresh fish to the fly. Many of these remote, rather pristine streams produce good to excellent fly-fishing conditions and reliable king returns. Some solid performers include the Kamishak River in the bear-studded region across from Kachemak Bay and the town of Homer and the Kustatan River of Redoubt Bay, both of which receive most of what pressure they do get from coho anglers.

The McArthur and Chakachatna River systems of Trading Bay and the Beluga River to the north also provide a quality king salmon–angling environment. All three of these systems are glacially influenced, however, so the fly-fishing opportunity is limited to mouths of clearwater feeder streams. The McArthur River has more tributaries suitable for king salmon fishing, all of which are unnamed. In the Beluga system, the fishing is also limited to the mouths of several clearwater tributaries, some of the best being Coal Creek, which empties

into Beluga Lake, and Pretty and Olson Creeks in the lower Beluga River. The best chinook fishing for the streams in these three systems usually occurs during the second half of June.

Between the Beluga River and the McArthur-Chakachatna system flows a salmon stream that appears relatively inconsequential next to its neighbors on a map. It's not, especially if you yearn to feel the authoritative tug of a chinook on the end of your line. The Chuitna River is a small freestone stream that hosts a substantial chinook return, with fish of above-average size not out of the ordinary. The river runs fairly shallow for much of its course, but its winding nature, moderately swift current, and shifting rock bottom combine to form a fair number of slow, deep pools where chinook like to hold. Tannins leaching into the water render it too murky for sight-

fishing in most sections, but because there is no big water to survey, determining where fish are holding can be managed by simply reading the current. A lack of good transition water also characterizes the stream. The kings will hold in the pools and then blow out upstream, not stopping until they reach the next bucket of holding water. Heads and tailouts fish well on the Chuitna, as do the pools themselves. Like the other salmon streams on the west side of Cook Inlet, the window is narrow on the Chuitna, with the bulk of the run typically entering the river in the last two weeks of June.

North along the Glenn and then Parks Highways from Anchorage lie the chinook fisheries of the Northern Cook Inlet Management Area. This sport-fishery management area covers some 23,000 square miles of Southcentral Alaska and is dominated by the Susitna

Battling a leaper on the upper Susitna system.

Bear tracks.

River watershed, which originates in the glaciers of the Alaska and Talkeetna Ranges and flows south about 200 miles into Cook Inlet. Eighty-eight streams in this region are known to contain spawning populations of chinook salmon, but just seventeen of them are responsible for over half of the production.

Accessed primarily by jet boat, the upper Susitna River above its confluence with the Talkeetna River can provide some impressive action for fly-rodding king salmon anglers. There are several clearwater tributaries that meet the river below Devil's Canyon, almost all of which hold kings during the early-July peak of the season. The confluences with the Indian River and Portage and Fourth of July Creeks are good places to start. Farther south, along the middle Susitna River, are two of the area's best king salmon fisheries, the Talkeetna River system and Montana Creek. The mainstem of the Talkeetna, a swift wilderness river, is fishable, but fly-anglers will have much better success fishing in or near the mouths of tributary streams. Clear Creek, which can be accessed by boat from Talkeetna, is a popular chinook hot spot in early July. The Parks Highway intersects lower Montana Creek, providing anglers easy opportunity to fish the gravel-bottomed stream's lower reaches. The best king salmon fishing is from late June through early July and takes place anywhere from the mouth of the creek to several good holes located upstream. The creek runs considerably clearer than the neighboring Talkeetna River, and as such is more suitable for fly-anglers. Plus, Montana Creek's smallish stature is not conducive to boat travel, making it an even more desirable destination for the wading angler.

From mid-June through late July, one of Southcentral Alaska's best spots for intercepting returning chinook is clear-flowing Lake Creek, a tributary of the Yentna River. Lake Creek chinook salmon, similar to those returning to Montana Creek, tend to run large, with fish over 40 pounds not uncommon. The best early-season action is usually had near the confluence with the silty Yentna, but as the year progresses, anglers can find kings holding in numerous spots along the middle and upper river. Several lodges and sport-fishing operations exist near the mouth of the creek, but an ever-popular alternative is to float the 54 miles from Chelatna Lake to the confluence with the Yentna. Due to the swift, rocky nature of the creek, however, this is not a trip recommended for the novice floater. Lake Creek is also a stream that can be blown out easily, so it's wise to check with locals before undertaking the expense of a trip.

One of the most significant chinook fisheries in Southcentral occurs in the Deshka River, which has rebounded from a forced closure just a few years ago. There is little opportunity for fly-anglers near the river's confluence with the Susitna, usually a chaotic scene anyway, with the water heavily stained by tannins. The upper and middle stretches are clear enough for presenting the fly, however. Here fly-anglers can wade and fish productively without feeling restricted by oppressive crowds.

Two other road-accessible streams of the Susitna River basin, Willow and Sheep Creeks, offer good numbers of above-average-sized kings. Roads lead directly to the mouths of these rivers, giving great incentive for the hardware crowds to come together, especially at the mouth of the Willow, which is a veritable zoo during the peak of the king run. A good alternative for fishing the mouth of Willow Creek is to motor upriver and fish the numerous clear sloughs and the mouth of Little Willow Creek, where many chinook temporarily halt their upstream migrations to recuperate.

In early June, Alexander Creek can provide outstanding action for the fly-angler, though there can be considerable jet boat traffic on this stream as well. Another long popular Southcentral Alaska float-fishing destination, the Talachulitna River, remains a classic fly-fishing stream despite large increases in pressure and in the number of lodge operations that have set up camp over the past two decades. In fact, when it comes to chinook, the Tal has held up remarkably well over the years and still offers good water and plenty of fish ripe for the right fly presentation. During most years, chinook will begin to show up at the river mouth in early June, with the heart of the run peaking around July 4. As with most of these streams, the best king-fishing locations are at the tributary mouths, especially Friday Creek, and at the confluence with the Skwentna River. With deep pools and plenty of long runs, however, the Tal offers floaters good potential throughout the trip.

KODIAK ISLAND

The Karluk and Ayakulik Rivers support the only populations of native chinook salmon on Kodiak Island, with the kings returning to the rivers from late May through mid-July. Half the immigration usually passes the weirs located in the lower rivers by June 15.

From its source at the outlet of Karluk Lake, the Karluk River flows approximately 22 miles to its terminus at Karluk Lagoon at the southwest end of Kodiak Island. It is a clear stream, with moderate flow and depth. Anglers fishing the river typically gain access in one of three ways: by flying into the village of Karluk via float- or wheel plane and then fishing the lagoon and lower river; by flying into Karluk Lake and floating downstream either to the Portage or all the way to the lagoon; or finally, by flying into the Portage area and either floating to the lagoon or fishing just this reach. Most early-season chinook anglers concentrate on the lagoon and lower river stretches for bright fish as they enter the system from Shelikof Strait. As the season progresses past the middle of June, fly-ins to the Portage area or floating down from the lake become a more viable option.

However, access is an important element of sport fishing the Karluk River, as land status is dynamic and complicated. Two Native corporations—Koniag, Inc., and the Karluk Tribal Council—own much of the landing surrounding Karluk Lake and Lagoon, along with the banks along the river. A very small percentage of the drainage is owned by private individuals, contains public easements, or consists of small tracts purchased by the state of Alaska. Anglers needing access must first acquire the proper permits, which the Native corporations offer for a fee.

The Ayakulik River, located about 25 miles south of the Karluk, contains the only other native population of chinook salmon on Kodiak Island. Most of the land surrounding the Ayakulik River is within the Kodiak National Wildlife Refuge, and anglers typically gain access to the river via float-equipped aircraft. In many ways, this is a better system for chasing chinook salmon on a fly. There are typically more fish in the Ayakulik than the neighboring Karluk; the former receives decidedly less pressure, and its classic stream conditions lend themselves very nicely to fly-fishing.

The distribution of spawning chinook in the river begins just above tidewater and extends upriver. One of the major spawning tributaries is the East Fork Ayakulik upriver from the Red River. Below the Red River–Ayakulik confluence is another tributary, Bare Creek, directly accessible by floatplane and where some of the most productive king salmon angling takes place.

SOUTHWEST ALASKA

Perhaps as close to paradise as the fly-angler can get, Southwest Alaska is home to some of the state's most scenic and remote watersheds. From the vast Kuskokwim River and its many tributaries south through Katmai and on to the Alaska Peninsula, a map of the area reads like an authentic *Who's Who* of North America's

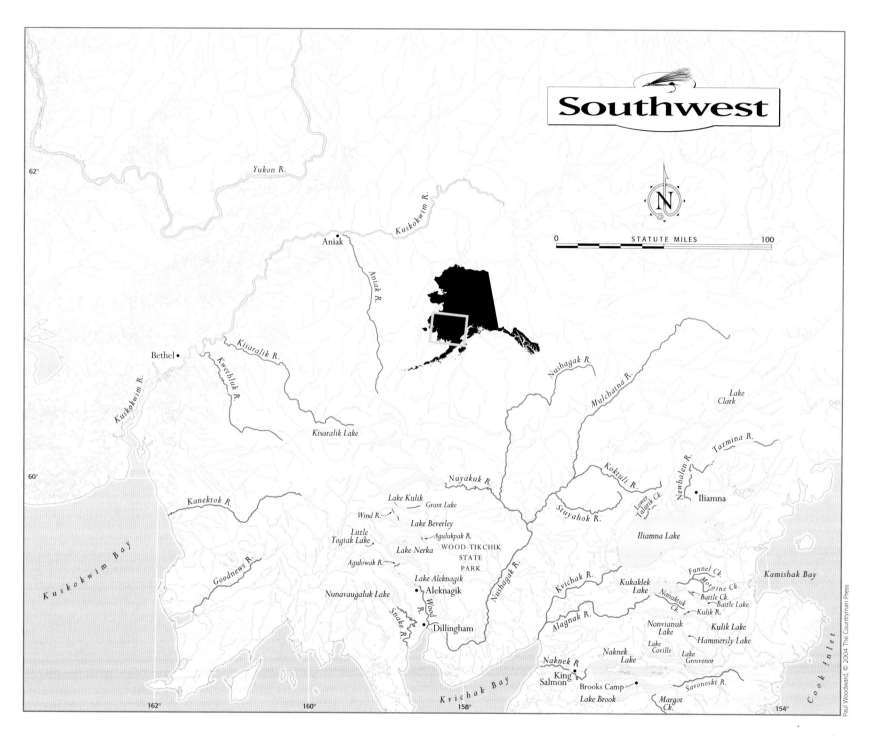

Southwest

STATUTE MILES
0 — 100

Yukon R.

Kuskokwim R.

Aniak

Aniak R.

Bethel

Kisaralik R.

Kwethluk R.

Kuskokwim R.

Kisaralik Lake

Nushagak R.

Mulchatna R.

Lake Clark

Tazmina R.

Koktuli R.

Newhalen R.

Iliamna

Nuyakuk R.

Lower Talarik Ck.

Stuyahok R.

Kanektok R.

Lake Kulik

Grant Lake

Wind R.

Lake Beverley

Iliamna Lake

Little Togiak Lake

Agulukpak R.

Lake Nerka

WOOD-TIKCHIK STATE PARK

Kuskokwim Bay

Funnel Ck.

Kamishak Bay

Agulowak R.

Goodnews R.

Lake Aleknagik

Nushagak R.

Kvichak R.

Kukaklek Lake

Moraine Ck.

Battle Ck.

Nanuktuk Ck.

Battle Lake

Nunavaugaluk Lake

Aleknagik

Wood R.

Kulik R.

Alagnak R.

Nonvianuk Lake

Kulik Lake

Snake R.

Dillingham

Hammersly Lake

Lake Coville

Naknek Lake

Lake Grosvenor

Naknek R.

King Salmon

Brooks Camp

Savonoski R.

Kvichak Bay

Lake Brook

Margot Ck.

Cook Inlet

Paul Woodward, © 2004 The Countryman Press

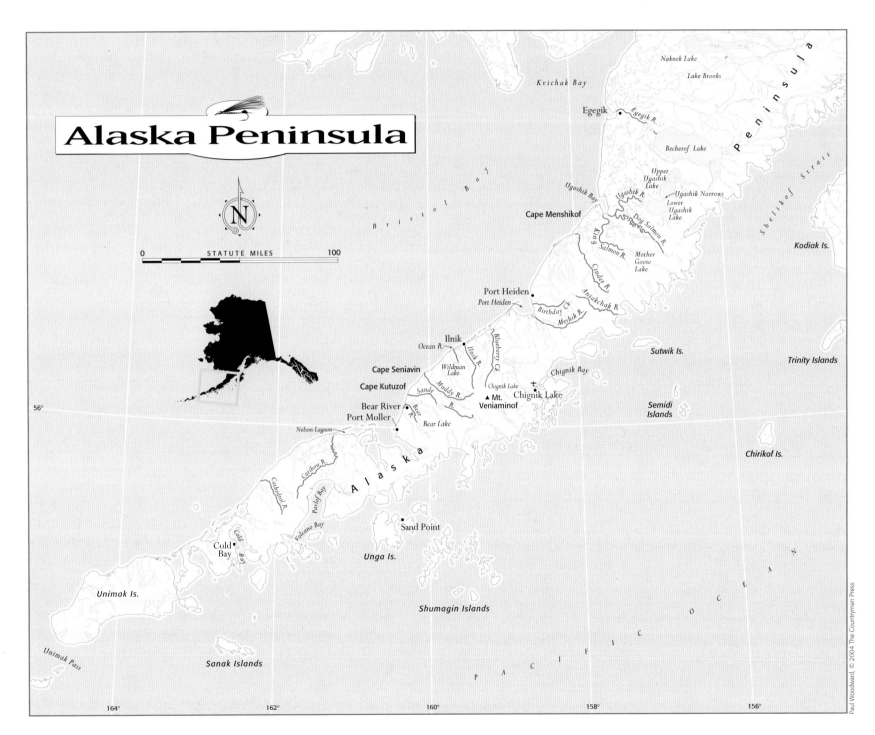

Alaska Peninsula

STATUTE MILES

0   100

Naknek Lake

Lake Brooks

Kvichak Bay

Egegik • *Egegik R.*

Becherof Lake

P
e
n
i
n
s
u
l
a

Upper
Ugashik
Lake

Ugashik Bay

Ugashik R.

Ugashik Narrows
Lower
Ugashik
Lake

Bristol Bay

Cape Menshikof

King Salmon R.

Dog Salmon R.

Cinder R.

Mother
Goose
Lake

S
h
e
l
i
k
o
f
S
t
r
a
i
t

Kodiak Is.

Port Heiden

Port Heiden

Birthday Ck.

Antiakchak R.

Meshik R.

Sutwik Is.

Trinity Islands

Ilnik

Ocean R.

Ilnik R.

Blueberry Ck.

Chignik Bay

Cape Seniavin

*Wildman
Lake*

Chignik Lake

Chignik Lake

*Semidi
Islands*

Cape Kutuzof

Sandy

Muddy R.

▲ **Mt.
Veniaminof**

Chirikof Is.

Bear River
Port Moller

*Bear
R.*

Bear Lake

Nelson Lagoon

56°

Caribou R.

A
l
a
s
k
a

Cathedral R.

Pavlof Bay

• **Sand Point**

Volcano Bay

Unga Is.

**Cold
Bay**

*Cold
Bay*

Unimak Is.

Shumagin Islands

P
A
C
I
F
I
C

O
C
E
A
N

Unimak Pass

Sanak Islands

164°   162°   160°   158°   156°

most productive wilderness rivers. And the best part for the chinook angler? Unlike other areas of the state, silt-laden rivers of strong glacial influence are the exception here rather than the rule. Many of these Southwest streams are sparkling clear, and because of that—and the fantastic numbers of salmon to be found—fly-fishing conditions could hardly be better.

The second largest river in Alaska, the 800-mile-long Kuskokwim has long been of great importance to Native Alaskans. Principally glacial in origin, the drainage's sport fishing is limited mostly to its clear-flowing tributaries, some of which, especially along the lower river, are quite famous among fly-fishers. The Aniak, Kisaralik, and Kwethluk Rivers should all come to mind. Above the Aniak confluence, sport fishing for salmon and other species has historically been very limited. In recent years, however, probing guides and anglers alike have been venturing toward the tributaries of the middle to upper Kuskokwim. The Holitna River system is the most productive sport-fishing tributary within this section of the watershed, supporting approximately half of the fishing effort, harvest, and catch in recent years for the upper Kuskokwim sport fishery. Even more recently, the sport fishery for chinook salmon has spread into other nearby tributaries of the Kuskokwim, including the Oskawalik, George, and Tatlawiksuk Rivers. There are currently about seven guiding–outfitting businesses operating on the Holitna and close to an equal number offering services on the nearby streams. Access to this portion of the Kuskokwim drainage is generally gained via floatplane from the communities of Iliamna, Aniak, or Bethel.

The longest history of active sport fishing in the Kuskokwim drainage undeniably belongs to the Aniak River. Beginning at Aniak Lake in the Kilbuck Mountains, the Aniak flows north to reach the Kuskokwim River at the community of Aniak. Major

tributaries include the Kipchuk and Salmon Rivers, both swift, alpine-natured streams. The upper two-thirds to three-quarters of the Aniak are moderately swift and shallow with much braiding among the numerous gravel bars. In the lower reaches, the river has a single deep channel that flows slower, with the water also becoming less clear. The chinook begin returning to the river in mid- to late June, with the run peaking during the first two weeks of July. There is ample holding water above the confluence with Doestock Creek, about 9 miles upriver from the confluence with the Kuskokwim, and that is where the best fly-fishing opportunities exist for king salmon anglers. If fishing in the silty, meandering mainstem below that, try the many sloughs and slow, deep pools where salmon like to hold. There are several lodge operations on the lower river, with powerboats the preferred means of travel. A number of experienced floaters also use the watershed each season, though it's not a system for the beginner. Spring runoff and periods of heavy rain cause frequent course changes in the river, and high-water events regularly deposit large numbers of trees and other plant material on gravel bars, occasionally blocking large channels of the river.

Between the Aniak confluence and the point where the Kuskokwim empties into the bay of the same name, there are several other outstanding possibilities for king salmon anglers, each a pristine drainage that receives relatively little in the way of fishing pressure. The Kisaralik, Kasigluk, and Kwethluk Rivers are the best known of these, and for good reason: Their clear, clean-flowing waters are typically favorable to the fly-angler. But just south of the Kuskokwim River and its tributaries, also draining into Kuskokwim Bay, lies one of the chinook fly-fisher's dream locations—the Kanektok River.

The Kanektok, located about 70 miles south of the community of Bethel in the Togiak National Wildlife

Refuge, issues from an outlet at Kagati Lake in the Ahklun Mountains and flows west to its terminus in Kuskokwim Bay. It supports significant fisheries for a variety of species, and according to information gathered from ADF&G mail-out surveys, the river is one of the top five destinations for anglers in the Southwest Management Area. The Kanektok is probably best known

as a chinook stream, with the king salmon sport fishery occurring primarily in the lower 10 miles of river, which is a meandering, braided section of water that stretches across a broad tundra floodplain. The crystal-clear waters, shallow and moderately swift (the river is primarily rated Class I, with some Class II stretches), lend themselves to fly-fishing on a world-class scale. The

Landing an Aniak River chinook.

chinook salmon | **63**

significant numbers of fish help. During even most below-average years, the Kanektok's chinook returns surpass twenty thousand fish.

Another sure highlight of Alaska's Southwest region is the Togiak River, an exceptionally scenic tundra river flowing through the heart of more than 4 million acres contained within the Togiak National Wildlife Refuge and Wilderness. The Togiak runs gin-clear and is especially suited to fly-anglers, as it's only 40 to 80 feet wide in most of the upper reaches. The sport fishery commences about the third week of June with the arrival of the first sea-bright chinook (the Togiak historically averages approximately thirty-six thousand returning kings per year) and is usually concentrated in the lower 20 miles of river.

Maybe Alaska's premier chinook salmon drainage, the Nushagak River, should need no introduction. In case it does, the river begins with headwaters that rise in the Nushagak Hills and flows nearly 275 miles to Nushagak Bay. It is the largest nonglacial system in Southwest Alaska and the largest producer of all species of Pacific salmon except sockeye in Bristol Bay. Also of interest to fly-anglers are the Nushagak tributaries, primarily the Nuyakuk and Mulchatna Rivers, as well as the Mulchatna's well-known feeder streams—the Stuyahok, Koktuli, and Chilikadrotna Rivers.

The Nushagak hosts one of Alaska's largest chinook runs, with average returns running 75,000 to 100,000 fish or more (2003 saw an estimated 136,000 king salmon return to the Nushagak, which—while roughly matching the most recent five-year average run size—was slightly below the preseason forecast). Most anglers seeking chinook utilize three areas within the drainage. Historically, the majority of the sport effort on the mainstem Nushagak River has taken place from Black Point upstream 12 miles to the village of Portage Creek. This stretch of river is approximately 300 yards wide and

remains tidally influenced. Farther upstream, and beyond the influence of the tides, a sport fishery has developed near the village of Ekwok. The third major fishery is located along the middle portion of the Mulchatna River from about 3 miles below the confluence with the Stuyahok River upstream to the mouth of the Koktuli. Due to its productivity, large numbers of the Bristol Bay lodges use the Nushagak as a primary angling destination during the chinook run. The lower section of the river is also home to numerous tent camps that offer clients direct access to the returning kings. This is big water, though, with a lack of noticeable structure, and the mainstem Nushagak doesn't lend itself easily to fly-fishing. Often its runs are very deep and unreachable by conventional techniques, with many anglers opting to use Spey rods and fish heavy sinking lines from boats that are kept under power. Farther upriver, along the Nushagak's plentiful gravel bars, beaches, and sloughs, higher-quality fly-fishing can be had during the peak of the run, typically between late June and early July.

Continuing south from the Nushagak drainage, anglers will find the renowned Katmai Country, home of world-class rainbows, otherworldly returns of sockeye, and high concentrations of brown bears. There's also a chinook run or two of note, with the best combination of numbers of fish and fly-fishing opportunity existing in the Alagnak River. Sometimes known locally as the Branch River, the Alagnak is sited in the Kvichak River drainage north of the community of King Salmon, making it an economical alternative to fishing the more crowded Naknek River, which offers fewer opportunities for the chinook fly-angler anyway. The Alagnak can be a great floating river, though there is a dearth of good camping sites along the way. Thus, most of the angling is done from the handful of on-river lodge operations or on day trips with fly-out operators. It enjoys National Wild and Scenic River status and hosts a significant chinook

Casting.

TONY WEAVER

Chinook anglers on the Alagnak River take a break to explore a little history.

fishery, with above-average-sized fish. The bulk of the angling effort takes place in the lower 12 miles of river and peaks in mid- to late July, roughly two weeks later than other chinook fisheries in the area.

Beyond the Alagnak lies the isolated Alaska Peninsula and some of North America's wildest surroundings. There are several king salmon streams along the coast, but the area is terrifically remote, with logistics a genuine nightmare. Relatively small returns are predominant, but since few anglers venture anywhere near these small clearwater drainages, chances of success are high if the timing's right. Streams flowing along the north side of the peninsula that are known to host returns of chinook include the Bear, Cinder, King Salmon, Nelson, Meshik, and Sandy Rivers, and Black Hills and Steelhead Creeks. There are but a handful of guiding operations available for anglers looking to access these streams,

though a few are near communities that can be used as jumping-off points. Access can be gained to the King Salmon River from the Port Moller cannery, either by ATV or via wheel planes landing on the beach. Black Hills and Steelhead Creeks are near the community of Cold Bay, while the village of Port Heiden is in the vicinity of both the Cinder and Meshik Rivers. Use levels are low for all of the above, with small returns of kings appearing in late June. Aerial survey counts from ADF&G average 580 kings for the King Salmon River, about 600 fish each for Black Hills and Steelhead Creeks, and 1,500 and 3,000 fish, respectively, for the Cinder and Meshik Rivers. All of these drainages—from the black-sand-bottomed Cinder River, which actually originates among the cinder beds from the nearby Aniakchak caldera, to the Sandy far to the south—run clear and shallow, are easily wadable, and provide considerable

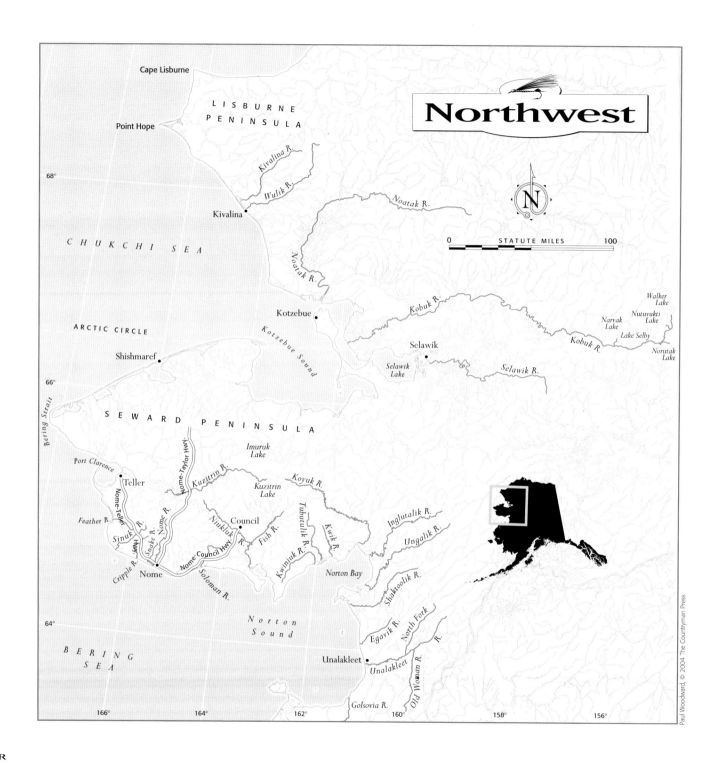

Northwest

Cape Lisburne

LISBURNE PENINSULA

Point Hope

68°

Kivalina R.

Wulik R.

Kivalina

CHUKCHI SEA

Noatak R.

Noatak R.

Kobuk R.

Walker Lake

Narvak Lake

Nutuvukti Lake

Kotzebue

Lake Selby

Selawik

Kobuk R.

Norutak Lake

ARCTIC CIRCLE

Kotzebue Sound

Selawik Lake

Selawik R.

Shishmaref

66°

Bering Strait

SEWARD PENINSULA

Port Clarence

Teller

Nome-Teller Hwy.

Feather R.

Sinuk

Sinuk R.

Cripple R.

Nome

Nome-Taylor Hwy.

Kuzitrin R.

Snake R.

Nome R.

Niukluk R.

Council

Nome-Council Hwy.

Soloman R.

Imuruk Lake

Kuzitrin Lake

Fish R.

Koyuk R.

Tubutulik R.

Kwiniuk R.

Kwik R.

Inglutalik R.

Ungalik R.

Shaktoolik R.

Norton Bay

Norton Sound

Egavik R.

North Fork

R.

BERING SEA

Unalakleet

Unalakleet

Old Woman R.

Golsovia R.

166°   164°   162°   160°   158°   156°

STATUTE MILES
0   100

Paul Woodward, © 2004 The Countryman Press

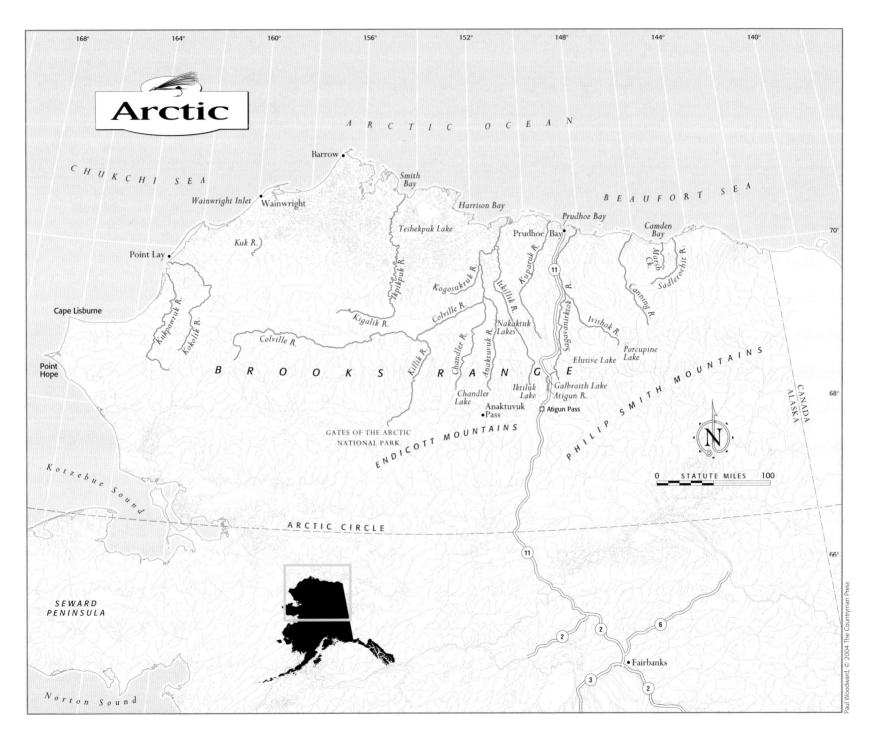

Arctic

ARCTIC OCEAN

CHUKCHI SEA

BEAUFORT SEA

Barrow

Smith Bay

Wainwright Inlet   Wainwright

Harrison Bay

Prudhoe Bay

Prudhoe Bay

Camden Bay

Point Lay

Teshekpuk Lake

Kuk R.

Ikpikpuk R.

Kogosukruk R.

Kuparuk R.

Marsh Ck.

Sadlerochit R.

70°

Cape Lisburne

Kukpowruk R.

Kokolik R.

Kigalik R.

Colville R.

Colville R.

Chandler R.

Itkillik R.

Anaktuvuk R.

Nakaktuk Lakes

Sagavanirktok R.

Ivishak R.

Canning R.

Point Hope

BROOKS RANGE

Killik R.

Elusive Lake

Porcupine Lake

PHILIP SMITH MOUNTAINS

CANADA
ALASKA

Chandler Lake

Iktiluk Lake

Galbraith Lake
Atigun R.

68°

Anaktuvuk Pass

Atigun Pass

GATES OF THE ARCTIC
NATIONAL PARK

ENDICOTT MOUNTAINS

N

Kotzebue Sound

STATUTE MILES

0   100

ARCTIC CIRCLE

66°

SEWARD PENINSULA

11

2   2   6

Norton Sound

3   2

Fairbanks

fly-fishing opportunities. It's near the sand-bottomed mouths of many of these streams that the state's best top-water conditions can materialize for chinook fly-fishers.

There is only one documented king salmon population returning to the south side of the Alaska Peninsula, and that stock belongs to the Chignik River. The ADF&G operates a weir on the river; over the past ten years, counts have averaged 3,863 king salmon, with a record 6,412 chinook returning in 2003. What there is of angling effort is primarily expended from skiffs in the 2-mile stretch from the weir to the outlet of Chignik Lake. With the local commercial fishery now a lot less labor-intensive, there is talk of several villagers from nearby

Chignik starting guiding operations. If so, access and opportunity to fish this gem of an Alaska Peninsula stream will soon increase.

NORTHWEST/ARCTIC ALASKA

North of the Yukon River, there is still plenty of opportunity to hunt chinook salmon in their native waters, but beyond some effort expended in the Unalakleet River drainage, sport fishing for the species is fairly rare. Far from just ice and snow, the scenery in this area of the state is exquisite, with good to great sport-fishing potential available to any willing to make the trip. King salmon streams in the area begin in Norton Sound and range

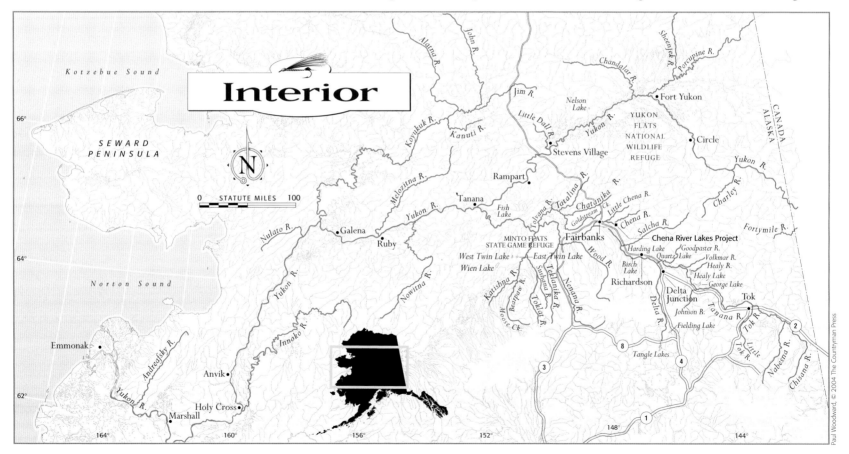

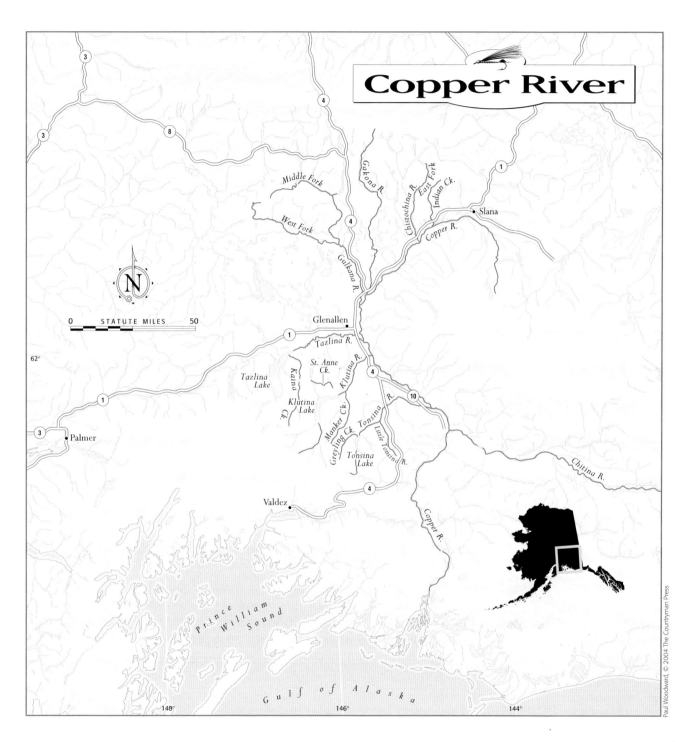

Copper River

N

STATUTE MILES
0   50

Middle Fork

West Fork

Gakona R.

Chistochina R.

East Fork

Indian Ck.

Slana

Copper R.

Gulkana R.

Glenallen

Tazlina R.

St. Anne Ck.

Kaina Ck.

Klutina R.

Tazlina Lake

Klutina Lake

Manker Ck.

Greyling Ck.

Tonsina Ck.

Tonsina R.

Little Tonsina R.

Tonsina Lake

Palmer

Valdez

Copper R.

Chitina R.

Prince William Sound

Gulf of Alaska

62°

148°

146°

144°

3

3

8

4

4

4

1

1

1

3

4

10

4

Paul Woodward, © 2004 The Countryman Press

north, generally thinning along the Seward Peninsula, which almost touches Siberia, until they end in the Chukchi Sea and Kotzebue Sound areas.

The rivers of Kotzebue Sound aren't known for their chinook populations; sheefish and trophy Arctic char are the primary draws here. There are a few fishable stocks, though, beginning in the Wulik River and its sister drainage, the Kivalina. The Wild and Scenic Noatak River and its tributaries also host a minor population, but all three of these Kotzebue Sound systems are undeniably more renowned for their unspoiled natures and the thousands of trophy sea-run char that clog their clear waters each year.

Most of the Seward Peninsula streams receive returns of spring chinook, including the Buckland, Pilgrim, Sinuk, Snake, and Solomon Rivers. The Nome River, just a few miles from the center of the town of the same name, receives the most attention from anglers, and has a small run of chinook. The Fish–Niukluk River system about 60 miles east of Nome may be the most consistent king salmon producer on the peninsula. The river can be reached via the Nome–Council Highway, and a number of sport-fishing operations have begun to offer services here.

The runoff streams of eastern Norton Sound offer Northwest anglers the best opportunity for consistent chinook action. Most of these systems drain the highlands west of the Yukon River, and access is generally limited to boats and the occasional floatplane landing. The Kwiniuk River, a short coastal stream that flows into upper Norton Sound, produces strong runs of kings, as does the Shaktoolik River, another largely unexplored sport fishery.

The Unalakleet River, located north of the mouth of the Yukon in Norton Sound, flows southwesterly through the spruce and willow forests of the Nulato Hills and supports an important chinook salmon run that sustains

BRIAN O'KEEFE

the largest subsistence, commercial, and sport harvests in Norton Sound. Access is almost entirely limited to boats from the community of Unalakleet, though there presently is at least one sport-fishing lodge on the river. For the Unalakleet and other Northwest king salmon streams, the best fishing tends to be in the first two weeks of July. In 2003, however, depressed returns caused both the Unalakleet and Shaktoolik drainages to be closed to chinook retention; unfortunately, both populations of salmon are currently on the list to be nominated by the Alaska Board of Fisheries as stocks of concern.

INTERIOR ALASKA

The fifth largest watershed on the continent, the Yukon, dominates the interior section of Alaska. Still, due to the remote nature of most clearwater spawning tributaries and the long migrations the salmon undertake, less chinook angling than you might think actually occurs in this region. Only in the Tanana Valley is there sufficient road access to allow noteworthy sport-fishing effort. Closer to the Yukon's mouth, most of the salmon angling takes place oin the Andreafsky River.

A major tributary of the Yukon, the Tanana River has its source high in the Wrangell Mountains and flows some 500 miles north to rendezvous with the Yukon near Manley. Sport fishing for chinook in the Tanana is chiefly accomplished in clear tributaries of the braided, glacial mainstem river. Most of the king salmon angling has historically taken place in the Salcha River, followed by the Chena and Chatanika. All three are accessible by car from Fairbanks, with the peak of the king season for the Salcha usually occurring in mid-July. Late July brings the best chinook concentrations to the Chena and Chatanika Rivers. Conservative management policies have recently helped expand what had been seriously depressed runs for the Yukon drainage; have chinook escapements in both 2002 and 2003 improved. However, since Yukon king runs are primarily made up of five- and six-year-olds, the weak Yukon system (including the Tanana River) salmon runs that were realized in 2000 and 2001 are likely to produce below-average returns through at least 2007.

The best king salmon angling to be had in the interior area of the state, however, occurs farther south in the region dominated by the massive Copper River. The Copper supports a large and commercially important run of chinook (recent four-year averages place this river's runs near eighty thousand returning kings annually), but as with many of Alaska's other large systems, the glacial nature of the river diverts much of the fly-fishing opportunity to the drainage's clearwater tributary streams.

A total of forty chinook salmon spawning streams have been identified throughout the Copper River drainage, nine of which are surveyed by the ADF&G

on a regular basis. In a 1999 study, these nine streams accounted for approximately one-quarter of the total escapement for the drainage, with the Gulkana River receiving about half of those fish, representing about 11.5 percent of the total Copper River escapement. The Gulkana begins with headwaters at the foot of the Alaska Range and flows through rolling hills on its way to meet the Copper River. A National Wild and Scenic River, the Gulkana supports the drainage's most significant chinook salmon sport fishery and accommodates fly-anglers nicely, with most of the action taking place from the Middle Fork confluence down.

Over the past few years, the chinook sport fishery on the Klutina has dramatically increased; it now rivals the Gulkana. Again, taken from the 1999 ADF&G study, about 24 percent of all fish returning to the Copper River are bound for the Klutina, which means there are plenty of fish for anglers to target. The Klutina is a large glacial system, though, and its gray-green, silt-laden flows are tough for presenting a fly. Thus, most of the best angling is to be found near the mouths of several clearwater confluences with the river. Klutina kings are larger than average, with fish over 50 pounds not beyond the realm of possibility, and the river's generally swift flows make landing these larger fish difficult if anglers are confined to the bank.

In general, Copper River chinook returns begin in early June and extend through July. Peak times are earlier for the upper Copper River systems, as radio-tag studies have indicated that the fish traveling the farthest upstream tend to enter fresh water earlier than downstream stocks. For the Gulkana River, the height of the king salmon season is generally near the end of June and beginning of July. The Klutina River, like the Kenai, receives two separate (but not always distinct) returns of chinook. The best times to fish the Klutina for kings are in early July and then again at the end of the month.

The falls isn't the only thing Brooks River sockeye salmon need to worry about.

sockeye salmon

HAVING BARELY RECOVERED from a rather severe run-in with dysentery, the Corps of Discovery floated through the canyons of the Snake River in less-than-stellar spirits. Traveling in dugout canoes fashioned from ponderosa pines that had been felled on Idaho's North Fork Clearwater, the men of Lewis and Clark's expedition found the going slow. Making matters worse, meat had been nonexistent since the Bitterroots. The thick forests of the western Rockies had offered abundant elk and deer, which had ably fed the party during the summer. But once they'd descended onto the largely treeless expanse of the Great Columbian Plain, bartering with the Nez Percé for dried fish and roots was the best they could manage. Hence, the dysentery.

An amazing sight greeted America's most famous travelers once they reached the gin-clear waters of the Columbia, however, as the fastidious William Clark noted for posterity.

RIGHT: *Spawning sockeye.*

"This river is remarkably Clear and Crouded with Salmon in manye places and I observe in assending great numbers of Salmon dead on the Shores, floating on the water and in the Bottoms which can be seen at the debth of 20 feet," chronicled the bewildered captain.

Meriwether Lewis had taken to ignoring his own journal through this stage of the trip, but it is believed that both men came to conclude the fish were succumbing to disease. The Nez Percé certainly knew better, as did the Yakimas, Wanapams, Wallawallas, and Chinooks, all peoples the expedition would encounter while continuing their voyage to the sea, and each a society built upon the backs of the anadromous fish. Appreciated for much more than the direct sustenance provided, the salmon held a central position within the Natives' esteem. For the people who lived and depended on the productivity of the great Columbia River watershed, all life was interconnected. They certainly hadn't traveled as far or witnessed as much diversity of ecosystems as the two great explorers, but they had seen enough with their own eyes to know their world depended on an annual invasion from the Pacific.

The fish Lewis and Clark encountered were probably fall-run chinook. Far to the north, in a land similar in some ways and very much different in others, another species of Pacific salmon was at the very least comparably vital. The sockeye, falling in the middle of North America's five species of Pacific salmon in terms of overall abundance, has three main areas of concentration—the Fraser River basin in British Columbia, along the Kamchatka Peninsula of Russia, and in the Bristol Bay region of Alaska. Here, as along the Columbia River, the species has long been at the center of life.

Alaska's Southwest presents a setting almost without equal. The rolling tundra lowlands are laced with meandering sapphire-colored streams, most of which begin in headwater lakes that cradle hundreds of millions of juve-

nile salmon. In fact, for the last four thousand years or so, the region has been home to some of the world's densest concentrations of fish. Both the area's boundless wildlife and the flourishing riparian habitat that rise up like an impromptu stockade from the muskeg tundra rely completely on the salmon, the sockeye in particular. The millions of dead fish that remain in rivers after spawning add to the nutrient base of the water system. This affects nitrogen levels, which in turn aid the growth of algae, a source of food for zooplankton. Plus, during the migrations, while on the spawning beds, and even afterward when the last of their energy wanes, the salmon are a tremendously important source of sustenance for the entire food chain: bears, other mammals, fish, and birds, each of which does its part to further spread the salmon's life-inducing nutrients. Some research has indicated that both the famous bruins of Bristol Bay and the area's equally celebrated rainbow trout can trace 80 percent or more of their body weight back to the annual invaders from the Pacific. "Crouded with Salmon," indeed.

Like the cultures Lewis and Clark encountered in the land now know as Idaho, Oregon, and Washington, Alaska's people have been drawn to the rivers since the earliest times. In fact, settlement of the Bristol Bay region first occurred over six thousand years ago. Central Yup'ik Eskimos and Athabascan Indians jointly occupied the area, utilizing the Naknek River system, in particular, as hunting and fishing grounds throughout the summer, with Sugpiaq (Aleut-Russian) Eskimos arriving to the same region in later years. By 1818, the first Russian traders had arrived in the area, and in about 1883 the first salmon cannery in Bristol Bay was opened east of modern-day Dillingham at the confluence of the Wood and Nushagak Rivers. Kiatagmuit Eskimos were living on the north bank of the Kvichak River in the village of Kaskanak and using the present-day site of Igiugig near the river's outlet from Lake Iliamna as a summer fish camp. Others dwelled in the Branch River village on today's Alagnak, which has its headwaters in Katmai National Park and Preserve. In 1890, another cannery was opened, this time on the Naknek River. By the turn of the century, at least ten more were operating in the region.

Today, these historic sites—and the sockeye salmon returns that were responsible for them—remain important. Igiugig, for example, is presently a primary landing point for sport anglers chasing the sockeye of the Iliamna system, as well as the giant rainbow trout that the sockeye feed. Katmai and, more specifically, the Naknek, Brooks, and Alagnak Rivers are world-renowned angling destinations and the centerpieces of a multimillion-dollar tourism industry. The community of Dillingham remains the gateway to the Wood-Tikchik, Togiak, and Nushagak drainages, each a watershed of nearly unimaginable productivity. For the longest time, though, the sockeye, an amazingly energetic fish capable of leaping over 10 feet of waterfall, wasn't even considered a sport fish. Fly-fishing for the species in Alaska didn't begin in earnest until around the early 1950s. Until then it was believed this most diffident of the Pacific salmon could only be taken in nets or by snagging, a practice the ADF&G mercifully ousted from freshwater regulations. Now, just a few decades later, fly-anglers see the sockeye for all that they are—feisty, robust, filled with desire. They are a premier quarry, and like the migrating salmon that met Lewis and Clark at the Columbia, these wild Alaska fish remain inseparable from the land and the people they sustain.

The Sockeye Salmon

(Oncorhynchus nerka)

Because of their significant commercial importance, Alaska's sockeye have been studied more extensively than have the state's other species of salmon. Consequently, much is known of their biology and life history. Viable

Sockeye salmon.

rakers on the first gill arch differentiate sockeye from sea-bright chum salmon. Once sexual maturation approaches, however, sockeye can be recognized without any inspection at all. Dramatic changes—sometimes bordering on the grotesque—occur in their appearance as the body becomes bright red and the dorsal surface turns a shade of dark green. Jaws and teeth become enlarged, and a distinctive kype is formed. Males eventually present a humpback profile like the pink salmon, while females will lack both the pronounced hump and the exaggerated kype but still display the same brilliant spawning hues.

Mature, pre-spawning sockeye begin appearing in rivers across the state as early as late May in rare cases, with peak freshwater migration periods usually occurring from the middle of June through late July. They are of relatively slight size among the North American species of Pacific salmon—only pinks are smaller on average. After leaving their saltwater feeding grounds, returning adults typically weigh between 4 and 8 pounds, although 15-pound and larger specimens have been caught in Alaska. Like pink salmon, sockeye tend to be socially oriented travelers, congregating by the thousands to push upstream. They'll remain in tight groups once in fresh water and will mill in tributary mouths, lake outlets, sloughs, and pools. Sockeye also have a habit of hugging close to the shoreline, selecting the shallowest water for their passage. The tendency to travel and hold in large groups and the species' obvious preference for shallow shoreline areas combine to make the fish a particularly inviting target for anglers and other shorebound predators, namely Alaska's coastal brown bears.

LIFE HISTORY

In some areas within its natural range, the sockeye can exist in a resident freshwater form, called the kokanee salmon. In Alaska, however, where nearly all the wild

populations of the species in North America occur from the Columbia River to the Yukon watershed, with some much smaller stocks returning to a handful of scattered streams as far north as Point Hope. Sporadic reports of sockeye existing outside this native range are based for the most part on strays, not established populations.

Sockeye salmon exhibit blunt snouts and bodies of streamlined proportion and are sometimes referred to as red salmon or bluebacks, the latter moniker derived from the metallic blue-to-green coloration evident along their backs. Ocean-fresh sockeye are also characterized by their glimmering silver sides and white bellies. Some fine black speckling may be present, but a lack of large black spots distinguishes the species from chinook, coho, and pink salmon. Only the numbers and shapes of gill

Bright sockeye.

sockeye are anadromous, separate populations still differ in the amount of time juveniles spend in fresh water before smolting and migrating to the sea, in the timing of spawning runs, and in the period when spawning itself commences. Indeed, the greatest diversity in life history patterns among any of the Pacific salmon can be found in sockeye, which maintain their unique compositions through fairly rigid spawning isolation.

Most populations spawn in the pea gravel of streams that are tributaries to lakes, though Alaska's sockeye frequently reproduce in the shallows along lake shorelines as well. When two or more populations of anadromous sockeye occur in the same lake system, as is common in the state, the species' refined homing instinct allows them to coexist without reproductive contact. Even when kokanee—stocked or native—are added to the mix, hybridization between populations is avoided because the varying stocks will use different spawning grounds or spawn at different times.

No matter the particulars of a life history pattern, Alaska's juvenile sockeye will usually emerge from the gravel by April through June. And whether hatched in inlet or outlet streams, the young sockeye will almost always travel into the system's lake to feed, where the vast majority will spend between one and three years. Sockeye are not entirely dependent upon lakes for feeding and rearing, however, as it's now known that some populations will rear in backwaters or areas along a river's floodplain. These sockeye will usually smolt and depart for the marine environment at only a few months of age, much like Alaska's pink and chum salmon. This completely fluvial life history pattern, likely a genetic rather than environmental mechanism, is common for sockeye native to the Kamchatka River in Russia and is also known to occur in some Alaska systems, namely the East Alsek River south of Yakutat. A handful of other Last Frontier populations, like those from a few streams in the Copper River drainage near Cordova, are known to rear in the streams of their birth rather than undertake a lake migration.

For the juvenile sockeye that do move into lakes, the first few weeks will be spent close to shore. Later, the fish will become pelagic and feed on plankton in the uppermost 60 feet of water. After at least a year in the lake (usually two in Bristol Bay watersheds), the young will lose their parr marks, turn silvery in color, and head downstream. Peak out-migration for Bristol Bay streams occurs in June, beginning when water temperatures

reach about 40 degrees. For the most part, they travel at night, usually between the hours of ten and midnight. However, sockeye salmon smolt in the Agulowak River of the Wood-Tikchik system defy this pattern and have been documented as leaving for Lake Aleknagik in mid-July, and then journeying throughout the day.

Once in the ocean, the young sockeye stay fairly close to shore at first, feeding primarily on various zooplankton and insects. As they get bigger and stronger, they head farther out to sea, and despite the widespread belief that sockeye are some form of saltwater herbivore, larval and adult fish, especially sand lance, will become important in their diets in some regions. The ocean-traveling fish will also feed upon squid and amphipods, copepods,

Fingers of Lake Iliamna, the world's most significant sockeye salmon rearing grounds.

BRIAN O'KEEFE

and euphausiids, which are organisms from three orders of crustaceans. Sockeye from areas south of the Alaska Peninsula head directly for the Gulf of Alaska. Those from Bristol Bay must instead move westward along the northern edge of the peninsula, eventually crossing into the gulf through the eastern and central Aleutian passes. In late winter, Alaska's sockeye are spread across the North Pacific in areas south of about 50 degrees N latitude. In late spring, the fish will move to feeding areas north of the Aleutians, and after a summer spent feeding heavily, the sockeye will split: Those that are to remain at sea for another cycle head south, while the mature adults will remain in the northern feeding corridor until spring, when they'll begin to stage near the mouths of their natal drainages.

In Alaska, most sockeye return in their fourth year of life, though five- and even six-year-old fish aren't completely uncommon in some areas. The pre-spawners return during the summer and fall, from July through early September in most of the state, with spawning occurring almost exclusively in streams that connect with large lakes. The salmon of Bristol Bay exemplify this lacustrine tendency in the species, as nearly every sockeye population in the region returns to spawn in the rivers feeding or draining the big systems: Lake Iliamna, Lake Clark, and Lake Becharof, as well as Ugashik, Naknek, Kulik, Nonvianuk, and Wood-Tikchik Lakes. An example otherwise are the sockeye of Southcentral Alaska's Copper River, of which approximately one in five are estimated to spawn in the lower river delta, never traveling near the giant upriver lakes within the system.

If there is any standard truth in regard to sockeye salmon returns, it's that across their range the event is not static and predictable. As with every anadromous fish species, both timing and abundance can vary widely. Fisheries managers and anglers alike have long sought to solve these riddles, many recently offering theories tied to El Niño, or La Niña, or trying to explain abundance fluctuations by way of Pacific Decadal Oscillation. But with fish that can spend over half their lives roaming far throughout the mysterious seas, it should come as no surprise that total comprehension has escaped our grasp. There are actually many factors involved in determining the abundance of a sockeye return, like brood-year escapement, the amount of rearing habitat available, instream predation, and ocean mortality, all of which a host of environmental factors could alter at any time. Perhaps it would be enough to admit that salmon returns are subject to change. And if that isn't enough, sometimes even the fish themselves will adapt.

Take, for instance, the unique circumstances surrounding three Gulf Coast drainages southeast of Yakutat and a twenty-five-year sockeye salmon "event" that occurred in one of them, the East Alsek River. Actually, only a hundred or so years ago, there was no East Alsek River—only the transboundary Alsek River, which drains a sizable area of the Yukon Territories, a portion of the southeastern panhandle, and, just a few miles south, the Doame River. It is assumed that the Doame system, which includes a clearwater lake, has supported anadromous salmon for several centuries. But around the turn of the century, the glacially occluded Alsek changed channels. Water was still funneled through a gravel berm into the old channel, however, giving rise to today's clear-flowing East Alsek, which extends for about 9 miles before emptying into an estuary lagoon.

Early on, anadromous salmon invaded the newly created stream, using the river's spring-type habitat for both spawning and rearing. The East Alsek never gained much acclaim as a sockeye producer, though its chum salmon returns were fairly significant. What was unique about the river's sockeye was that they migrated to the sea the year they hatched, spending very little time in fresh water, just like the chum. When combined with the river's exceptional spawning habitat—crystal-clear water, favorable water temperatures, excellent substrate, and ideal flows—the adaptation of sockeye to this life history form allowed the East Alsek stock to explode in magnitude from the mid-1970s through the 1980s, sometimes with runs reaching up to a quarter million fish.

A few other events helped create the necessary circumstances for this sockeye boom to take place. First, in 1959 an earthquake was responsible for the Alsek River shifting from a westerly to an easterly course, which most likely left more water available for upwelling in the East Alsek River. Second, another earthquake, this one in 1966, caused the Doame River to be sealed off from the ocean. The stream then formed a new channel just inside the beach line and joined the mouth of the East Alsek, adding a large amount of rearing habitat to the estuary lagoon. Likely even more important were the four major

Sockeye.

floods that occurred in the Alsek River from 1964 through 1983. During each one, the Alsek overran its banks and poured down the East Alsek channel, scouring the spawning gravel and clearing out the emergent vegetation. By itself, the East Alsek is not powerful enough to scour the algae, even in flood stage, and since 1983 there have been no more major floods of the Alsek. For the past decade, then, the upper East Alsek River has been choked with vegetation, rendering almost two-thirds of the spawning gravel inaccessible to sockeye salmon. The population has declined proportionately, and what had been a fishery of great potential has returned to producing small runs of sockeye.

In other areas of Alaska, events haven't been as dramatic. Some of the state's most significant stocks, like those of the Kvichak River, have endured consecutive depressed returns recently, while others, such as the sockeye of the Alagnak system, are enjoying booms of their own. Still, with ever-changing environmental conditions and increasing development near remote, formerly pristine watersheds, the sockeye's future is anything but assured. Thankfully, the great majority of Alaska's red salmon populations can still be found in excellent health. With any luck—and some careful management—they'll remain that way for generations to come, not only for our sake, but also for the bears, the birds, the other fish, and even the rivers they support.

Fly-Fishing for Alaska's Sockeye

Fly-fishing for sockeye salmon in the Last Frontier is marked by extremes. In many drainages, more than a million fish will stream in from the sea in less than a month's time. In others, it might seem as if equal numbers of anglers are packed into about a mile of beach. The trick for fly-fishers, then, is to find the one—

big numbers of chrome-bright fish—without being forced to endure the other. What this usually means is forgoing an easy trip to the state's more famous sockeye locales, especially the notorious combat zones along the Kenai and Russian Rivers, and instead journeying a little deeper into Alaska's backcountry.

Despite the species' culinary reputation and long history as a staple for indigenous cultures, fly-fishing for sockeye salmon remains a relatively fresh development. As recently as the 1970s, in fact, institutions like the International Game Fish Association still hadn't recognized the species as a legitimate target for sport anglers. For years, fly-fishers lobbied to have their Alaska-caught sockeye salmon considered for records. For years, they were denied. Then in 1977, the kokanee salmon—the landlocked version of sockeye—was finally added to the IGFA record books; a year later the sea-run sockeye, too, received its just recognition as sport fish. Some minor and usually poorly informed quibbling might still be found, but for the most part questions over whether or not the species will take a fly have been amply answered. Today, despite the foul-hooking charades that occur on some of Alaska's most popular and accessible streams, fly-fishing effort for the species is burgeoning. Sockeye salmon's legendary spunk when hooked makes them an exciting and worthy target, and contrary to popular belief, it takes much skill to produce consistent angling success.

RUN TIMING

When pursuing any species of anadromous sport fish, timing efforts to coincide with the heights of the runs is imperative. This basic angling tenet is even more true when a species tends to display as little aggression as do migrating sockeye. While absolute precision is probably unattainable, anglers can review historical run timing for a particular drainage and, by coupling this with current

DARYL PEDERSON

forecasts and weather trends, predict with decent accuracy the best chances for intercepting a run at its zenith. Good planning should include timing an outing for the best incoming tides as well. In areas with a significant commercial fishing presence, fly-fishers will also want to make sure their trip doesn't coincide with an opening, as the sockeye runs in a few major rivers will shut off like a faucet when the nets are deployed.

In general, strong numbers of sockeye can be found almost anywhere in the state during the month of July. Specific peaks will vary from population to population, sometimes drastically. Some Alaska streams will receive multiple returns in a season, each of varying strength and displaying differing times of peak migration. There are also occasions when the sockeye salmon runs of neighboring drainages are off by a month or more. For example, reds typically begin to enter the Doame River by early June, while East Alsek spawners won't arrive at the systems' shared lagoon until late July, with some past

Fly-fishers often arrive in Southwest Alaska to find other anglers already there.

GREG A. SYVERSON

LEFT: *Rainbow trout can commonly be found near schools of spawning salmon, where they wait for the eggs to drop.*

RIGHT: *There's only one way to get to the world's best sockeye fishing.*

migrations continuing into September. In cases where separate runs of sockeye return to the same drainage for spawning, one is almost always more productive than the other. The Kenai is one such river, with early-returning fish available in late May and June, and a second, more significant wave of fish arriving around the middle of July.

GEAR FOR SOCKEYE

Thankfully, deciding on equipment for a sockeye outing is an immeasurably simpler task than choosing when or where to fish. Pound for pound one of Alaska's feistiest fish, the species is responsible for a lot of broken rods each year. Thus, 7- or 8-weight, fast-action outfits are normal, chosen more for their ability to apply the pressure required to move stronger fish than for any need to punch out long, accurate casts. Big-water rivers like the Kvichak or Kenai, with their often heavy, swift currents and fish approaching 14 pounds, may even necessitate stepping up to a 9-weight outfit. As always, reels should balance with the rod. For sockeye, capacity needs not range much above 200 yards of Dacron or gel-spun backing, though anglers should look for reels with carbon fiber, cork, or synthetic drags. Clicker or palm reels without a compression drag system are not recom-

mended for sockeye, as break-offs, busted knuckles, and line cuts are already the norm even when using a higher quality disc-drag reel.

The standard Alaska setup for targeting sockeye is a floating line, long 9- to 10-foot leader, and various amounts of split shot above a 2-foot tippet section. The most important component of this rig is the weight. No matter the depth of the water and the velocity the current is traveling, the weight should be enough to quickly make contact with the bottom but not so much as to slow the drift of the fly. At other times, when fishing in still or frog water, anglers working a large group of milling fish will also want to use a floating line and long leader, only on this occasion it's usually better to forgo the split shot and instead employ a lightly weighted fly, which will slowly sink to the proper depth, where it's more likely to be picked up by a cruising fish. Hand-tied leaders constructed from abrasion-resistant, stiff monofilament are preferred, though fly-fishers may opt for fluorocarbon when fishing in ultraclear water and for spooky fish. Tippet strength should be from 8- to 12-pound test.

Carrying a range of sinking lines instead of a floater and lots of split shot will allow anglers to pick a line to suit the water and enable better depth control, always a most important factor when fishing for Pacific salmon, even more so with sockeye. Teeny Mini Tips and other short sinking tips can probably be used in more circumstances than any other line, though there are enough situations when presentations will need to be made in heavier water that having a variety of grain weights to choose from will seem prescient. Leaders of 4 feet are about right for sinking-line presentations.

FLIES FOR SOCKEYE

Many of the early patterns designed for red salmon in the Last Frontier developed big reputations in no time. By the 1980s, an angler shopping for sockeye patterns in any one of the fly shops in Southcentral Alaska would have had a hard, if not impossible, time walking out without at least a few of the most ubiquitous creations. Some, such as the Comet, the Sportsman Special, and the Coho or Russian River Fly, are still widely used today.

Like those, all effective sockeye salmon patterns seem to exhibit a few basic traits. One, they're simply tied. None is encumbered with anything more than sparse hackle, and relatively few materials are utilized, with most usually nothing more than thread, yarn or chenille, and a bucktail wing. Some patterns might call for bead-chain or barbell eyes for weight, but that's about as fancy as it gets. Flies that ride upright are encouraged, since sockeye in close confines are prone to being foul-hooked. Color combinations are relatively limited as well; black, red, yellow, chartreuse, orange, pink, and white are the predominant choices. And finally, most effective sockeye patterns have slim profiles and are tied on hooks that range from size 4 to size 10.

An effective commercial sockeye pattern that exhibits exactly those traits is the Teeny Nymph, which was designed for precisely this type of sinking-line presentation. Even the Crazy Charlie, a famous bonefish pattern with similar characteristics, seems to be singularly suc-

cessful when fished for sockeye. Guides on the Kanektok and a few other exceedingly clear streams speak of situations where sockeye will also take well-presented stonefly nymphs. Other flies currently in vogue include the Montana Brassie, the Sockeye Orange (or Red, Blue, or Green), and the Boss, plus a host of local derivations that'll be available in different fly shops around the state. Tiers wanting to create their own patterns will have little trouble designing a consistent producer, as long as the general guidelines above are followed, and the fly is then presented effectively and with the necessary persistence.

Some of Alaska's experienced sockeye anglers believe the species' saltwater preference for luminescent, shrimplike euphausiids makes them particularly susceptible to chartreuse, orange, and vibrant red flies upon their freshwater returns. Some guides in the state only fish flies that imitate the euphausiids, even though sockeye will stop feeding like the rest of the Pacific salmon

An arrangement of Teeny Nymphs and Leeches.

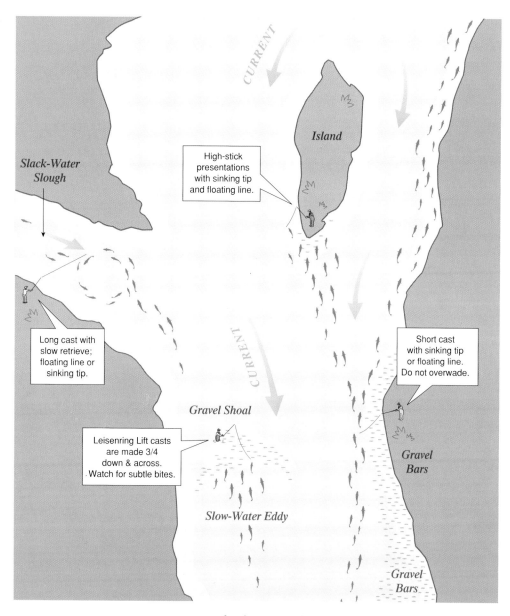

Slack-Water Slough

High-stick presentations with sinking tip and floating line.

Island

Long cast with slow retrieve; floating line or sinking tip.

CURRENT

CURRENT

Short cast with sinking tip or floating line. Do not overwade.

Gravel Shoal

Leisenring Lift casts are made 3/4 down & across. Watch for subtle bites.

Gravel Bars

Slow-Water Eddy

Gravel Bars

ANGLING STRATEGIES

Fly-fishing for sockeye can drive anglers to the summits of frustration one minute and seem ridiculously simple the next. This is probably due at least in part to the species' capricious freshwater demeanor. Sometimes, however, altering an element of the presentation— perhaps the size or color of the fly or the length of a leader—will allow an angler to turn the bite back on after the river seems to have gone dead. Sometimes the fish just need to be rested, too. But by dispensing with the dogmatic, fly-anglers will inevitably allow themselves more room to be successful.

For reasons both obvious and obscure, locating strong concentrations of fish should be the first step for all sockeye fly-fishers. Even though they lack the strong predatory response common to other species in fresh water, sockeye seem more prone to strike when pressured by the crowded conditions of an overloaded run or pool. Thus, anglers should look for shallow areas where stress factors will be highest upon a group of fish. Of course, remembering the sockeye's unique near-shore migration tendencies is a first step. In the Alagnak River, for instance, aerial surveys have documented large groups of sockeye completing the entire freshwater journey as a unit, moving nose to tail from the river's mouth to the headwaters at Nonvianuk Lake, hugging the banks, holding in certain types of water for recuperation, and then crossing to the opposite riverbank in areas of defined transition to continue progressing upstream. Lake outlets and inlets, river mouths, and areas of defined structure, such as waterfalls, the lee sides of islands, and boulder-lined rapids, can produce the kinds of natural rest stops preferred by migrating fish and the high concentrations necessary for productive fly-fishing of the species. A few examples are the areas preceding the Kukaklek Rapids, the mouth of the Newhalen River, and the Russian River Falls, where thousands of reds will stage.

once they've entered their natal drainages. These patterns, like many of those above, center on a theme of simplicity, as they can be tied by just palmering red yarn on a standard nymph hook. For sockeye, there's often nothing more to it than that.

Working the fly in front of a sock-eye school.

In large off-color or glacially influenced rivers, sockeye are also extremely prone to holding in the areas where clear streams mix with the larger river's flows. Despite the high numbers of fish these areas often hold, they are shunned by many anglers, who buy into the myth that sockeye won't bite in these milling scenarios. It is a fallacy unfortunately perpetuated by many of the anglers who visit common fish-holding areas and simply attempt to line the fish, inevitably foul-hooking the majority of their catch. Contrary to popular belief, however, large concentrations of holding fish present fantastic opportunities for the sockeye fly-fisher. Basically, these fish will often be found milling in circular schooling patterns. Anglers should use a floating line or light sinking tip and make longer casts over the holding fish. A slow, hand-twist retrieve should be employed, with aggressive strips avoided. When fishing these areas correctly, the sockeye will rarely spook, and repeated casts can be made over the schools.

Good Alaska sockeye water can also include areas of fairly strong current. After all, most experienced sockeye fly-fishers believe that moving fish are more apt to respond to strike stimuli, whether because of aggravation, oxygen stress, or reflexive feeding behavior. To fish traveling sockeye, anglers must first locate migration corridors along the edges of shallow gravel bars and in long slots close to shore, preferably where the water is less than 3 feet deep because of the effect water depth has on fish concentration, visibility, and fly presentation.

For presentation, remember that it's rare for a sockeye to break ranks even slightly for a fly moving above or below in the water column. For this reason, blind-fishing is not the best idea. Either way, anglers should position themselves in the best possible casting locations, slightly up and across stream from the holding fish. One of the most consistent techniques is to then cast down-and-across and employ a modified, highly controlled wet-fly swing, usu-

The scene on the Brooks River when a fresh wave of sockeye moves in is one angler won't soon forget.

Sockeye are known for their spirited fights, like the one being put up by this Alagnak River leaper.

ally with a sinking tip rather than the floater/split-shot setup, with the line kept taut at all times. Shorter casts work better, not just because the fish are usually close to shore, but also because this allows for more line control.

Another standard nymphing technique, the Leisenring Lift, can be very effective when fishing for traveling sockeye. To put James Leisenring's technique to work on Alaska's sockeye, anglers should use a floating line and a 9-foot or slightly longer leader. Begin by wading into position across from the suspected lie or travel corridor and then cast upstream, above the fish. As the fly drifts, hold the rod high, keeping the line off the water, and follow the progress of the fly with the tip. By not allowing the fly line to belly in the current, anglers not only

enable their fly to sink more quickly—and stay down—but produce a more realistic dead-drift presentation as well. As his fly would approach a fish's suspected position, Leisenring would temporarily halt his rod's motion, and the slight tension would cause the wet fly, nymph, or, in his particular case, "flymph," to rise slightly and breathe, looking more like a real living insect. However, as Alaska sockeye fly-fishers typically aren't trying to replicate the lifelike movements of a particular organism, they can either follow the fly with the rod tip without hesitation or, if the bite is off, mix in an occasional stop to try to induce a take.

One of the most difficult things for beginning sockeye salmon fly-anglers to pick up is the subtle nature of the overwhelming majority of sockeye takes. Many will be barely perceptible, perhaps just a slight hesitation in the downstream progress of the line. By intently following their fly's progress, anglers can better anticipate a strike and react in time to avoid foul-hooking the next fish in line. In clearwater sight-fishing situations, fly-fishers can also be sure of a pickup when they see the telltale white of the inside of a sockeye's mouth. A last item to keep in mind is that many anglers make sockeye fishing more difficult by overwading. Again, the fish prefer the shallow shoreline corridors for migration, and in most circumstances knee-deep is plenty far to wade. Otherwise the fish will just be pushed into deeper water, making the fishing that much more technical.

Although few anglers have caught or even tried for sockeye in salt water, there are numerous areas of such high and accessible concentrations that success is readily available. For instance, major staging areas occur in the clearwater bays, coves, and estuaries of Prince William Sound, the Kenai Fjords, the inshore waters surrounding Kodiak Island, and throughout much of Southeast Alaska's Inside Passage. In late May, June, and early July, before the fish make their move into their freshwater streams, fly-anglers can locate huge schools of sockeye and fish for the species in a totally new and completely different manner. For starters, jumping and porpoising fish will often give away the locations of intensely packed groups. Anglers can target these fish by making a long cast to the front of a school with a floating line and a small shrimp- or nymph- imitation pattern. Some popular flies include Crazy Charlies in pink, Gotchas in pink or green, Twister Shrimps in orange or pink, and Teeny Sparkle Nymphs in hot green. Sight-casting to sockeye from a high vantage point on the deck of a boat or skiff will increase the odds of detecting the subtle pickups. But once again, as with freshwater angling for the species, anglers should be careful in their approaches:

Saltwater sockeye are often spooky. Intense pressure from predators like seals and sea lions in these staging areas often puts fish off the bite.

Sockeye Salmon in Alaska

Though local abundance varies widely, fly-rodders can pursue sockeye salmon virtually anywhere in Alaska. The species ranges from streams near Petersburg and Ketchikan in the far southern drainages of the state north to the rivers emptying into Kuskokwim Bay. Some scattered returns occur even farther north, the most northerly population of any size being that of Salmon Lake on the Seward Peninsula. The most populous stocks exist in the clear-flowing waters of the Bristol Bay region, which is home to the largest annual harvest of the species in the world, the commercial fisheries of the area taking an average of twenty five million fish per year from 1982 to 2002 (Bristol Bay sport fishers averaged 13,700 harvested sockeye during that same twenty-year span). In other areas of Alaska, like Cook Inlet, Prince William Sound, and Chignik Lagoon on the southern side of the Alaska Peninsula, commercial fisheries operate at a clip of about one to six million sockeye per year.

Despite the fact that the state's—and the world's— most significant sockeye salmon populations return to spawn and rear in the immense lake–river habitat of Bristol Bay and the northern Alaska Peninsula, where individual runs can number in the millions and fly-fishing conditions are ideal, the great majority of the angling for the species occurs in a few Southcentral streams. The actual numbers are quite staggering.

Sockeye are adored for their culinary appeal. Here, shore lunch simmers on the coals.

BRIAN O'KEEFE

In the early 1990s, ADF&G studies for a quartet of the most popular Southwest Alaska rivers found that none averaged more than fourteen thousand angler-days of effort per year directed at sockeye. Effort on the Naknek River came closest, while sport fisheries on the Alagnak, Newhalen, and Kvichak Rivers recorded averages of ninety-seven hundred, fifty-seven hundred, and five thousand angler-days, respectively. Contrarily, effort expended on the Russian River during the same early-1990s time frame exceeded 65,000 angler-days per year, while the mainstem Kenai River saw sockeye effort top 340,000 angler-days.

Beyond the overwrought Southcentral fisheries and the sockeye mecca that is Bristol Bay, there are a few areas of the state that should interest fly-fishers. Kodiak Island, in particular, is home to several smaller clearwater drainages with explosive angling potential. Likewise, fly-fishers can encounter great numbers of returning sockeye—and few fellow anglers—in many of the tea-colored coastal streams in Southeast. Upstream tributaries of the glacial Copper River drainage in interior Alaska also support wild stocks of sockeye salmon. In fact, about 125 Copper River tributaries host spawning populations of sockeye salmon. Of these, the Gulkana River has historically supported the largest fishery. However, the semiglacial Klutina River offers good opportunities as well, primarily near the mouths of its own tributary streams and away from the crowds that gather along the river near Copper Center downstream of the Richardson Highway. Together, the Gulkana and Klutina Rivers have accounted for over 90 percent of the angling effort expended for sockeye salmon in the Copper River system.

Finally, for anglers bound for the northwestern corner of the state, an emerging sockeye fishery has developed in the Pilgrim River. Not traditionally known as a sockeye destination, fertilization of the headwater

Salmon Lake during the 1990s has resulted in an increase in the size of the returns. Fishing for all salmon species is closed in the lake itself, but in 2003 ADF&G counted over forty thousand sockeye in the river during the late-July migration. If these numbers remain strong, the Pilgrim River could provide an excellent sockeye salmon fishery for years to come.

SOUTHEAST ALASKA

The prolific angling opportunities for sockeye aren't as common in Southeast Alaska as in Southwest or on the Alaska Peninsula, but there remain fisheries of note, especially in the far southern panhandle near the communities of Petersburg, Wrangell, and Ketchikan. And much as it is with other sport fish species, Prince of Wales Island features some of the most concentrated freshwater angling opportunities in the region.

The severely stained waters of the Sarkar Creek and Lake system in the northwest corner of the island can be particularly good for sockeye in late June and early July. Some of the best fly-fishing can be had just up from the lagoon at the river's mouth, where the fish stage before pushing upstream during high tides. The fishing can also be good near the other outlets and tributary mouths in Sarkar Lake. The stream, which in total drains four freshwater lakes in the area, isn't very long, and most of the sockeye fly-fishing opportunities exist in stretches of water that remain tidally influenced. However, the numerous deep holes between the mouth and the outlet of Sarkar Lake provide excellent holding water, and the sockeye tend to stack up for days at a time, meaning that the stream can be fished with good success even during slack- and low-tide periods. The better-known Prince of Wales streams—Kegan Creek and the Karta and Thorne Rivers—provide equal if not better sockeye fishing, especially the Karta, which receives tens of thousands of in-migrating fish during the late-July run.

Not on Prince of Wales Island but still within the general Ketchikan area, the McDonald Lake system offers phenomenal prospects for Southeast sockeye fly-fishers, especially near lake inlets and outlets. The run occurs later here than in most other areas of the state, with the bulk of the sockeye entering Wolverine Creek and then moving throughout the system in mid-August through early September. As at many of the areas in Southeast, there is a Forest Service cabin and skiff available here for anglers who book early enough. Farther north and among the maze of channels, straits, and tidewater estuaries that make up the Inside Passage, strong returns of sockeye are more sparsely located, though both the road-accessible Thoms Creek near Wrangell and Petersburg Creek can provide consistent action during their short peaks, as can a few of the freshwater lake–stream systems on Admiralty, Baranof, and Chichagof Islands.

At the northern tip of the panhandle lie a pair of river systems of note to the sockeye fly-fisher. Dissecting the mountainous terrain of northern British Columbia, the glacial, braided Chilkat River flows south to rendezvous with Chilkat Inlet near the community of Haines. The area is primarily known for the approximately thirty-five hundred bald eagles that gather each fall in the tall cottonwoods lining the river, making the watershed the largest eagle council grounds in the world. A nice run of sockeye ascend the stream as well, and good fly-fishing prospects exist at the mouths of tributaries and in lake outlets, particularly where Chilkat Lake pours into the Tsirku River (*tsirku* is Tlingit for "big salmon"). During the summer, heavy silt loads make the mainstem river unfishable for the most part. The neighboring Chilkoot River system, also accessible by car from Haines, provides yet more fly-fishing opportunity for area salmon enthusiasts. Most of the sockeye fishing takes place in the boulder-strewn lower mile or so below Chilkoot Lake during both of the river's runs, the first of which peaks in

RIGHT: *The point where the clearwater Russian River mixes with the Kenai's glacial flows has long been one of Alaska's most popular sockeye fisheries.*

late June or early July. A second wave of bright sockeye makes its way through Lynn Canal and into the Chilkoot system in August. This drainage takes on some silt in the summer months as well, and it flows fairly fast for much of its length. Fly-fishing success can still be had, though, especially in the river's many long seams and slower-moving pockets, where large groups of sockeye will hold.

Several excellent chances for fly-fishers to work large concentrations of sockeye also exist in drainages of the immense Copper River Delta near Cordova (the same Copper River with upstream tributaries like the Gulkana and Klutina Rivers that lie in interior Alaska). The Eyak River, Alaganik Slough, and Martin River systems all produce healthy sockeye populations, and anglers willing to work a little to travel deeper into the watersheds—and farther from the Cordova road system in the case of the Eyak and Alaganik drainages—will be rewarded with solitude and some spectacular scenery to go with the

outstanding fly-fishing. Other, more remote North Gulf Coast drainages are sure to receive quality returns of sockeye salmon. A few, like the Katalla and Bering River systems, already see some steady though light traffic from summertime salmon anglers. For the most part, however, these short coastal streams, many of which originate in the vast St. Elias ice fields, remain unmolested as fisheries. Limited to beach landings, anglers will find access to be tough and the weather unforgiving, but the area's tremendous upside will continue to draw interest from the country's more passionate and adventurous fly-anglers, those interested in prospecting unknown streams for fish that have never seen a fly.

SOUTHCENTRAL ALASKA

To paint with a broad brush, Southcentral Alaska is home to two kinds of sockeye fishery. One is extremely fertile and based in some truly beautiful wilderness settings. The other certainly lacks nothing in productivity or scenic grandeur, though the zoo-like atmosphere so often encountered can belie the *wilderness* tag. Within some Southcentral drainages, both scenarios can be found within a few miles of each other. In fact, there may not be two more divergent scenes on any single river in Alaska than those found on the opposing ends of the Russian River.

At one end—the river's mouth—a U.S. Forest Service campground off the Sterling Highway provides the staging area for one of Southcentral's most infamous scenes, the combat fishing that takes place where the clear waters of the Russian mix with the Kenai's glacial green flows. Tens of thousands of sockeye salmon arrive here with the top of the summer season, and so do the anglers who chase them. At the other end—near the river's twin source lakes—a fly-fisher can access not only the fantastic fishing the Russian River is known for, but a fairly remote and scenic section of water as well.

Cordova, Alaska: gateway to the bountiful Copper River region.

DARYL PEDERSON

Visitors to the upper river can even witness one of nature's most dramatic spectacles, as the sockeye try to negotiate the falls and reach their spawning grounds at Upper Russian Lake.

The turquoise-colored Kenai, too, can offer fly-fishers experiences at both ends of the spectrum. While some areas, most notably the stretches leading up to the confluence with the Russian, will be well and truly packed with anglers during the heights of the sockeye runs, others allow a chance to fish the same productive waters without experiencing the crush of humanity common to the most popular and accessible sites. Areas of the middle river, like the confluence with the Moose River in Sterling, provide much of the best angling opportunity for shoreline-migrating sockeye. However, most of the land in this area is privately owned. Where public access is available, crowds are as much a feature of the fishing as the middle Kenai's wide, powerful nature. The upper Kenai offers anglers another option. Probably the state's most famous day-trip float destination, the upper river, much of which lies within the Kenai National Wildlife Refuge, somehow clings to its wilderness quality despite heavy summertime raft traffic.

Though getting off the road system and away from the crowds often means arduous backcountry travel or pricey fly-outs to remote lodges, there is another option, especially for those with a mind to experience some phenomenal sockeye fly-fishing in an area insulated from the Kenai Peninsula crowds. That option is the west side of Cook Inlet, where nearly a dozen streams tail off the eastern slopes of the Alaska Range and cut their way through the muskeg flats to join Cook Inlet just a few miles away. Most of the best sockeye streams are within half an hour's flight, and any number of Kenai- or Anchorage-based air taxi operators offer trans-inlet flights and packages that begin with as little as a day's fishing. Some highlights of the region include clearwater

BRIAN O'KEEFE

TONY WEAVER

*Donna Teeny shows off a huge
14-pound Kenai River sockeye.*

fertile as any other concentration of freshwater fisheries in North America.

A rugged spine of mountains splits the length of North America's second largest island, which is alternately blanketed by thick spruce forests, lush, grassy hummocks, and alpine tundra. With the exception of a few larger rivers, most of the freshwater fisheries of the archipelago are located in short, coastal streams that flow just a few miles from headwater lakes to meet the sea. Many of these systems will be literally brimming with sockeye during the peak of the migrations, allowing fly-fishers a chance at some rapid and often frenetic action. About 70 miles of roads originating in the town of Kodiak and running toward Chiniak Bay provide some easy-to-access fishing, but for the most part the Emerald Isle's best sockeye angling is reached only by floatplane or boat.

Of the roadside streams, the best bets for sockeye are the Buskin and Pasagshak Rivers, though a few smaller creeks offer good potential when the timing is right. The narrow, winding Saltery River, which can sometimes be reached by four-wheel-drive vehicles, is loaded with sockeye during the first half of July, and the stream's confined nature is very conducive to fly-fishing. The more famous sockeye locales require a flight, however. The Karluk and Ayakulik Rivers, both of which receive a pair of distinct returns, are good for sockeye, as is the Uganik River. On the Uganik, sockeye can be targeted in the lower portion of stream between Uganik Lake and the bay of the same name, or throughout the multiarmed upper river system. The Afognak River, the largest watershed on spruce-covered Afognak Island, offers quality angling throughout both a June and a late-July run of reds. Fishing can be particularly good near the outlet of Afognak Lake. Also on Afognak Island, short, shallow, and clear-flowing Malina, Pauls, and Portage Creeks can be great in the second half of June.

Coal Creek in the Beluga River system, Wolverine Creek at Big River Lakes (due to large numbers of sockeye and dependable brown bear traffic, twenty or more charter skiffs may be operating here throughout the season), the Chuitna River system, including Threemile and Chuit Creeks, and the blue-green waters of Crescent River and Lake.

KODIAK ISLAND

Some of the most productive sockeye salmon streams to be found in the Last Frontier lie 30 miles from the Alaska mainland, across Shelikof Strait in the Kodiak Island complex. The area is world renowned for its population of brown bears, approximately three thousand of which inhabit the archipelago, though the clearwater drainages that thread through the varying terrain are as diverse and

Even the most jaded, most widely traveled adventurers would have a hard time explaining away the wonders of Southwest Alaska, the sheer breadth of its pure, pristine wilderness, the diverse bounty of its tundra-carving watersheds. For Alaska-bound fly-fishers, the region is an undeniable jewel, perhaps the diamond in a land of pearls. And if sockeye are the target, those anglers can safely say they've arrived at the best place in the world.

During the month of July, many of the clear-flowing watersheds will be literally choked with fish, the planet's greatest concentration of the highly prized sockeye moving inland toward their spawning beds. Along the way, and with their eventual deaths, they'll disperse millions of tons of nutrients from the rich marine environment to the tundra's nutrient-poor fresh waters, increasing production at all levels of the food chain, from aquatic insects and rainbow trout to bald eagles and coastal grizzly bears, as well as providing crucial sustenance for the surrounding riparian and lacustrine ecosystems. Sockeye-seeking fly-anglers new to Southwest will soon discover that planning a successful trip in this region isn't so much about where the fish will be—since they can be found in numbers virtually everywhere—but about where they feel like visiting and what sorts of things they hope to see.

Recreational fisheries for sockeye salmon are becoming increasingly popular in the region, and there are many lodges, guide operations, and air taxi services to help anglers access the often remote waters. The Kvichak River drainage, including Alaska's largest lake, Iliamna, as well as Lake Clark (the sixth largest) and many smaller tributaries, has historically been the most significant sockeye producer in the state—indeed, the world. Since 1979, up to forty-two million fish have ascended the Kvichak River in a single season. Many of those fish are bound for other streams within the watershed, where they can be targeted by fly-fishers; of these, the Newhalen has long been the most popular with sockeye anglers. Most of the fishing that takes place in the main-stem Kvichak occurs in the upper 10 to 15 miles of the river, with effort concentrated near the village of Igiugig during late June and early July. However, Kvichak salmon are in serious decline. Once producing over half of the sockeye caught in the multimillion-dollar Bristol Bay fishery, the Kvichak watershed's continued declines have resulted in the region begin declared an economic disaster area in multiple years. In an effort to rebuild the populations, managers have even been forced to close fishing in the Kvichak area a few times since 2000. In 2003, when sport fishing for the species was again closed, the 1.7 million sockeye counted by ADF&G personnel at the Igiugig tower fell far below the department's forecast of 2.6 million fish.

West of the Iliamna system, several other high-quality opportunities exist for fly-fishers interested in sockeye salmon. The largest stocks of the species found in drainages emptying into Kuskokwim Bay occur in the Goodnews and Kanektok Rivers, both among the Great Land's most renowned float-trip destinations. In the lowlands between this area and the Iliamna drainage, the entire roster of Southwest's fabulous salmon fisheries offers good to excellent sockeye populations, the Togiak, Wood-Tikchik, Nushagak, and Mulchatna systems especially. However, to the other side of Lake Iliamna lies an area that can never be far from a discussion of the state's grandest angling settings.

Katmai National Park and Preserve, which houses accumulations of natural wonders that rival those found almost anywhere else in the world, has long been one of Alaska's most celebrated remote destinations. But today the region is perhaps most famous not for its volcanoes, rugged wilderness, and brown bears, but for the tremendous populations of fish that inhabit the myriad cool,

*The Katmai caldera speaks to
the region's volcanic past ...
and future.*

sapphire-colored waters. In fact, one of Alaska's most
recognizable scenes occurs in Katmai, when forty to sixty
of the region's sockeye-hunting bruins congregate along
the Brooks River and the nearby shorelines of Naknek
and Brooks Lakes, where they can be readily viewed by
travelers. Katmai sport fishing didn't get untracked until
the early 1940s when pilots like Ray Petersen began flying workers from the Naknek and Nushagak canneries to
Brooks Lake and other prominent fishing holes. At
around the same time, the U.S. Army built a pair of
rest-and-recreation camps on the Naknek River. One,
informally called Rapids Camp, was located at the foot
of the river's rapids, while the second, Lake Camp, was
constructed about 7 miles upstream. From those fairly

humble beginnings, word of Katmai's outlandish fecundity spread quickly. By the end of the decade Petersen's
newly created Northern Consolidated Airlines was flying
in anglers from across the United States. His family operates the fly-in fishing operation today, called Katmailand,
which remains centered in the three camps Ray initially
opened, Brooks, Grosvenor, and Kulik.

While the Brooks River and its waterfall-leaping sockeye salmon garner a fair share of the area's notoriety,
there are certainly other sockeye fisheries associated
with Katmai that are of equal or even more productivity.
The region's glacier-carved valleys and lowlands are dotted with a profusion of freshwater lakes and their interconnecting streams. Many present fantastic fly-fishing

potential for sockeye, and a number, like Brooks, are part of the immense Naknek Lake and River system, which welcomes returns of more than a million sockeye during most years. A perhaps lesser-known but still excellent Katmai sockeye locale is American Creek, a short, swiftly flowing stream that boasts a significant late-July/early-August salmon migration. Tailored to fly-fishing and strewn with rocks and other debris that create deep pools for holding salmon, American Creek would probably draw more interest from anglers, but relatively limited access and a healthy population of Katmai grizzlies tend to dissuade many potential visitors.

Another major sockeye producer in the Katmai neighborhood is the Wild and Scenic Alagnak River, which actually empties into the Kvichak River near Kvichak Bay. Unlike the larger Iliamna-system stream, Alagnak sockeye populations have not fallen on hard times but are in fact booming. In past years, when six hundred thousand or more sockeye would return to the Alagnak, fly-fishers could inevitably find prime concentrations of bright fish gathered in the river's numerous upstream braids. The ideal fly-fishing landscape found in the Alagnak was obviously much aided in 2003, when ADF&G estimated 3.7 million sockeye returned to the river. If future runs continue at anything resembling this level, it's sure more midsummer attention will be focused here. As it is now, booking a week at a Kvichak- or Lake Iliamna–based lodge during the summer will probably land anglers in a floatplane, making the early-morning flight south to the Alagnak.

For those adventurous souls who may be looking for something even more on the wild side, the pellucid waterways of the Alaska Peninsula beckon like Aztec gold to a sixteenth-century conquistador. The land offers more than raw, unspoiled wilderness, too, for only the distant geography has kept many of these drainages off the worldwide "must-fish" list. Two national wildlife refuges make up much of the region, and within their environs over one thousand salmon-producing streams are known to exist.

Within the 1.2 million acres of the Becharof refuge lies Alaska's second largest landlocked body of water—and the third largest freshwater lake in the United States—Becharof Lake. A nursery for the world's second largest run of sockeye salmon, the Becharof system, when combined with the drainages of the neighboring Alaska Peninsula National Wildlife Refuge, produces in excess of thirty million sockeye per year, even when conservative estimates are used. Virtually any of the clear-water streams that proliferate in either refuge are worth exploring, especially the inlets and outlets of creeks connecting with Becharof Lake or those within the Ugashik system. Many have a mixture of fine sand and cinder bottoms due to the area's intense concentration of active volcanoes like the stately Mount Peulik that towers almost 5,000 feet above the southern shore of Becharof Lake and is last known to have erupted in 1852.

The Aniakchak National Monument and Preserve, which shares a boundary with the Alaska Peninsula National Wildlife Refuge, rivals the two larger refuges for wilderness-fishing potential. Here, the Meshik River, one of the few area streams with a name known to outsiders, begins in wide, saddlelike headwaters that interrupt the Aleutian Range. Undeniably productive, the Meshik and a number of short, fairly shallow tributaries provide excellent fly-fishing potential. For that reason, a few lodges do operate in the area. On the southern, Pacific side of the Alaska Peninsula, yet another little-fished treasure trove for sockeye salmon exists in the Chignik River system. Both Chignik and Black Lakes are headwaters to the system and are important rearing grounds for the salmon. Most of the fishing that does take place occurs in the Chignik River between the lake and the lagoon.

coho
salmon

WORLD-CLASS FLY-ANGLERS tend to be a discerning but opinionated bunch when it comes to their game fish. Avowed steelheaders might look at other angling options as minor-league pursuits better left for those without the chutzpah necessary to perform in The Show. Most devotees of Bug Latin, on the other hand, will almost surely defend to the death the sublimity of a riseform, eschewing as gluttonous any reasons tendered for dipping beneath the surface. Then there are the flats anglers, who see more backing in an average year than a fly-shop shelf and who must listen with a certain amusement as the keepers of the Rocky Mountain tall-tale tradition regale audiences with stories of violent, reel-squealing runs and the hot fish that cause them.

Part of the beauty of fly-fishing is derived from this diversity and the never-ending discourse it spawns, of course. Beautiful, too, are fish that can arouse such passion. Fly-fishers will

Casting to saltwater silvers in the waning light.

BRIAN O'KEEFE

necessarily brave terrific distances and defy many of life's conventions as defined by the nonangling world to chase them. For beyond the incessant and truly irrelevant comparisons, welcome only for their ability to extend coffee breaks and encourage happy-hour attendance, no angler can resist the siren call of the world's great game fish and the lure of the places where they'll be found.

Even the most well-traveled fly-fisher will get weak in the knees when pondering the salmonfly hatch on a handful of rivers of the West. A case of the shakes might be induced by memories of the windblown pampas of Tierra del Fuego or hazy recollections of boreal forests, gin-clear water, and the coastal steelhead of northern British Columbia. Likewise, nearly everyone who has ever tied a fly dreams of casting to the King of Sport Fish from the autumn-soaked banks of the Miramichi or in the fish-addled flows of Russia's Ponoi. Many anglers wait a lifetime to fish the Keys, the Bahamas, Christmas Island, or Mexico's Yucatán, and once they've fulfilled the wish, they'll almost certainly insist on returning every year.

Each new season, in fact, fly-fishers will grab their passports and their gear bags and head for destinations laden with treasures enough to make Marco Polo swoon. From the blue-ribbon trout streams of the American West to the name rivers of Scotland, there's always one last sweetwater stream, one more perfect pool, another flat that's yet to be fished. So while the heart of the matter can often be found in any of a hundred thousand pieces of home water, even the most adamant introvert will have composed some form of travel agenda. Not surprisingly, a species or two from Alaska waters will be found on most of those dockets.

The fish that demands that ink be put to calendars across the globe might not be one that immediately leaps to mind, however; for most anglers, the Last Frontier's reputation as a premier fly-fishing destination has more to do with resident rainbows than it does any of the anadromous fish that return by the millions each year. Plus, the methodical nature of pursuing a bottom-hugging fish that isn't even slightly interested in eating might seem like enough to bore a tax attorney. But unlike tight-lipped sockeye and occasionally obtuse chinook, at least one species of the Pacific salmon is prone to the attack—the coho salmon.

The natural ferocity of Alaska's coho is already well known, of course, as is the fact that they're tailor-made for fly-fishing—willing biters, able and in a lot of cases, spectacular fighters, with spawning congregations tending to favor the more lithe coastal streams. And if all that wasn't enough to lure the angling cognoscenti north, coho fresh from the sea are also the most prone of the Pacific salmon to rise and explode on a surface presentation.

The Coho Salmon
(Oncorhynchus kisutch)

Coho salmon, commonly referred to as "silver salmon" in many areas, are the second least abundant of the Pacific salmon, after chinook. The species was originally distributed in North America from the area around the San Lorenzo River in California northward to Point Hope. Within the forty-ninth state, silvers range continuously from the far southern panhandle to Norton Sound and from there sporadically to the aforementioned Point Hope on the Chukchi Sea. They are an extremely adaptable fish and occur in nearly every accessible body of fresh water in much of this range, from large, glacially influenced drainages like the Stikine or Susitna to small clearwater tributaries and coastal rivers. In Southeast Alaska alone, spawning populations of coho salmon are known to exist in at least twenty-five hundred streams.

In appearance, the coho closely resembles the larger

chinook salmon. In fact, in inshore marine waters where the two species will sometimes be found together, young chinook can be mistaken for coho—both are silver in color and display irregular black spots and markings across their backs. However, with silver salmon, the spots only exist on the upper lobe of the caudal fin, whereas chinook display the black markings on both the upper and lower lobes. Chinook also exhibit black pigment on their gums, while in coho the area around the teeth will be grayish, with white at the crown of the gum. Once they've entered fresh water, coho, like the other species of Pacific salmon, begin to undergo rapid physiological changes. Body coloration darkens, especially along the back, which in coho usually turns a dark, dull, greenish brown to maroon color. Sides are flanked with a red stripe, which can spread across the body, though females typically don't undergo quite as drastic a conversion as males. Males of the species also develop a pronounced kype as the spawning condition intensifies.

Adult coho returning to Alaska waters average between 8 and 12 pounds and are usually 24 to 30 inches long, though specimens of over 25 pounds have been caught. In some areas of Alaska, wild fish better than 20 pounds are actually a fairly common occurrence. Some Kodiak Island streams and the rivers of the Gulf Coast south of Cordova in particular have been noted for the large average size of their coho.

LIFE HISTORY

Throughout most of its southern distribution, the coho salmon shows little diversity in life history. In drainages that receive spawning runs from about the middle of British Columbia southward to the Monterey Bay area, returns generally occur in September and October. The young hatch the following spring, spend one year in the river, and then migrate to the sea in late spring (usually early May). However, from approximately the Skeena

BRIAN O'KEEFE

River system northward, including throughout the species' Alaska range, the shorter growing season and widely varying water temperatures make generalizations dangerous.

What all coho do share is an innate aggressiveness. Emergent fry begin to feed immediately upon leaving the redd in the spring of their birth. They tend to take up residence in the shallows of stream margins at first, later establishing territories in lakes and the deeper pools of rivers, which they'll rigidly defend. From there they'll cruise the shorelines (especially in lakes) and dart out from beneath debris or among other submerged vegetation to take prey organisms. Both terrestrial and aquatic insects, especially midges in many areas of Alaska, and a little zooplankton, make up the bulk of the young silvers' diet at this point. As the juvenile coho grow, they begin to feed on progressively larger prey. In many Alaska streams, they eventually can become serious predators of young sockeye salmon. Past studies have even indicated that in some systems, young Alaska coho consume up to seven times as many sockeye as do Dolly Varden, a species once under a state bounty for what was perceived as a penchant for victimizing salmon stocks.

Throughout their range, young coho will begin to head for the sea after their first year, though in Alaska several stocks will remain two, three, or even four years in fresh water before smolting. Research on coho of the Karluk River has shown that the longer freshwater residence frequently results in fewer but larger smolts that are probably better equipped for ocean survival. The young initially remain close to shore, moving farther from their home river as they grow. Some southern populations are known to stick close to the coast throughout their saltwater tenures, though Alaska coho are believed to move farther into the open ocean. Tagging has shown that Southeast Alaska fish will migrate north along the coast and eventually assemble in the central Gulf of Alaska until maturation is complete. While in the oceanic environment, coho feed voraciously; growth is rapid. Herring and squid make up the bulk of their diet where abundant, though the opportunistic predators will also consume large numbers of crustaceans and other fish, like sand lance.

In Alaska, coho typically return to their home streams after sixteen to eighteen months at sea. Entry into natal drainages can occur anytime between midsummer and winter, usually during periods of high runoff. Although as a rule the earlier spawning returns are associated with the more northerly stocks, each separate population of coho salmon will have evolved a distinct run timing based on its particular circumstances. For instance, coho that must traverse a falls during their in-stream migrations might arrive in July when water flows are lower and the barriers easier to navigate. Other stocks, such as

Topwater coho.

TONY WEAVER

The rich heritage of Southeast is impossible to ignore.

the Yukon River fish, may arrive early because of the distances they have to travel to reach the spawning grounds. Water temperature also plays a part: In northern streams with colder average temperatures, coho have developed earlier spawning times to allow for longer periods of egg development.

Even though coho salmon are known to spawn in clearwater tributaries of the Yukon River at least as far upstream as the Tanana system, most populations seem to prefer short coastal drainages. Whether an evolutionary trait developed from the great distances they travel or not, coho that undertake long migrations to their freshwater areas of reproduction have a distinct morphology, with slimmer, more streamlined bodies than coastal

silvers. After entering fresh water, coho in these shorter river systems will hold in deep pools until they ripen, when they'll move the typically short distance to their spawning locations. In rare cases, such as the coho salmon of the Pasagshak system on Kodiak, the fish will mill in a lake near tributary outlets and only enter the tributaries themselves to spawn. For this reason, Lake Rose Tead, not the actual spawning streams, is a primary fishing ground for float-tubing anglers interested in fishing the Pasagshak system.

An abrupt change in any of the environmental conditions can drastically alter run timing. A good example of this occurrence was the 2000 coho return to the Buskin River on Kodiak Island. A late-summer drought occurred

coho salmon | 101

in the area that year, with less than 4 inches of rain falling during August and September (average precipitation for those two months is over 12 inches). Stream levels were very low, and the coho delayed their entry until after some heavy rainstorms in early October. The next year, rainfall was near average levels for August and September, and the silvers accordingly returned right on schedule.

Fly-Fishing for Alaska's Coho

In many ways, the coho salmon could be considered the premier fly-fishing quarry of the Pacific Coast's anadromous species. Most would immediately rank the steel-head trout, especially, or maybe even the chinook salmon higher. Of course, there is much merit in doing so. Like those species, the silver salmon is an exuberant fighter, usually quite acrobatic, with both good size and stamina. Plus, the species is normally more willing to chase a fly than the chinook and generally occurs in higher concentrations than either of the two. Being the most willing topwater target of Alaska's anadromous fish certainly doesn't hurt the coho's reputation, either.

The coho, as a game fish, offers fly-fishers an incredibly diverse range of angling scenarios for which any number of techniques, presentations, and patterns may be appropriate. Added to that variety, coho can be taken in nearly any of Alaska's angling environments, from the rock-strewn creeks that tumble through the old-growth

Hooking up with an estuary silver.

TONY WEAVER

timber of Southeast to the wide-open artesian streams of the Aleutian coast. Aerial maneuvers, long, sizzling runs, and the willingness to actively chase flies are just the icing on the cake.

RUN TIMING

Across most of their Alaska range, silver salmon can be found entering their natal fresh waters from mid-July through the beginning of November. Barring significant environmental aberrations, like the 2000 Kodiak Island drought or the 2002 Kenai Peninsula floods, the great majority of the runs occur from late July or early August through September.

Generally, Southeast silver returns peak later than their counterparts to the north, in September and October. The specific time is particular to unique stocks, however, with some, like the coho of the Wrangell area, arriving in multiple waves. A first run of silvers returns to the freshwater streams around Wrangell from early July to mid-August, with a second, primary return occurring from the middle of August through the middle of October. Anecdotal evidence from the region's guide fleet suggests that not only do the early runs comprise fewer fish, but that these coho are typically smaller, too, averaging only 3 to 4 pounds, while the autumn-arriving silvers can weigh 10 pounds or more. The period from the beginning of August through the end of September usually holds the peak for fly-anglers wishing to target area coho in the salt before they reach their home streams.

For Southwest Alaska stocks, silvers can begin to show by late July, with runs peaking in August and tapering off by early September. Likewise, the few quality coho opportunities available for Northwest-bound anglers usually occur during the month of August. In Southcentral Alaska, runs can begin in late July and sometimes stretch into November, with late August and

early September seeing the highest numbers of fish migrating into fresh water in most areas. In Southcentral, too, a few drainages host dual coho returns, most notably the Kenai River, where an early return occurs in August and a second, smaller run begins to enter the drainage around the middle of September. This second Kenai return can occur throughout October and even November, with bright fish often available well into Alaska's winter season.

GEAR FOR SILVERS

Once the fish are located, most of Alaska's coho aficionados vary little in their choice of weapon, whether they're targeting the feisty fish in salt water, a boulder-filled clearwater stream, or the surface of a back-flooded river mouth. Seven- to 9-weight fly rods are the norm, usually 9 to 10 feet in length, with fast actions and strong butt sections. The longer rods are appreciated for the greater control they give anglers when mending line. Fast actions are also needed to cast bulky salmon flies and subdue large, powerful fish. In saltwater scenarios, 9-weight rods are typically preferred simply to cope with the heavier sinking lines that must be cast.

Line weights to match a rod's rating or, more important, that load a rod properly are recommended. As is the case when fishing most of Alaska's game species, coho anglers can benefit greatly from specialty tapers with most of their mass in the front 30 feet of line. These lines load fast and shoot far and can aid in turning over the bulky deer hair creations often used for topwater coho angling. In fact, when hunting topwater silvers, experienced fly-fishers will frequently keep 30 to 40 feet of line out to quick-load the tip of the rod and cast quickly to fast-moving fish. Again, as with the other salmon in the state, coho anglers will want to carry a range of sinking tips and full-sinking lines.

For saltwater anglers, even more variety will be

Fighting Southwest Alaska coho.

RIGHT: *Tying flies on the mother ship.*

needed; everything from intermediate shooting heads to hybrid express lines is used. The extra-fast-sinking lines, 500 grains or more, are best utilized when fishing the deep-water bays, straits, and Inside Passage canals of Southeast, though the same applications will be needed if fishing in the generally more open environment found off the coast of the Kodiak Archipelago or in Resurrection Bay.

Also similar to much of the state's other fly-fishing, proper leader construction is of fundamental concern when preparing to fish for coho salmon, whether in salt or fresh water. Most leaders, especially the commercially available extruded leaders, perform poorly when casting big salmon flies. They'll do even worse with a water-soaked 'Wog. Hence, unlike the case of traditional dry-fly fishing—where soft leaders are preferred for making delicate dead-drift presentations—most salmon leaders are tied with stiff monofilament, the kind designed for salt water, and range from 7½ to 9 feet in length. Mason

Hard Mono, Rio Saltwater, and Maxima Clear are all good choices for Alaska silvers. To construct a generalized coho leader, start with a butt section that is at least 65 percent of the diameter of the fly line (diameters are included in fly-line literature) and then design the leader using a formula that will get you to the desired tippet strength. For example, begin with a 3-foot butt section of .030 monofilament, stepping down via a blood knot to 3 feet of .020. Then, following another blood knot, attach 1 foot of .015 mono, which will be connected to 2 feet of .012 or .010 tippet. A leader like this, with the proper stiffness, will kick over most bulky flies with ease.

When using a sinking line in freshwater-fishing situations, such leader lengths aren't typically desired. Other than in supremely low and clear waters—when it's doubtful a sinking tip would do much good anyway—4 to 6 feet of standard monofilament leader will be plenty. An exception is in preparing saltwater leaders, when anglers may need to go to longer, 10- to 14-foot constructions. This is typically the case when silvers are pooled near the surface of tidal estuaries, where spooking the fish is of utmost concern. Anglers might also want to step their tippet strength up to 15-pound test in the salt, again using stiff monofilament leader material, as saltwater tippets need to be able to withstand abrasion from kelp, barnacles, and, in some areas, jagged rocks.

FLIES FOR SILVERS

Within Alaska, more original efforts have probably been extended toward tying new coho flies than patterns designed to entice almost all of the other Pacific salmon combined. Perhaps this is because coho are so prone to reward a tier with a follow and take. Or probably more likely, fly-tiers are as attracted to the bright, sometimes gaudy materials as the fish are. In either case, both traditional patterns and a never-ending array of variations, deviations, and, depending on who's judging, hallucinations are tied up and sent swimming in search of coho. From Flash Flies or Conehead Buggers adorned in kaleidoscopic colors to marabou and rabbit-strip leeches, only one truth seems certain when applied to silver salmon flies: Nearly everyone with some thread and a vise can become a successful innovator.

Most freshwater coho flies are tied on hook sizes from 6 down to 1/0. As with chinook flies, many of the most popular patterns include fluorescent colors, especially pink or chartreuse, though patterns tempered with black or purple to offset tonal values can be the most effective. Another important element prospective coho anglers should keep in mind is movement. A fly that flutters or swims will be immeasurably more effective than heavily weighted patterns when fishing Alaska's silver salmon. Toward that end, supple materials like marabou, rabbit strip, and Arctic fox can be used in a wide variety of creations. For fishing faster water, where soft materials lose much of their effectiveness, stiffer, hackled flies will be needed. If weight is required to get down to low-lying fish, patterns tied with barbell or bead-chain eyes will be better than those fashioned with numerous lead wraps beneath the body, despite most Alaska tiers' preference for doing just that.

Before thinking about a surface pattern for coho, it's important for anglers to remember that the fish have stopped eating by the time they reach their natal streams. Thus, fly selection should be predicated less upon specific colors or shapes than it might be for many other applications, such as when particular forage fish need to be replicated for fly-fishing salmon in the salt. Topwater coho anglers are looking to create a surface disturbance that will activate a territorial, not feeding, trigger. If the fly gurgles or pops, so much the better.

Some patterns used for topwater trout, like shrew, mouse, or other waking flies, will also work for coho,

BRIAN O'KEEFE

as will basically any big, high-floating fly that makes a noise when it hits the surface. Probably the most identifiable fly for topwater coho is the Pollywog or 'Wog. The 'Wog is often tied in a variety of styles; most common are cigar and hammerhead shapes. Although effective, these flies often require extensive labor to create, as stacking and trimming deer hair can take time and skill. And the flies are typically good for only one or two fish, because slime and water absorption, not to mention the silver's notorious ability to wreak havoc on feathers and fur, finally combine to make them unfishable. This is also why some traditional surface flies, primarily the summer steelhead patterns of the Pacific Northwest, are not more widely utilized for coho, even though they can work quite well in certain situations.

With some of the synthetics presently available to tiers, many of the past impediments to creating both effective and durable topwater silver flies are now easily overcome. Flies can often be tied faster with synthetic materials, which also shed water easier and are more likely to withstand repeated strikes. Closed-cell foam and popper bodies can be used in a variety of fashions in combination with dyed deer hair to construct hybrid, high-tech coho flies. These patterns, some of which are the Hot Lips, Kamikaze, Gurgler, and Techno Spanker, are beginning to replace earlier favorites. Plus, with a slimmer profile than popular patterns like the Pink Pollywog, these flies float higher and are much easier to cast. The latter factor may be the most significant to consider when designing coho surface flies.

For saltwater flies, anglers will of course be looking to imitate the coho's prevalent food forms as closely as possible. This means baitfish patterns that look and act like the real thing. For herring, many anglers use a vari-ety of color combinations of Bill and Kate Howe's ALF, Homer's Herring, or Sea Habits. Sand lance, important forage fish throughout Alaska's saltwater environment, are very realistically imitated by Kodiak tier Hank Pennington's Sand Candy and Needlefish patterns. The two are similar, tied in the Thunder Creek style, with an epoxy coating over a reversed, synthetic hair and buck-tail body. They're tied slender and range from 2 to 4 inches in length, the epoxy coating rendering the bodies nearly indestructible. They're also tied on short-shank hooks, like most Alaska saltwater patterns, which allow the fly to ride nose-down, mimicking the action of a wounded baitfish. For the Sand Candy, white and brown Super Hair are combined with aqua Krystal Flash and gold peacock herl beneath pearl Mylar tubing and the final epoxy coating. Generalized saltwater patterns like the Clouser Minnow, many of the Popovics-style epoxy flies, or Lefty's Deceivers, also have their place in Alaska's salt water, especially when fishing a new area or over eager fish. The Clouser in chartreuse and white, tied

RIGHT: A coho that came up for a 'Wog.

BELOW: A selection of coho patterns.

BRIAN O'KEEFE

about 2 to 5 inches long, seems to be particularly effective in a range of locations and may be one of the best multipurpose choices Alaska saltwater anglers can make.

ANGLING STRATEGIES

Fly-anglers visiting the Last Frontier for the first time during the height of a coho return will soon discover that like chinook, these salmon are much more active and willing to chase flies during the low-light hours of the day. Thus, while steady silver salmon action can be had throughout the day in many instances, well-planned excursions will include fishing during and just after high tide in coastal areas, as well as during the first three hours of morning and the few hours of midnight-sun twilight.

Coho tend to travel and hold less in primary river channels than chinook, shunning the stronger flows of a mainstem river except where unavoidable. Also similar to fly-fishing for chinook and the other Pacific salmon, the closer to saltwater the fish can be intercepted, the better it is for the angler. Silvers are brighter and full of fight near the sea, as well as being much more prone to actively chase a fly. In a lot of instances, fly-fishers can pursue the fish right in the bays, estuaries, or river mouths, where the fish stage for the first big push upriver. Once they've cleared the tidewater area and moved into the stream proper, the holding water anglers are looking for doesn't differ much from that of silvers to the other salmon. Side sloughs and confluences with tributary streams are almost always productive areas to fish, as are eddies, long seams, and the tailouts of pools, as well as the belly of the pools themselves. During the height of a run, strong numbers of coho will stack in the most desirable lies, and often an angler will be able to ascertain their location without a lot of blind-casting. Active silvers tend to roll and show themselves more than chinook or, at times, even sockeye.

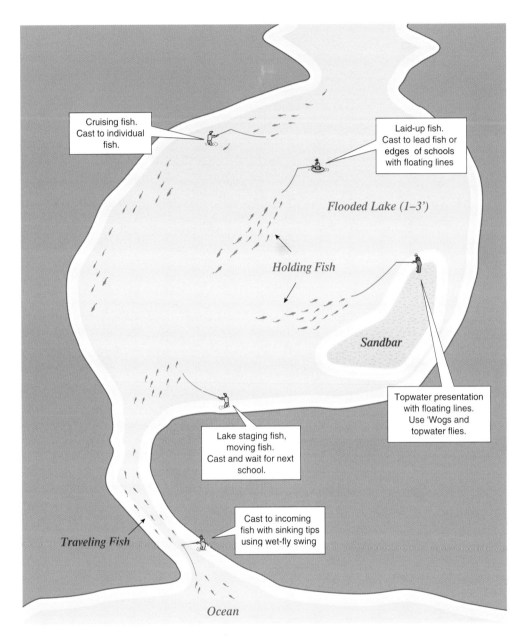

BRIAN O'KEEFE

For the most part, presentations need not be artful in order to entice bright silver salmon to strike. A controlled wet-fly swing is the most common tactic utilized, where conditions warrant. Because of the coho's territorial impulses and general aggressive nature, the swing is sometimes combined with short, erratic strips, which seem to be effective. If fishing a wide pool or riffle, anglers will position themselves just upstream and across from the holding fish. The fly is cast about 10 feet in front of the fish and allowed to sink, then stripped as it drifts toward their position. If the fish seem reticent after several casts, anglers can increase the length or frequency of their strips before swapping out flies or making other significant alterations. For coho, the retrieve and action of the fly, not the severely controlled depth, can be the most important elements in successful

angling. In extremely low and clear situations, it's usually best to put the standard, brightly colored coho flies back in the box and go to a more subtle, darkly colored pattern. Leeches and Woolly Buggers are two of the most common clearwater coho patterns. On these occasions, a lot of disturbance can actually be counterproductive as well, so anglers should fish the subdued patterns dead-drift, forgoing the action and strip of earlier presentations. In large, wide rivers like the Nushagak, coho angling is usually best done from a boat. There are times, even on the Nushagak, when anglers can get out and wade a beach to fish, but for the most part, operators can place a boat above holding fish and give anglers repeated shots to make their presentations. The technique here is very similar to the boat tactics used for other salmon. Casts should be made at a slightly steeper downstream angle than usual, and the fly allowed to drift in front of the holding fish, hovering across their noses.

Once the coho does strike, there are often no second thoughts. Unlike chinook, coho only rarely mouth a fly. In fact, they'll often hit and turn so hard that they hook themselves. All that's left to the angler is to hang on through the repeated runs and watch the aerial show.

TOPWATER COHO

For those willing to do a little looking, there are a few broad characteristics that will aid in locating waters across Alaska that afford the opportunity to take coho on the surface. Generally speaking, anglers should scout for streams with shallow, clear water and a rather gentle flow. Four feet deep or less is a good benchmark, and anything more than a slight ripple should be avoided, as the broken current will tend to keep the fish trained on the bottom. It's also best to concentrate on areas close enough to the surf that the fish are still bright and aggressive, while not being so close that the salmon have yet to acclimate to the drastic change in their environment;

Judith O'Keefe with a chrome coho.

recently arrived coho are often lethargic as they habituate themselves to fresh water.

The best topwater fly-fishing in the state may be found in the streams of the Lost Coast area south of Cordova, where numerous sand-dune flats dominate the bottom structure in the lower few miles of the short coastal drainages. Not unlike their tropical counterparts, these flats will have a hard sand bottom and commonly run shallow. Usually within a mile of salt water, a back-flooded effect is created in most of these drainages, and the rivers will run like a big, slow-moving lake. Fish will stack up in these regions while they adjust to the fresh water. Often they'll rest near the surface, with their fins protruding, allowing anglers an opportunity to wade and sight-cast to coho much as they would to bonefish off the coast of the Bahamas or Christmas Island.

However, casting over the top of holding silvers in the topwater milieu will often spook them out of striking a surface presentation. Instead, anglers should begin in the proper position and then generate enough line speed during the cast to make a fly-first presentation, which is again similar to the techniques needed for fishing tarpon or bonefish, when ticking the water with the fly line can spoil an otherwise fine cast. In smaller tributary streams and creeks, like the upper reaches of the Susitna and Yentna drainages, this can be even more important. Here, after exiting the big glacial rivers, coho will stack up like cordwood in the flush of clean water to rest before beginning another push upstream. Anglers can stalk and then sight-cast to these fish by keeping a low profile and approaching each pod with as little disturbance as possible. In this scenario, the first cast is always the most important—it will almost always take a fish if they aren't lined. By then working the edges of the pods methodically, fly-fishers can take fish after fish. It's only after being spooked by a big splash in the middle of the school that the coho will usually disperse in numbers.

Unloading on the Lost Coast.

Casts should be made at a face-to-face angle downstream from the holding fish. After the cast, anglers should let the fly drag across the current, keeping tension on the line to create a wake. If needed, a slight strip can be added to the swing, furthering the surface disturbance created. Also, if fishing over slow-moving, unrippled water, fly-fishers may need to throw a downstream mend to get more line on the water, which will create greater surface tension and a more significant wake. Most strikes will come at the apex of the swing, because the fish follow the waking fly and finally take it as the line straightens below the angler's position.

In other topwater coho locations, stealth is not as important. Some, like the Tsiu and other large systems south of Cordova, contain so many fish that missed shots are immediately replaced with new opportunities as the next wave of silvers enters. Mortensen's Lagoon near Cold Bay on the Alaska Peninsula is another such choke point for migrating silvers, sometimes holding as many as three thousand milling fish during the big tidal pushes. Likewise, the Tsiu and Tvisat Rivers of the Lost Coast are both prime hunting grounds for topwater silvers, complete with large flooded-lake backwaters where thousands of fish mill. When fishing these river-backflow lakes, look for nervous water or fins protruding from the surface before committing. Often these lakelike waters will have a nearly imperceptible current, and the fish can seem to be moving in a multitude of directions. The trick is to find the orientation of the majority of fish and then to aim for the head of the school.

In either circumstance, whether stalking small-stream silvers or sight-casting to huge schools, anglers should look for laid-up rather than moving coho for the best

Birds often indicate the presence of salmon.

TONY WEAVER

surface action; fish that have moved in from the saltwater edge and settled down often become territorial and more aggressive. There are a few successful alternate presentations that can be made to milling fish once they're found. For instance, topwater coho anglers might want to make short, fast strips across the current to induce surface commotion and noise. That should be altered to fit the fish and conditions, however. Aggressive fish might be persuaded to attack a splashy, popping retrieve of a 'Wog, while more acclimated fish might not be so inclined to chase. Sometimes these fish will show a penchant for sipping rather than inhaling flies like their more assertive counterparts. In this case, try a subtler, slow strip of a Kamikaze, leaving only a minutely noticeable wake. Sometimes even a heave-and-leave technique will prove most productive. Then fly-fishers should cast to the fish as they mill in a shallow pool. Leave the fly nearly motionless, only twitching or otherwise barely moving it to get the coho's attention. Sooner or later, if fishing over a good concentration of coho in the right type of water, a fish will wake up and come to get a better look at the intrusion.

SILVERS IN THE SALT

In regions like Southeast Alaska, coho salmon tend to trace the steep, rocky shorelines of the coastal islands and are readily available to anglers wanting to enjoy some of the most thrilling salmon fly-fishing to be found anywhere on the Pacific Coast. Finding coho in the salt can seem tough, however, especially without the aid of electronic fish finders and graphs. After all, it's a big ocean.

Fly-fishers willing to search a little can do much to aid their cause by beginning in the many straits, bays, estuaries, and sounds of Alaska's Inside Passage. Some areas, like Icy Strait near Juneau, are more productive fish corridors than others. But even in areas of significant fish concentration, where jumping or rolling silver salmon can sometimes be found, experienced, localized knowledge is probably the single greatest asset an angler can tote along. Knowing the locations of the coho's regional feeding and migration lanes, which usually don't change from year to year, is of the utmost importance. When those lanes are unknown, or when prospecting a new area, there are still a number of clues fly-fishers can use to help locate the saltwater salmon.

During the late spring and summer, the sight of birds working above the surface almost guarantees there will be salmon feeding in the immediate area. If the flocks of gulls or terns aren't engaged near the water's surface, but are instead seen flying in a group around a certain area, not traveling or appearing to be actively searching, it can indicate the presence of deeper schools of baitfish. Coho will often herd these deeper baitfish into tight balls that will eventually push toward the surface. Anglers should remain back from the bait balls and cast to the sides of the schools. The coho will typically slash through the baitfish and then circle back to pick off the wounded, which is why short-shank patterns that wobble slightly and ride nose-down during the retrieve can be such effective saltwater silver salmon flies.

Because of their curious natures, coho in the salt can also provide fly-fishers with an easy option for maintaining contact with a school. Because the fish will frequently chase stripped flies to the stern of the boat, anglers can keep their interest by immediately recasting or by employing a teaser presentation. Large charter boats often create this scenario unintentionally, simply because they often have a multitude of rigs in the water, and a number of coho will follow a hooked fish to the surface, attracted to the boat by the amount of flash and bait in the water. Small groups of fly-anglers can mimic this effect by rigging multiple hookless flies on a teaser rod to bring the coho in to investigate. Hootchie skirts

rigged on a casting rod, with enough weight to get the rig deep as quickly as possible, can work exceptionally well; lowering and raising the flies will draw silvers to the surface, where fellow fly-fishers can cast to them.

When nothing quite so obvious is present, anglers must rely on structure and their knowledge of the coho's preferences to help locate fish. The edges of the kelp forests that shelter thousands of sand lance and herring is never a bad place to begin. Coho will travel the circumference of the kelp beds in search of a meal, and during low tides the kelp will be more exposed and easier for anglers to locate. The idea is to then cast to the deep-water edges of the bed and start a fast retrieve, imparting a swimming motion to the fly, as if it were a typical baitfish darting back to the shelter of the kelp.

Bays or estuaries with a salmon stream emptying into them are other obvious good places to start searching for saltwater silvers, as are tide rips and the back eddies that form off the rear of islands and mainland points. The shallow, grassy flats sometimes found between islands can be productive, drawing large numbers of baitfish to the cover they provide. During flood and ebb tides, baitfish can also be flushed toward rock cliffs and windward shores. The saltwater angling grounds accessed via the port of Seward, which are exposed to the extreme tides of the Gulf of Alaska, feature many such cliffs and rocky pinnacles where baitfish are pushed by the wind and tides. The area's coho inevitably follow.

Obviously, for the open-water fly-fisher, the above barely touches on the importance of structure. Armed with a good depth finder, the appropriate array of sinking lines, and an armful of National Oceanic and Atmospheric Administration bathymetric charts, anglers

Rich Culver with a saltwater silver.

can stake out key interception points in a host of locations prime for coastal-cruising silvers. Fishable structure changes dramatically with the tides, however. On incoming tides, for example, baitfish will draft in behind the back sides of intertidal rocks. When the tide ebbs, the other side of the same structure will now fish better.

A up-to-date tide book will be one of the most important pieces of equipment a saltwater angler can have. Tides play a critical role in salmon-feeding activity, and understanding their effects is a prerequisite for success. Broadly speaking, there are no best tides, either; just different. Kelp beds will fish better on ebb or low-slack tides, while flood tides will push baitfish into windward faces of rock cliffs, ledges, and beaches, where they'll be trapped, making easy pickings for the aggressive coho. The necks of rocky bays and coves, as well as tidal estuaries, will also fish best on the flooding high tides.

A pair of fly-anglers work an estuary from their skiff.

As far as timing for saltwater coho, fish begin to concentrate in offshore waters in early July, though they tend to still be feeding deep at this time—40 to 60 feet. By late August and September, however, when they're much closer to entering their natal drainages, the coho will tend to be found in the top 30 feet of the water column. When fishing for coho in the brine, tactics necessarily need to be adjusted from the standard freshwater plans of attack. In areas with deeper holding fish, anglers should cast and let the fly sink, using a countdown method, then swim it back toward the skiff as rapidly as possible. In general, a retrieve rate of 6 to 12 inches per strip will be acceptable. In calmer estuaries, the fish may prefer a slower swimming retrieve, and anglers will have to adjust accordingly. For either scenario, the key is to get the fly into the feeding zone and have it stay there, all while looking and acting like the natural forage fish it represents.

Coho Salmon in Alaska

Though silvers are known to be fond of short, coastal drainages, it is the massive Kuskokwim River, the state's second largest, that hosts the most significant returns of chrome-bodied coho, with up to a million fish entering the glacially tinted waters in some years. From there the fish enter the river's many clearwater tributary streams, including the Aniak, Kasigluk, Kisaralik, Kwethluk, and Holitna Rivers, where fly-fishing opportunities are magnified.

While other watersheds in the state may not receive coho runs that equal the Kuskokwim's in terms of the sheer number of fish, many, due to their more manageable natures, present even better fly-fishing potential. And since Alaska's coho salmon can be found continuously from Dixon Entrance south of Ketchikan to Norton Sound, and sporadically to Point Hope, there

BRIAN O'KEEFE

TONY WEAVER

are inevitably a host of drainages that receive little to no angling pressure at all. The area surrounding Cordova, most of it reachable via a short road system, plus the Tsiu, Tsivat, Kiklukh, and other North Gulf Coast rivers, the upper Susitna and Yentna systems, and the Cold Bay region are all known producers of top-flight silver salmon action. In each, the chance of discovering anything resembling a crowd is nearly nonexistent. Along the Gulf Coast and on the streams of the Alaska Peninsula, even encountering another group of anglers is rare.

Via the aforementioned Kuskokwim River and the vast Yukon system, coho are also able to penetrate the state's interior watersheds at least as far inland as the Tanana, pouring into the spawning streams that run off the glacier-stuffed Alaska Range. The foremost silver salmon fishery in the region occurs in the Delta Clearwater River, an otherwise insignificant 23-mile-long tributary of the Tanana. The Delta Clearwater has averaged returns of over thirty thousand fish for the last decade or so, its springlike, oxygen-rich flows remaining open throughout the state's bleakest season and providing excellent spawning and overwintering habitat. But because the river's coho run doesn't typically peak until

Many of the best silver salmon destinations are far away from the crowds.

A saltwater fly-fisher does battle in the heavy fog of Southeast.

Goodnews, and Kanektok Rivers—are all good candidates, as are the wild and hardly visited streams of the Alaska Peninsula, most of which boast coho runs of merit.

SOUTHEAST ALASKA

Alaska's isle-dotted southern coast, drained by myriad short, relatively small streams, provides fantastic habitat for coho salmon. Indeed, fly-fishers would be hard-pressed to locate an angling environment offering a more complete experience than can be found among the innumerable scenic and secluded freshwater streams of tree-shrouded Southeast. Over twenty-five hundred primary anadromous streams are already documented to host populations of sea-bright silvers. Little is actually known about the wild coho populations from most of the watersheds, many of which are little more than narrow, winding rivulets that interconnect a few low-lying lakes and then drain quickly to the sea. Though individual production is small, certainly when compared to returns from the state's large glacial river systems, Southeast coho salmon stocks as a whole are currently held to be in excellent condition. A prolonged period of low abundance had extended for about twenty-six years into the early 1980s, when the region's coho populations began to recover. For most stocks, escapements peaked in the early to mid-1990s when runs were exceptionally strong. They've reached relatively high levels again in the past few years as downward-spiraling salmon markets have substantially curtailed effort levels in troll and net fisheries, a trend that appears set to continue in the years to come.

The rich and still virtually unexploited Cordova area is one place where coho-minded fly-fishers can access this burgeoning production. A number of small freshwater streams drain into Orca Bay in eastern Prince William Sound, many just outside of town. Major road-

the middle of frostbitten October, with the fish having traveled a good 1,000 miles from the sea, pressure remains light, even in recent records years when more than eighty thousand silvers have completed the voyage (well over a hundred thousand returned in 2003).

Not to be outdone, Southcentral Alaska offers several quality coho streams as well, from the Kenai River and the tannic-colored creeks of the Bachatna Flats directly across Cook Inlet to the clearwater tributaries of the Susitna. The coho salmon fisheries of Kodiak Island rival those found anywhere else, and while roadside streams like the Buskin, American, and Pasagshak Rivers can see good numbers of anglers turn out, the island's more remote rivers still pair great fly-fishing with an unimpeachable wilderness milieu. Southwest Alaska, too, has boundless potential for eminent coho angling. The old reliables—the Togiak, Alagnak, Naknek, Nushagak, accessible coho fisheries exist in the Eyak River and several of the clearwater streams and lake outlets within the Alaganik Slough system. A number of islands in the bay also host fantastic coho fisheries, most of the best of which take place during high-tide periods in back-flooded freshwater lagoons. Fly-fishers can reach these little-visited silver salmon hideaways by boat or float-plane from Cordova or from the handful of lodges springing up on places like Andersen Island. The area also serves as the gateway to even more outstanding silver action, north by jet boat to remote Prince William Sound streams between Cordova and Valdez that offer coho within half a mile of the coast. Nevertheless, the most exciting fly-fishing opportunities associated with the area, and some of the very best in all of Alaska, occur to the southeast, along the fabled Lost Coast between Cordova and the community of Yakutat.

Often overlooked among Alaska's seemingly limitless numbers of top angling destinations, the area can actually be one of the most productive in the state. It is immaculate, pristine country—perfect for the adventure angler looking to sample some of the last truly wild fisheries on earth. Plus, these winding coastal drainages present what are perhaps the state's most outstanding locations for finding trophy silver salmon. From the Kiklukh River, 145 miles northwest of Yakutat, to the isolated Kaliakh, 30 miles farther south, coho can be encountered returning with a vengeance. The Tsiu River, situated between the two, is undoubtedly the area's premier coho stream and produces epic returns of silver. Clear, meandering waters with long runs and abundant pools predominate, and the area is replete with classic fly-fishing conditions. Distinct possibilities for taking coho on dry flies exist in most of the drainages, especially near the usually wider and slower-flowing intertidal reaches.

There are several other fabulously productive tributaries and small streams along the Lost Coast, from the Katalla and Bering Rivers closer to Cordova and the Copper River Delta to the Tsivat River system, which joins with the Tsiu, and the Kaliakh's Kulthieth and Chiuki Rivers. Farther southeast toward the Yakutat end of the Lost Coast, those with a mind for pioneering can find some of the world's hottest edge fisheries in the freshwater streams throughout the Icy Bay area. With an ice field larger than several states as a backdrop—the Malaspina Glacier—freshwater havens like the Yahtse River and Yana Stream are virtually exploding with silver salmon during the peak of the mid-August through September runs. The area is extremely remote and lies at the southern edge of Wrangell–St. Elias National Park, where the weather can be almost as rough as the fishing is good. The logistics of a trip to this area are daunting and the usually required beach landings a bit dicey, but a knowledgeable guide and good planning will park fly-fishers in the middle of a piscatorial paradise sure to impress.

In the vicinity of Yakutat itself, all the fly-fishing activity centers on the region's most famous and widely utilized stream, the crystal-clear Situk River, which, during the first half of September, presents anglers with good concentrations of silvers, some of trophy potential. Like Cordova, this midsized Alaska coastal community can also be used by fly-fishers for a lot more than direct access to the nearest streams. Anglers willing to venture farther southeast from Yakutat will find a handful of prolific—and attractive—streams and rivers, none of which entertains Situk-like effort. The Italio River system, just 25 air

TONY WEAVER

Jake Jordan with a Tsiu silver.

miles from town, is actually world famous for its silver salmon runs, while the nearly unmolested Doame system just south of the Alsek can also boast of a solid coho return. Even the Akwe River, which is probably better known as a trophy-cutthroat producer, presents fly-fishers with good chances to stalk dime-bright coho from late August through the middle of September.

Moving toward the true Southeast panhandle, the individual coho populations tend to get smaller, though they occur frequently along the coast and in drainages whose fly-fishing conditions are in no way diminished. The third or fourth largest stock that exists in the region returns annually to the Chilkat River near Haines, while the freshwater streams of lower Lynn Canal north of

The harbor at Wrangell, Alaska.

Juneau also offer good and at times excellent angling potential. In fact, the glacially influenced Taku River, which saw a sharp increase in the size of its silver salmon returns in the early 1990s, is probably the single largest coho producer in all of Southeast Alaska. Several Sitka-area watersheds present opportunities for freshwater fly-anglers as well, on both Chichagof and Baranof Islands. Near Wrangell, in the heart of the Inside Passage, some tremendous fresh- and saltwater coho fisheries occur. Clarence Strait, which runs across the north and east coasts of Prince of Wales Island west of Wrangell, offers a particularly compelling saltwater locale, as the water is so clear an angler can often see the schools of offshore fish moving throughout their feeding corridors. The region includes many islands, and the corresponding straits, bays, and channels serve as migratory, feeding, and staging points for mature salmon. The area's coho are also fishable in clearwater tributaries of the Stikine on Mitkof Island and in other coastal rivers of the Petersburg/Wrangell area, such as Kadake and Duncan Saltchuck Creeks and the Castle, Harding, Kah Sheets, and Eagle Rivers.

Never far from any discussion of Southeast Alaska's best freshwater-fishing locations, Prince of Wales Island's heavily forested coast is home to several high-quality coho salmon streams, among them the tea-colored Thorne and Klawock Rivers and Kegan Creek. Several additional stocks exist in the Ketchikan area, though most waters, like Chuck Creek on the southern outside coast, rarely host runs totaling more than a few thousand fish. An exception is the Unuk River on the mainland northeast of Ketchikan, which has seen recent coho production trend upward from about 12,500 mature fish in 1997 to almost 58,000 spawners in 2001. Another above-average coho producer in the area is the Naha River, located less than half an hour northeast of Ketchikan by boat and one of the most popular silver salmon fishing streams in the region. The river flows for—about 19 miles and drains seven lakes on western Revillagigedo Island before entering Naha Bay in west Behm Canal. The coho's anadromous reach extends only about 7 miles from the mouth at Roosevelt Lagoon, with returning fish traveling as far upstream as just above Heckman Lake, the second lowest lake in the drainage. As in many of the areas in Southeast, the U.S. Forest Service maintains three small cabins and a streamside trail to facilitate access to the Naha.

SOUTHCENTRAL ALASKA

As with the other species of Pacific salmon, perhaps the defining characteristic of the Southcentral Alaska angling environment for coho is the amount of effort that's expended. Without a doubt it's the most heavily fished area of the state, and during the height of the runs, it's doubtful a fly-fisher can find a roadside salmon stream without bumping into at least a few fellow anglers. The wild coho of the Kenai River are a primary component of the area's silver returns, and as is usual for the drainage, these coho support the largest freshwater sport harvest in the state. In fact, the Kenai contributes an average of about one of every five coho salmon harvested in sport fisheries in Alaska.

Beyond the Kenai, also as is the case with the other Pacific salmon species, the region does offer autumn fly-fishers a nice variety of coho opportunities, some just minutes away and far less fashionable. On the western shores of Cook Inlet, several drainages spill off the slopes of the Alaska Range, crisscrossing the short, muskeg-dotted forelands and eventually emptying into the sea. Some are phenomenal sockeye fisheries, a few provide quality chinook salmon angling, but the real treasure of the area lies in its silver.

While the coho runs to these west Cook Inlet drainages aren't necessarily prolific in numbers alone, the lack of attention they get from the overall Alaska angling community—despite their proximity to the population center of the state—and the usually compressed nature of the streams make the fishing hard to beat. Big River Lakes, a series of four interconnected lakes on the Bachatna Flats, probably get the most visitors during the silver salmon run, along with the Kustatan River, located a short distance away and featuring similar angling prospects. The Kustatan is a solidly glacial system, however, that offers little in its mainstem for fly-fishers, who are instead limited to fishing in the upwelling tributary water, where the coho stack to refresh themselves and clean their gills during the upstream migration. Coho of the Big River Lakes area, on the other hand, have less chalky gray flows to hide beneath, and the drainage is known as a top locale for pitching Pollywogs and other surface skaters to milling silver salmon.

Probably the area's best chinook salmon stream, the Chuitna River, also doubles as an exceptional coho destination. The Chuitna, not unlike the other drainages on the west side of Cook Inlet, runs fairly shallow for much of its course, but its winding nature, moderately swift current, and shifting rock bottom combine to form a fair number of slow, deep pools for holding coho. Tannins leaching into the water render it too murky for sight-fishing in most instances, but as the stream is just a few miles long, the silvers usually remain sprightly from their ocean sojourn and repeatedly show themselves on top. Silver Salmon Creek and the Kamishak River, both farther to the southwest, also offer superb coho angling set amid the sweeping coastal scenery. The Kamishak is located but a few miles from the McNeil River, though, so visitors will definitely want to prepare for bear encounters.

For those anglers bound to the roads of the Kenai Peninsula, venturing a little farther up the Sterling Highway from the state's most famous salmon locale

might be in order, as the Anchor River receives a decent return of silvers, enough to nearly clog the narrow stream. Before even reaching the Kenai, travelers from Anchorage will also pass the Placer, Portage, and Twentymile Rivers near the head of Turnagain Arm. The Seward Highway crosses the lower sections of these systems near tidewater in open country left virtually sterile after flooding with salt water during the 1964 earthquake. Though the best fishing almost always involves a jet boat trip deep into the thick spruce that veils these streams, each can be an exciting and productive alternative to the more crowded fisheries farther down the highway. The runs in the area aren't enormous, though, so timing can be critical, with returns commonly peaking anywhere from the second half of August into the first two weeks of September. Another prime though often overlooked coho destination on the peninsula is the Swanson River, which is probably better known for the trout and grayling fishing found along the popular canoe trails through its headwater lake system. The area near the river's terminus at Cook Inlet can be crowded, but anglers who put in at the Swanson River Campground and float the 24 miles of middle and lower river will see more silvers and fewer people. The river runs shallow, and there are almost always a number of exposed gravel bars that can make the coho skittish during the height of the day. Fly-anglers will do best by searching out the cutbanks and deepest holes in the river and then concentrating efforts there. On its worst day, the Swanson presents a pleasant float, while on its best the coho fly-fishing can equal much of what's found on the more famous Kenai.

And actually, despite the acclaim, the Susitna drainage, not the Kenai, is the most prolific coho producer in Southcentral. The mainstem Susitna, like the Yukon, Kuskokwim, and Copper Rivers, is much too large and silty to provide for quality fly-fishing, leaving the best opportunities concentrated in the many clearwater tributaries of the system. Most of the Parks Highway streams offer good coho angling during August and early September, especially for those willing to use a raft or jet boat to access the lonelier stretches of water. The glacial Yentna system also receives a healthy run of silvers, which can be best fished in the numerous clear-water sloughs and tributary mouths that dot the drainage.

KODIAK ISLAND

Home to some of the best coho salmon streams in Alaska, the glacier-carved Kodiak Archipelago sees plenty of anglers targeting the autumn-arriving species. However, the great majority of those anglers can be found on only a handful of streams—naturally, those that flow within reach of Kodiak's short road system. Of the many coho populations located within the Kodiak road zone, very few are of much size. The largest occur in the biggest systems, though, namely the Buskin, Pasagshak, Saltery, Olds, and American Rivers. Throughout the 1990s, 56 percent of the islandwide silver salmon harvest came from road-system streams, and nearly three-quarters of that from the Buskin, Pasagshak, Olds, and American.

Smaller drainages within reach by car include the Miam and Roslyn Rivers and Salonie, Pillar, Monashka, Sargent, Russian, and Chiniak Creeks, where, for the most part, the coho stocks are small and relatively fragile. For most of the systems, fly-fishers tend to concentrate on the lower, intertidal regions, where the returning salmon will stage, especially during periods of low water. With the small nature of many of these streams, and the relatively small returns, salmon fishing in the middle and upper systems is often closed or intensely regulated, depending on the particular drainages, of course.

Certainly, by getting off the road system and prospecting nearly any one of the wilderness streams on either

TONY WEAVER

Angling in front of a float camp.

Kodiak or Afognak Islands, anglers will greatly increase their chances of success, and usually the overall quality of their experience. After all, the remote fisheries of the archipelago offer very little to dissuade the potential fly-fisher, except perhaps the more demanding logistics, the unpredictable weather, and a few thousand Kodiak brown bears.

Primarily very short coastal streams, nearly all the Kodiak road-system drainages require good timing for consistent coho success. During the early part of a run—or on a high tide—fishing can be superb in lower reaches, while fly-anglers will want to concentrate their efforts upstream as the season wears on toward October. Most of these rivers are part of a lake system, too, and in a few cases, most notably that of the Pasagshak River, the lake itself can offer excellent coho angling. The Pasagshak is a sluggish, meandering stream that flows just over a mile from the outlet at Lake Rose Tead to Pasagshak Bay. Due to its extreme coastal character, the river's coho are almost always right on time, as even in drought years the Pasagshak's flows are unaffected. The entire river, in fact, is influenced by the tides, and the depth and direction of the water flow will fluctuate proportionately. Because the Pasagshak generally lacks much in the way of good holding water, incoming coho are liable to streak straight

for the lake or, at the very least, for the wide, slow-moving outlet area. Because it's shallower than many other bodies of water near the road system, like Buskin and Saltery Lakes, Lake Rose Tead can actually present excellent fly-angling opportunities for coho, mostly for float-tubing anglers. The fish tend to roll or jump once in the lake as well, often giving away their holding positions in the wide-open water.

Saltery Lake, on the other hand, is deeper and extremely turbid, not to mention much more difficult to reach. In fact, in many years calling the Saltery River a road-accessible stream is a stretch only possible in Alaska. What remains of the unimproved dirt road leading to the drainage is, at the best of times, navigable only by all-terrain vehicle or serious four-wheel drives. The road washes out easily, too, and in years like 2003, the only access left in autumn is via floatplanes landing at the lake, where a sport-fishing lodge is currently in operation. Once arrived, however, fly-anglers will usually find the coho fishing spectacular. As in the Pasagshak River, Saltery coho tend to be of above-average size, with fish near 20 pounds not at all uncommon. Short at just about 2½ miles and narrow for most of its course (usually about 30 feet across), the Saltery is an easy river to read and fish, with the in-stream holding water being obvious. The upper eighth of a mile or so before the lake is almost frog water and takes on the lake's thick glacial-green tint. Silvers tend to pile up in this deeper water before pressing into the lake itself, but it is less conducive to fly-fishers than the rest of the stream.

For the really exquisite coho-angling opportunities within the archipelago, anglers will have to board a float-plane for a short hop to a headwater lake, or sometimes take a boat on a longer journey around the coast to a stream's mouth. And, as always when talking salmon or steelhead fly-fishing on Kodiak Island, the Karluk River leaps to the forefront of the conversation. This is for good reason: The coho fishing can be excellent on the river throughout the month of September, with bright silvers available at times anywhere from the lagoon to the Karluk Lake outlet. Several remote systems beyond the Karluk host noteworthy coho returns as well, foremost among them the Ayakulik and Uganik Rivers. In the Uganik system, some of the best coho angling occurs among the cottonwood-surrounded lower river and lake outlet. Good fishing for salmon can also be found at the upper end of the lake, where the braided upper Uganik River enters. The Sturgeon and Silver Salmon Rivers and Akalura, Dog Salmon, and Olga Creeks receive their own healthy shares of the fall-returning fish, though none of them commonly see runs that reach ten thousand fish. Fly-anglers finding themselves on any of these drainages during the month of September will doubtless find that the lack of angling contemporaries more than compensates for the smaller returns.

Afognak Island is another prime coho destination within the overall Kodiak Archipelago, offering four quality drainages for pursuing the species with a fly rod. The Afognak River is always a viable choice for silvers, with the most exceptional coho fishing taking place at the lagoon near the mouth of the river, in the lower few miles of river, or at the lake outlet. Cutting through the Sitka spruce that dominates the island, you'll find a pair of lake systems that eventually drain into Perenosa Bay on the northern end of the island offer a second excellent opportunity for Afognak coho anglers. The first, the Portage system, includes the approximately 2-mile-long lake and a short (less than a mile) creek that drains into Discoverer Bay. Just to the north of there is the Pauls Lake system, which empties into Pauls Bay. In both, the best fishing is usually found during high tides in the intertidal stretches of the creeks and sometimes in the lake outlets. Pauls Bay, however, also provides one of the archipelago's best opportunities for taking silvers

in the salt, as the coho stage in the narrow-walled bay and can be found near the surface in good concentrations.

SOUTHWEST ALASKA

There's a reason a handful of rivers in Southwest Alaska are so well known. Almost without variance when recounting the best salmon streams in Alaska or the best rainbow or lake trout, Dolly Varden, or Arctic grayling destinations, anglers will eventually be forced to recognize the supremacy of the same few rivers in Southwest Alaska. With coho, too, the pattern continues, and fly-fishers would be well advised to visit just about any of the big-name Southwest drainages, as strong coho populations annually visit systems like the Naknek, Alagnak, Togiak, and Kanektok Rivers. And let's not forget that the state's single largest silver salmon producer, the giant Kuskokwim, has several clearwater runoff tributaries that offer outstanding fly-fishing opportunities.

Of the more famous Kuskokwim tributaries, most of which fish very well for coho, the Aniak, Kisaralik, Kwethluk, and Holitna Rivers probably present the most consistent populations. The Aniak has long been a favored, if advanced, float-trip destination for salmon-hunting fly-fishers, but the larger and more remote Holitna is only beginning to be seriously explored for its bountiful fly-fishing potential. It's a meandering interior Kuskokwim drainage, with fairly gentle current for most of its length. As on the neighboring Aniak, the Holitna's riverbanks continue to slowly erode into the forests of the area, and the felled logs tend to create abundant sweepers and logjams. The obstacles are great for creating deep pools and otherwise exemplary fish habitat, but they're not so swell for floaters. A good bit of the coho angling is accomplished either near the river's confluence with the Kuskokwim (near the village of Sleetmute) or upstream at the mouths of several tributary streams.

To the north, a few tributaries of the mammoth Yukon

Coho fishing along the Aleutian chain can require the use of a beach for a landing strip.

River system also present some good fly-fishing opportunity. Unlike the coho that travel all the way up the river to the Tanana drainage, which are often well into their spawning adaptations by the time they reach fishable waters, the silvers of the lower Yukon system are the same bright, aggressive fish that patrol the other coastal drainages of Southwest. The Andreafsky River in particular is a name worth remembering for adventurous fly-fishers. Unlike most of the drainages within the Yukon Delta, this 105-mile-long clearwater tributary, and its twin the East Fork Andreafsky, traverses a broad range of ecosystems, including alpine tundra, rolling hills, and a

few sparse forests of spruce. Much of the lower river, after the Andreafsky and East Fork have joined to form one channel about 5 miles above the village of St. Mary's, can be reached by jet boat, but to access the entire watershed, anglers have to find a gravel bar in the upper stretches that's of suitable size for a small wheel-plane landing, a sometimes difficult but never impossible task. The coho typically begin to arrive in the system during August and continue in fishable numbers throughout the first few weeks of September.

South of the Kuskokwim River, the chance for fly-fishers to intercept populous concentrations of bright coho only increase. All three of the major rivers draining into Kuskokwim Bay—the Kanektok, Goodnews, and Arolik Rivers—present outstanding prospects, their clear, fairly shallow flows ideally suited to fly-fishing. The Kanektok, which begins at Kagati Lake and flows through a broad, mountain-lined valley and then across the flat tundra floodplain of the Kuskokwim Bay area, produces good numbers of the fall-returning salmon, which tend to receive less angling pressure than the river's chinook. The Arolik River sees even fewer visitors, primarily because it's a more difficult trip to make, though the fishing can be superb. The coho fishing on both rivers, as well as on the nearby Goodnews, primarily takes place in the lower 10 miles or so of water.

The Nushagak and Togiak systems, as well as the Alagnak River farther to the south, are home to coho salmon stocks worthy of their immense reputations as well. Fly-fishers hoping to cast Pink Pollywogs and other waking flies will certainly want to take a hard look at these drainages, as each in certain circumstances will offer some of the region's best opportunities for taking silvers on the surface. On the wide, meandering lower Nushagak, the twentieth largest river in the United States by volume, fly-anglers will want to concentrate on the fairly shallow seams that run off the river's sizable gravel bars or in one of the many clearwater tributary streams such as the Nuyakuk River, a deep, gin-clear waterway that flows from Tikchik Lake through black spruce forests and heavy brush to its confluence with the Nush. The Alagnak River, too, presents ample 'Wogging grounds. In fact, thanks to a couple of former guides from Katmai Lodge, located just below the famous braids, the Alagnak is actually the birthplace of the Pollywog as we know it today.

Even given the prolific coho territories just described, perhaps the most significant occasions in Southwest Alaska for fly-fishing silver salmon fresh from the salt occur to the south of Katmai, on the forlorn Alaska Peninsula. Truly ubiquitous, unlike chinook or sockeye, silvers will even be found in good numbers on a few of the larger islands of the Aleutian chain. For instance, the itinerant game fish return to the Nateekin River near the city of Unalaska, where good fly-fishing can be found, though it honestly pales in comparison to what awaits fly-anglers heading for a few areas on the peninsula's mainland.

The streams of the Cold Bay area and outlet areas like Mortensen's Lagoon will literally become choked with silvers during the high tides of late August and early September, and fly-fishers who travel to this region can be sure there will hardly be any others around to share in the bounty. Rivers, like the Sandy that flows 15 miles through the muskeg-covered tundra, feature long, deep runs, wide-open plains ideal for fly-casting, and incredible numbers of coho, some of trophy size. The nearby Ocean River, running about 12 miles from Wildman Lake to the Bering Sea, sees even more coho return than the Sandy, and its slower, less choppy flows are much more conducive to taking fish on top. Farther north on the peninsula, the Meshik, Ilnik, and Cinder Rivers can all provide exceptional coho angling, and though the entire area sees few visitors, at least four sport-fishing operations are available to put fly-fishers on any one of these systems. There is even a pair of permanent lodges in the area, one at Wildman Lake, the other on the upper Sandy. For wilderness floaters and other fly-in anglers, the options are practically endless.

BRIAN O'KEEFE

A deep pool on
Prince of Wales
Island.

DARYL PEDERSON

chum and pink salmon

OF THE FINAL TWO SPECIES of Pacific salmon
that annually return to Alaska's waters, not much is usually said
and even less is written. Or at least not much that's nice. For a
lot of fly-anglers, neither the pink nor the chum salmon deserves
any better. In the case of the chum especially, that's probably
because the anglers have never bothered to fish for them.

Every summer in Bristol Bay, about the time we North
Americans are rising before dawn to try to beat the next lodge
to the best rainbow runs of the region's many fly-out destinations, squads of European anglers will show at a handful of
fly-fishing camps. Inevitably they'll be packing big sticks,
exceedingly long double-handed rods, and they'll surely bristle
every time some impertinent Yank lets the tag *Spey rod* fall from
his lips. It's just as likely that they'll be pleased to leave the trout
alone, having lugged 15 feet of graphite halfway around the
world for a date with a chum instead. Pink salmon, too, receive

First skiff out in the morning.

BRIAN O'KEEFE

little direct angling attention. These species are held in such low regard as sport fish, that they haven't managed to acquire a cultlike following even from foreigners.

The chum and the pink probably owe much of their lowly reputations to the condition of the returning fish in their southern range, where many fly-fishers first encountered them—and then proceeded to spread the bad news to the rest. The fact is, both species tend to spawn very soon after arriving in fresh water, especially in areas like California, Washington, and southern British Columbia. They can even begin to undergo the drastic pre-spawning metamorphosis common to the species while still in salt water, arriving at their home streams already in a state of rapid deterioration. This understandably fails to ignite the flames of passion in most fly-fishers, aesthetic dilettantes or not. Surely not, helping matters, may be that most Alaskans refer to the chum as dog salmon.

But appearances—and names—can indeed be deceiving, as vacationers arriving in Greenland might be able to explain. Both chum and pink salmon are a testament to that, for each specie can make a fine quarry for the Alaska-bound fly-angler. Each is as aggressive as Pacific salmon come, often more than willing to eat a fly and sometimes downright greedy about it. Both make themselves available to anglers in salt and fresh water and are also known to occasionally chase down a surface presentation. Anglers who know when and where to look can find each in startling fresh condition. And as many of Alaska's regular European visitors already know, the chum salmon is an exhausting adversary, prone to displays of brute strength, incredible stubbornness, and endurance enough to shame a Kenyan marathon runner. The experience of hooking one on a fly rod may not be enough to make anglers disavow Bristol Bay's rainbows—the most serious of blasphemies western fly-anglers could make—but it's certainly enough to make them forgo matters of national solidarity and start buying bright pink deer hair.

The Pink Salmon
(Oncorhynchus gorbuscha)

In comparison to the other species of Pacific salmon, pinks reach sexual maturity at the smallest size, usually averaging just 3½ to 4 pounds upon their return to Alaska's coastal fresh waters. But they're also the most abundant of the salmon species, a fact that no one who has ever been to one of those streams during a heavy pink return needs reiterated.

The abundance is at least partially due to the pink's unique life history, which is the least variable of all the Pacific salmon: Pinks mature, spawn, and die at two years of age. The lack of variance results in even- and odd-year age-classes that never mix with populations spawning in the following year. And although the small size of the pink in comparison to the other species of Pacific salmon does not vary, individual sizes of returning spawners will—from region to region and from year to year. Some Alaska stocks will even show definable size differences between even- and odd-year fish, with only the largest ever nearing 10 pounds.

Pink salmon can be found from the Monterey Bay region of California north to the Arctic Ocean. The species' range also extends from Kidluit Bay in Arctic Canada west to northern Siberia's Lena River and from there south along the Asian coast to Korea and the Japanese island of Kyushu in the Sea of Japan. The areas of greatest abundance occur in the central portions of that range—in fact, over 70 percent of the total marine catch of pink salmon in North America comes from the waters of Southeast Alaska.

While their small size immediately sets them apart from the other salmon, pinks at sea are silvery in color with steel-blue to green backs, distinguished by large black spots that adorn their bodies above the lateral line and on both the upper and lower lobe of the caudal fin. However, the chrome coloring of their seaward state doesn't last long once sexual maturity approaches; the secondary characteristics associated with spawning appear rapidly. By the time they enter spawning streams, or shortly thereafter, male pink salmon will have developed the large hump that gives the species its common name, the humpbacked salmon or, more commonly, just humpy. Dark, dull brown and greenish colors overtake the upper half of the body, with purple splotches extending from midbody to the ventral area. Females will display similar coloring, but without the hump and the extended kype of the spawning male.

Jim Teeny with a Kanektok River pink salmon.

JIM TEENY

The Chum Salmon
(Oncorhynchus keta)

Though the pink salmon is the most numerous of the Pacific salmon, the chum is the most widely distributed and the most abundant in terms of total biomass. This is due to its size: Chum can reach maximum weights second only to the chinook salmon, with specimens reputed to reach as much as 46 pounds.

The historical distribution of chum salmon in North America is expansive, completely overlapping the range of the pinks from Monterey Bay northward along the Pacific Coast around Alaska, including the larger Aleutian Islands, and on to Arctic Ocean drainages at least as far east as the Mackenzie and Anderson Rivers of Canada. The Noatak and Kobuk Rivers of Northwest Alaska have been known to support runs of about one million fish apiece, but north of there the returns are scattered and much less prolific. The Yukon River is North America's greatest producer of chum salmon, which arrive in two waves, unlike returns in almost every other watershed on the continent. For most rivers, a single run of chum salmon enters fresh water in either summer or fall.

TROY LETHERMAN

Chum salmon.

If taken in the salt or soon after they arrive in their freshwater streams, chum salmon can actually be quite difficult to distinguish from ocean-fresh sockeye or coho. They're usually chrome-bright on their sides and bellies, with fine dark speckling sometimes present, and it can take a close examination of their gills or caudal fin scale patterns to set them apart. Once the transition to fresh water is complete, though (and it often occurs very rapidly), chum salmon need no close inspection. Dusky red sides and vertical bars or stripes of green and purple give them the common name "calico salmon" in some areas. Males develop significant kype and very large teeth that at least partially account for the chum's other common moniker, the dog salmon. (The remainder of the reason for the name's lasting power lies in the fact that many rural Alaskans use chum salmon to feed their dog teams throughout the winter.) Females tend to look similar to males, except they feature dark horizontal bands of color along the lateral line and their green and purple vertical bars are less prominent.

LIFE HISTORIES

Pink and chum salmon are more closely related to each other than any of the remaining species of Pacific salmon. In particular, they share a limited dependence on fresh water for feeding and rearing, much less than any other anadromous species of the family Salmonidae. Neither chum nor pink young undergo a distinct smolt transformation, both instead migrating to salt water as alevins. This allows more time for feeding and growing in the fertile waters of the Pacific Ocean and at least in part accounts for the greater abundance of the two species.

Their spawning tendencies and early life histories are nearly identical, with reproduction typically occurring in small coastal streams. Both species can travel farther inland to spawn, especially chum salmon in certain watersheds, but those situations are relatively rare. For the most part, spawning areas are near river mouths, where eggs are subjected to varying levels of salinity as they develop. Upon hatching, pink salmon alevins immediately migrate to saltwater estuaries and bays, while chum salmon young generally don't depart for the salt until their yolk sacs have been consumed. In Southeast Alaska, these out-migrations can begin as early as late March, with peak periods of movement from early to mid-May. More northern watersheds with overall cooler temperature regimes will produce populations with later periods of peak migration, generally early to mid-June.

Once in the sea, juvenile chum salmon remain close to shore for several months before dispersing into the open ocean, feeding on small crustaceans and young herring in the brackish water of estuaries and bays. Once they've moved farther out to sea, chum salmon feed opportunistically, though invertebrates rather than fish make up a larger percentage of their diets than is the case with chinook and coho salmon. Pink salmon, too, feed opportunistically on invertebrates and small fish in the sea. After first migrating, the young salmon cruise shoreline areas, foraging near the surface on zooplankton, fish in the larval stage, and small crustaceans. Predation is heavy but growth is rapid, and soon the pinks shift

their interest more toward amphipods, euphausiids, and small fish.

While they're at sea for a relatively short period of time compared to the other species of Pacific salmon, pinks can migrate thousands of miles. The Alaska fish may in fact be found spread across most of the northeast Pacific, from the Bering Strait to about Kiska Island in the Aleutians and then southeast to the California coast. The waters near the Aleutians are particularly important feeding grounds for both North American and Asian pink salmon stocks. Alaska's chum salmon tend to be found in the Chukchi and Bering Seas, westward along the Aleutian chain, and southward in the Gulf of Alaska. The average time spent at sea varies according to geography, with most fish from the southern part of the range

A coastal lake system, prime breeding and rearing grounds for both chum and pink salmon.

DARYL PEDERSON

Pink salmon holding on a flat in a Prince William Sound drainage.

returning during their third or fourth years of life and those from the Yukon and probably other far northern rivers initiating spawning runs in year four or five. This long period of saltwater feeding explains the fact that mature chum are relatively large, some exceeding 30 pounds, although their growth rate in the ocean is less than that of coho and chinook salmon. For pink salmon, the sizes attained during the fourteen to eighteen months they spend at sea varies by both individual population and in different regions, and sometimes even between even- and odd-year-classes. However, the most distinctive attribute of the pink salmon isn't their small size or short migrations but the tendency of the species to stray. With pinks, runs can suddenly appear where none were before, sometimes even outside the species's native range. Chum, like chinook, coho, and sockeye salmon, home in on their natal waters with much greater precision.

Pink salmon in Alaska return to freshwater streams from late June to early October, with the later in-migrations typically occurring in the southern parts of

their range. They do not travel far upstream to spawn, either, a notable exception being populations returning to the Yukon and Kuskokwim Rivers, which have been known to travel 100 miles or more before reaching their preferred spawning sites. For coastal spawners, the drastic morphological changes associated with reproductive maturation generally begin to appear while the pinks are still in salt water, becoming more apparent as the fish near their home streams. Chum salmon also begin to deteriorate both internally and externally as they approach their home systems. Chum salmon tend to spawn near the coast within days of entering the river as well. Some populations, however, have a distinctly different life history. These fish will instead migrate long distances, surviving for as much as two or three months after entering fresh water. The most dramatic example are the chum salmon of the mainstem Yukon River, which can travel all the way to the great river's headwaters in British Columbia and Teslin Lake, Yukon Territory— some 1,750 miles from the sea.

The Yukon watershed is also home to a pair of distinct annual returns of chum salmon, another departure from

GREG SYVERSON

the norm for the species. The summer chum enter the river for the most part in June, almost all of them destined for lower Yukon tributaries downstream of the mouth of the Koyukuk River. By contrast, the fall chums typically do not arrive until late June or July. The fish of this run are larger on average and spawn in spring-fed streams upstream from the Kantishna River. For most other chum salmon streams, which generally only receive a single run of fish, run times vary widely, though in general summer runs are typical for streams in the northern part of the species' range, with fall runs occurring in most southern drainages. Because they sometimes spawn in the same places, reproductive isolation between chum and pink salmon is not total and hybridization is known to occur. While these natural hybrids are fertile, none have thus far been documented as self-sustaining populations.

Fly-Fishing for Alaska's Chum and Pink Salmon

In truth, the pink salmon is undoubtedly the single species of game fish in the world most frequently hooked fair, but by utter accident—or even when attempts are made to absolutely avoid doing just that. In fact, at some times in Alaska, fishing for coho can mean trying to thread a fly through hundreds of pinks. On these occasions, the eagerness of the pink salmon actually works against them, as anglers out for silvers are often heard to utter less-than-complimentary ideas about hooking up yet again with another pink. However, if those same anglers would just give in to circumstances, put the big 8- or 9-weight coho rods away, and instead pick up a 4- or 5-weight, they might see the species in a different light.

The pink salmon is a fine light-tackle pursuit, and the species' sheer willingness to chase a fly has rescued more

than one outing when bigger, prettier, more spectacular-fighting species decided not to show up. Pinks can also be targeted in the salt when they're still actively feeding, and are in prime condition, adding another dimension for anglers looking for new challenges.

Chum salmon fresh from the sea, on the other hand, should need no shilling. They're large, strong fish with amazing stamina, actively eating properly presented flies—in the salt, on the surface, or below. Accordingly, fly-fishing for the species is steadily gaining in popularity, especially on the tundra rivers of Southwest, where good concentrations of bright fish can often be found in an environment perfectly tailored to fly-anglers, even those who prefer to use a double-handed rod.

RUN TIMING

Both chum and pink salmon return during the height of the Alaska summer, when fishing for kings and sockeye is usually on the wane and the big pushes of chrome-bright coho have yet to build. However, since both also tend to spawn in extreme coastal areas, with the spawning condition and associated bodily changes coming on fast, it's usually best to target runs at their outset and as close to salt water as possible. This is especially the case with pink salmon.

Most chum salmon runs peak from early July to early September, though returns can begin in early May and extend to mid-December in some locations. In general, runs will begin earlier to the north and commence at progressively later dates the farther you travel south. In Southeast Alaska, for example, runs typically span the months of July through October, peaking from late July through the first two weeks of August. In Southwest, runs will begin to pick up in the second half of June and peak near the end of that month and the beginning of July.

As always with Pacific salmon, run times will vary according to the local region, as some watersheds can have significantly different run times than neighboring rivers. For instance, the Alagnak River in Southwest Alaska typically won't get its first good numbers of chum until July, and then the run can proceed for seven weeks or more into August, with groups of fresh fish pushing into the river throughout that time.

Pink salmon also appear in fresh water from mid- to late summer. Runs tend to peak during July and August throughout most of their range, but bright pinks may be present in fresh water anytime between early June and late October, depending on the region and even the particular stream. Many regions of the state also have stronger runs of pinks in even-numbered years, with smaller runs during odd-numbered years or vice versa.

GEAR FOR CHUM AND PINKS

Eight- or 9-weight rods are preferred for chum salmon and are typically coupled with large-arbor reels that have quality compression-drag systems. Chum salmon usually won't go on any line-burning distance runs, instead just settling into a pool, content to slug it out in the deeper

RIGHT: Pink salmon often give away their location when staging near the coast.

DARYL PEDERSON

TROY LETHERMAN

TONY WEAVER

LEFT: *Using a Spey rod can be of great assistance to anglers fishing big water, like the lower Alagnak.*

RIGHT: *A waking chum follows a topwater presentation.*

water, so exorbitant amounts of backing are not needed. Double-handed rods should also handle an 8- or 9-weight line. For rivers like the Alagnak and other larger Southwest Alaska flows where anglers frequently have to contend with wind, the 14- and 15-foot models are a good choice.

Leaders for topwater presentations should be at least 9 feet long, hand-tied and tapered with stiff monofilament capable of turning over large, wind-resistant flies. For sinking presentations, no more than 4- to 6-foot leaders are typically needed. When the fish are found holding in thigh-deep shallows, anglers can utilize unweighted flies and a short sinking-tip line. To reach fish in deeper lies, or faster water, heavier-grain sinking lines will be needed.

Anglers specifically targeting pink salmon will want to go with a lightweight outfit. As most who've caught the species accidentally while fishing for coho or another species already know, pinks aren't much sport when subdued with a big 8-weight outfit. A 4- or 5-weight system will be plenty to handle the fish and still let the angler encounter some of their finer qualities, one of which includes a fairly feisty nature when fresh from the sea. Under typical circumstances, pinks will be found in

dense concentrations in fairly shallow water, too, making a standard weight-forward floating line a good all-around choice.

FLIES FOR CHUM AND PINKS

Far and away the most popular chum salmon flies in Alaska share one common trait—they're pink. For reasons completely unknown to anglers and fly-tiers, chum salmon will at times become extremely color-selective. While no one's determined the exact cause—whether temperature, light conditions, water clarity, or something else entirely—many do believe the way around the phenomenon is to carry a variety of pink-colored flies. In some places, in fact, like Katmai Lodge on the Alagnak River, chum guides carry nothing else.

While that may be taking things to the extreme—and treading perilously close to the shadows where the dogmatic hang out—it can be safely said that color and not design is the chief principle for fly-tiers to keep in mind when designing chum salmon patterns. Otherwise, chum flies differ very little from other popular salmon patterns, most including some flash, supple materials that swim well like marabou and rabbit fur, and usually weight in the form of bead-chain or barbell eyes.

Pink is the color of choice for Alagnak River chum.

Excluding the latter, of course, is the family of topwater salmon flies. In some areas, a simple deer hair mouse or shrew pattern in muted colors has proven successful for chum, though there is no doubt that the most popular pattern for the species is the Pink Pollywog.

Probably more renowned as a surface pattern for coho, the 'Wog as we know it today was actually born on the Alagnak River. Walt Krau, a Katmai Lodge guide, had begun by using pink deer hair creations in the design of the standard mouse. When those flies proved successful on the river's tidewater chum, another pair of Katmai guides, Dec Hogan and Ed Ward, took the experiment one step further by adding a long tail of cerise or hot pink marabou mixed with a few strands of Flashabou. They called the refined pattern the Pollywog, and it hasn't stopped taking fish on top yet.

Currently, many guides and fly-fishers are experimenting with smaller topwater flies—Micro-'Wogs, Techno 'Wogs, Ultimate 'Wogs, and even brightly colored versions of traditional patterns like the Humpy. There is no consensus yet as to which versions produce better, though the new 'Wogs, usually tied with closed-cell foam and other synthetics, are certainly more durable, float higher in the water, and are easier to cast. Under some circumstances, however, chum seem to prefer a fly that sits lower in the surface film and pushes more water. With the jury still out, anglers would be well advised to carry a few of both styles and formulate their own opinions, which is a good choice in any case.

Another advantage of the smaller topwater patterns is that they can double as pink salmon flies. While pinks won't be drawn to the surface with the regularity of chum or coho, they will rise and follow under the right circumstances. The rest of the time, anglers will need to dip beneath the surface. Flies should be tied with some flash and in sizes 6 through 10, though pinks will eat much larger patterns. And that's about as complicated as it gets. Almost any of the standard Pacific salmon fare or traditional streamer pattern in a variety of colors will perform admirably with pinks—unfortunately, even when they're not the intended target. The ubiquitous Egg-Sucking Leech produces results worthy of its widespread reputation, as does almost any other fly with some color contrast in its design. For pink salmon in the salt, fly-anglers need to be a little more detailed in their choice. In general, though, most small baitfish or smolt patterns will be effective when fished over large concentrations of pinks in at least moderately clear water.

ANGLING STRATEGIES

Fishing for pinks is often fast and frenzied, and the numbers of fish in many coastal areas can be truly astounding. Plus, they tend to be as aggressive as they are plentiful. The best place to find them is in the extreme lower stretches of coastal streams and the deep holes and runs right above intertidal areas. In large, glacial systems like the Kenai, however, bright fish can also be found miles upstream near the mouths of clearwater tributary streams. Still, small, shallow spawning streams, such as many of the Southeast Alaska coastal drainages, might never see a returning pink in top form, as their rapid maturation will have begun while still in salt water in most cases.

When targeting chum salmon, anglers should be most intent on locating milling fish. During in-river migrations, chum will frequently stick close to the shore in the same traveling corridors as used by sockeye, sometimes even mixing with their cousin fish. At these times the fish are usually too concerned with reaching the next piece of holding water to bother with a fly that's presented even inches off their route—although these same fish will often stop at the entrances to sloughs and side channels and pool up. It's here that they'll aggressively chase flies, and the bite can remain steady for hours at a time. In tidally influenced regions, the rapid occurrence of a large outgoing tide can also leave hundreds of chum salmon nearly exposed in 2 or so feet of water on sandbar flats that may have been covered by 4 or 5 feet of water minutes before. At these times, anglers can simply swing unweighted flies just beneath the surface, using floating lines and short, controlled casts. Time will be of the essence, however, as not long after the tide goes out, the stranded chum will look to move upriver in search of less compromising holding positions.

In deeper water, chum salmon will assertively move toward flies that swing across the current with some speed. For this reason, leading the fly—even throwing a large downstream mend—can increase an angler's chances. The salmon fly-fishers with double-handed rods mentioned earlier typically employ floating lines and long, tapered leaders with moderately weighted flies, using the greased-line presentation the British invented for Atlantic salmon.

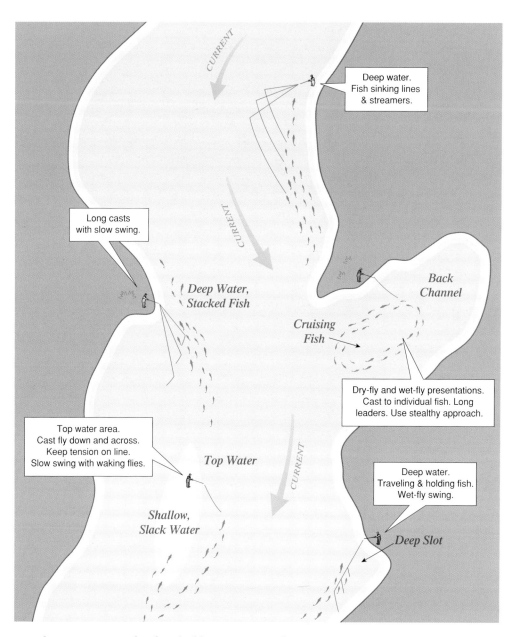

When prospecting for the ideal locations to make a surface presentation, anglers should look for long, steady slick water, shallow tidal flows less than 3 feet deep, and back channels. Chum will take a fly in deeper holding

Working for chum salmon during last light on the Alagnak.

water, too, especially side sloughs where large schools can often be found milling for extended periods of time. A classic example is on the Aniak River, a major tributary of the mighty Kuskokwim, where numerous side sloughs are available for salmon needing to pull over and rest before resuming their upriver journeys. Anglers can spot laid-up chum in the 15- to 20-pound range in these sloughs and make straight-line presentations with subtle topwater flies in muted colors. Fish in these sloughs are often skittish and very aware of predators, namely bears, and perhaps the drab, subtle nature of flies like the stan-

dard mouse pattern makes for better choices. Slow retrieves with short, steady strips will usually bring a boil. Anglers can initially employ a quick strip to get the fly noticed, then settle into a slower retrieve that will give a fish time to home in and grab the fly after it's within its range of vision.

In tidal areas and faster river flows, fly-fishers will want to use the classic Pollywog. In moving water, anglers should also refrain from stripping the fly, instead casting at a 45-degree downstream angle and allowing a short belly to form in the line, which will speed up the drift and create a discernible wake behind the fly. A riffle hitch can sometimes help keep the fly skittering nicely across the surface, especially after the deer hair has had time to soak up lots of water. Takes can come at any point, but a good number will occur as the fly quarters downstream. The takes can be slight, too, with just a snout appearing before the fly disappears.

For pinks, tactics are often the very definition of *simple*. Any of the regular techniques employed for other salmon will work when targeting the fish in fresh water. In the saltwater environment, the most consistent pink fishing can be had in bays and coves with clearwater spawning streams in the immediate vicinity. Big schools will turn up near freshwater outlets, with the pinks commonly spotted porpoising not far from shore. Surf casters will encounter profitable fishing during incoming tides when the movement of the ocean current will push fish toward shore areas.

Chum and Pink Salmon in Alaska

Because they're the two most widely distributed species of Pacific salmon in Alaska, a state certainly not lacking in runs of the remaining trio of salmon species, it stands to reason that you don't have to search very hard to locate a quality pink or chum return. In a lot of areas, they can't be avoided.

For fly-anglers, only the Interior and Southcentral regions are really lacking in opportunities for one species or the other. The fact that pinks tend to stick near coastal regions for spawning precludes much of the water in Alaska's expansive inner regions. On the other hand, there are plentiful returns of chum salmon to the Interior, and sport fisheries do exist in some Yukon tributaries like the Nulato, Nowitna, and Chandalar Rivers, as well as in the Salcha and Delta Clearwater, two Tanana

River–system drainages. But the distance the fish must travel before reaching these waters, combined with the chum salmon's proclivity for rapid deterioration, mean anglers are left to target less-than-prime specimens. Likewise, the primary chum salmon producer in Southcentral Alaska is a massive glacial system—the Susitna River—and sexually mature fish have a long way to travel before reaching clearwater tributaries where they can be effectively targeted.

Southcentral Alaska is not short of pink salmon fishing destinations, though. On the contrary, Prince William Sound offers some of the world's best saltwater potential for fly-anglers. Coastal streams near Valdez can be explosive, as can many Cook Inlet streams. Resurrection Creek, a small, shallow stream that enters Turnagain Arm near the historic mining community of Hope, is famous for its even-year pink return. And there's probably no location in the state that can match another of the region's rivers when it comes to trophy potential, as the Kenai's even-year pink run has produced several IGFA world records. Still, runs in these areas, particularly the chum salmon returns, can pale in comparison to those in other regions of the state, where both chum and pink salmon returns frequently turn the phrase *fish-choked stream* from cliché to apt description. In fact, the runs are typically so numerous and so often encountered that no two books could likely list them all.

Some of the best fly-fishing opportunities for chum and pink salmon exist in the northwest corner of the state, though the area is so remote that nothing approaching the pressure found in other regions of Alaska occurs here. Chum runs to the area's watersheds usually peak in the first part of July and extend into

A Susitna chum in spawning colors.

August in most years. While many rivers and streams in the area receive runs, their frequency and abundance tending to thin north of Norton Sound, the real headliners are the Kobuk, Noatak, and Wulik Rivers.

All three empty into Kotzebue Sound north of the Seward Peninsula, and adventurous fly-fishers probably know each as a prime fly-fishing destination, only for a species other than chum salmon—sheefish on the Kobuk and Alaska's largest trophy Dolly Varden on the Noatak and Wulik Rivers. Both the Kobuk and Noatak receive runs of up to a million chum in strong years, however, and when coupled with light competition, angling can be spectacular. The Kobuk is a gentle-flowing though large river that begins in alpine Walker Lake and meanders about 140 miles to Kobuk village and then at least another 200 miles to meet Kotzebue Sound, along the way passing one of the area's most distinct—and well-known—geological formations, the great sand dunes of the Kobuk Valley (summer temperatures can reach up to 100 degrees in this Sahara-like desert of the high Arctic). Most of the best chum salmon fishing takes place below the village of Kobuk, especially in or near the mouths of the numerous clearwater tributaries, a few of which have great fishing potential of their own.

For pink salmon, anglers interested in Northwest Alaska can find excellent fishing in most of the drainages flowing into Norton Sound. Though run strength varies from year to year, a quality pink return can be found somewhere in the area at virtually any time of the late summer, either in the road-system streams near Nome or those flowing into eastern Norton Sound, particularly the Ungalik, Shaktoolik, and Unalakleet

Rivers. Fishing during incoming tides in coastal areas near river mouths is by far the best bet for anglers, because pink salmon of the area will show signs of the spawning condition after as little as a day in fresh water, and sometimes much less.

Similarly, the chum and pink salmon fly-fishing opportunities waiting to be realized in Southeast Alaska are tremendous. In all seriousness, finding a stream in the region that doesn't host a run of one or the other would probably be much more difficult than locating water with good potential. However, a great majority of the systems that host returns in the area are small coastal streams, meaning that neither salmon species tends to reach fresh water in top condition, often already well along the path to sexual maturity. Luckily for anglers, Southeast Alaska also offers some of the best saltwater fly-fishing opportunities to be found anywhere in the state.

For pink salmon, very few places can rival Southeast's panoply of unparalleled fishing destinations. Anglers working from skiffs in estuaries, bays, straits, or narrows can find large schools of the fish traveling and feeding near the surface. Larger boats often do just as well in the tight passages they can access, as well as providing anglers access to the salmon migration corridors in areas of open water. Just some of the saltwater locales known for their productivity include Chatham Strait near Sitka and the Wrangell Narrows/Duncan Canal area. For chum salmon of trophy size, with some fish exceeding 30 pounds, nowhere in Alaska is better than Behm Canal near the top of the panhandle. Saltwater fly-fishers will also encounter schools of feeding fish, both chum and more frequently, pink salmon, in the waters of Cross Sound, Icy Strait, and Stephens Passage.

In any of these areas, the beaches of bays and estuaries home to stream mouths are fantastic places for the shorebound angler to cast a fly. In some places—like

Releasing a pink salmon.

Starrigavan Bay and the creek of the same name on the western edge of Baranof Island—fishing in the freshwater stream is prohibited for salmon. But during the July peak of the pink return, so many fish are usually stacked into the saltwater bay it'll be nearly impossible to fish without success. Small baitfish and shrimp imitations will be needed, and anglers can generally stick with a floating line, as the staging fish school near the surface.

Kodiak Island, which is home to healthy populations of both chum and pink salmon, is much like Southeast Alaska in its character. For pink salmon especially, the best fly-fishing is located in inshore areas, before the fish enter their freshwater streams of origin, where spawning will commence almost immediately. All of that means one thing—anglers looking for exceptional fly-fishing opportunities, which combine classic water conditions and big numbers of large, bright chum salmon, will once again want to think about traveling to Southwest.

An ideal example of the type of chum salmon river that's become popular in Alaska—with Europeans and their double-handed rods especially—is Katmai's Alagnak River. Blessed with exorbitant numbers of fish that avoid taking on the calico colors of spawning for days after entering the river, the Alagnak typically presents nonstop action for fly-fishers throughout much of July. Most of the chum salmon of the system—and of greater Bristol Bay as well—average around 8 to 12 pounds, not as large as average fish from areas like Behm Canal but more friendly to the fly-angler. The first Alagnak chum usually begin to arrive in the beginning of July, streaming in on flood tides large enough to reverse the flow of the lower river. Not surprisingly, these lower stretches are where a lot of the chum salmon angling takes place. Thousands of fish will be found milling in the very lowest reaches throughout the high slack tide, but then the impetus to head upriver will overtake the fish as the falling tides returns the river to shape.

Preparing lunch on the Alagnak.

Alagnak chum push upriver in sizable groups, large enough to disturb the water's surface, and anglers wading the sandbar flats can typically scan for nervous water and then make very precise presentations without ever really seeing the fish. For the most part, the fishing remains good on the river through the beginning of August, with bright chum salmon showing up throughout the run. Still, there are many, many more great locations for the fly-fisher in the Southwest, from the Nushagak to the Togiak and on to the tributary streams of the immense Kuskokwim River. Most of the region's rivers fish similarly to the Alagnak for chum, with the addendum of tributary mouths and clearwater side sloughs to the list of sites to prospect.

Floaters on a Southwest Alaska tundra river stop to work an inside run.

BRIAN O'KEEFE

rainbow trout

IN THE CLASSIC Ernest Hemingway short story "Big Two-Hearted River," it doesn't take long for Nick Adams to remember just what it was he missed while away. "As the shadow of the kingfisher moved up the stream, a big trout shot upstream in a long angle, only his shadow marking the angle, then as he went back into the stream under the surface, his shadow seemed to float down the stream with the current, unresisting, to his post under the bridge where he tightened facing up into the current." The words flow as clearly as the water Hemingway must have imagined. "Nick's heart tightened as the trout moved. He felt all the old feeling."

Language left to its own devices might never suffice to explain such emotion. The reader must already own such images, must have already felt that same quickening of the pulse near a promising stretch of water. Undoubtedly many do—and have. And like Nick, they probably find the memories more closely tied to the trout than anything else.

Indeed, in the western United States at least, there's little doubt the grandest cathedrals of fly-fishing fantasy were raised in worship of the rainbow trout. From lonely spring creeks to the never-ending seams of a mammoth coastal river, the species is by turns voracious and tight-lipped, ebullient and bashful, unparticular and quite finicky. 'Bows require all of an angler's guile, the very best skills, and even a little faith. They're more than a worthy adversary; they're the definitive sport fish, the benchmark all anglers must eventually be measured against.

In Alaska, the fly-rodders of today enjoy wild rainbow opportunities that have long been lost to anglers just about everywhere else. Only the streams of Russia's Kamchatka Peninsula can rival the forty-ninth state for

Casting for 30-inch rainbows on the Naknek.

big, beefy, and abundant 'bows. From the celebrated stomping grounds of 30-inch trophies—the Kenai, Naknek, and Iliamna watersheds—to lesser-known, though not necessarily less prolific ribbons of blue criss-crossing the state in areas both remote and right-next-door, the rivers that hold Alaska's wild *Oncorhynchus mykiss irideus* may escape the accumulated body heat of salmon-fishing fervor, but whatever lack of numbers trout anglers bring to their waters is more than made up for by a healthy outpouring of passion.

There's little chance the trout-bewitched will ever cease chasing all that old feeling, either. Regret for them is as foreign as poetry is to bait slingers and Wall Street tycoons. Worry, however, is felt in abundance, as trout anglers can fret over their shadow, tailing loops, a drag-

BRIAN O'KEEFE

ging fly, dull hook, and poor knots all at the same time. Curiously enough, even when tippet and leader forever part ways, fly-fishers, like playwright Henrik Ibsen's oblivious Peer Gynt, will somehow refuse to accept dejection in any form. The magic of the rainbow trout, then, must lie in its ability to still give while taking everything else away. And in truth, perhaps no other fish save the rainbow's sea-run cousin can inspire such hopes, dash them so pitilessly, and leave nothing but contentment swimming its vacated wake. Those who understand that, who've *felt* that, can never be turned away. For them, a day spent streamside only amplifies the zeal to return. And though it's doubtful the rainbow trout, despite the intelligence assigned the species by its most pious disciples, even notices the power it holds, it hardly matters. For there is no need for the beautiful to understand what beauty means.

The Rainbow Trout

(Oncorhynchus mykiss)

Although it's easily the most recognizable trout in the world, the rainbow actually varies considerably in both physical appearance and general life history across its range. Much of this diversity can be attributed to the regional—and hence, dietary and climatic—differences between populations. Two subspecies of the North American rainbow also have a seagoing component, as was discussed in the first chapter, which amplifies the divergences. All of Alaska's rainbow trout, both sea-run and stream-resident, belong to the coastal subspecies *Oncorhynchus mykiss irideus*. But even within that subspecies, and within its Alaska range, several notable differences can be discerned.

Most of the coastal rainbow trout, which exist from California north to Alaska and in the streams of Russia's Kamchatka Peninsula, are profusely marked with small,

BRIAN O'KEEFE

irregularly shaped black spots both above and below the lateral line. Trout that display this general pattern can be found all across Alaska, from some of the lake systems of Southeast to Kuskokwim Bay. Most will have backs that are colored anywhere from a dark, greenish brown to a steely blue. But some of Alaska's rainbows, hailing from a handful of the state's colossal lakes—Naknek, Kenai, Iliamna—will have backs that are more lightly hued, usually closer to the emerald green of the steelhead. These resident rainbows will also display the bright silvery body color of the seagoing steelhead throughout much of the year, their small spots only discernible after close inspection.

There are also several stocks of rainbow trout in the state that take body coloration to the other end of the spectrum. Most recognizable of these are the leopard rainbows of Bristol Bay, brilliantly hued, heavily speckled fish with large, bold black spots and sides of copper to gold. Even the trademark band of red can differ among trout populations in Alaska. In the Bristol Bay rainbows, and several other stocks in the state, the block of deep red can nearly cover the entire width of their sides. In the fish of the largest lake systems, a light pinkish stripe will only invade the overall silver coloring of the fish as the spawning season progresses. Still others will look exactly as most expect a rainbow to look, with copper sides, small black spots, and a perfectly pink stripe.

Rainbows from Alaska's large lake systems are often more silvery in color, with fewer and less distinguished spots.

Where Alaska's rainbows don't differ from one another is in their sleek, streamlined shape, with barely forked caudal fins that are broad at the base. Most populations of Alaska rainbows also share one other trait—a propen-

sity for attaining world-class sizes. This, like the differences in appearance that make some populations of fish unique, is primarily a product of the distinctive lives many Alaska trout lead.

LIFE HISTORY

A wide variety of factors influences the growth rates and patterns of the rainbow trout, among them a stock's genetic composition, the type and availability of food, the type of habitat, including the average water temperature, and the overall region of distribution. So, what enables so many of Alaska's rainbows to grow so large? Well, after reading the above, a reasonable angler might say, *It's in the water.*

The resident rainbow trout of the Last Frontier's cold waters grow at a slower rate, reach sexual maturity later, and live longer than their more latitude-challenged cousin fish. Most trout of western North America join the spawning pool at an age of two or three and live to reach only six or seven years of age. On the other hand, Alaska rainbows, which can live for upward of ten years, might not enter into reproduction until after their fourth or fifth year of life. Some resident rainbows from drainages like the Kvichak and Naknek Rivers have been estimated to be fourteen years old or more and have recovered from the rigors of the spawning beds on multiple occasions.

Another Alaska growth incentive is the amount of biomass made available in the state's more productive river and lake systems. As might be expected, environments conducive to hosting large rainbows contain both rich and stable food sources. Depending on availability, larger rainbows will mostly eschew insect and other invertebrate morsels to feed on sticklebacks, sculpins, leeches, freshwater shrimp, snails, and even small rodents such as voles, mice, and shrews—and in Alaska especially, eggs, alevins, fry, and out-migrating salmon smolt.

Just being piscivorous, however, won't necessarily make a trout large. To continually gain mass and reach truly large proportions, a resident rainbow trout must be able to take in more energy from food sources than it expends throughout the course of a day. Efficient feeding practices combine nicely with some other attributes of Alaska's cold waters to create what is virtually the world's best trophy-trout habitat. Alaska's resident trout not only enjoy a higher caloric intake of food than many other wild stocks in North America, due to the immense numbers of salmon returning to the state's most prolific waters, but the cold water temperatures also impart lower metabolic rates to the trout, a trait that is further amplified by the amount of food available—in many areas these rainbows don't have to work very hard to eat. Thus, Alaska rainbows aren't often prone to rise and devour the minuscule nutrition found in a *Callibaetis* hatch. And why would they, when thousands of pounds

of decomposing salmon flesh and high-protein salmon eggs are floating right through their watery dens?

Beyond the fact that most populations of Alaska rainbows enjoy similarly large and productive sources of nutrition, their life histories tend to vary greatly according to the specific environmental conditions of a watershed and the genetic makeup of the population that inhabits it. Spawning stocks, which maintain their unique identities through reproductive isolation, can diverge in appearance from other rainbow trout within the same drainage. And they will almost certainly differ in migratory patterns. In fact, it's their migratory tendencies, or lack thereof, that are responsible for the most drastic variances among different populations of rainbow trout in Alaska.

Some are not that dissimilar from most rainbow trout of the Lower Forty-eight, traveling little and primarily utilizing the same feeding grounds throughout their lives. However, the life histories of a few Alaska trout stocks are much more analogous to those of seagoing steelhead than they are to more characteristic resident rainbows. These fish also tend to look the part, displaying the bright silver sides, the sparse to nearly imperceptible black spots, the lack of a prominent pink or red flank stripe, and the well-proportioned, powerful shape of the steelhead.

By late fall, Kenai River rainbows have had plenty of time to gorge on salmon eggs and flesh.

Take, for instance, the life history of rainbow trout that spawn in the upper Naknek River. Like steelhead, they attain large sizes (a 30-inch Naknek fish isn't all that uncommon), and they migrate into a large lentic system after spawning. Naknek Lake isn't quite an ocean, but it

In the very early spring, Naknek system fish will often be found in the river. Here Dave Doucet displays a healthy rainbow caught in late March.

is a large oligotrophic body of water (with a surface area of approximately 238 square miles) that houses a significant source of high-protein food for the trout, without many of the threats steelhead encounter while at sea.

The sexually mature rainbow trout of the Naknek River tend to exhibit an allacustrine migration pattern—that is, their travels take them from a lake to a river outlet to spawn and then back again to feed. Thanks to the thesis work undertaken by Craig Schwanke in 2001 and 2002, much more about this stock's specific migrations is known. In the spring, Naknek fish will move downstream from the lake to spawning grounds in the upper 10 miles of river. After spawning, the trout will move back into the lake for summer feeding, though they'll return to the river in the fall. Most fisheries biologists figure that the post-spawning movement of the Naknek rainbows is a feeding migration, as Naknek Lake provides such a significant rearing area for juvenile sockeye salmon. However, a percentage of the rainbow trout present in the Naknek drainage will reenter the river to feed for a select few weeks during the smolt out-migration, usually in early through mid-June.

There is a second theory that can account for the migration of Naknek River rainbow trout into the lake for summer feeding: The fish may be seeking refuge from the explosion of salmon entering the river throughout the summer months. For systems without large headwater lakes, where the rainbows show similar summertime movements away from the mainstems and into upper tributaries, this refuge response takes on even more credence. At any rate, the rainbow trout from the Naknek River will use both the lake and the river for overwintering, with the river being the preferred winter habitat, which again is a life history aspect with parallels to the steelhead, many populations of which enter their natal streams in the fall and overwinter near their spring spawning beds. It's also believed that the Naknek rainbows return to the river in the fall not only to seek out their winter lairs but also to feed on the flesh of deteriorating salmon carcasses as it washes downstream from the lake.

While differing from many resident rainbow trout

TONY WEAVER

populations, the Naknek fish have brethren in Alaska, most prominently the neighboring rainbows of the Kvichak system and some of the trout from the Kenai River in Southcentral Alaska. Both of those populations have life histories that more closely resemble seagoing steelhead than resident rainbows, and each uses a large, oligotrophic lake for summer feeding. Predictably, both also enjoy the tremendous numbers of sockeye salmon returning to their systems.

Within the overall Naknek drainage, Schwanke's thesis also noted that there are at least five distinct spawning stocks of rainbow trout: one each above and below the falls of the Brooks River, one in Idavain Creek, an American Creek population, and the Naknek River stock discussed above. ADF&G telemetry data suggest that there is some limited mixing of the Brooks River, Idavain Creek, and Naknek River stocks during the summer and fall, though no mixing on the spawning beds has been documented. None of the other four stocks exhibits steelheadlike tendencies to the extent of the Naknek fish, however, and none is known to produce trophy specimens with such regularity, either.

Another watershed that's home to multiple groups of reproductively isolated rainbow trout is the Alagnak drainage, where some of the trout also display a high degree of seasonal movement, though they don't have an expansive freshwater lake for summer feeding like the Naknek trout. The observed groups within the Alagnak River system include lake residents, a lake–river group or ecotype, and a riverine group. Alagnak River rainbows aren't necessarily migratory, though, as some of the fish in both the riverine and lake-resident ecotypes spawn, feed, and overwinter in the same general area within the system.

Lake-resident Alagnak fish utilize a combination of one lake—either Kukaklek or Nonvianuk—and the respective lake outlet and inlet tributaries for spawning, summer and fall feeding, and overwintering. The lake–river fish, on the other hand, tend to use the lakes, their inlet tributaries like Battle, Moraine, and Funnel Creeks and the Kulik River, and the mainstem Alagnak River throughout their annual life cycles. In various telemetry projects, these fish have been tracked to their spawning beds in the braided section of the Alagnak, where some remain throughout the summer feeding season, which coincides with the spawning activity of chum, pink, and chinook salmon in the same area. Others within this ecotype migrate back to the lake-inlet tributaries, where they focus their summer-feeding efforts on the eggs of spawning sockeye salmon. And all the lake–river fish eventually migrate back to their respective lakes for overwintering purposes (it's currently believed that these fish display lake basin fidelity and won't move between lakes from one season to the next).

Within the riverine ecotype, fish exhibit both seasonal migratory patterns like the lake–river rainbows, as well as nonmigratory behavior. The general pattern for river migratory fish involves an upstream migration to the braided reaches of the mainstem Alagnak River during the spawning season, another upstream migration to the braided reaches during the post-spawning season, and finally a downstream movement to overwintering areas in the lower and middle portions of the river. The majority of river nonmigratory trout were located in the braided reaches of the mainstem during all seasons. These fish do make upstream migrations during the spawning and post-spawning seasons, but on a relatively smaller scale in comparison to migratory fish. With all three of these groups, however—whether they display seasonal migratory tendencies or not—temporal and spatial distribution is very obviously dictated by the presence of spawning salmon. This one pattern doesn't change in Alaska, whether it's fish of big lake systems like the Kenai or trout such as those from the Togiak and

Susitna drainages that roam mainstem river and tributary corridors throughout their existence. For both, the bulk of the year's sustenance arrives every summer from the Pacific, and where spawning salmon can be found, rainbow trout won't be far behind.

Fly-Fishing for Alaska's Rainbows

In *Trout Madness*, Robert Traver wrote, "The amount of Machiavellian subtlety, guile, and sly deception that ultimately becomes wrapped up in the person of an experienced trout fisherman is faintly horrifying to contemplate." He was referring to the equal amounts of deftness and deception it took for a fly-fisher to fashion a lifelike ensemble of feather and fur that would then have to be deployed in the stream with just the right animation to fool a fish into thinking it was the real thing. Long before and definitely ever since Traver penned his masterpiece of wit and wisdom, this notion of the advanced skill needed to consistently take trout has pervaded fly-fishing literature, mostly because it's true. In most decent trout locales, neither a sloppy presentation nor a silly-looking fly is likely to bring about much more than the need to cast again. That's not necessarily so in Alaska, where, frankly, anglers can often perform with appalling clumsiness and still take a few nice rainbows, just as long as they can find them.

As their migratory tendencies would seem to suggest, fly-fishing for Alaska's rainbows is a traveling affair. That shouldn't present any problems for anglers accustomed to working the freestone streams and large trout rivers of the West. Eastern U.S. fly-fishers, on the other hand, who might prefer to diligently mine a short section of water for hours at a time, will want to observe a more transitory approach. In the springtime, rainbow fishing techniques for Alaska will be as closely allied with the

tactics used in the Lower Forty-eight as they're going to get. The trout will be found feeding on insects, crustaceans, and forage species like sculpins throughout their range. One event particular to Alaska's trout systems occurs a little later in the year, when the fish move into position to intercept the out-migrating salmon smolt, often providing some frenetic topwater fly-fishing action. In the summer, the rainbow trout angling scene shifts to areas ripe with migrating salmon. This emphasis on the salmon for trout anglers only heightens as the year progresses. Understandably, anglers the world over frequent the many quality streams of the Bristol Bay region and other salmon magnets during the autumn spawn. This time of seasonal change is when Alaska's rainbows will start their power-eating binge in an effort to store winter fat. Fly-fishers who park themselves in the right locations during this time of year will likely experience some of the most prolific trout fishing on the planet.

Yet for all the numbers of fish and the size they routinely attain, Alaska's rainbows can disappoint the angler undertaking a first fishing trip to the Great Land. Much like the majority of the population of the forty-ninth state, Alaska rainbows eschew excessive pomp. The artful presentation means less here than just about any other place on the continent. Food is obviously abundant in the waters they inhabit, and locating the big 'bows is often the most difficult obstacle an angler will face—next to landing them, of course. A beautiful cast and perfect presentation help, no doubt, but neither seems to be nearly as important as providing the trout a selection of what they're already eating, which in the Last Frontier often means salmon flesh and eggs. It's enough to drive traditionalists to the verge of public hysteria and certainly blow Alaska-sized holes in Traver's Machiavellian hypothesis, but for the trout purist, it's a heaven-sent sign of the world as it was meant to be: rivers full of hefty fish with the finicky left far behind at home.

LEFT: *An angler battles a rainbow trout set against the autumn foliage of Brooks River.*

Timing

The large rainbows in Alaska are migratory, that much has been settled. Some streams will have plenty of trout during major salmon-spawning activity but then be devoid of fish after the salmon are gone. Then there are the resident rainbows that occupy the large lake systems, fish that display characteristics very similar to those of steelhead. These resident rainbows will use the lake systems like a freshwater ocean, sometimes overwintering but always using these bodies of water for the large populations of forage fish and the ample nutrients they contain. In this scenario, it's the spring out-migration of smolt that triggers the first big rainbow migration, as the system's large trout actively pursue this phenomenon.

The Bristol Bay trout opener usually falls in the middle of the migration, when lake temperatures initiate a mass exodus of the ocean-bound smolt. This major migratory event can begin either earlier or later than the early-June opener, contingent on the weather and how fast the lake's surface temperatures heat up. In recent years, this event has occurred earlier as warmer temperatures have triggered earlier migrations, but even then the spring migration of smolt can last until mid-July in some rivers, most notably within portions of the Wood-Tikchik system. Fantastic fishing can be had during this period, with diving birds and swirling fish, and rainbows that can be caught with smolt-imitation surface flies.

In the late-summer to fall time period, the resident trout migration is tied to another trigger: the salmon moving to their spawning beds. At this time of year, Alaska's rainbows are no longer looking for juvenile smolt, but mature adults—they're in search of eggs and, a little later, flesh. Autumn rainbows can travel many river miles in the hunt for food, this highly migratory nature being somewhat akin to wolves scouring the tundra for prey. Part of the autumn game for Alaska anglers is thus fishing egg and flesh flies for ravenous rainbow trout, wherever they can be found.

Gear for Rainbows

Anglers will use anywhere from a 5-weight to a 9-weight rod for most trout conditions in Alaska, a favorite being a 6- or 7-weight, 10-foot rod that will fish well with lines up to 200 grains. Some overline their rods when fishing smaller water. This helps load the tip of the rod when fishing short and using long leaders. When fishing heavier flows like those encountered in the fall on the Kvichak or Naknek, anglers might move up to a 9-weight, which allows the use of lines up to 400 grains and aids in casting larger flies and fighting healthy autumn fish in the stronger current.

Most reels should be equipped with at least 150 to 250 yards of backing, for when fishing bigger water from the bank or an anchored boat, anglers can routinely find themselves spooled by large fish. Gel-spun backing will allow almost double the yardage on most reels, which will help to prevent this from happening.

BRIAN O'KEEFE

Spring trout are especially susceptible to well-presented fry and smolt imitations.

TONY WEAVER

When fishing floating lines with indicators, anglers will normally choose lines that load fast and shoot far. Some of the newer lines, like Teeny's Whitlock Bass Bug taper and the Rio Clouser, work well with strike indicators and heavy flies. Scientific Anglers also has a specialty Nymph Taper that is designed to load quick and turn over heavy flies. Leaders should vary along with the conditions—length and tippet size are regularly dictated by spooky fish and shallow or deep flows—but a standard leader setup for average Alaska nymphing conditions would be 9 feet of stiffer monofilament, hand-tied and tapered down to a 2X (.009) tippet section. Anglers can start with 32 inches of 30-pound-test mono connected via blood knot to 21 inches of 25-pound test. Following another blood knot, 12 inches of 20-pound test will lead to an identical 12-inch section of 15-pound monofilament, then 8 inches of 12-pound and another 8 inches of 1X, which is knotted to the 18-inch tippet section.

Also, a tag end left off a blood knot at the tippet can serve as a dropper to keep split shot from damaging the main line.

Anglers who wish to can attach a strike indicator between the first blood knot and the loop-to-loop connection with the fly line. The most commonly used indicators in Alaska are high-visibility Corkies pegged to the leader with a toothpick or Antron yarn heavily treated with floatant. For surface presentations, anywhere from 9 to 12 feet of leader is usually plenty to avoid spooking the fish. And although they occur rarely, there are situations when Alaska fly-fishers will need to utilize fluorocarbon tippet material for making presentations, either on the surface or below, to extremely wary fish.

Finally, lots of different knotless tapered leaders do exist commercially, but anglers willing to spend the extra time tying their own can construct better leaders with just the right combination of turnover, stiffness, and abrasion resistance. In general, leader length should be about one and a half times the depth of the water, and by hand-constructing their leaders, fly-anglers can very easily alter the length to fit the conditions. Learning how to tie blood and surgeon's knots with speed will save valuable time on the river, as will tying up a handful of leaders in advance, especially for nymph or bead-egg anglers who'll more than likely lose a few rigs to the bottom or a foul-hooked sockeye.

TROUT FLIES

The perfect Alaska fly would be easy to tie, work in a variety of conditions, mimic many food forms, and catch every species. Although the Egg-Sucking Leech catches pretty much anything that swims in Alaska and may at first seem like the quintessential fly for fishing the Last Frontier, it's not ideal for every occasion. Fortunately, fly-fishing is more complex than that.

For Alaska's rainbow trout anglers, who enjoy the luxury of fishing for a species that's actually interested in eating, the task is to figure out what the prevalent food source is for the area and time of year and then to imitate that food as closely as possible. Anglers should generally choose a fly that closely mimics the size, shape, movement, and color of the prey, in that order. One of the real beauties of fly-fishing is figuring it all out and having a system for selecting just the right fly at just the right time. Trout flies are especially abundant, however, and the Alaska neophyte could easily become lost in the maze of choices. To make fly selection for fishing the state's rainbows a tad simpler, it's usually best to think of trout patterns as belonging to distinct groups of flies, each of which will perform better than the other possibilities under certain circumstances. Below are some of the major fly categories for Alaska's trout fly-fishing.

First, of singular importance to the Alaska trout angler are the rainbows' two dietary mainstays: eggs and

flesh. Glo-Bugs, chenille eggs, and even beads (although not technically classified as flies) provide anglers with accurate imitations of salmon spawn, while most flesh flies—usually simple rabbit strip creations tied in a scale of colors—can replicate the varying stages of decomposition quite well. Flesh in its early-season form (late summer and early autumn) is darker in color, often orange or a fuller pink hue. Lighter shades of pink will be more productive as the year wears on, while tans and whites gain prominence later in the fall, during the winter, and again in the spring when rainbows will feed on flesh that's washed into the stream with the higher flows. Flesh flies tied in sizes 2 to 6 on streamer-style, unweighted hooks are the most popular, though many anglers are experimenting with larger, articulated flies at present. Anglers can also use a few standard streamers to imitate salmon flesh, most notably the White Woolly Bugger and the Battle Creek. Patterns in the mold of the Babine Special that combine both flesh and egg characteristics can also be effective at times, although they're nowhere near as widely used as the most ubiquitous Alaska trout pattern, the single egg.

Seasonally there is a transition point when the trout really start to feed on eggs. At first when the salmon are beginning to pair up, the competition on the spawning beds makes egg fishing difficult, and fly-fishers can still do well with a variety of patterns. However, as the eggs start to drop and the intense rivalry subsides, no other fly pattern will do as well. In fact, during the peak of the egg drop, the feeding is typically so intense that anglers can present an egg-imitation fly anywhere within the general area of spawning salmon and have reasonable success. It is not until the late transition from egg to flesh, when there is an abundance of eggs in the water, that the fishing becomes challenging again. Accurate imitations and flawless presentations will then regain their importance.

Chum eggs.

LEFT: *For spring fly-fishing, fry patterns are hard to beat.*

particular species' eggs, which are at a particular stage of development or debilitation, manifest in the color they appear underwater.

Alaska's salmon don't attract interest as a source of nutrition from the state's rainbow trout only when they're producing eggs or dying and shedding flesh. The juvenile salmon, whether as alevins or smolt, can provide a significant forage base and should be of immense interest to anglers, especially in the spring. The alevin is a salmon in the immature stage, often still attached to the yolk sac. Alevins are not strong swimmers, and hence, they are often washed from the stream margins or up from the gravel substrate into the main current, where they become prey for hunting trout. Alevin patterns can also be extremely effective in watersheds that have significant populations of chum and pinks, for these salmon migrate to the ocean early in their juvenile stage, usually during the first year of life and not as second-year smolt like chinook and sockeye young.

Most alevin patterns are tied on 4X-long streamer hooks in sizes 6 through 10 with orange marabou throats to mimic the egg sac. Some tiers are also using hot glue and synthetic materials for an alternate version of this fly. Most alevins should be weighted with light bead chain, which when fished with a floating line and a long leader will help get the fly in the gravel. For most Alaska fly-fishers, alevins are of secondary concern, though. Every spring, the migration of the salmon smolt from the rearing lakes downstream to the sea sends myriad birds and fish in pursuit and can provide for some of the year's most blistering action. For those who've experienced it, this two- to three-week event is a must. Flies to imitate the out-migrating smolt vary from 2 to 4 inches in length. Polar Fiber and other synthetic hair creations typical of baitfish patterns have become popular for smolt imitations, as have Popovics-style epoxy flies. Anglers can also continue to find many of the standard

To be fair, it must be mentioned that some fly-fishers hold a strong aversion to fishing egg patterns. While there is no debating their effectiveness, beads in particular draw a lot of scorn. For anyone willing to fish a wet fly or nymph, however, there shouldn't be a lot of resistance to using egg imitations. In fact, there are obvious similarities between matching emerging nymphs and trying to discern and duplicate the color and size of the salmon eggs a river's rainbows are feeding on. Although not as critical early on, making a suitable dead-drift presentation with just the right color and size of egg becomes paramount when the fish are keying in on a

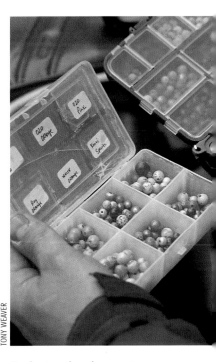

TONY WEAVER

By the time the salmon arrive, Alaska fly-anglers better be prepared for the egg drop.

During the smolt out-migration, topwater gurglers often work as well as any of the more realistic baitfish imitations.

RIGHT: *The quintessential Alaska trout pattern: the deer hair mouse.*

flash patterns that have been used for years. All are tied on 4X-long streamer-style hooks in sizes 2 through 8, both weighted and unweighted.

The entirety of rainbow trout angling in the Last Frontier doesn't revolve around the Pacific salmon, though. In fact, the assumption that Alaska is devoid of good dry-fly and nymph fishing could not be further from the truth. The stoneflies of the Iliamna region's Copper River, those of the genus *Pteronarcella* in particular, can come off regularly in the right weather conditions in June and July, accounting for the stream's reputation as the best dry-fly river in the state. Black stonefly nymphs fished deep or midcolumn and Olive Stimulators on the surface will produce well on warm summer days. Good dry-fly and nymph fishing extends to many of Alaska's other freestone streams, especially in June before the salmon arrive. Some have prolific, though sporadic caddis and mayfly hatches, which when encountered can be fished with success. Doubtless, the Gold-Ribbed Hare's Ear and an Elk Hair Caddis are the most versatile patterns fly-fishers can stock for spring and early-summer outings.

Alaska's lakes, however, present virtually untapped potential for bug-loving fly-fishers. The Matanuska Valley, adjacent to the Anchorage Bowl, is one such haven for anglers, though for the most part these are stocked, not wild trout. The Swanson River–Swan Lake system is another. On these and many more Last Frontier still waters, midges, leeches, sticklebacks, and both damsels and dragonflies provide the bulk of the trout's diet. The lake leech, weighted and tied with black, brown, or olive marabou, can be an effective searching pattern. Chironomids are a second season-long producer, while in some Matanuska Valley locations, the June damsel fishing is hard to top.

Anglers searching for surface action in Alaska aren't necessarily limited to dead-drifting tiny insect replica-

tions; nor must they pinpoint exactly the smolt out-migration. In fact, for many the pinnacle of topwater trout fishing in the state involves neither of these. Rather, the chance to skate mouse patterns has long been one of the most considerable draws for Alaska-bound trout aficionados, and certainly those headed for the southwestern portion of the state, where packing a mouse or shrew imitation in the fly box is nearly mandatory. Most of the best mouse patterns are simple, spun deer hair creations tied with rabbit strip or suede tails. Most store-bought mice, with their eyes, suede ears, and the correct number of whiskers, are good for wowing fly-shop browsers, but their performances are often lackluster when compared to those of bushy, buggier-tied styles. Wide-gapped and light-wire hooks (stingers or dry-fly salmon styles in sizes 2 and 4) dressed with spun deer hair, antelope, or another buoyant material work great for standard mice patterns.

Still, a few of Alaska's most consistently successful

rainbow trout patterns—indeed, a few of the world's—have yet to be mentioned. One is Don Gapen's original masterpiece, the Muddler, which features a clipped deer hair head that mimics the widely distributed sculpin. Sculpins can make up a large portion of the trout's diet. They range in length from ¾ inch to over 4 inches, and their coloration will vary, often closely matching a river's bottom. Greens, blacks, browns, and combinations thereof are the most frequently used colors by fly-tiers. Spun ram's wool or deer hair is typically utilized to construct the sculpin's most prominent feature, the large head. Some other popular and effective sculpin patterns for Alaska are the Black Marabou Muddler, the Woolhead Sculpin, the Zoo Cougar, and Whitlock's Sculpin, which is designed to swim hook-point-up to eliminate hang-ups when fished directly on the bottom, where the majority of sculpins will be found.

Another trout food form in Alaska waters are the freshwater eels predominantly found in the bigger lake systems. For instance, the rainbows of both the Naknek and Iliamna systems feed heavily on the eels in the spring, early-summer, and late-fall time periods. Articulated Leeches in larger sizes, even up to 10 inches, work quite well in these environs. Without a doubt, though, many effective fly patterns really don't imitate anything in nature. The Woolly Bugger in all its forms can loosely represent many things, but it's meant to look nothing like any specific forage. And then there's the Egg-Sucking Leech, probably the most identifiable and productive fly across Alaska's fly-fishing spectrum. It's really not an accurate leech imitation, though like the Woolly Bugger, the slim profile could conceivably fool a trout into thinking it's a minnow. The salmon-colored egg at the head certainly doesn't hinder its effectiveness, either. In the end, the sheer adaptability of the pattern and its many triggers—profile, wiggly marabou tail, and the fact that it might look like some type of critter eating

BRIAN O'KEEFE

salmon spawn—makes it irresistible to a number of Alaska fish, including rainbow trout.

A Southwest rainbow that succumbed to a topwater mouse.

ANGLING STRATEGIES

As has already been mentioned, the primary differences between trout angling throughout much of the Lower Forty-eight and fishing for the Last Frontier's rainbows lie in both the latter's highly migratory natures and their reliance on the life cycle of the Pacific salmon for food. However, that very dependence on the salmon makes Alaska's rainbow trout at least mildly predictable, even in their seasonal migrations.

In the spring, as the ice recedes, fly-anglers will find the rainbow fishing to be much like it is anywhere else, with the fish slowly moving toward their spawning grounds or already there, holding in typical trout water, and feeding ravenously on insects, crustaceans, and forage fish. Some fly-fishing guides, like Steve Fickes of the Great Alaska Adventure Lodge on the Kenai River, will target the big rainbows almost solely with deer hair and

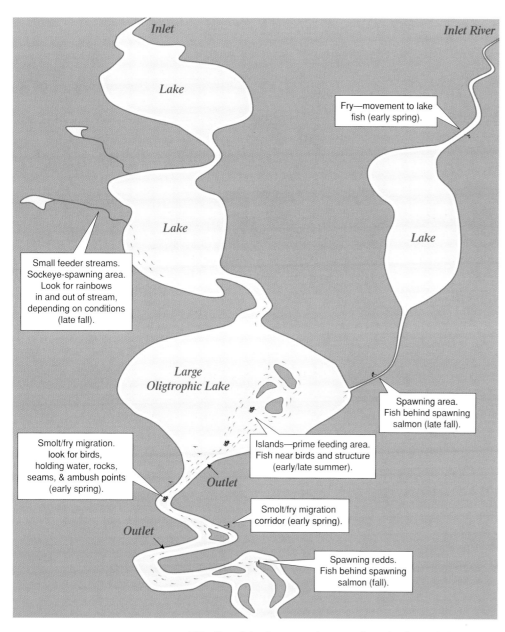

Inlet

Inlet River

Lake

Fry—movement to lake
fish (early spring).

Lake

Lake

Small feeder streams.
Sockeye-spawning area.
Look for rainbows
in and out of stream,
depending on conditions
(late fall).

Large
Oligtrophic Lake

Spawning area.
Fish behind spawning
salmon (late fall).

Smolt/fry migration.
look for birds,
holding water, rocks,
seams, & ambush points
(early spring).

Islands—prime feeding area.
Fish near birds and structure
(early/late summer).

Outlet

Smolt/fry migration
corridor (early spring).

Outlet

Spawning redds.
Fish behind spawning
salmon (fall).

RIGHT: *Summer trout anglers
must work to pick out rainbows
from among the sockeye.*

Woolhead Sculpins until June when the first of the chinook and sockeye reach the spawning grounds. Salmon flesh patterns, too, can be very effective in the early spring, when higher flows scour the banks and flush the remnants of autumn's decay downstream. The best colors will be white or washed-out pinks. Probably the most anticipated spate of spring fishing, however, occurs in the state's large lake and river systems, such as the Iliamna, Naknek, Wood-Tikchik, and Alagnak drainages, when rising water temperatures trigger the smolt out-migration.

The mass exodus of millions of sockeye salmon smolt generally occurs when water temperatures reach 40 degrees—from late May to the end of June in most Southwest Alaska lake–river systems. Mainly a nocturnal occurrence, this event is seldom seen by most lodge anglers, as the smolt slowly slip downriver under a cloak of darkness. There are exceptions, though. The best-documented variation takes place in the Agulowak River within the Wood-Tikchik Lake system. Over the course of many years, the sockeye smolt of this short clearwater river have been observed using the middle of the day for the bulk of their movement. Added to that, this migration occurs not only in the spring but also during the height of the Alaska summer, in mid-July.

For fly-fishers intent on intercepting rainbows on the smolt feed, perhaps nothing will be as important as following the birds. Both terns and gulls will often appear when large schools of smolt are present, and quite randomly, too; there will be no birds in sight and suddenly, within a few seconds, a congregation will descend on a point in the stream, hovering, feeding, and vocalizing their find. Naturally, the birds are often joined by predatory rainbows. Fishing from the bank makes locating and then accessing those areas of concentration difficult, mainly because most smolt movements appear to occur randomly and on different spots of the river. Thus, bank anglers are usually relegated to a waiting game, staking out narrow corridors or traveling conduits in the river where smolt are likely to be channeled into good concentrations. Sooner or later, a school will surface and the action can begin.

To more effectively cover water, anglers will want to stay mobile, which in larger rivers means employing a powerboat. While the advantages are obvious, boats don't come without their pitfalls. Number one is the difficulty of landing fish. However, having a catch-and-release net will minimize the stress on rainbows landed from the boat, as well as saving valuable fishing time, since anglers won't have to travel to the bank when landing fish. A second concern for boat anglers is the need to make accurate casts to moving targets while drifting. To make matters worse, winds can constantly shift directions and speeds, and casting angles are usually difficult. It's actually quite similar to fly-fishing the saltwater flats, differing only in the nature of the pursuit. Here, birds are spotted at a moment's notice, and boats are run quickly to areas of intense activity. Motors are shut down, and with a bit of luck the birds and fish will be in a direct-intercept point from the boat, where casts can be made to the edges of the smolt schools. The attacking rainbows will slash through the group and then circle to pick up the cripples. In this scenario, a strip–pause–strip–pause retrieve will often bring hard charges from ravenous trout. Short strikes are also common, making it easy for anglers to pull the fly from chasing trout. Leaving the fly motionless instead of continuing the retrieve in this case can bring a rainbow back around to finish the kill. Short strikes can be circumvented by a stinger or trailing hook as well. If regulations in an area don't permit the use of a second, trailing hook, simply clip the point of the lead hook.

As spring transitions to summer, the character of Alaska's trout fishing also undergoes a change. Both are marked by the arrival of the first waves of salmon to the state's waterways. In a number of watersheds, the rainbows will have moved. Some entire streams will nearly be empty of fish, while others that may provide little or no spring fishing will receive a large influx of trout,

BRIAN O'KEEFE

which is probably close on the heels of the king or sock-eye salmon. Anglers with a mind to will still be able to locate some dry-fly fishing in the state, namely in rivers like the Copper of the Iliamna system or in tributaries that hold rainbows seeking refuge from aggressive salmon. Summer in Alaska also presents the peak of the mousing season, especially in the clear runoff streams of Southwest. Near grassy overhangs and cutbanks are good areas to try, though skating a mouse across midstream runs can also bring bone-jarring strikes. There is potential for mousing in other regions, too. The clearwater tributaries of the upper Susitna area in particular could offer some quality mousing water, though anglers typically haven't fished the patterns with enough consistency to yield much success. A large part of the reason why lies in the fact that a great number of Alaska fly-anglers, like the trout themselves, turn their attention to salmon eggs as soon as they become available in the stream.

In general, most of the trout will be congregated below schools of spawning salmon, jockeying for prime real estate to take advantage of drifting eggs. They are quite serious about finding some, too. From campfires to saloon stools, anglers can hear from guides and other fly-fishers who've watched as dozens of rainbows have herded large chinook salmon toward gravel bars, bumping them in the sides in an attempt to dislodge eggs.

To get in on this action, as when preparing to fish any other fly, it helps to first understand the food source. The size and color of certain eggs are very important, as not all salmon eggs are the same. An obvious example is the difference in size between smaller sockeye eggs and the larger eggs dropped by spawning kings and chums. Although the entire range of eggs may be available in the same river system, rainbows seem to prefer sockeye eggs where large runs of those fish return. Then again, in some rivers with rather large populations of chinook salmon, the resident trout will show a distinct preference

for their eggs instead. Despite the difference in diameter, most salmon eggs are very bright orange when first dropped, and they will carry an almost translucent sheen to them. This will change; the eggs begin to take on a milky white tint as they either decompose or begin to develop. The overall orange color will also fade through various stages of pink along the way. It pays for anglers to understand the differences, too, as the trout are certainly aware of what they're eating.

Fish keyed in to orange eggs will usually refuse pink or lighter-colored imitations, as well as beads or egg flies that are of the incorrect size. This phenomenon is very similar to a complex hatch, where anglers must utilize all of their deductive reasoning to crack the code. Curt Trout, one of Alaska's premier nymph-and-egg anglers, explains that the trout's preferred egg, and thus, an angler's imitation choice, could vary in just a few miles of river. "The Kenai will have a multitude of different salmon spawning in the river in August," he says. "The main channel might have a pair of chinook salmon spawning with rainbows feeding on their eggs, while farther downriver on an inside seam, a number of sockeye will also be dropping eggs." This scenario can be frustrating, as the angler can fish dozens of color and size combinations before finding the right imitation. For this reason, ardent bead anglers like Trout and his guides at Alaska Troutfitters are constantly sizing, Soft-Texing (dipping the beads in solution to give them a more natural feel), and custom-blending paint to "match the hatch." If you were to inspect Trout's fly box during the height of the Kenai trout season, the different beads and Glo-Bug combinations would number in the hundreds.

Beads are also difficult to fish; the technique for detecting nuances in the line requires a vigilance and skill cultivated only through thousands of hours on the water. Although the occasional village-idiot fish will always amaze anglers with its voracity, most egg bites are subtle.

Double eagles.

DARYL PEDERSON

In fact, many go undetected. A good nymph angler can "see" the ever-so-slight hesitation in the line that signifies a pickup, but for the most part, fish will lift and reject egg imitations without the angler ever knowing they were there.

As autumn matures, days get shorter and termination dust settles atop most Alaska mountains. Another change occurs as well, this one beneath the surface of the state's many productive trout streams. On the banks and in the water of these once-busy rivers, the decaying remnants of thousands of salmon carcasses breathe new life into the food chain. Flesh from these rotting carcasses will provide high-calorie nutrition for insects, birds, and plant life. Trout will start to feed heavily on decaying flesh and washed-out eggs as these float by. At this time of fall, the rainbows are particularly vulnerable to a well-presented flesh fly. Normal fishing will dictate that the early-fly colors be oranges and reds, which resemble newer flesh. Pinks, tans, and whites should be used later in the season; washed-out or bleached flesh is quite common when the tissue becomes thoroughly oxidized. These latter colors are normally fished from late September until freeze-up. Although flesh is readily available as a food form in late autumn, it is not unusual for rainbows to eat other parts of the salmon as well. Seeing big rainbows ingest a large pectoral fin from a decaying salmon can change an angler's thinking on fly design. Using a salmon-fin fly probably borders on the sacrilegious, but having a varied assortment of trout patterns to complement the variety of flesh flies can pay dividends during the late fall.

When fishing over spawning salmon, devising strategies tailored to the waters is paramount, as fishing the Kenai will be different from autumn angling on the Naknek, and neither are anything like Moraine Creek. For example, because the Kenai River water is silty, trout there are not leader-shy. Casting over these fish and using

a heavier leader will not affect anglers' success rates. However, when fishing the very clear Brooks River, sloppy presentations will spook fish, as will heavy leaders and nonstealthy approaches. Then again, when trout are on the heavy feed, they tend to be impervious to external stimuli and will continue to feed no matter what is tossed at them. A classic example can be taken from the Kvichak River, where anglers will motor over spawning fish and then cast from a moving boat into prime lies. The fish will momentarily move away from the commotion created by the outboard, but they'll also stay within the vicinity of the spawning fish, set to continue feeding.

Speaking of the Kvichak, potential travelers to Alaska should be aware of the sometimes overwhelming size of some of the state's better trophy-trout locations. While many of the prolific rainbow destinations are classic free-stone streams with the standard riffle–run–pool structure, many others are simply mammoth waters. Rivers like the Naknek, Kvichak, Kenai, or Nushagak can be

Little rivals the thrill of watching rainbows strike mouse patterns skated on the surface.

daunting and seem impossible to read. Fly-fishers must break down this type of big water into more manageable quadrants and then dissect it thoroughly. Even then, covering all the prime-looking lies will be tough. For this reason, two-handed or Spey rods have become much more popular with Alaska trout anglers. Two-handed rods can be used to cast large flesh flies, sculpins, leeches, and other bulky creations into zones normally reserved for all-tackle anglers. On the Naknek and Kvichak especially, anglers have combined the use of the longer, more powerful trout rods with powerboats, making quartering casts downstream from either side of the craft while anchored or under power but moving slower than the current. In this manner, immeasurably more water can be covered, which will eventually lead to more trout being caught.

Rainbow Trout in Alaska

All trophy-trout hunters share in one bit of knowledge—to catch big trout, you must first go where they live. That search will inevitably lead toward Robert Peary's pole, as the last strongholds for large resident rainbows exist far to the north, in Alaska and on Russia's Kamchatka Peninsula. These two northernmost populations of wild coastal rainbow trout share more than superficial resemblances: Biologically, the Kamchatka rainbow is virtually identical to its Alaska counterpart. Both have captured the hearts and minds of trout-mad anglers worldwide, for whom dreams come tailor-made with 10-pound 'bows leaping in front of sunsets that frame both the wild fish and their equally pristine surroundings. These are anglers who share in a second bit of knowledge as well—trophy trout are just as likely to hook an angler as that angler is to ever hook them.

Many familiar with Alaska's angling landscape may have heard the old saying, *As the reds go, so go the rainbows.*

While this adage holds a certain veracity, there is much more to consider in searching out Alaska's most likely lairs for trophy rainbows. Alaska is a vast state, with a diverse range of environmental circumstances that result in a variety of river, stream, and lake ecosystems, and, in turn, some distinct differences among the state's resident trout. After all, from the leopard rainbows of Bristol Bay and the silver-sided behemoths prowling mammoth lake systems like the Naknek and Iliamna to the resurrected stocks of the Talachulitna and the fabled 'bows of the Upper Kenai, the one sure similarity may be the presence of trophy potential. Which is why trout anglers flock to Alaska with something like the reverence of the maybe more theologically minded pilgrims who annually trek to their own holy shrines. For these anglers, and probably even many of those who've yet to pull a fly tight against a 30-inch leviathan, none of this will likely approach revelation status. Ten-pound trout, unfortunately, have a way of making secrets hard to keep. Thus, without further gilding the lily and no more ado, the following represent the ten top spots for finding trophy trout in the Last Frontier.

NAKNEK LAKE AND RIVER SYSTEM

Jason Dye, the ADF&G's area management biologist for Bristol Bay, has much to rave over when discussing the trophy-trout possibilities in his area of operation. "It's a great place to go rainbow fishing," he says of the region, seriously understating the case. At first, choosing a destination among the region's plethora of overly productive trout systems might seem like it would be a difficult task. That's not so if trophy size is the primary concern, however, because a pair of the region's rivers shoulder reputations that dwarf just about every other trout stream on the planet. "I would characterize the Naknek and Kvichak Rivers as two of the premier wild rainbow trout fisheries in the world and certainly in North

America," Dye continues, before closing with a compelling recommendation: "The Naknek has large numbers of 30-inch fish."

That, along with its booming salmon sport fishery and relatively easy accessibility, are some of the reasons the river receives the highest amount of angling pressure of any sport fishery in Southwest Alaska, over fifteen thousand angler-days annually. Naknek Lake and the river of the same name lie some 300 air miles to the southwest of Anchorage. Accessible via commercial flights from Alaska's largest city, the community of King Salmon sits on the river and is the launching point for the great majority of the trout-angling activity, whether lodge based, guided, or of the do-it-yourself variety.

Deep, jade-colored Naknek Lake provides both remarkable and consistent trophy-fishing potential, while the Naknek River, equally productive, drains the lake and flows about 30 miles west before emptying into Kvichak Bay. There are five distinct spawning stocks of wild rainbow trout within the system as a whole, as was previously mentioned. Though the Naknek River stock currently holds the most trophy potential, the rest of the drainage is not immune to producing the occasional 30-incher. In fact, the Brooks River, which flows barely a mile in connecting Naknek Lake to Brooks Lake, was responsible for a large number of trophy catches in the past, though that number has dwindled with the increase in fishing pressure throughout the 1980s and 1990s.

Idavain Creek is a small clearwater stream that flows about a dozen miles from Idavain Lake to its terminus in the North Arm of Naknek Lake, just west of the Bay of Islands. The trout population is strong and can be sight-fished with good success both in the spring when the fish are concentrating on the juvenile sockeye migrating from Idavain to Naknek Lake and then again in the fall, once the sockeye have taken up their positions on the spawning beds. Between those two periods, however, most of

One of the world's greatest trophy-trout locales: the Naknek River from the air.

the Idavain rainbows—the bigger specimens in particular—will be in the Bay of Islands area of Naknek Lake. Access to the stream is limited to floatplanes and boats as well, which means relatively few other anglers will be found on the river at a given time—except the four-legged variety. Idavain Creek and its surrounds are teeming with Katmai grizzlies, and in the fall especially, encounters are nearly guaranteed.

If bears, solitude, and rugged country are the quest—along with strong numbers of wild rainbow trout, of course—then American Creek is an even better bet. Issuing from Hammersly Lake to the northeast of Naknek Lake, the stream rushes, and sometimes rages in about 40 miles to Lake Colville. American Creek pre-

sents an advanced challenge for floaters, with abundant sweepers, some Class III rapids, and lots of grizzlies. Because of the speed much of the river flows at, combined with its narrow confines (especially in the canyon section), anglers can find themselves right on top of a bear before either realizes what's happening. The trout fishing, however, can reach the spectacular. In the river's upper stretches, the rainbows are generally smaller, rarely going over 20 inches, but the area does present the best potential for dry-fly fishing. Hammersly Lake also sends sockeye fry swimming for Colville Lake early in the spring, and trout anglers with impeccable timing can find the action furious. In the fall, the creek probably fishes better than it does at any other time of year, particularly in the pools and tailouts of its middle and lower sections, where beefier 'bows will be gorging on sockeye eggs and flesh.

The widely migrating Naknek rainbow trout population first moves from the lake to the river for spawning, which occurs downstream from the lake outlet in the upper 9 river miles during April and May. There is a limited sport fishery for pre-spawners that coincides with breakup, and fly-fishers can do extraordinarily well with large Black Articulated Leeches, though the area is hampered by inclement weather at this time of year. Currently, the section of the river where the majority of spawning activity occurs, from Rapids Camp upstream to the lake outlet, is closed to angling from April 10 until June 7 to protect spawning stocks. On June 8, Naknek rainbow fishing resumes as anglers begin to target trout feeding on sockeye salmon smolt migrating downriver from Naknek Lake.

Not all of the Naknek's trout are available to river anglers at that time, however; a number of post-spawning trout migrate back to the lake for the summer, where there is abundant forage in the form of millions of juvenile sockeye salmon. Whether some of the trout retreat to the lake primarily to feed or as a refuge response brought on by the large influx of salmon entering the river—or simply because some of the larger rainbows prefer expending less energy in the lake's lighter current—might never be known. It could be a combination of these factors as well. In any case, great trophy-rainbow fishing can be had in the lake during the summer months, particularly in the area known as the Bay of Islands, where the usually turbid water is clearer and allows the predatory trout to more effectively utilize their visual acuity. Some studies have found that by the month of August, over half the rainbow trout in the lake can be found in this eastern arm. Numerous others have determined that on average these summer lake fish are the largest of the system's rainbows.

The lake-feeding rainbows eventually return to the river in the fall, though, some as early as August, when fishing in the Naknek heads toward another peak of activity that continues into October. As the autumn months progress, the number of total fish and the number of larger fish both increase in the river as the trout return to their preferred overwintering habitat (some use Naknek Lake for overwintering as well). Their primary forage at this time will be eggs and the flesh of deteriorating salmon carcasses, both of which will be washing downstream.

Even with all the targets, the Naknek is not a trouble-free river to fish by any means. Obvious holding water is not easy to locate, especially during the higher water of late summer and fall when prime lies are often disguised beneath deep, heavy flows. Still, the presence of the big, silver-sided lake fish that frequent the river make it part of a very small group of North American rivers that pump out 30-inch rainbows with regularity.

KVICHAK RIVER

As the primary outlet for giant Lake Iliamna, the Kvichak River harbors some of the world's largest wild rainbows and has long been at the head of the list for Alaska's trophy trout. The river runs clear and deep, providing perfect habitat for these spectacular resident 'bows, whose life histories are very similar to those of the lake-resident Naknek trout. Both rivers' wild trout populations are very similar to that of steelhead as well, except that the large lentic systems the Kvichak and Naknek fish migrate to after spawning are immense freshwater lakes, not open ocean. Kvichak's (and Naknek') resident rainbows sport the same bright silver, lightly spotted coloration characteristic of the sea-run versions of *Oncorhynchus mykiss irideus*, and they attain similar hefty sizes, carried on sleek, well-proportioned frames.

The Kvichak River lies approximately 250 miles southwest of Anchorage and is most commonly accessed from either King Salmon or the village of Iliamna. The good fishing starts right in Igiugig at the river's outlet from Lake Iliamna. A number of outfitters operate from the village, and fly-fishing lodges for every budget dot the river, which winds from its outlet through the broad muskeg tundra for some 60 miles before emptying into Kvichak Bay about 10 miles north of the mouth of the Naknek River. It's a big, fast-flowing river, where two-handed rods fished from either a boat or the bank can be productive. Fly-fishers will find most of the river difficult to fish, however, and should look for a few of the better-suited stretches, most of which exist in the upper dozen miles of water. Good possibilities include the lake outlet, near the Kaskanak Flats (a braided section of water beginning about 5 miles below Lake Iliamna), and the mouths of the two upper tributaries, Pecks and Kaskanak Creeks. Below the braids, there will be some big Kvichak rainbows in both the early spring and fall, though this section of water is wide, fast flowing, and deep, and can be exceedingly tough on fly-fishers. In the top stretch of the Kvichak, between the Lake Iliamna outlet and the braids, the river is broad and fishable, particularly near the many islands that break the current.

In the early spring, before the post-spawning trout leave the river for the summer, fishing can be exceptional in this stretch, as big, hungry rainbows patrol the island

Relaxing back at the lodge.

flats in search of out-migrating sockeye smolt. As with the Naknek, trout fishing on the Kvichak really revs up again in the late summer and fall, when the usually heavy returns of Iliamna sockeye turn the river's rainbow fishery into one of the best autumn trophy-trout regions in the world. From the braids to the outlet, anglers can use first eggs and then flesh imitations to ply areas behind spawning salmon. Much of the fly-fishing is best accessed by powerboat, though wading anglers can find success in spots.

KENAI RIVER

It should come as no surprise that the most popular sport fishery in Alaska is also one of its best trophy-trout streams. After all, especially in Alaska, big reputations are made upon the backs of big fish. And like it or not, the Kenai River has both.

For the longest time, the best-known trophy-trout fishery in Alaska existed in the upper Kenai River. Slowly but surely, as the numbers of anglers using the river have exploded over the past decade or two, some of that focus began to shift, albeit only a few miles downstream. "The upper river garnered the reputation for trout fishing," agrees ADF&G Area Research Biologist Bruce King, "but the rainbow population is healthy and growing throughout the whole river." Southcentral Alaska anglers have noticed. Lately, the number of true trophy-sized fish caught in the upper river has declined, while below Skilak Lake, tales of 28-inch and larger trout are becoming almost commonplace. Predictably, the pressure is shifting, too. While commercial-use permits are limited for the upper river, no such restrictions currently exist for the middle-river-guiding operations. In recent autumns, the wide-open effects could readily be seen in the large numbers of boats and anglers fishing at the Skilak Lake outlet.

The upper river, a designated trophy-trout area, issues from the outlet of Kenai Lake and flows swiftly west through a panorama of scenic mountains and forests until its emerald waters pour into glacial Skilak Lake. From there, the section known as the middle river begins, and good numbers of large trout are taken in the first few miles of water after Skilak. But, as King notes, trout fishing remains good all the way past the mouth of the Moose River, though the number of potential trophies may be diminished. "Trout average 18 or 19 inches in the middle river," King explains. Almost anywhere else in North America, those would be trophies. Not here. "In general, in Alaska, we're kind of spoiled," he continues. "A 16- or 17-inch fish is such a common occurrence, it's overlooked. I don't really start getting excited until a fish reaches 24 inches in length." Of that class of trophy trout, the Kenai still maintains an abundant population, though there might not be as many as there used to be.

King describes the thinning of some of the river's largest stock as a natural by-product of the increase in angling pressure through the years. "The Kenai has followed the classic pattern in a fishery as participation increases," he says. "High-pressure fisheries tend to lose their very large fish, the fish that have something going for them other than an average growth rate." And, according to the Soldotna-based research biologist, who has spent years studying the river's rainbow populations, that's exactly what has occurred on the Kenai: "There are fewer fish in the 24-inch or longer size class than there were in the mid-1980s or 1990s, while the total numbers of trout are increasing."

Whether or not that increase in fishing pressure has also "educated" the Kenai's trout and made them harder to catch is another matter. King explains that any difficulty in hooking Kenai trophies stems more from the amount of food available than any learned behavior. "Part of the issue is, you have a population of fish that don't have to work very hard to eat. They literally don't have to move." Recent underwater video footage has confirmed that fact. "There's a blizzard of fish parts floating by in the fall," King continues, "and if a fish moves 3 inches to feed, that's a lot."

But even with the angling pressure the Kenai receives, and even with fewer trophies at present than in the past, anglers still have a good chance of hooking a monster trout from one of the planet's most famous rivers. "The Kenai has to rank very high worldwide for road-accessible trout fisheries," King concludes. "Especially ones where 20-inch fish or greater can be found."

ILIAMNA LAKE SYSTEM (EXCEPT THE KVICHAK)

The world-class productivity of the Iliamna Lake system certainly doesn't end with the Kvichak; several of the lake's other drainages provide anglers with trophy-trout potential that remains virtually unrivaled. The lake itself is Alaska's largest body of fresh water at approximately 1,000 square miles, and it is the world's most productive sockeye salmon system, supporting annual runs that reach into the millions. It follows, then, that the system would also be home to some of the world's highest concentrations of trophy rainbow trout.

Recently, with the Iliamna region experiencing consecutive years of depressed sockeye returns (in 2003, for the third straight year, the sockeye run failed to meet escapement projections), some concern has been raised about the future of the drainages' trout populations. Jason Dye, however, notes that the ADF&G has been closely monitoring the situation, and that so far there is little reason for alarm. "We're keeping a close eye on the Iliamna system," he explains. "But so far, it appears the stocks are healthy, with catch rates and historical size composition remaining in place."

That's good news for the thousands of anglers worldwide who flock to the region every summer and fall to fish for wild rainbow trout in streams like the Newhalen and Copper Rivers and the diminutive Lower Talarik Creek. Big, fast, and deep, the Newhalen River flows for about 25 miles in connecting Sixmile Lake and the adjoining Lake Clark to immense Lake Iliamna. It's a major migration corridor for the sockeye making their way into the far reaches of the drainage. September and October usually provide the best action for beefy Newhalen 'bows, though the down years have seemed to take a higher toll on the Newhalen and neighboring Tazimina River's trout stocks. The fishing can still be good, especially compared to many other areas, but size compositions appear to be less than the historical average, with neither drainage currently producing rainbow fishing most associated with the Iliamna region.

Unlike most of Alaska's best trout streams, Iliamna's Copper River was made famous by dry flies. This clearwater stream originates in a series of lakes in the Chigmit Mountains and runs swiftly from there the 15 miles to Iliamna's Intricate Bay. Its lower 10 miles or so are perfectly suited for the wade-and-fish angler, and, of course, the Copper remains one of the state's best dry-fly streams, especially during June and early July. This is because most of the Copper's rainbows are river-resident fish that don't retreat into the expanse of Lake Iliamna like the Kvichak fish. Also derived from this season-long residency, however, is the fact that the Copper River rainbows rarely reach the trophy dimensions of the migratory rainbows. Stoneflies and caddisflies account for the bulk of the river's angling-worthy insect life, and like almost any western North American stream, the bigger fish are usually taken on a nymph rather than a dry. Lots of pocket water and some isolated deep pools are ideal for traditional nymphing tactics. And, as in the other tributaries of Lake Iliamna, Copper River rainbow fishing is also good in the fall after the salmon have paired up over their preferred gravel, with the usual egg-imitating fare affording anglers the best results.

Lower Talarik Creek's size is in no way suggestive of the massive reputation the stream carries; it has been one of the Iliamna area's most popular trophy-trout fisheries since at least the 1950s. "Lower Talarik Creek is a phenomenal fishery," echoes Dye, "an unusually small creek with unusually big rainbows." A small isthmus separates the creek from Lake Iliamna, where many trout over 25 inches congregate well within most casters' range. However, the rainbows of Lower Talarik are often on the move, wolves searching for a quick meal, and the fishing can be spotty, as Dye also points out. "The fish are in and out of Lower Talarik Creek from day to day," he explains, "so you can get skunked." For most anglers, though, the possibility of hooking a 25- to 30-inch trophy makes the stream plenty worth taking that chance. Because of its notoriety, Talarik has gotten hit hard by the Bristol Bay lodge crowd over the years, and the likelihood of landing a 10-pound or better rainbow today is definitely less than it was ten years ago, though the chance does exist. Floatplanes arrive at first light as guides try to get their clients on the best water, especially in The Ditch or near The Rock, two of Alaska's best-known angling landmarks.

WOOD-TIKCHIK LAKE SYSTEM

Bearing a striking resemblance to the deep fjords of Northern Europe, the dozen lakes that make up the Wood Tikchik chain at the head of Bristol Bay are as stunning to behold as they are enjoyable to fish. Best accessed by making a commercial flight from Anchorage to Dillingham and then a short floatplane hop to one of the lakes, the system presents nearly peerless rainbow trout angling possibilities, especially from August through late September. It's a giant area, though, and opportunities are nearly endless. Wood-Tikchik State

The Rock on Lower Talarik Creek.

Park covers some 2,500 square miles, and the lakes and streams that flow throughout are literally stuffed with wild Alaska rainbows. There is actually a pair of drainage systems originating here—the upper lakes end up draining into the immense Nushagak River system via the Nuyakuk River. In this case, however, both the northern and southern lake groups will be considered a single, though immense, watershed. The Nushagak system will be addressed in a later section.

The southern lakes of the Wood-Tikchik drainage are interconnected and eventually funnel into the Wood River below Lake Aleknagik. The Wood joins with the Nushagak near the community of Dillingham. It is in this lower system that the best trout angling is to be found, though a few areas of the northern (Tikchik) section have good reputations, especially the Tikchik Narrows, which connects Tikchik and Nuyakuk Lakes. In the Wood River system, the river's outlet at Lake Aleknagik can be excellent, but the big rainbow producers in the area are two of its smaller streams, the Agulukpak and Agulowak Rivers—called the 'Pak (*pack*) and 'Wak (*walk*) by locals.

The Agulukpak River flows only about a mile and a half between Lakes Beverly and Nerka. The rainbows can move in and out of the stream rapidly, but from midsummer on, good concentrations can always be found milling behind the salmon. There is also some of the state's best dry-fly fishing available in the 'Pak throughout the spring and early summer, with much of it accessed by boat. The Agulowak is at least an equal trout producer, its 4 miles of sparkling blue water usually loaded with nice-sized rainbows. This river fishes much like the 'Pak (better from a boat or raft), with sizable concentrations of fish found during the smolt out-migration and throughout the fall after the salmon have begun to drop their eggs.

The pristine nature of the surroundings and the high numbers of trout have not gone unnoticed, however, as fly-fishers especially have made the Wood-Tikchik region one of Alaska's top fly-in destinations. For example, according to the ADF&G, the estimated sport-fishing effort on the entire Wood River Lake system ranged from approximately seventeen hundred to five thousand angler-days per year from 1977 through 1988. Pressure began to rise by 1989, though, in some years ballooning to over ten thousand angler-days, but since the mid-1990s that has stabilized to around nine thousand angler-days of fishing per season. Still, when it comes to the two most popular areas—the Agulukpak and Agulowak—the trout fishing hasn't been diminished in either numbers of fish or the level of difficulty in catching them.

UPPER NUSHAGAK RIVER SYSTEM

Long renowned for the squadrons of salmon that swarm its lower reaches, the Nushagak River and its tributaries also present a phenomenal trophy-trout fishery along the upper sections. "The upper Nushagak above Harris Creek is similar to the 'Pak and the 'Wak," explains Area Management Biologist Jason Dye. "There are 20- to 22-inch fish, occasionally larger, with strong numbers and good fishing potential mixed with relatively light effort."

The immense Nushagak drainage features headwaters that stretch from the Tikchik Lakes to the highlands near Lake Clark, and its hundreds of miles of tributaries, two of which are National Wild and Scenic Rivers, encompass a wide variety of both terrain and angling opportunity. The trout fishing of the upper mainstem Nushagak above Koliganek begins to heat up later in the summer and on into fall as the returning salmon reach their spawning grounds. Access to the extreme upper stretches of the Nushagak is limited to a few scattered tent camps and guiding operations, or do-it-yourself float trips. The rainbow fishing is great in spots in this section, with dry

Anglers step out to work good holding water on the Agulowak River in Wood-Tikchik State Park.

BRIAN O'KEEFE

flies, nymphs, and streamers working well until salmon arrive. The trout fishing remains good into the braids that begin below the confluence with the King Salmon River, though there will be more competition here, especially from powerboats. The mouths of the river's tributaries are also extremely productive areas to wet a line.

Both the Koktuli and the Stuyahok Rivers, which drain the highlands west of Lake Iliamna, as well as the Mulchatna and its other Wild and Scenic tributary, the Chilikadrotna River, are perfectly tailored for the float-minded rainbow angler (the upper Mulchatna River, in particular, requires an experienced hand). One of these headwater floats, especially when undertaken late in the summer, can land an angler amid superb and steady trout fishing as the rainbows line up to feed behind the spawning salmon. The Koktuli should garner a closer look from travelers searching for a wilderness float where they'll encounter fantastic scenery, few people, and good numbers of trout holding in crystal-clear water.

ALAGNAK RIVER SYSTEM

The Alagnak is very similar to many of the other rivers in Bristol Bay—a few just discussed—in that it's not quite at the level of the Kvichak and Naknek Rivers for trophy-trout angling, but remains a high-numbers fishery that produces the occasional 30-inch rainbow. The mainstem Alagnak originates at the outlet of Kukaklek Lake and flows 70 miles before spilling into the Kvichak River just before the bay of the same name. Its primary tributary, the Nonvianuk River, originates at Nonvianuk Lake south of Kukaklek Lake and joins the Alagnak after a short flow.

The two lake outlets, particularly Kukaklek, have long been famous trout locales, with participation increasing both there and in the Alagnak River over the years. Fishing at the outlets is prevalent during the early-June Bristol Bay trout opener, when fly-fishers look to work

Southwest Alaska's myriad streams feature some of the best trophy-trout habitat on the planet.

the groups of aggressive rainbows schooled up during the peak of the smolt out-migration. Moving downstream, the confluence of the Alagnak and Nonvianuk will almost always hold trout in the long, conspicuous seam that marks the two flows' convergence. Just below there, the best trout fishing on the river is encountered in the famous Alagnak braids. Streamers and smolt patterns are extremely effective in the late spring, and though most of the larger rainbows will follow the July-arriving sockeye out of the Alagnak and into the two headwater lakes and their tributaries, the summer offers steady mousing action.

Beyond the mainstem Alagnak, several of the system's smaller lake tributaries offer trophy potential. Moraine and Funnel Creeks have relatively large rainbows in strong numbers, with some fish pushing 30 inches every year. The Kulik River and Battle Creek are noteworthy as well, with fall being the prime time to search for 24-inch and larger rainbows. The Kulik, much like the Brooks River, is a tiny 1½-mile-long stream connecting two larger bodies of water, in this case Nonvianuk and Kulik Lakes, and can also present some exciting spring fishing when the trout congregate to chase the sockeye fry and smolt heading for the safety of Nonvianuk.

Moraine Creek is a classic piece of Alaska trout water, with nice riffles and pools that hold big fish scattered throughout. This used to be one of the Last Frontier's most closely held trophy-trout secrets, but the word has long since gotten out and now the lodge crowd descends

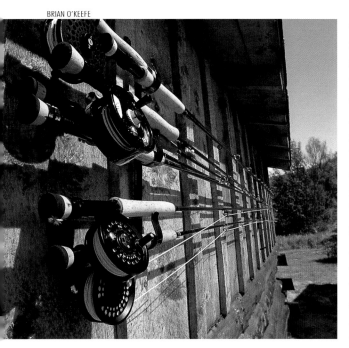

The lineup of trout rods at Kulik Lodge in the heart of Katmai Country's phenomenal rainbow milieu.

FAR RIGHT: *The prominent red stripe on the flank of Alaska's leopard rainbow is visible long before a fish is in hand.*

on the stream in force. The fishing picks up in July, when squadrons of sockeye move through Kukaklek Lake and distribute themselves along the Moraine's spawning gravel. The rainbows traveling with them can be fished with streamers and other traditional trout patterns for a few weeks, until the eggs begin to drop and the feeding frenzy begins. By mid-August, Moraine Creek is usually an egg-only affair, at least until later in the fall when the salmon begin to die off in numbers. Nearly identical angling circumstances exist in Funnel Creek, the primary tributary to Moraine Creek. Both also share another trait—lots and lots of salmon-munching bruins, enough that the pair of streams stands out as favored grizzly locales even among the other bear-infested streams of Katmai.

LOWER KUSKOKWIM AREA

Draining the western Alaska Range, the 800-mile-long Kuskokwim is Alaska's second largest river. The best sport-fishing opportunities in the area, and the trophy-trout waters, exist in clearwater streams that flow from headwaters in the highlands west of the Togiak River Valley into either the lower Kuskokwim River or directly into Kuskokwim Bay. The rugged Aniak River, accessed via commercial flights from Anchorage to the village of Aniak and then by float- or wheel plane to several upper- and midriver points, is perhaps the most significant of these.

The Aniak flows clear and fast off the western edge of the Kuskokwim Mountains in three forks, which—with

their series of logjams, sweepers, and channels—can heap disaster on even experienced boaters. Still, the substantial braids and river debris also make for fantastic trout habitat. The area from the confluence of the three headwaters (Aniak, Kipchuk, and Salmon Rivers) downstream about 9 miles to the mouth of Doestock Creek provides the best trophy-trout potential, both in the main river channels and in some of the off-river clearwater sloughs, where rainbows can be found following the schools of spawning chum salmon in the late summer.

There are a few other lower Kuskokwim River tributaries worth exploring for rainbow trout. Nearly all of them hold good to excellent potential for 20-inch-plus fish in strong numbers. Plus, it's remote, beautiful country, and nowhere near as heavily utilized as the trout streams of Katmai, which also means that the trout of the area are much less sophisticated. The Kwethluk River makes for a fine wilderness float, as do the Arolik and Eek Rivers, offering healthy populations of wild trout, especially after the spawning salmon begin to arrive. The Kwethluk in particular offers a more relaxed, less demanding journey than the Aniak presents. A third Kuskokwim tributary that provides both solitude and potentially explosive trout fishing is the braided, clear Kisaralik River.

The Kisaralik originates in the startlingly clear waters of Kisaralik Lake, which is nestled between peaks of the Kilbuck Mountains at an altitude of about 1,200 feet, and flows first through gentle, rolling hills and then a broad plain that surrounds its confluence with the Kasigluk River. Ten river miles on the Kasigluk separate the mouth of the Kisaralik from the sprawling Kuskokwim. Mostly a float-trip destination, and still hardly visited at that, the Kisaralik's best trout fishing begins after the upper falls, a nasty set of rapids that requires portaging.

The fishing can be spotty near the mouth of

Quicksilver Creek, but trout anglers will enjoy steadily increasing action as they approach the river's braids. Throughout this section, the Kisaralik River features rich rainbow trout habitat, and it produces accordingly, especially during the summer months when the salmon are in. Another section of Class III whitewater at the head of the braids, nicknamed the Golden Gate, signals the start of the most exceptional summer rainbow action. Carving through a narrow rock canyon at about river mile 40, it's a beautiful piece of water, with productive seams and deep pockets tailing behind numerous large boulders. After this stretch, the Kisaralik tames considerably. For the final 30 miles, it's a meandering, braided tundra river, with ample holding water for the migrating salmon, which means the rainbows are abundant. According to *Fish Alaska* magazine publisher Marcus Weiner, the Kisaralik's biggest trout will often be found in this stretch, lurking in one of the several clearwater back channels that'll be stacked with spawning chum salmon. But because the salmon are so plentiful in the side waters, so are the bears, something bushwhacking fly-fishers should keep in mind.

The sparkling, sapphire-blue Kanektok River flows off the edge of the mountains in Alaska's extreme southwest corner. Accessed via commercial flight from Anchorage to either Bethel or Dillingham, then by floatplane to the headwater Kagati Lake, the Kanektok is undoubtedly one of the world's premier wilderness float rivers. And this river was meant to be floated, with long gravel bars, medium flows, and exceedingly clear water. At one time, when only a few had ventured to this gem buried within the expanse of the Togiak National Wildlife Refuge, it was known only as the Chosen River, a fictitious name dreamed up to try to prevent other fly-fishers from discovering the Kanektok's exact whereabouts.

The moniker may have worked for a while, but eventually the rumors of an angler-friendly, fly-fishing

BRIAN O'KEEFE

paradise grew too widespread to deny. The best rainbow trout habitat, of which there is plenty, seems to be from Klak Creek down, along the braided middle and lower sections of the river. Trophy trout are harder to come by here than in some of Southwest's other rivers, but the numbers and beauty of the fish make up for it. These are the much-celebrated leopard rainbows, and to make the destination even more desirable, the Kanektok is also one of Alaska's best locations for skating deer hair mouse patterns, either midstream or in the back channels, where a properly skittered mouse can bring the bigger 'bows up from their hiding places among the root wads and tangled deadfall. In the autumn, these areas are also ripe for presenting flesh flies, as the dying (and dead) salmon get hung up instead of being washed downstream, providing a steady avalanche of high-calorie nutrition to the waiting trout.

A second Kuskokwim Bay stream worth prospecting for trophy rainbows is the sometimes fabulously productive Goodnews River. Flowing 375 miles southwest of Anchorage, the Goodnews is a short tundra river with outstanding opportunities for abundant and occasionally very large resident rainbows. The river comprises three forks, with the middle fork and mainstem being the most commonly fished portions of water. And though it doesn't appear overwhelming in size, many of the best trout lairs are in the Goodnews's deepest holes, deep enough to require sinking lines up to 400 grains. Egg imitations are the river's standard fare during the sockeye drop, but like the neighboring Kanektok, the Goodnews also offers excellent mousing potential in June and early July and then again for a short period in August before the coho land on the spawning gravel.

Susitna River Drainages

Beginning in the runoff from massive glaciers in the eastern Alaska Range, the Susitna River is one of South-central Alaska's most significant and consistent fish producers. Most of the fishing opportunity is centered in clearwater tributary streams, almost all of which already carry healthy reputations among the Alaska angling crowd. Trout anglers, especially, enjoy the Susitna drainage for its easy access, good rainbow potential, and opportunity to get away from the really big crowds.

Speaking of the region's trout populations, Dave Rutz, ADF&G area management biologist for Northern Cook Inlet, says that true trophy specimens can be hard to come by, but the drainage's abundant populations of nice-sized rainbows are hard to beat. "We can't grow them as big as they do out in Southwest," he explains, "because we don't have the big warm-water sinks with 4.5 to 11 million sockeye returning each year." However, Rutz notes that for roadside fisheries, both Willow and Montana Creeks put out a lot of trout each year, and that as many as ten thousand fish are annually caught in Lake Creek and the Talachulitna River. He also has much praise for a fishery that may have dropped off the radar for many Southcentral trout anglers.

"The Deshka's come back in the last ten or fifteen years, having been rebuilt by steps, and the population is currently as high as it's ever been," Rutz continues. The feel-good story of the Deshka is reminiscent of another Susitna tributary that had fallen on hard times, the Talachulitna, which in 1977 was the first stream in Alaska to have total catch-and-release regulations imposed on its rainbows. "The Tal as a system was in a very depressed state," Rutz says, observing that the combination of a lot of weekend floaters and very liberal retention limits (ten trout per day, twenty in possession) nearly decimated the river's wild stock. "But within six or seven years of catch-and-release that system totally rebuilt to what it is now—a fantastic rainbow trout fishery."

When planning to search these Susitna tributaries for trophy 'bows, as in almost every other trout river in the

Great Land, anglers would be wise to mind the salmon runs. "The seasonality of these fisheries depends upon the spawning nature of the salmon," Rutz explains. "Most pick up around July 15 when the kings start spawning. Before that, the fish are spread out. During spawning, however, these fish are concentrated and better targets for anglers."

Rutz adds that autumn is another good time for Mat-Su—bound anglers to find large concentrations of fish. "In places like Lake Creek and the Tal, rainbows move into the lakes or down to the mouths of the rivers where there's better holding water; plus that's where all the food is available, mainly the accumulation of salmon parts drifting downstream." Lake Creek, he notes, is especially productive during the fall, with almost no angling pressure. "Both Lake Creek and the Tal have a lot of fish in the 20-inch category," he finishes. "The health of these fisheries is better now than it has been for probably thirty-some years, and maybe longer."

TOGIAK RIVER SYSTEM

Sandwiched between the renowned streams of Lower Kuskokwim Bay and the Wood-Tikchik Lakes lies the Togiak River system, a network of nine lakes, the main-stem Togiak River, and six major tributaries in the heart of the 4.7-million-acre Togiak National Wildlife Refuge.

Out of all the drainages on this list, however, the Togiak system may offer the fewest chances to catch rainbows in any numbers. Wilderness float guide and author René Limeres agrees, noting that when compared to other, more trout-jammed waters of Southwest Alaska, the Togiak requires a little more effort on the part of the angler. "You have to know how to fish it," he explains, "as the trout for the most part confine themselves to the mouths of the clearwater tributaries." Limeres adds, however, that there's plenty of reason to put in that work. "There might not be that many fish, but the ones

that are there all seem to be 7 pounds."

An intensely scenic water-way, the 63-mile-long Togiak drains the Togiak Lakes into Bristol Bay. It's most commonly accessed via commercial flights to Dillingham, followed by a floatplane hitch to one of the headwater lakes, usually Togiak or Upper Togiak, or selected points downriver. A deep, wide tundra river, the Togiak is easy to float but difficult to fish. As Limeres notes, the majority of the system's rainbows, trophy or otherwise, are concentrated in the mouths of the tributaries, most notably the Gechiak, Ongivinuck, Kashaiak, and Kemuk Rivers and Pungokepuk Creek, though they're rarely found in high numbers. During the spring, the trout will usually be found concentrated near the tributary mouths, positioned to intercept out-migrating fry and smolt. Once the sockeye arrive and begin to move toward upstream spawning sites, most notably in Pungokepuk Creek and the Gechiak River, the rainbows will follow. During the summer, these tributaries of the Togiak will far out-fish the mainstem for rainbow trout. In the autumn, fly-fishers will again be able to pick up rainbows near the tributary mouths as they await the flesh and eggs that'll no doubt be coming their way.

The end is near—a fly-fisher prepares to land a healthy rainbow.

Locked in battle with a shallow-water lake trout.

DARYL PEDERSON

CHAPTER SEVEN

lake trout

VERY FEW FLY-ANGLERS have much to say when speculation turns away from the freestone streams, the spring creeks, and the giant Northwest rivers they know so well. Where there are no tailouts, no pocket water, no 200-yard seams, there is little chance of meeting another member of the feathers-and-fur crowd. Even in places where stillwater angling is something less than an esoteric pursuit, fly-fishers are rarely found in quest of much more than the usual suspects. Those who regularly eschew surface-sipping rainbows or elegant Arctic grayling and aim instead for fresh water's greatest predators, however, have already learned to love a lack of moving water.

Most of these hunters of both lake and slough are after the voracious northern pike, a monster marauder that in wild Alaska must be stalked like a lion on the Serengeti. A few others are in search of something else, a species that most may not envisage as prey to the well-fished fly—the lake trout.

In search of lakers during the summer, anglers must first find the location of their primary forage.

Lake trout, the largest of the char, are also Alaska's largest resident freshwater fish, routinely reaching weights beyond 20 pounds. They are extremely opportunistic predators, preying on almost any obtainable food source, including other fish species that might be available. But despite the sizes they can attain and their indiscriminate appetites, lakers have yet to gain much of a reputation among fly-anglers, mainly because they are one of the least accessible of all North American freshwater game fish. In Alaska, however, that maxim doesn't necessarily hold true. Neither do many of the other traits once thought to describe the fish continentwide.

The vile reputation assigned the lake trout in fly-fishing circles is primarily a product of the environs the species haunts within its Lower Forty-eight range. Lovers of the dark, deep nether regions where water temperatures are more to their liking, lake trout force anglers in

most areas to cope with heavy rods, heavy metal, downriggers, and the tedium of a day spent trolling. Thankfully, a host of environmental factors bestows some distinction to the northern populations of lake trout.

In many Alaska lakes, the water never warms up enough to stratify and establish a definite thermocline. While more latitude-challenged lakers must head for a lake's nadir as soon as the summer sun begins to warm the water, the lake trout of Alaska can offer themselves to fly-anglers year-round. And these aren't the lethargic, bottom-loving lakers many visualize. Rather, Alaska's lake trout frequently display a determined and aggressive nature worthy of the best of sport fish, sprinting for the depths when hooked and showing anglers their backing in a matter of seconds. Often these Alaska lake trout are caught on or right near the surface. In select areas at just the right time of year, fly-fishers can even hunt sand-floored shallows and sight-cast like they might for bone-fish in the tropics.

Still, few fly-anglers can be found chasing these old men of the lakes, even in Alaska. In the realm of adventure and discovery that encompasses fly-fishing, this peculiarity should only serve to make the species more desirable. And the lake trout, large and powerful, gluttonous predator, habitué of wild and remote waters, is already a fish worth the taking of some notes.

The Lake Trout

(Salvelinus namaycush)

The most differentiated species of char, the lake trout isn't as controversial in its classification as some of its cousin fish, specifically Arctic char and Dolly Varden. Nonetheless, at one time it was grouped into a separate genus, *Cristivomer*. Under today's taxonomy, the fish is classified within the genus *Salvelinus* with brook trout, Arctic char, and Dolly Varden.

The members of the genus *Salvelinus* are some of the most arresting freshwater tenants in the world, especially when doused with spawning hues. The lake trout exhibits a much more muted coloration than the other species of char, however. Its body color can range from gray to dark green or even black, while large, irregularly shaped spots and vermiculations cover the whole body down to a creamy white ventral region. The spots are usually white to pale yellow, never red, orange, or pink as on other char. In northern populations especially, red or orange tints can be observed upon the pectoral, pelvic, and anal fins of the lake trout. The color of lake trout is not static, though, and can vary with the season or by specific population. Generally speaking, the specimens of an overall darker coloration usually hail from the less fertile, tannin-influenced lakes of the north, while the lighter fish are dwellers in the deep southerly lakes.

Male and female lake trout appear similar, with the males exhibiting a slightly larger, more pointed snout. Tail fins are deeply forked in comparison to most freshwater fish, and scales are minute. Highly piscivorous, lake trout have a large head and large jaws with well-developed teeth. Extremely heavy specimens have a distended belly and a less elongated shape; otherwise lakers are normally shaped very much like other salmon, trout, and char.

Native exclusively to North America, the species has

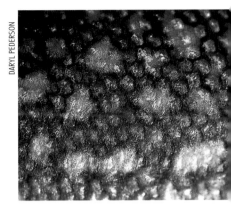

Lake trout scales.

LEFT: *Lake trout.*

RIGHT: *Autumn lake trout.*

been introduced into a few other parts of the world, including Scandinavia, South America, and New Zealand, but has never become as widely transplanted as rainbow, brook, or brown trout, largely due to its carnivorous penchant for exterminating other fish stocks. Its North American range relates quite directly to the limits of the last glacial epoch. Thus, while the lake trout can be found from the Alaska Peninsula east to Nova Scotia and from the islands of the Canadian Arctic south to northern New York and the Great Lakes, the fish, having survived the Pleistocene period in unglaciated refugia, is absent from lowland regions like Alaska's Yukon and Kuskokwim River Valleys. In the more isolated regions of its range, the lake trout remains rather abundant; you could even say it's thriving throughout much of Alaska. On the other

hand, for many areas, especially the Great Lakes, only careful management and, in some cases, artificial propagation has allowed the species to endure.

Lake trout live longer than any other salmonid, the oldest on record having reached sixty-two years of age. It's also the second largest of the salmonids, after the chinook salmon, and the largest member of the genus *Salvelinus*. Officially, the largest lake trout on record is a 50-inch, 102-pound fish netted in Lake Athabasca, Northwest Territories, in 1961. Throughout most of its range, and in Alaska specifically, a 20-pound lake trout is considered a trophy catch, although fish of 30 to 45 pounds are caught every year in some of the most productive northern waters.

The average size of Alaska's lake trout varies but is approximately 4 to 8 pounds. Ten-pound fish are not uncommon in much of the state, particularly in lakes that continue to receive less-than-systematic effort. In recent years, though, overfishing in many of the most popular and accessible lakes has left a higher proportion of smaller fish. It's hoped that more active management policies and a growing emphasis on angling ethics will restore the state's most easily reached lake trout waters to their former quality.

LIFE HISTORY

Understanding the life history of the fish, and then being able to extrapolate that knowledge to angling, may be more important for lake trout than for almost all other freshwater species. The reason? Lake trout are typically found in large (and frequently deep) lakes, and they tend to roam extensively throughout those waters. Hence, knowing where they're going to be and when is a must for any successful fly-angler. Knowing why is the first step.

Clouding this issue for Alaska anglers is the fact that research on the state's lake trout stocks has been limited.

BRIAN O'KEEFE

Almost nothing is known about early life history, with information on migration, habitat requirements, sources of mortality, and factors that influence year-class strength almost completely lacking. In fact, most of the quantitative information on the life histories and habits of lake trout that is available comes from Canada and the Great Lakes. However, with the exception of the large lakes in the Northwest Territory, Alaska's lake trout encounter markedly different climatic conditions than their southern counterparts. Thus, at present, only general inferences about the species's life history can be made with absolute confidence.

To begin with, the degree of adaptation to and preference for cold water differentiates members of the genus *Salvelinus*, especially lake trout and Arctic char, from species of *Salmo* and *Oncorhynchus*. A trait that makes the species unique even among the other members of the genus *Salvelinus* is its inclination toward lake habitat for the entire life cycle, which is a product of the species' temperature and oxygen tolerances. The other species of char primarily use lakes for spawning but tend to migrate to streams (and, in some cases, the sea) for feeding purposes.

Lake trout favor water temperatures of roughly 50 degrees, and they tend to avoid areas with less than about 4 parts per million of oxygen. In the more temperate regions of the species' range, those requirements can usually only be met near the bottoms of large, deep lakes that are low in nutrients. During the summer, only the upper layers of water in nutrient-rich lakes contain adequate oxygen concentrations, but these water layers are usually too warm for lake trout. Low-productivity lakes, with more suitable water, also have fewer food sources available. Thus, it usually takes an oligotrophic lake of more than 500 surface acres to sustain an abundant lake trout population.

In some areas of Alaska, especially in the lakes of the state's Southwest, Northwest, and central Arctic plain regions, these requirements are readily met. By determining a lake's thermal habitat volume (THV)—defined as the volume of water within the temperature range of 46 to 54 degrees during the period of maximum thermal stability (usually July and August)—biologists can estimate potential lake trout yields with reasonable accuracy. Most lakes in these regions of Alaska, however, tend not to stratify to the degree common in other areas. A temperature profile between 46 and 54 degrees can usually be found, but 54-degree water typically starts right at the lake's surface, rendering the entire body of water suitable lake trout habitat, even during the height of summer. In fact, when comparing results from a 1994 ADF&G THV study of fourteen Southwest lakes, yield estimates were found to be considerably higher than those procured from earlier studies of lakes in Southcentral Alaska and Ontario, Canada. This lack of a higher temperature regime allows Southwest fish to follow their food sources throughout an entire lake, no matter the time of year.

Some of Alaska's lake trout stocks will evidently follow that food beyond the lake as well. During the early-spring and fall time periods, anglers can often catch lake trout feeding near the outlets or inlets of their lakes, but stream surveys such as those conducted for the Arctic gas pipeline have turned up fish many miles from their home lakes. Very little is known of why or for how long these stocks use the flowing waters, but most of the rivers and several relatively small streams of the North Slope have been found to hold lake trout during the summer months, most notably the Colville River and its tributaries, the Anaktuvuk, Chandler, Ikagiak, Etivluk, and Killik Rivers. Data from additional lake and stream surveys also point to the presence of lake trout in the Sagavanirktok and Canning Rivers, as well as in a few Northwest Alaska rivers, including the Kobuk, Noatak, Nimiuktuk, and

Cutler. As of yet, however, no cases of river-spawning lake trout in Alaska have been recorded.

Alaska's lake trout instead gravitate toward the rocky substrate of a lake bottom for their spawning activity. Like the other char, lake trout are fall spawners, generally commencing with reproduction during periods of declining temperatures and shortening days. The exact time of spawning, however, varies with latitude and temperature. Over the entire range of the lake trout, spawning occurs from late August and early September in the north to as late as early December in the far southern reaches of its range. In Susitna Lake, simultaneous to fall turnover, spawning begins in the middle of September at water temperatures of 49 to 50 degrees. In Paxson and Summit Lakes in the Alaska Range, lake trout also spawn in mid- to late September. But on the North Slope, ripe females can be encountered by the end of August. The spawning season may be as short as seven days in small, shallow lakes such as those of the high Arctic or extend beyond a month in large lakes.

The lake trout's spawning act itself is unique among salmonids, as they do not excavate a redd. Lakers instead broadcast their large, ⅕- to ¼-inch eggs over the spawning beds, which are typically areas of rubble and cobbled rock with abundant crannies and crevices for the eggs to fall through. In areas where there is no typical lake trout spawning habitat, like the isolated lakes of the central Arctic plain, the eggs and milt are still broadcast, only the sand and silt bottoms of these lakes must at least moderately lessen rates of survival.

Also, research shows that while spawning is an annual affair in southern areas, it occurs only every other or even every third year in the lakes of the north. The lake trout of Northwest and Arctic Alaska are believed to be at least every-other-year spawners. In Southcentral Alaska, evidence indicates that females do not spawn each year, though males generally do. Spawning itself is primarily a nocturnal activity, with the fish more or less dispersed during the day. In the late afternoon, lake trout begin to return to the spawning beds in considerable numbers.

Age at maturity varies as well, with lake trout populations from southern and interior Alaska spawning at an earlier age than stocks in the northern regions of the state. Based on its research, ADF&G reports that lake trout first spawn in Paxson and Summit Lakes at ages seven and eight, respectively. Age at maturity for Kuskokwim Bay lake trout is generally reached between ages nine and ten, with almost all fish mature by age twelve. In some lakes of the Brooks Range, male lake trout were found to mature as much as three years earlier than females. Samples from lake trout populations from sixteen North Slope mountain lakes and from other lakes on the Arctic coastal plain ranged from nine to twenty-five years in age of first maturity.

Despite their reputation for attaining great size, lake trout from most populations are slow growing and rarely weigh more than 10 pounds, even at age twenty or older. The coldest waters with the shortest growing seasons produce the oldest lake trout. In more temperate regions with longer growing seasons, lake trout older than ten years are actually rare. Among these relatively short-lived stocks, first spawning can occur in four- and five-year-old lake trout.

A key to lake trout abundance is a food supply adequate for the fish to attain lengths of about 18 inches, the point at which they are capable of preying upon forage fish. Without fish in its diet, lake trout tend to grow very slowly, and their life span is shortened. The young begin to feed on zooplankton, benthic invertebrates such as chironomid larvae, and small crustaceans, and then at a length of about 10 inches in most of their native range, they graduate to the slimy sculpin and the deep-water sculpin, as well as threespine and ninespine sticklebacks.

Schools of juvenile sockeye like this are an important food source for lake trout during spring.

As lake trout grow, they generally switch from invertebrates to a primarily piscivorous diet in waters containing forage fish. Most populations in Alaska prefer Arctic, Bering, and least cisco, many different varieties of whitefish, and sculpins for prey species, but grayling, pike, burbot, and other lake trout have all been found in dissected stomachs. An adult lake trout can devour prey fish up to one-half its size.

Beyond the regular range of meals, seasonal changes in the food habits of the lake trout have been observed in several areas, most notably those regions of Alaska that host both a significant sockeye salmon return and a population of lake trout. During the spring out-migration in these waters, lakers frequently forgo the other food sources available to concentrate on the smolt.

But no matter the amount or variety of food available, abundance will always remain low when compared to other species such as rainbow or brown trout. This is largely because lake trout feed at the top of the food chain in nutrient-poor lakes while rainbows and browns feed at many different levels of a food chain, tolerate a broader range of temperatures, and have shorter life spans and therefore higher production rates. All the direct evidence that's been compiled bears this out, and the results are decidedly lopsided. High-abundance lake trout populations will have biomasses over two hundred times less than those of the most productive rainbow and brown trout waters.

The lake trout's situation at the top of the food chain in most areas does mean that natural mortality remains low. However, slow growth rates, long lives, and alternate-year spawning leaves trophy lake trout populations extremely susceptible to overharvest. After seeing some of their significant lake trout stocks depleted, Canadian officials instituted strict catch-and-release policies for many of their better waters, a trend that seems to be catching on in some of Alaska's more urban-accessible waters. At the very least, Alaska's fisheries managers have recognized a need to reassess and amend many of the liberal regulations in place since the early days of statehood. In the end, a knowledge of the lake trout's unique life history and proper conservation will ensure that this ancient evolutionary strain of salmonid remains alive and thriving for future generations of anglers to enjoy.

Fly-Fishing for Alaska's Lake Trout

Some myths persist so long that even those who know better will end up one day defending their absolute veracity. For example, every year legions of American schoolchildren are taught that an adventurous Italian skipper braved the stormy Atlantic to the ridicule of a citizenry who just knew the world was flat. Likewise, at least once during every fishing season for the past century, a guy in some fly shop has expounded upon the failings of the lake trout as a game fish. Too deep to reach, sluggish fighters . . . any fly-fisher residing north of the Kispiox has heard the repartee.

Legend, folklore, and plain old bad information are actually quite central to angling tradition, but when it comes to certain fallacies concerning the lake trout and the sockeye salmon and a few other species, popular opinion has done much to build secrets too good to keep.

The truth? Lake trout are not leviathans of the impenetrable deep, but rather sleek, versatile predators that are sometimes more likely to sip a size 12 Adams than they are to crush a spoon jigged off the bottom. In some areas, the fishing during the smolt out-migration is fast and ferocious, more akin to schooling bluefish than it is to jigging for walleye, with anglers wading shallow sand flats and sight-casting to streaking lakers up to 20 pounds. Even summertime lake trout will routinely cruise the shoreline and chase sculpins and baitfish-

imitation patterns. Once hooked, the shallow-feeding lake trout offers anything but humdrum resistance, often bolting for deeper water and sounding within seconds, a deed that is followed by headshakes and gyrations enough to make the stoutest rod shudder, or enough to make any tapestry of angling myth come apart at the seams.

Yes, just as sockeye will most certainly take a well-presented fly, Alaska's lake trout are more than worthy quarry for the discerning fly-angler. And while popular myths are on the chopping block, it's worth remembering Aristotle wrote conclusively that the world was indeed round a full eighteen hundred years before Chris Columbus ever put ship to sea.

TIMING

As the ice melts and spring slowly makes its return to the North Country, lake trout become very active, gliding through the shallows and feeding near the surface, violently assaulting anything that even resembles a food source. In Alaska, this spring haste to eat can be heightened by the presence of hundreds of thousands of out-migrating salmon smolt.

DARYL PEDERSON

IMMEDIATE RIGHT: *Fishing during the spring in many lakes takes place on large, shallow flats.*

FAR RIGHT: *Fishing is often at its best as soon as the ice begins to clear.*

Though always important for anglers, timing and location become even more critical at this time of year. A key to spring lake trout success can be arriving just as the ice begins to recede, though in some of the more northern lakes, there is no access available until the ice has melted enough to allow for floatplane landings or boat navigation. Ice-out typically occurs soonest around inlet and outlet waters and beaches that lie on the windward side. In these areas, anglers can almost always find fish during the sweet of the year, especially on bright, sunny days. For lakes with a population of juvenile salmon, ideal timing will coincide with the one- or two-week period when the bulk of the young smolt up and begin their journey to the sea (more often than not around the first two weeks of June).

After the ice has completely receded, lake trout may not be as easy to find, though they can still generally be found in the mornings and evenings scouring shoals and shallow bays for concentrations of baitfish. Once the results of the nonstop northern sun truly begin to take effect, Alaska's lakes will undergo stratification, though exactly how much depends on the region, weather, and type of lake. During this time of year, anglers need to pay particular attention to water temperature, bottom structure, and the availability of food. Fishing imitations of the prey available, at a depth the lake trout feel comfortable in, is the necessary starting point. Also, smaller lake trout, customarily 2- to 8-pounders, will sometimes remain near shore throughout the summer months, especially in Southwest Alaska and lakes of the Far North. Cloudy or windy days, as well as the low-light hours of early morning or late at night, are the most productive times for fly-fishing summer lakers.

In late August and September, when cooler temperatures again prevail throughout much of Alaska, lake trout begin to assemble for reproduction. Autumn is easily the shortest season in the state—sometimes it seems as if

there is nothing but a direct switch from summer to winter—but the right timing can land anglers among the very best lake trout fishing of the year. Because they are migrating to spawn, look for fall lakers to be concentrated near gravel beaches and above the kind of jagged, rocky substrate that accommodates their unique reproduction needs.

GEAR FOR LAKERS

While equipment needs for many other species of Alaska game fish hardly deviate from a slight range of line weights, the fly rods requisite for lake trout fishing vary considerably. If fishing small dry flies in the summer from a float tube, when 2- to 8-pound lakers are the predominant quarry, a 5- or 6-weight rod will be plenty. However, in the spring and again in the fall when large baitfish patterns and other streamers are the norm, a 7- or 8-weight rod will make casting much more efficient, not to mention enjoyable. A 9-weight is at the top of the

range of rods that can be used effectively for lake trout. The chance for larger fish at these times of year adds to the need to gear up with a little stouter rod. These heavier rods are also a better choice on windy days or when utilizing sinking lines.

As with rods, there is no standard solution for lake trout fly lines. Sometimes—both when fishing surface smolt patterns during the out-migration or casting a Royal Wulff on a summer evening—a floating line is all an angler needs. At other times, however, a variety of sinking lines will likely come in handy. Fast-moving lakers on the hunt for salmon smolt and other baitfish don't usually hang around one place for long, and anglers can find themselves fishing a sharp 15-foot drop-off one minute and a gently sloped beach in 3 feet of water the next. Well-prepared lake trout anglers will arrive equipped with a floater, and several sinking an intermediate, lines ranging from 200 to 500 grains.

Leaders need not be fancy for the pursuit of lake

trout. Standard 4- to 6-foot mono leaders will suffice for sinking-line presentations, while longer, 7- to 10-foot constructions will be needed for surface action. Again, commercial extruded leaders might perform fine when casting small dry flies, but when anglers need to turn over size 2 Woolhead Sculpins, it's best that their leaders be hand-tied with hard mono. The standard step-down formula will work, beginning with 25-pound test and ending with a 10-pound tippet section. If fishing shallow waters, a 10-foot tapered mono leader attached to a floating line, with a lightly weighted streamer tied on, will be enough to get down to the fish, though anglers may have to wait a moment or two longer before beginning the retrieve.

During certain times of the year, when lake trout can consistently be found feeding in the shallows, the wading angler can encounter great success. Still, no matter the lake trout's penchant for feeding along the shorelines, anglers with access to a boat, portable or otherwise, will undoubtedly find the going easier. Float tubes, transportable pontoon boats, catarafts designed for still waters, and powerboats can all be applied to angling on Alaska's lakes, though large, windswept bodies of water can be hazardous to small craft. With prudent attention to developing weather, however, anglers with portable boats can still fish calmer back bays and shelf drops close to shore. Covering big water will be more effective with a powerboat, of course. Ideal models look very similar to saltwater flats boats and allow anglers to stand toward the bow and spot fish from the deck. This type of boat with an open front end also provides plenty of room for casting.

FLIES FOR ALASKA'S LAKE TROUT

Winter in Alaska is nothing if not harsh, and everything that doesn't find an excuse to flee south greets the arrival of spring much as an inmate must look at a favorable parole board. It must be even more extreme for the resident fish, which have spent three or so months trapped under sheets of ice that can be up to 5 feet thick. No wonder breakup finds the lake trout positively ravenous.

During this time of year, logic might suggest that any kitschy streamer will work. To tell the truth, that isn't entirely off the mark. However, anglers who reach for patterns more closely resembling the baitfish of the local area will inevitably finder greater success. After a winter spent beneath the ice, these lakers are interested in eating more than anything else.

There are any number of existing patterns to emulate fleeing forage fish, including the Alaska Mary Ann, the Black-Nosed Dace, Mickey Finns, Gray Ghosts, Matukas, Glass Minnows, the Stacked Blonde, and Zonkers. Virtually any of Dave Whitlock's baitfish patterns perform well for Alaska's lake trout, as will traditional saltwater flies like ALF patterns, Sea Habits, Lefty's Deceivers, and Clouser Minnows. If fishing the smolt outmigration, however, it's best to use baitfish patterns that match the size and color of the naturals. To mimic juvenile salmon and give the fly some sense of both flash and translucence, most use synthetics like Super Hair or FisHair. The Bristol Bay Smolt, an imitation that like most of the above is sold commercially, has a silver body followed by bands of white, olive, and peacock herl. Unlike smolt imitations, which generally need to be sized very closely to their counterparts in nature, most of the baitfish patterns generally can't be tied too large. A 3X- to 6X-long size 2 is a nice all-around fly, though some flies necessarily call for hooks that are either larger or smaller than that. In general, for spring lakers a size 4

This spring laker fell for a fry imitation fished near the surface.

or 6 streamer-style hook is about as small as you'll want to go. On larger fly patterns, especially baitfish imitations, the use of stinger-style hooks will increase solid connections, as lake trout tend to chase and nip or cripple prey fish before turning and taking them headfirst.

Fish-imitating flies remain productive throughout the season, naturally, but as the year progresses other streamers should be added to the arsenal. For example, when no surface-feeding activity is encountered, large subsurface flies like Purple, Black, Brown, and Olive Woolly Buggers, leeches, Woolhead Sculpins, and Muddler Minnows can be just the ticket. Olive or Brown Zonkers are terrific for imitating sticklebacks, an important food source for lake trout where found.

A mix of searching patterns for fall lake trout.

When there are signs of surface-feeding lake trout, nothing beats breaking out the floating line and watching a cruising laker come up to inhale a small dry fly, even if these fish are usually of the smaller, 3- to 5-pound variety. Again, pattern size isn't typically that important. Even if the fish are feeding on chironomids, there's no reason to fool with tiny midge larvae patterns. Instead, try a general dry-fly attractor, as long as it looks buggy. Humpies and any of the Wulff family of flies will find success with summer lake trout inclined to feed at the surface.

Autumn is the time to find the big lakers as they move into the shallows in preparation for spawning. But with the fish so aggressive at this time of the year, fly choice isn't that important. Almost any of the streamers mentioned earlier will work fine, as will most bucktail patterns and sculpins.

ANGLING STRATEGIES

After reviewing research on the habits particular to lake trout, it's easy to see why most fly-anglers who target the species are very selective when it comes to the time and place for their outings. All three seasons of the Alaska fly-fishing year demand a different strategy, and when fishing is so dependent on ancillary factors like temperature and the lacustrine migrations of baitfish, it pays to be dialed in to your fishery. In the spring, both lakers and Alaska's famous rainbows key in on the annual smolt out-migration. Where there are no salmon smolt to chase, lake trout might still be found in outlets and small bays, only in these lakes they'll likely be preying largely upon spring-spawning suckers and aquatic insects, as well as sculpins, leeches, and sticklebacks if they're available. The onset of summer heralds a slower time for stillwater anglers, though lake trout can still be found feeding in the shallows very early in the morning and again late at night. The action heats back up in the fall. In fact, autumn fly-fishing for lake trout in Alaska can be every bit as productive and exciting as it is in the spring, only now anglers will be casting large streamers and baitfish patterns to sizable concentrations of feeding fish.

When winter's icy grip finally recedes from Alaska's lakes, fly-fishers are afforded a rare opportunity to have consistent success in the shallows, or sometimes on top. At this time of year, lake trout can be found anywhere in the water column, and after a long winter spent beneath the ice pack, they're more than willing to chase a fly. Add an annual smolt out-migration and you have all the ingredients for an explosive fishery. Lakes like Iliamna, Kukaklek, Nonvianuk, Tikchik, and Clark are nurseries for significant to staggering numbers of sockeye progeny. The warming of these large oligotrophic lakes each spring (anywhere from late May through June) triggers a mass exodus of juvenile salmon bound for the sea. Lake trout stage at points of interception in shallow, shoreline waters or at the head of a stream outlet and capitalize on this most important staple of their diet. However, the out-migration usually doesn't last for long, ranging from as little as a few days to as long as three weeks in length, depending on temperatures, the lake, and the fecundity of the native salmon.

Anglers in quest of these smolt-slashing lakers will have their best success during the low-light hours of late evening. As a relative June darkness falls, smolt activity usually begins to peak, with daily runs reaching their height between the hours of 9 PM and midnight. Anytime a group of smolt has been located, schools of feeding lake trout will be seen splashing in the surface film with reckless abandon. Watchful anglers can use other signs to locate feeding fish, too, particularly other predators. "We can catch lakers simply by watching the birds," says Kirk Wilson, whose Club Crosswinds sits on the shores of one of Interior Alaska's best lake trout locales. "We'll sit in the lodge playing cards, drinking coffee, and casually

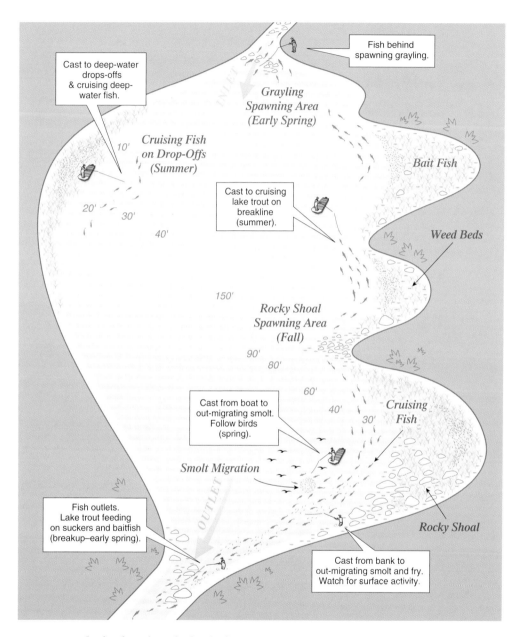

prospecting for birds. When the birds show, we jump in the boats and motor to the areas of heaviest activity."

Smolt imitations, baitfish patterns, and even poppers will catch fish during these short but intense feeding frenzies. And this is one of the few times anglers can reliably find lake trout willing to boil on a surface fly. In river mouths, lakers will ambush smolt from strategic locations; look for them to be on the lee sides of large boulders, in deep channels, and holding off points. The sand-bottomed flats along a lake's lee shore just upstream from an outlet are other prime areas for spring lake trout. Some of the shallower areas near lake outlets will also have nearly indiscernible channels and bottom rocks that the fish will use for cover while waiting for the smolt to pass by. Anglers can usually wade within casting range of these interception points and position themselves to strip smolt patterns through the areas of greatest activity.

During summer in the Last Frontier, lake trout can be found almost anywhere, but refining your search to areas with irregular topography (points, islands, cove mouths, or points of rapid transition between deep and shallow water) will help. The summer feeding and movement habits of Alaska's lake trout are also greatly influenced by the food sources available, which is why they can sometimes be found in the streams of the North Slope, many miles from their home lakes. Plus, in lakes that do experience some thermal stratification, temperature-sensitive lake trout will retreat to cooler water levels, dispersing and remaining within their comfort zones. This is especially true throughout the warmest periods of the day, when fish in most lakes are beyond the reach of fly-fishers. The smolt, a rich and easy food source, are gone as well. To be successful now, fly-anglers must ascertain what food is available and then when and where the lake trout are finding it.

Lakes bottoms are commonly divided into three major zones: the littoral, sublittoral, and profundal. Littoral zones are the shallowest areas of a lake, and are usually shoreline regions. They're also the most productive areas, as they receive more light and frequently har-

bor the vegetation that produces good numbers of aquatic insects. Hatches of these insects attract forage fish, and—during evening hatches especially—the forage fish attract hungry lake trout. Here is where the summer fly-angler can find success.

Littoral zones with steep drops provide the ideal feeding grounds for summer lake trout, which can access the areas to feed during heavy forage fish activity in the evening and early morning and then slip back to their resting zones where temperature and oxygen contents are more favorable. In northern lakes with small populations of baitfish, like many of those on the Arctic coastal plain, lake trout will even be found taking advantage of the hatches directly. At these times, anglers with floating lines and a box of traditional dry flies will do well.

Corresponding with the progression of the season, anglers can also begin to utilize their larger baitfish patterns to greater success. In a lot of areas, the coregonids that lake trout feed so heavily upon are absent throughout the winter and spring, many of those species being at least partially anadromous. Bering cisco, for example, winter in salt or brackish water and return only after the ice is clear. Least cisco, too, are seasonal residents of the freshwater lakes and streams of the Far North. Arctic cisco begin their spawning runs in the summer, as do the truly anadromous humpback whitefish, which returns to many lakes north of the Kuskokwim River for fall reproduction. Lake whitefish, residents of the Interior part of the state, never leave their lake environment and are available to lake trout throughout the year in the systems they share.

As temperatures dip, days shorten, and autumn colors dominate the shoreline foliage, perfectly mimicking forage fish or choosing a realistic sculpin imitation becomes less important than at other times of the year. For maybe more than anything else, aggression marks lake trout behavior in the fall. They will begin to return to the shallows for spawning in late August in the Northwest and Arctic regions of Alaska. Late September to October is an appropriate time to search for these shore-cruising lakers in the lakes of Bristol Bay. Wherever you fish, however, look for water between 5 and 15 feet deep with a rocky bottom that might be utilized for reproduction.

For any of these times of year, GPS units and bathymetric maps will facilitate finding fish. And as mentioned previously, having a boat will allow anglers to cover more water and reduce the downtime involved in prospecting new areas. To effectively fish a large—and new—piece of water, transpose an imaginary grid over prime areas and cast into 5-foot squares, dissecting the potential water. Depending on water clarity, feeding fish can often be spotted as they cruise the littoral flats. Floating lines with weighted flies and mini tips can both be successful here. Cast ahead of the moving fish at an angle designed to intercept their path. Stripping the fly back across their route will usually result in a follow. Lift-and-settle retrieves are also effective, especially when fishing sculpin and leech patterns. Likewise, for deep-water tactics, using the rise-and-fall retrieve from a drifting or anchored boat is a successful tactic.

Lake Trout in Alaska

Called a trout but actually a char, the lake trout also presents something of a paradox in its history. The species, an ancient strain of the genus *Salvelinus*, has an extremely long life span in comparison to other salmon, trout, and char. For over ten thousand years lake trout have persevered in some of North America's harshest and most desolate extremes, even surviving an ice age. But today in many former centers of abundance, the species has encountered some trouble, with trophy-angling practices and general overfishing threatening the fish with developments Mother Nature never intended.

The lake trout occurs naturally from Quebec, the Maritime Provinces, and Labrador in eastern North America, and its range stretches west across Canada and the north-central United States to the Pacific coastlines of British Columbia and Alaska. It's most widely distributed in the northern tiers of that range, throughout Alaska and in Nunavut, Yukon, Northwest Territories, and the Arctic islands of Canada.

Within Alaska, lake trout can be found in the high-elevation lakes of the Brooks Range and the lakes of the central and eastern Arctic coastal plain. They are distributed throughout the upper Tanana, Susitna, and Copper River drainages, in the alpine lakes of the Alaska Range, and in the watersheds draining into Bristol and Kuskokwim Bays. Lake trout are also found in good

Fishing the surface for behemoths like this is an exhilarating experience.

DARYL PEDERSON

Soaking out the kinks after a long day battling Alaska's trophy fish.

numbers on the Kenai and Alaska Peninsulas. But the species's range in Alaska is not continuous, for they are not found in the coastal drainages of the southeastern panhandle or in the lakes of Kodiak Island. Lake trout are generally absent from the lowland lakes of the North Slope and the Yukon and Kuskokwim River valleys, as well as from the Seward Peninsula and, for the most part, the Wood River system. Finally, Alaska's lake trout do not appear in the lakes and streams on the south side of the Alaska Peninsula or in northern Alaska Peninsula systems south of Mother Goose Lake.

Traditionally, across its entire North American range, the lake trout has been sought by commercial, sport, and subsistence fishers, and some subsistence fishing still exists among the Native peoples of the Far North. However, overfishing during the decades between 1950 and 1980, amplified by the lake trout's unique life history patterns, drastically reduced the number of large fish in the northern regions of the species' range. Because of the low production rates in lake trout stocks and their long life span, most of the biomass of a population will consist of fish five to fifteen years of age. When older, larger fish are removed, it will necessarily take several years—and in the case of the ultraslow-growing populations of the Arctic, maybe even decades—for the original abundance to be restored.

In Canada during the early 1980s, the lake trout populations began to rebound from the effects of overharvest, but only after stringent conservation measures were enacted. Today almost all of that country's trophy lake trout are protected by regulations that mandate catch-and-release and the use of barbless hooks. In Alaska, very little has been accomplished in assessing the status of any but the most accessible lake trout populations. Where research has been conducted, all signs point

to a healthy and even thriving fishery, even though the most heavily fished populations have shown a decline in average size of fish and in the number of trophy specimens.

Potential lake trout anglers should immediately see the relevance of all this. First of all, it's obvious that trophy lake trout, more than many other game fish species, are tremendously vulnerable to overfishing. Every angler should be inclined to insist that these fisheries remain viable and productive for the generations to come. Second, a glimpse of the specifics of the lake trout's range makes clear that distribution is greatest in the most remote areas. Most of the populations that are in danger are easy to get to; most of the others are hardly fished. In many cases, not even fisheries biologists know much about these remote stocks.

Such is the case in Alaska, where the great majority of angling activity is concentrated on the state's world-class salmon and rainbow trout fisheries, so much so that even the best-known lake trout fisheries continue to escape the level of pressure seen in some of Canada's better destinations. Popular spots like Paxson and Crosswind Lakes and Lake Louise turn out trophy fish over 20 pounds every year even with mounting pressure. And the more remote but still road-accessible lakes off the Dalton and Denali Highways can provide exceptional lake trout action for the fly-angler, along with a good dose of solitude. But like everywhere else in North America, the best lake trout angling to be had in the Last Frontier can't be accessed by automobile. A short flight from Palmer, Talkeetna, Glennallen, or Willow will land anglers among the pristine alpine lakes of the Wrangell or Talkeetna Ranges, while Alaska's crown jewel of angling opportunity, Southwest, is home to an abundant number of sparkling blue lakes that are rarely, if ever, systematically worked for lake trout. Add to that the primeval wilderness fisheries of the Northwest and the Arctic plain, where lake trout are known to be present in hundreds of drainages and can probably be found in a hundred more. In the Great Land, lake trout fly-fishing isn't even limited to lakes—anglers fishing from the Alagnak to the Noatak often drift smolt patterns and subsurface leeches for spring lakers holding below their headwater lakes. Thus, Alaska's current generations of adventure fly-fishers are afforded great opportunity to pursue a species that not only survived Pleistocene glaciation, but has also continued to elude most of the fly-angling community at large.

SOUTHCENTRAL ALASKA

In this most populated and road-traversed region of Alaska, lake trout are widely spread throughout the upper Susitna River drainage. They can also be found in a few bodies of water on the western shores of Cook Inlet, as well as in some of the lakes of the Matanuska and Knik watersheds. The species is present in many of the lakes on the Kenai Peninsula, including those within the Kenai and Kasilof River systems. Lake trout have even been reported in Little Tokun Lake of the Martin River drainage in the Prince William Sound area.

As mentioned above, several decent lake trout fisheries lie among the dense conifer forests, towering mountains, and copious wetlands of the Kenai Peninsula. Five glacial lakes in the area host native lake trout stocks, including Tustumena Lake, the largest lake on the peninsula, where fishing is best near the Kasilof River outlet in early spring and again in the fall. Skilak, Kenai, and both Upper and Lower Trail Lakes are also home to populations of lake trout, though the size, depth, and turbid natures of the two Kenai River lakes make them less-than-prolific destinations for fly-anglers. Those who do have lake trout success here usually find it in the early and late parts of the season when fishing the inlet or outlet regions of the in-river lakes. The lower end of Skilak Lake, especially, is noted for the occasional laker, and Muddlers, sculpin patterns, and dark-hued Articulated Leeches seem to be the most consistent producers of spring lakers.

Of the clearwater lakes on the Kenai Peninsula that host lake trout (Hidden, Juneau, Swan, and Trout), Hidden Lake often provides the most productive destination for the fly-angler. Just after ice-out in the spring and then again in the fall, reasonable numbers of lake trout can be found near the shorelines of Hidden Lake, which can be accessed via the Hidden Lake Campground on Skilak Lake Road. Casting leeches, sculpins, or other streamer patterns during the low-light hours works well during these times of year. Boaters should use caution, however, as high winds can sometimes descend on the lake in a hurry, their intensity magnified due to a funneling effect created by the narrow mountain valley that holds the lake.

The peninsula's other lake trout fisheries of note lie along the Resurrection Pass Trail, a well-used summertime hiking path that begins in the town of Cooper

Kulik Lodge sits near a great point for anglers to intercept lake trout keyed on the sockeye fry and smolt moving between Kulik and Nonvianuk Lakes.

BRIAN O'KEEFE

Landing and winds through a portion of Chugach National Forest to its terminus at the historic village of Hope. The trail, first used by miners swept up by gold fever in the late 1800s, is used by anglers to access a number of lakes in the Kenai highlands. Juneau Lake, which along with Trout Lake is tributary to the Kenai River via Juneau Creek, is a fairly significant body of water and features a large lake trout population. A few miles farther up the trail, Swan Lake offers even better lake trout angling, especially near the lake's west end where the Chickaloon River begins. A healthy run of sockeye salmon migrating up the Chickaloon every July means that spring lake trout anglers can target the smolt out-migration for best success.

Just across Cook Inlet, a few lakes are worth mentioning for their lake trout potential, most notably Crescent Lake, a turquoise-colored body of water just 75 miles southwest of Anchorage by air. The lake receives a tremendous return of sockeye salmon through the river of the same name, and fishing the smolt out-migration in mid- to late June, just after ice-out, can be phenomenal. Moving farther north, the upper Susitna drainage provides ample, and Southcentral's steadiest, lake trout action, with trophy prospects as good in select locations as they are anywhere else in the state.

The Tyone River system about 35 miles northwest of Glennallen, a labyrinth of lakes and small streams that dissect the high plateau country east of the Talkeetna Mountains, is home to the best lake trout angling in the Southcentral region of the state. According to the ADF&G's sport-fishing surveys, since 1977 the Tyone drainage has accounted for about 16 percent of the annual lake trout harvest in Alaska. Lake Louise, the largest lake in the drainage and a major source for the Tyone River, has long been a renowned lake trout destination, by harvest statistics the most popular in Alaska. Lakes Susitna and Tyone are also notable, but like Lake Louise both are large, deep lakes that can prove immensely difficult for the fly-angler. Lake Louise covers 16,102 acres and is up to 167 feet deep in places, while Lake Susitna, which is connected to Lake Louise by a narrow channel, is slightly smaller at 9,426 acres and a maximum depth of 121 feet. Paramount for fly-fishers is to hit these clearwater lakes in late May or early June, just as the ice has begun to vanish, and to work the open water as it appears.

For the fly-in Southcentral angler, great lake trout fishing can be had in some of the wilderness lakes near the upper Susitna River, including Clarence, Deadman, and Watana Lakes. In fact, the 47-pound state-record lake trout came from Clarence Lake in 1970. Chelatna Lake, near the Kahiltna Glacier in the foothills of the Alaska Range, can also provide fly-anglers an occasion to cast for surface-feeding lake trout, though most travelers only use the lake as a put-in for their float trips down Lake Creek, largely ignoring or unaware there's much good lake trout angling to be had.

In some lakes, like massive Skilak Lake in the Kenai system, lake trout can be very hard for the fly-fisher to find.

BRIAN O'KEEFE

SOUTHWEST ALASKA

Gorgeous and, for the most part, utterly pristine, Southwest Alaska seems like a dream. For those who can remember what the Kenai Peninsula was like seventy years ago, it might seem like a long-lost memory. Either way, the area is the crème de la crème of fly-fishing destinations. Judging by the number of anglers this salmon and trout Shangri-la receives each season, that's already a well-known fact. Much less celebrated is the region's marvelous lake trout potential.

Pete Raynor, manager of Sonny Pederson's Katmailand in Bristol Bay, agrees that a dichotomy exists between potential and effort. "Normally we don't book any exclusive trips for lake trout," Raynor says, "even though the fishing in front of the lodge can be excellent

in mid-June." That's when the bulk of the sockeye smolt are departing Kukaklek Lake, and for about ten days to three weeks, any fly-fisher willing to spend the time chasing birds to the smolt will be rewarded with a maelstrom of lake trout activity on the lake's surface. Why more don't take part is anyone's guess. If anyone did care to chase large, sleek ambush predators feeding on top, then Southwest would be a prime spot to pick.

As the previously cited 1994 ADF&G study revealed, most of the lakes in Southwest Alaska hardly stratify during even the warmest parts of the year. This analysis of fourteen geographically representative lakes—Brooks, Goodnews, Heart, Kagati, Kanuktik, Naknek, Lower Ugashik, Tikchik, Kontrashibuna, Lower Twin, Upper Twin, Turquoise, and Telaquana, along with Lake Clark—

The striking beauty of Alaska's Kenai Peninsula.

lake trout | **193**

discovered that the thermal habitat volume of Southwest lakes was higher than THVs for similar-sized lakes in both Ontario, Canada, and Southcentral Alaska. However, even with significant numbers of lake trout available, and no strict temperature regime to force the fish deep, the lakes receive little to no fishing pressure.

That makes the lake trout perhaps the single most overlooked sport-fishing species in the region. Flourishing populations exist in the Naknek, Kvichak, and Nushagak River drainages, as well as in the systems of Kuskokwim Bay, and considering the numbers of anglers who access the area's waterways by raft each year, usually putting in at a headwater lake, it's somewhat of a surprise that more don't take the time to ply the lake shallows a little before hustling along to search for rainbows and greet the incoming salmon. However, for those interested in sight-casting to 10-pound fish in some of the world's most stunning scenery, the lack of neighbors is most assuredly a good thing.

All fourteen of the lakes in the ADF&G study are situated within a state or national park or a national wildlife refuge. From the rugged and forlorn Lake Clark National Park and Preserve, which houses five of the study's lakes—Kontrashibuna, Lower and Upper Twin, Turquoise, and Telaquana, as well as Lake Clark itself—to the glacially carved tundra of Wood-Tikchik State Park, lake trout anglers in Southwest Alaska are delivered into a setting of profound beauty. Naknek and Brooks Lakes are located within the nearly 4 million acres of Katmai National Park and Preserve, a sort of natural wonderland complete with the lofty, snowcapped peaks of volcanoes, dense riparian forests, rolling lowlands, and an eruption-influenced valley that's as barren as the face of the moon. North of there, stretching from ocean beaches to the treeless alpine tundra of the Ahklun Mountains, the Togiak National Wildlife Refuge encompasses another 4 million acres of one of North America's

last unspoiled wilderness areas, as well as the four remaining lakes in the study. Each of them provides almost boundless possibilities for stalking lake trout with a fly rod, but for most, the intensity of journeying among these surroundings for the first time makes the fishing seem almost secondary.

Almost every significant body of water within the region will have a good to excellent stock of lake trout for anglers to hunt, though. Whether the bedrock basin lakes of the Kuskokwim Bay drainages or the clear, fish-filled waters of Kukaklek and Nonvianuk Lakes, it's obvious that angling potential is not limited to the fourteen study lakes. Noteworthy salmon returns to most lakes in the region provide a good supply of forage fish each spring in the form of smolt. Freshwater leeches, sculpins, sticklebacks, and plenty of coregonids are also available to Southwest's lakers, which during the few hours of Alaska's midnight sun can be found feeding in the slight depths near shore. Even if the plan is to spend a week floating for rainbows or salmon fresh from the sea, scheduling an extra day to sample a headwater lake for the largest of the char is highly recommended.

INTERIOR ALASKA

Since 1977, over 40 percent of the lake trout taken annually in Alaska hail from the upper Copper and Susitna watersheds. Nearly half that total comes from a single drainage, the Gulkana River, a major tributary of the mighty Copper, the most significant waterway completely within the bounds of interior Alaska.

Four lakes within the Gulkana watershed provide the bulk of the lake trout opportunity: Paxson, Summit, Crosswind, and Swede. Paxson Lake lies beside the Richardson Highway and is by far the most heavily used of the group. All present fantastic potential, though, especially near their inlets and outlets, as the Gulkana system's vast numbers of forage fish continue to support outstanding lake trout populations. In fact, Crosswind Lake, accessible by a short floatplane hop from Glennallen, hosts one of the state's better spring fisheries, with at least one commercial lodge operation directly targeting lake trout following the smolt outmigration. For the lake trout angler, this is wade-and-cast fishing at its finest, presenting fast and thoroughly exciting action.

The milky Klutina system can also offer a shot at shallow-feeding lake trout, especially near the clearwater mouths of tributary streams, but it's a third branch of the massive Copper River drainage that should pique the interest of most fly-fishers. The raw and isolated Tebay River system—which, much like western Alaska, combines rugged, spectacular scenery with unmatched angling potential—is a series of high mountain lakes and streams that flow through the boreal forested uplands of the Wrangell Mountains until eventually emptying into the Chitina River. With the exception of the copper-seeking miners who scrambled to the area in the early 1900s, the region has received few visitors, but strong populations of wild lake trout inhabit most of the drainage, most notably Hanagita and the Tebay Lakes. As other lake trout waters in the state become more crowded, these remaining dens of seclusion will only become more extraordinary.

Also isolated, but much easier to get to, the alpine lakes near the Denali Highway present even more chances for the lake trout angler to escape the masses and find good fishing along the way. Situated almost exactly halfway between Anchorage and Fairbanks, the 126-mile highway runs east to west and connects the towns of Paxson and Cantwell. Lake trout anglers will want to concentrate on the Tangle Lakes region of the road's eastern end, a system of eight lakes and their interconnecting streams. This is high tundra country, with lightly carpeted hills rolling into distant mountain

DARYL PEDERSON

peaks, and one of the few places in the state where anglers can hike along trails for reasonable distances without meeting an impenetrable wall of brush. Some of the lakes right on the highway do provide decent fishing, but of course those willing to travel deeper into the system will be rewarded with the steadiest action. Again, it's usually best to fish the inlets and outlets of the lakes, especially in the spring and fall. However, lake trout aren't present throughout the entire drainage. Round, Landlocked, and Long Tangle Lakes, as well as Landmark Gap and Glacier, all contain documented populations and can be fished effectively by canoe, float tube, or wading.

NORTHWEST AND ARCTIC ALASKA

In this region of the Last Frontier, sometimes desolate, entirely feral, and above all beautiful, lake trout are numerous, occurring in most of the higher-elevation lakes and streams of the Brooks Range. This includes a

Sleep? Fly-fishers on a float trip set up camp at ten forty-five on a summer night.

limited distribution in Northwest Alaska, chiefly among the headwater lakes of the Noatak and Kobuk River drainages, though lake trout are occasionally found in both mainstem rivers as well. The species is also distributed widely in the mountain and foothill lakes on the north slope of the Brooks Range, as well as in the Sagavanirktok, Colville, and Canning River systems. Lake trout are generally absent from the Seward Peninsula, the drainages of Norton Sound, and the lowland lakes of the central coastal plain, except those lying between the Ikpikpuk and Colville Rivers. They are, however, quite common in the lakes of the eastern Arctic coastal plain.

Some of the watersheds in Northwest Alaska and the Brooks Range host both returns of Pacific salmon and lake trout, and the angling action in these can be quite good near outlets during the smolt out-migration. Still, forage fish like cisco and whitefish are the prevalent prey in most of these northern waters. Anglers would do well to search shallow coves and bays, confluences with tributary streams, and shoals near islands for concentrations of these baitfish. In many of the Arctic coastal plain lakes, lake trout aren't presented the option of smolt for dinner and instead subsist almost entirely on aquatic insects and other invertebrates such as snails. Lake trout in this far northern part of Alaska enjoy long lives, but they rarely reach sizes of 10 pounds or more.

As mentioned before, the most prominent lake trout fisheries in Northwest Alaska occur in the beautiful mountain country of the upper Kobuk and Noatak River drainages. The alpine reaches of the upper Kobuk watershed contain several large lakes that host populations of lake trout and several species of whitefish, most prominent among them being mountain-rimmed Walker, Selby, and Nutuvukti Lakes. The Noatak River drainage begins above the Arctic Circle in the Schwatka Mountains and also hosts several significant lake trout

BRIAN O'KEEFE

destinations, almost all of which can be reached only by floatplane. Feniak, Desperation, and Matcharak Lakes should be of interest to adventurous lake trout anglers.

Some other exceptional lake trout fisheries can be found in the foothill and mountain lakes on the north side of the Brooks Range, all of which lie within or originate in the Gates of the Arctic National Park, which sits astride the Arctic Divide. To the north is the broad, flat, treeless tundra of the North Slope, while to the south lie the conifer-and-hardwood forested valleys typical of the Brooks Range. Near Anaktuvuk Pass, both Chandler Lake, the largest alpine body of water on the North Slope, and Amiloyak Lake entertain excellent lake trout potential, though neither is ice-free for more than a short two months or so each year. The Anaktuvuk River system is also home to good populations of lake trout, as are the lakes of the Killik drainage. Probably the most popular lake in this region is Itkillik Lake just north of Atigun Pass, its attractiveness heightened by a proximity to the Dalton Highway.

The 414-mile-long highway (sometimes referred to as the North Slope Haul Road) was built in 1974 to facilitate the construction of the Trans-Alaska Pipeline. Opened completely to public travel in 1995, the roadway allows fairly decent access for anglers willing to hike a short way in to the area lakes, which were only previously fished by local Natives and the occasional oilfield worker. Besides Itkillik Lake, several other good lake trout possibilities are located just off the west side of the highway, including Galbraith, Tee, Atigun, Toolik, and Itagaknit Lakes. The Campsite Lakes, almost all of which hold lake trout, are also quite well known for waters this far north. A trail leads from the Dalton Highway to this cluster of twelve or so headwater lakes that serve as sources for Oksrukuyik Creek, a tributary of the Sagavanirktok River.

North of the Brooks Range lie the barren tundra foothills and flatlands of the Arctic coastal plain. The region is dotted with shallow streams and lakes, many of which are home to healthy lake trout stocks. Some present twenty-first-century fly-fishers the rare experience of angling in virgin waters.

The longest river on the slope (and the seventh longest in the state), the Colville is undoubtedly one of the most significant drainages in Arctic Alaska. A big, deep river, the Colville presents its best opportunities for lake trout in its many tributaries and near the mouths of its headwater lakes. The Killik, Anaktuvuk, Chandler, and Itkillik systems are all tributary to the Colville. Between the Colville and the tea-stained Ikpikpuk Rivers on the central coastal plain, there is also an ample number of lake trout fisheries to be prospected, including several shallow coastal lakes. Teshekpuk

BRIAN O'KEEFE

Lake is the best known of these and is believed to hold an abundant population of hefty lakers. Nearer the Ikpikpuk drainage, dozens of shallow, almost totally isolated (except during spring high-water events), and generally unnamed bodies of water hold lake trout.

On the eastern Arctic slope, from the Canning River east to the border with Canada, the plain is crowded down to a narrow strip of rolling tundra by the towering peaks of the Brooks Range to the south and the frigid waters of the Arctic Ocean to the north. Lakes Schrader and Peters, a pair of headwater lakes in the 19-million-acre Arctic National Wildlife Refuge, present anglers' best chance for lake trout success, with catches of trophy size reputed. There are certainly more prospective lake trout waters, but due to its fantastically remote nature and the logistics of traveling this far north, much of the region remains unexplored.

RENÉ LIMERES

One thing float-trip
anglers can almost
always count on is
plenty of eager
Dolly Varden.

arctic char and dolly varden

ONE OF THE MORE ignominious chapters in the
history of Alaska's fisheries came decades before statehood had
even been achieved. Though many surely knew better, Dolly
Varden were proclaimed an official enemy of the salmon. In a
place where the salmon runs—and the money to be made from
them—took precedence over everything else, this made them
an enemy of the state. By 1921, with reputations thoroughly
sullied, the Dolly Varden of the Last Frontier found a two-and-
a-half-cent bounty levied upon their heads. Or to be more
precise, their tails, as the monetary reward was handed out for
every tail fin turned in.

Nearly twenty years later, the program had paid out bounties
for millions of tails. Then, as if this was the plot of a bad western, an injustice was discovered. Close examination of twenty
thousand of the tails revealed that over three-quarters of them

weren't even from Dolly Varden. More than half were coho tails, one of the species the program was supposedly designed to aid. There were even more rainbow trout tails among the examined sample than those from Dollies. The bounty payments were then halted, though there was no acknowledgment of the fact that Dolly Varden aren't nearly the piscivorous predators the simple-minded initiative made them out to be.

In reality, they're not even at a level with their close cousin, the Arctic char. The two, both native to Alaska's fresh waters, are often mistaken for each other, and elsewhere in the species' range the bull trout can be added to the mix, no pun intended. Digging a little deeper, the inconsistencies, controversies, and plain old fallacies that surround the species of the genus *Salvelinus* seem to know no bounds. Even their names—*lake*, *brook*, and *bull*

trout, *Arctic char*, and *Dolly Varden*—are capable of sparking controversy.

When early settlers from Europe found a North American game fish that in shape and size closely resembled the trout they knew, they naturally referred to the fish as trout. But these fish weren't true trout, and later, they were grouped together as "charr," from the Celtic *charre*, probably because of the deep red colors many of the fish can display as they near the spawning period. In today's common usage, all the names can be correct—*char*, *charr*, and *trout*—even though the American Fisheries Society has chosen *char* as the official moniker.

Overall, the members of the genus *Salvelinus*—the char—can be exceedingly beautiful fish, well marked with reds and oranges when doused in spawning hues, and shaped in the streamlined, aesthetically pleasing shape of the trout. They're distinguished from species of *Oncorhynchus* by those colors, as char don't have the characteristic black spotting of North American salmon and trout. However, they might not always be so easy to distinguish from each other, which is why for many years the world record Dolly Varden was a 32-pound fish taken from Lake Pend Oreille, Idaho, an area biologists now know never held the species. Instead, that record fish was likely a bull trout (recognized as a distinct species in 1978). Similarly, the Alaska state record for Arctic char had long been a 19-pound Wulik River fish, a river that hosts only Dolly Varden, not Arctic char. Even into the early 1990s, in fact, many biologists classified the Dolly Varden of northern Alaska as Arctic char. Once the Northwest Alaska fish were properly classified, that record "Arctic char" became the world-record Dolly Varden. Since then, even larger fish have been taken from the Wulik, including the current state

TONY WEAVER

record—an immense 27-pound, 4-ounce Dolly Varden. The two species are now clearly separated by biologists in Alaska, even if they're sometimes hard to tell apart, and even if many of the old char-classification arguments still prevail.

The Arctic Char

(Salvelinus alpinus)

Robert J. Behnke writes in his definitive *Trout and Salmon of North America*: "The Arctic char is the most complex and controversial of all North American salmonids." And as that statement portends, even fisheries scientists and anointed char experts can find reason to disagree when the northernmost distributed freshwater fish in North America is the concern. At the least, it can be said that a variety of differences do exist among most Arctic char populations—some even in char that inhabit the same system—in both physical appearance and life history. After that, things are a touch murkier, as the differences are such that no general description of the species is truly possible.

Broadly, Alaska's Arctic char display light-colored spots on a dark body background, the colors or shades of which vary across their range. The back is usually cast in a brownish or olive hue, with the sides lighter and fading to a pale cream-colored or white belly region. As reproduction nears, the spots, belly, and fins of the char take on bright orange, red, or gold coloring. They prefer both lake environments and cold waters.

The char debates, however, usually center on things that can't be seen. Different ideas on species classification come into play when questions of whether variant Arctic char populations should be considered separate species altogether or just subspecies of *Salvelinus arcticus* are considered. Currently, a majority of fisheries scientists recognize a pair of Arctic char subspecies as

BRIAN O'KEEFE

Underwater Dolly Varden.

occurring in Alaska. Fred DeCicco, the ADF&G management biologist for the Northwest Management Area and one of the state's leading char experts, says that it is likely these two subspecies are present in Alaska and that their presence is based on two invasions of the Arctic char into North America, one from the east consisting of char from Europe via Greenland (*Salvelinus alpinus erythrimus*), and one from the west (*Salvelinus alpinus taranetzi* or Taranetz char). DeCicco adds, however, that the two are not well differentiated, with their relative distributions undocumented.

The Dolly Varden
(Salvelinus malma)

Dolly Varden was the name of a character fond of brightly colored, spotted dresses in Charles Dickens's 1841 *Barnaby Rudge*. The first char to receive this name was probably a bull trout, but today the Dolly Varden is the coastal char of Alaska. It exists in two forms in the state, southern and northern. The northern form—or, depending on which biologist you're talking to, subspecies—occurs from both sides of the Alaska Peninsula

north to the Arctic. Some of the Susitna River drainages also contain populations of northern Dolly Varden. The southern form of the Dolly Varden occurs south of the Alaska Peninsula, including drainages on the Kenai Peninsula, along the Southeast Alaska coast, and on Kodiak Island, many islands within the Aleutian chain, and the islands in Southeast large enough to have streams that flow all year, every year.

At one time, it was believed that a population of char known only in headwater areas of the Brooks Range was a full species of its own called Angayukaksurak char. Now, however, it's generally thought that this population is simply a resident Dolly Varden of the northern form. Most of these stocks are confined to their headwaters by falls or other impediments to migration, but across its Alaska range, the Dolly Varden exists as both an anadromous and resident fish, with lake, river, and "dwarf" populations found among the resident stocks. Little is known about the nonmigratory Dollies, other than the fact that at times they don't differ greatly in appearance from the seagoing fish, though they are generally smaller in size.

Sea-run Dolly Varden fresh from their summer travels will be silvery in color with dark green backs and a number of pink to red spots on their sides. As the spawning season approaches, males will turn a shade of brilliant orange or red on their lower body surfaces, with their lower fins turning reddish black with white leading edges. Males also develop an extended kype, and while females show similar changes, the degree of morphology isn't as drastic. By spring the anadromous fish will feature a darker overall coloring, usually green to gray, with the same pale white to red spots, looking basically the same as resident fish do year-round.

As far as differences between the northern and southern form of Dolly Varden, there seem to be none that can be discerned with the naked eye. So far, scientists can only distinguish between the two by counting the number of gill rakers, vertebrae, or chromosomes. Differentiating between Dolly Varden and Arctic char is measurably easier, as the latter generally displays a more blunt head, a narrower base of the tail, and a deeper tail fork. Arctic char can also display larger, less numerous spots. Where the two species' ranges overlap, however, it can sometimes be quite difficult to tell which is which. At these times, biologists again rely on gill raker counts.

Like Arctic char and the other members of the genus *Salvelinus*, Dolly Varden are well adapted to cold-water environments. In fact, excessively warm water has been shown to be lethal to the species, just as with the others (a 1991 study determined that water temperatures of 74 degrees were lethal to Arctic char). Knowing this, it should be easy to see that one of the most significant threats facing Dolly Varden today is the impact of human development on watershed habitat, since young char often utilize small tributary streams for rearing purposes. The Chakok River, a small Anchor River tributary, is a good example. On this small stream and thousands of others like it, overhanging vegetation and riparian forests deflect much of the sun's direct influence, minimizing the warming influence on the water, which can be significant in Alaska's tannic-colored streams. Plant transpiration also buffers the severity of runoff from periods of heavy rainfall. However, when a portion of the natural ecosystem is removed, such as in areas along the Chakok River and many other feeder streams on the southern Kenai Peninsula where extensive logging or development has taken place, water temperature and runoff are expected to fluctuate dramatically, adversely affecting young Dolly Varden populations.

LIFE HISTORIES

Like all members of the genus *Salvelinus*, Dolly Varden and Arctic char spawn in the fall. And even though they sometimes share a watershed in many systems on Kodiak Island or within the drainages north of the Alaska Peninsula, the two species are believed to maintain reproductive isolation through slightly different spawning times and different preferences for spawning sites. Still, because of the difficulty in sometimes distinguishing between the two, and the ongoing confusion in the species' classification, there's not much chance a hybrid would be noticed right away or at all.

In actuality, the simplest manner in which to distinguish the Arctic char from the Dolly Varden in Alaska is by environment and life history, for in the great majority of cases Alaska's Arctic char are a lake-adapted species of freshwater fish, like the lake trout of the genus *Salvelinus*, while Dolly Varden, like brook and bull trout, are much less choosy. In Alaska, sea-run, lake-resident, and stream-resident populations exist for both the northern and southern forms of Dolly Varden, the majority being sea-run. Some anadromous Arctic char populations are also known to exist throughout the species' worldwide range,

Sea-run Dolly Varden.

especially char of the Russian Far East and Arctic Canada, where the fish have shunned their lacustrine tendencies to summer at sea. But as of yet, no sea-run Arctic char populations from Alaska have been documented. As Fred DeCicco notes, that doesn't necessarily mean they don't exist.

"If there are any anadromous Arctic char in Alaska, it's likely they would occur in the Bristol Bay region where they have easy access to lake systems," DeCicco explains. "It's not unreasonable to believe that there may be anadromous populations down there somewhere; they just haven't been documented yet."

The Northwest Alaska biologist also says that a member of the ADF&G office in that area, Brendan Scanlon, had recently conducted tests on the Arctic char of the Becharof Lake region and found evidence of high strontium levels in several otoliths. "This would suggest that [the Arctic char] had spent some time in salt water," DeCicco continues. "Strontium could also be acquired by a diet composed largely of marine-derived items such as salmon eggs or flesh. Whether this would account for the levels found, however, remains unknown."

Even if there were some anadromous Arctic char populations waiting to be discovered, the vast majority of the stocks in Alaska occur as lake-resident fish, where little is known of their actual life histories. After reaching maturity, it's believed the state's Arctic char spawn every other year, usually from August to October, depending on the precise temperature range of a lake. Growth and maximum size vary significantly, too, depending on the productivity of the lake, the competition the char face for forage, and probably genetics. In many areas, an Arctic char of 2 pounds would be a truly large specimen, while other Alaska lakes regularly produce 10-pound fish.

As to Dolly Varden, much more is known about their life histories, which, typical of the genus *Salvelinus*, only seem to lead to more questions. Generally speaking, Dolly Varden exist in stream, lake, and seagoing populations and spawn in streams from mid-August through November. There is no definite distinction between the life histories of northern and southern populations of the species, either, except that in Alaska, southern Dolly Varden are known to utilize lakes widely. That's not the case for the northern form. In fact, in much of the range of the northern Dolly Varden, a good number of the lakes are inhabited by Arctic char. The fact that this northern form of Dolly Varden occurs almost entirely as sea-run or stream-resident populations means the two char species will only rarely encounter one another.

Stream-resident fish, like the Angayukaksurak char, might live their entire lives in a short section of water and are believed to spawn annually, while oceangoing Dolly Varden, especially those of the northern form, enter into reproduction only in alternate years. The anadromous fish typically reside in their home streams for three or four years before undertaking their initial late-spring migration to the sea. From then on, Dolly Varden spend the rest of their lives wintering in fresh water—southern fish in lakes, northern in streams, though neither reach full sexual maturity until after their second summer of ocean feeding. Research indicates that the stream-born southern fish will seek out lakes for overwintering, even if there isn't a lake within their home system. This searching for winter sites after spending a summer feeding at sea is not unique to the southern form of the Dolly Varden, however.

Anadromous Dolly Varden do eventually return to their home streams for reproduction, meaning that distinct stocks remain genetically segregated, but in non-spawning years both the northern and southern forms of the species tend to seek lakes and large or spring-influenced rivers outside their natal watershed for over-wintering purposes. One example is the Dolly Varden

population of the Anchor River. A spawning river for the species, the Anchor is inhabited by both juvenile fish and adults. Sexually mature Dollies return to the Anchor in the late summer or early fall, enter into reproduction anywhere from September through November, and then remain in the stream throughout the winter. In the spring, the adults that have survived, and the juveniles that have reached three or four years of age, will migrate to Cook Inlet. During nonspawning years, many of these fish will not return to the Anchor River, instead using other coastal watersheds for overwintering, probably areas like the English Bay Lakes, Packers Lake, and the Kenai and Kasilof Rivers. When ready to spawn again (or for the first time), Dolly Varden of Anchor River origin will return to the stream. This pattern is consistent throughout most of Southeast Alaska and also for the Dolly Varden of Kodiak Island, where Buskin Lake serves as the primary overwintering site for Dollies from the Buskin, American, and Olds Rivers.

Dolly Varden of the Beaufort Sea area of Alaska's North Slope also return from the sea each winter, avoiding the subzero temperatures of the near-shore marine environment by moving into river sections in the Brooks Range that are near groundwater or spring sources. The springs are probably essential to the survival of the species this far north. Like the southern Dolly Varden of Southeast Alaska, the Kenai Peninsula, and Kodiak Island, the North Slope fish are believed to remain close inshore throughout their marine migrations.

Typically, returning Dolly Varden range from 14 to 18 inches in length, whether of the southern or northern form. Individuals of some populations, like the Kenai River fish, Dollies from some of the Bristol Bay systems, and Kodiak Island char, can reach much larger sizes,

Searching for returning Dollies in Southeast Alaska.

though this may be attributed to the significant sockeye salmon populations of those systems and the subsequently large amounts of freshwater forage available. Still, the largest Dolly Varden are routinely taken from Northwest Alaska, where sockeye stocks are not significant. Dolly Varden from the Kivalina, Wulik, and Noatak River systems can reach maximum sizes in the 15- to 20-pound range, and current research, much of which was conducted by biologist Fred DeCicco, has brought to light some heretofore unknown aspects of the species' life history—specifically, the potential for long migrations.

The three systems each host spawning populations of anadromous Dolly Varden char, which then migrate to the sea for summer feeding. Like the fish of other populations, all of these Dolly Varden return to fresh water for the winter, whether mature or not. In the southern part of their range, most Dolly Varden populations aren't believed to roam more than about 100 circuitous miles and even then never very far offshore. Dollies tagged on

the Seward Peninsula, however, have been recaptured across the Bering Strait in Russia. The Wulik River in Northwest Alaska hosts wintering populations of fish native to the Noatak, Kivalina, Kobuk, and Pilgrim Rivers, as well as Dollies born to the system. Tagged fish from these drainages have also been found in locations near Point Hope, in streams on St. Lawrence Island, and in the Anadyr River in the Russian Far East. This latter locale requires Alaska Dolly Varden to undertake migrations of 1,000 miles or more.

While at sea, both southern- and northern-form Dolly Varden feed opportunistically on large crustaceans and numerous types of small fish. In fresh water, the Dollies tend to be bottom-oriented foragers that prefer invertebrates, mainly insects. In Alaska's numerous salmon streams, however, the Dolly Varden will feed on eggs, flesh, and some juvenile fish, though they're nowhere near the scourge of the stream they were once made out to be. In fact, as biologists like DeCicco will tell you, Dolly Varden feeding on salmon eggs are for the most part just doing their part in the overall ecology of the stream: Most of the eggs they consume are not rooted from incubatory redds but are already dislodged, free-floating eggs that wouldn't survive to hatch anyway.

Fly-Fishing for Alaska's Arctic Char and Dolly Varden

With the surrounding hills and tree-lined river corridors gone twenty different shades of red and orange, the overwhelming grass and underbrush thinned and passable, and the creeks running low and crystal clear, autumn is an ideal season for fly-fishing places like Alaska's Kodiak Island. Steelhead are a popular target for many, and over a dozen streams of the archipelago are known to host fall runs. Anglers can find a deep pool behind a riffle, cast a Glo-Bug or Polar Shrimp, and catch fish after fish. Only,

Anglers search a northern lake for Arctic char.

BRIAN O'KEEFE

chances are the eager fly-eaters won't have a crimson stripe running down their flanks but white, pink, or orange spots and bellies instead. The angler intent on steelhead can go to extreme lengths at these times—a Freight Train, a Skykomish Sunrise, a Dark Spruce—and still find the Dolly Varden willing to chase. As a final act of desperation, the drys might be broken out, or, if one is actually handy, a traditional Spey or Dee pattern. More than likely, this will simply have the effect of making certain nothing but Dollies come calling. Yes, autumn steelhead fishing on Kodiak Island is a great time for char.

All across Alaska, actually, coastal streams will be brimming with pre-spawning Dolly Varden so aggressive that arms will weary and fly boxes be emptied long before the fish go off the bite. It's not always as easy as it can be in some of Kodiak's remote clearwater rivers, but frankly, whether the Dollies are just less fastidious than trout or simply voracious, the fall char fishing is red hot more often than it's not.

Because most of the char encountered in Alaska will be Dolly Varden—and because the great majority of those are sea-run fish—successful fly-fishing begins with understanding the migratory and life history inclinations of the species. Good angling can be had anytime from ice-out to freeze-up, too, though location, tactics, and flies will necessarily change with both season and locality. But once anglers decide when to target them, then where, they can proceed to the how. For Alaska's Dolly Varden, the how is the easiest part.

TIMING

Broadly speaking, anadromous Dolly Varden migrate to the sea from April through early June, with the fishing often good throughout this window in both the migratory streams and the associated beaches near river mouths. In drainages south of the Alaska Peninsula, where the sea-run Dollies are prone to overwintering in lakes, the stream-outlet areas will also present good opportunities during peak migration times. Dolly Varden fly-fishing in Alaska reaches its zenith in the fall, when the large fish return to fresh water, some of them to spawn. In autumn, especially in streams with spawning salmon or those that commonly host both spawning and overwintering fish, fishing can be off the charts. A ready example is the upper Kenai River in Southcentral Alaska, a renowned but still incredibly productive Dolly Varden fishery. Throughout the months of August and September, anglers floating through the Kenai National Wildlife Refuge will find concentrations of fish waiting for loose eggs behind nearly every pair of spawning salmon. Toward the end of September and into October, flesh patterns will become more important, with fish congregating at points where large quantities of drifting eggs and flesh are funneled, such as the area below the Kenai Canyon just before the river empties into Skilak Lake.

Arctic char are available throughout the Alaska fly-fishing season as well. Primarily a stillwater fish, Arctic char will be found in different parts of their lakes and at varying depths during certain times of the year. Thankfully, their movements are largely predictable, dependent as they are on water temperature and the abundance and type of forage. For the most part, spring char can be found closer to the surface, as lake temperatures at this time of year will be largely uniform and

TROY LETHERMAN

Autumn on Kodiak Island features some of the most prolific Dolly Varden fly-fishing to be had anywhere. Here Marcus Weiner displays a typical Saltery River Dolly Varden.

cool. Areas near outlets can be excellent during the early season as well, particularly in the headwater lakes of Bristol Bay, where the fish can home in on groups of out-migrating salmon smolt. During the height of the summer, anglers may have to employ full-sinking lines for char. In lakes that stratify, they'll move to stay in the cooler waters, traveling back to the shallows only in the late evenings and early mornings to feed. In the fall, Arctic char will again be found cruising throughout the lake environment, eating salmon eggs or flesh where available. This is always a great time of year for fly-fishers—whether the still waters they're targeting hold spawning salmon or not—because the char become exceedingly aggressive as they try to build fat reserves for the coming winter.

GEAR FOR DOLLIES AND CHAR

There is little difference between the equipment needed for most of Alaska's trout streams and the gear recommended for the state's Dolly Varden and Arctic char. For most locations, a good 4-weight outfit will be plenty, though when fishing areas known for trophy fish, like the Kenai or, particularly, the Wulik, Noatak, and Kivalina Rivers in Northwest Alaska, a 7- or 8-weight rod will be a much better choice. In areas crammed with spawning salmon, the heavier rods will again be needed, since good presentations often require drifting flies right through the spawning fish. More than once bright-red sockeye have made splinters of a high-priced graphite fly rod after taking an egg pattern meant for the Dollies holding just a few feet downstream.

While both Dollies and Arctic char can be brought to the top by an inviting dry-fly presentation, the great majority of the fly-fishing for the two species will take place beneath the surface. This often means sinking lines. For stream angling, a short sinking tip will cover most situations, though when nymphing or utilizing an egg pattern, most anglers prefer weight-forward floating lines and, when necessary, split shot. For lakes, a couple of density-compensated full-sinking lines will stand fly-fishers in good stead. In particular, a Type III and Type V line will handle the bulk of the workload.

Leaders need not be long for char: the standard 4 to 6 feet for most subsurface presentations and 7½ to 9 feet for dry-fly applications. When fishing eggs on rivers like the Kenai, the leader formula will be identical to the nymphing leader for rainbow trout: 9 to 10 feet of tapered monofilament, hand-tied to the same specifications.

DOLLY VARDEN AND ARCTIC CHAR FLIES

After studying their life histories, their habits, and their preferences, it is perhaps predictable that effective flies for Arctic char and Dolly Varden hardly differ at all from the favored patterns of Alaska's rainbow trout anglers. Egg patterns, flesh flies, traditional trout nymphs, like the Gold-Ribbed Hare's Ear and the Pheasant Tail Nymph, and to a lesser extent sculpins and leeches, all produce as well when fishing for Dolly Varden as they do for the rainbows that often haunt the same watersheds. The major difference, of course, comes when targeting Dollies in the salt, with small baitfish and shrimp patterns particularly successful.

For Arctic char in lakes, the best patterns are usually predicated on the time of year. Smolt and other baitfish patterns will draw the most interest during the spring smolt out-migration, while summer is the time to imitate the various stages of aquatic insects common to the stillwater environment. Streamers, which are equally effective for Arctic char and Dolly Varden in both lake and stream, should be carried throughout the season and fished deep. Woolly Worms, Woolly Buggers, Muddlers and other sculpin patterns, and leech imitations are common favorites. During the fall when the salmon have begun to deteriorate, flies should include flesh colors.

Streamers tied in oranges, pink, and whites, such as the Polar Shrimp and the Battle Creek, have long proven themselves as top char patterns.

Hook sizes for Arctic char and Dolly Varden fly-fishing tend to run small by Alaska trout standards, with sizes between 6 and 10 the most common. Also in regard to size, Dolly Varden keyed in on the egg drop tend to be more discerning when it comes to the size of the egg rather than the color. Dollies in relatively heavily fished areas like the upper Kenai and the Kodiak road zone streams have been known to consistently reject 8mm beads in favor of the 6mm versions, while still chasing four different shades of pink.

ANGLING STRATEGIES

In a lot of ways, everything that anglers need to know about fly-fishing for Dolly Varden was already covered in the rainbow trout chapter. After you figure out their migratory patterns and can predict with relative consistency the times they'll be available in the stream, any

From midsummer on, Dollies can't resist a well-presented egg imitation.

BRIAN O'KEEFE

standard trout technique will produce at least as well with char. In Alaska, this is never more true than in the fall, when all things wild—and especially rainbow trout, Dolly Varden, and Arctic char—turn their concentration to the Pacific salmon returns. Fly-fishing the upper Kenai after the sockeye have reached the spawning beds serves as a perfect example. Anglers will float the river, most drifting bead eggs, with every strike a question mark until the fish makes its first run and defines itself as either trout or char.

If the salmon are indeed in and spawning has commenced on the Kenai and the thousands of other streams in Alaska that are home to both Dollies and salmon, hold-ing in downstream pools—it's almost scripture in the Last Frontier. Nymphing tactics tend to work best on these occasions, though especially in areas where the fish see little pressure, anglers can do nearly as well when swinging streamers as they can with egg patterns. In rivers where the Dollies might be a touch more sophisti-cated, they're known to sometimes show preferences. For instance, one day—or one hour—the fish might like the dead drift or a steady swing, while the next they won't budge until a fly begins to be pulled toward the surface on the retrieve. At other times, anglers will notice that nearly every take is coming as the line straightens downstream at the end of the swing. The key

On one end of the spectrum, anglers can fish for sea-run Dollies amid the natural beauty of Tongass National Forest.

BRIAN O'KEEFE

then is to vary tactics when fish are present but the bite is off. Most likely, the fly is the last thing that needs to be changed.

Most fly-fishing techniques for Alaska's Arctic char are different from those previously discussed, primarily because of the species' nearly universal lake distribution. In fact, other than when intercepting char positioned for the smolt out-migration, the skills needed are of an entirely different sort than the ones used for taking trout, salmon, and char in flowing water. What hasn't changed is the need to first find the fish. Some of the lakes in Alaska that hold char can be intimidating in their size, and for anglers more comfortable on a freestone stream, the lack of readable seams and current breaks might be frustrating at first. Nonetheless, fish will typically be found in certain locations at definite times, and lacking experience on a particular body of water, anglers can learn these patterns and apply them in their fishing.

First of all, the best indicator of fish is the presence of significant hatches. While Arctic char won't be seen breaking the water's surface with the frequency of, say, grayling, that certainly doesn't mean they're not in the area. Especially early in a hatch, or if the adult insects are coming off only sporadically, char will concentrate a great percentage of their feeding attention on the emerging nymphs headed for the surface. To fish nymphs effectively in a lot of stillwater scenarios, fly-fishers can use floating lines and long, 12- to 15-foot leaders. Retrieves should be kept short, varying between ultraslow hand-twist presentations and foot-long strips. In a few of the alpine lakes in the Arctic char's northern range, an effective combination can be a hand-twist retrieve coupled with a size 18 through 22 chironomid pattern. Of course, it should go without saying that by far the best, if not the only, opportunities for raising char to a lake's surface occur during the best hatches. Often, the best technique to employ as insects are coming off or spent

adults are falling back to the surface is the well-documented heave-and-leave presentation, with the angler only responsible for keeping enough slack out of the fly line to maintain a direct connection to the fly.

If a hatch is in progress somewhere on a lake, chances are that it's occurring in the shallows. Rocky points, silt-bottomed coves, and areas with plenty of vegetation or submerged structure hold potential for aquatic insect life, and stillwater anglers would be well advised to look for these areas when prospecting for fish on unfamiliar water. Even if nothing's happening at the moment, checking back in the evening will sometimes land fly-fishers in the middle of an intense feed. Without the obvious signs of a hatch, of course, the char can be more difficult to locate. On windy days, one of the most productive areas of a lake will be in isolated coves or to the lee side of points. In both areas, the wind will drive debris into discernible accumulations, where char will often be found beneath the surface feeding on the insect life and baitfish below the debris.

When water temperatures are relatively uniform throughout a lake and the char aren't keying on a definable event (a hatch, the smolt out-migration, or the like) or driven to predictable locations by conditions, prospecting becomes, well, prospecting. Anglers heading to new water should expect this type of scenario and be prepared with full-sinking lines and an array of streamers. Often bead-chain or barbell eyes will be added to

On the other hand, fly-fishers can chase Dollies and Arctic char into some of the wildest regions of the Far North.

ABOVE: *Aniak, Alaska: hub to the prolific fisheries of the lower Kuskokwim River system.*

FAR RIGHT: *An aerial view of the upper Kenai River, one of the state's best Dolly Varden fisheries.*

searching patterns for these stillwater situations. One tactic for fly-fishers to employ under the circumstances is to isolate a section of water and then systematically make casts in a pattern designed to cover as much of the water as possible before moving on to another section. And since many of the lakes within the Arctic char's range in Alaska don't stratify completely, the fish can generally be found feeding throughout the water column. Thus, thoroughly dissecting a piece of water will also include fishing at different depths, which is commonly accomplished by using the countdown method after completing a cast and before beginning the retrieve.

Arctic Char and Dolly Varden in Alaska

While anglers might not be terribly worried about whether the fish they're catching are Arctic char or Dolly Varden, the answer can usually be found by simply taking note of where the fishing is taking place. For the most

part, Dolly Varden are more stream-oriented in Alaska, and Arctic char are far more prone to inhabit lakes. There are plenty of exceptions, though, especially south of the Alaska Peninsula, where Dolly Varden are known to overwinter in lakes a great deal of the time. But then again, very few Arctic char populations exist within that range anyway.

Generally, Arctic char can be found in the headwater and foothill lakes of the Brooks Range, in some lakes in the upper Kobuk watershed—most notably Walker and Selby Lakes—in some lakes in the Kigluaik Mountains north of Nome, and within a small area of the Interior in Denali National Park. Arctic char are also distributed in many of the lakes in the Kuskokwim Mountains, where exceptional fly-fishing destinations like the Kisaralik, Aniak, Kwethluk, and Kanektok Rivers get their starts, as well as in lakes within the Goodnews and Togiak systems. The many headwater lakes of Bristol Bay also host populations, as do a few Kenai Peninsula lakes and several bodies of water on Kodiak Island. Arctic char are also resident to lakes on the Alaska Peninsula at least as far south as Lower and Upper Ugashik Lake.

Throughout much of that geographic range, Dolly Varden occur as well, though it's believed the two rarely intersect. For example, both Dolly Varden and Arctic char are present in waters of the North Slope, but the Arctic char occur only in lakes of the coastal plain and foothills and a few mountain waters like Galbraith, Chandler, Itkillik, and Elusive Lakes, while the region's Dolly Varden are found mainly in freshwater streams from the Colville River eastward. Most of the North Slope Dolly Varden are anadromous, though a few systems do host both sea-run and stream-resident forms, the Kongakut River of the Arctic National Wildlife Refuge being a prime instance.

To the west lie Kotzebue Sound and the Chukchi Sea. Some of the largest Dolly Varden in North America are caught every year in the large Northwest Alaska rivers that terminate there, even though the region's remote character prevents a great deal of visitation. There are three primary char populations in the area, belonging to the Kivalina, Wulik, and Noatak River drainages. The Wulik River, while supporting its own spawning population, is more important as a major overwintering location for nonspawning Dolly Varden. During ADF&G aerial surveys, which have been known to consistently produce numbers on the low end of the actual population total, over ninety thousand Dolly Varden are generally counted overwintering in the Wulik.

These sea-run char normally begin entering the Wulik during the second or third week of August and are well distributed throughout the river by the beginning of September. Significant numbers of anadromous Dolly Varden also utilize the 400-mile-long Noatak River for both spawning and overwintering. The Noatak, draining an area of approximately 12,600 square miles, is one of the largest watersheds in North America left relatively unaffected by any human development, and its Dolly Varden, while among the world's largest, receive relatively light fishing effort. The river begins on Mount Igikpak and meanders through treeless alpine tundra, two canyons (the Grand Canyon of the Noatak is approximately 65 miles long), and the rolling Igichuk Hills before spilling onto the coastal flats near Kotzebue Sound. The entire route remains above the Arctic Circle, and anglers can usually find a few extra hours of sunlight to pursue the late-summer-arriving Dollies. Fishing in any one of these three systems can be good just after ice-out, too, when the char will be preparing to return to the sea. In the Noatak River especially, small fry patterns can be used to great success, as the river is also home to a large chum salmon population.

Moving south, fly-fishers will encounter strong populations of Dolly Varden all along the western coast of

TONY WEAVER

Alaska, from trophy specimens on Nunivak Island to prolific numbers of small char in the upper Togiak River. Almost any stream that receives a run of salmon will also host Dolly Varden, with good concentrations found downstream from the spawning beds as the summer progresses. Many of these Southwest Alaska streams are best accessed by floating, and a lot of times fly-fishers will encounter Dolly Varden miles (sometimes days) before the first returning salmon or the best congregations of rainbow trout begin to appear. There will still be plenty of char in the middle and lower river sections, and, depending on the time of year, probably even more. Since both species' late-summer to fall feeding revolves around the same source—spawning salmon—rainbow trout and Dolly Varden will be found in similar locations by fly-anglers. In fact, there's little doubt more Dolly Varden are caught in Southwest Alaska than any other species.

Some rivers of the region, though, are just Dolly Varden streams. No one has offered a substantive answer as to why, but in some cases strong populations of Dolly Varden will exist in streams only a few miles away from trophy-trout rivers of legendary proportions, and yet these streams might have only a few, if any, rainbows. A textbook example is Margot Creek, a Naknek Lake feeder stream located just over 5 miles from the Brooks River. And while Brooks is famous, few have heard of Margot Creek, probably because the Dollies are abundant and the trout scarce. Also, many of the small, intimate streams that flow into Lake Iliamna will have plenty of voracious Dolly Varden stacked up behind the spawning sockeye but none of the rainbows that have made the lake and its tributaries famous the world over. For fly-fishers looking to escape the Bristol Bay lodge crowds while still enjoying the region's prolific angling, setting aside a day to prospect any one of these often gin-clear streams can be well worth it.

Throughout Southwest Alaska, Dollies can best be targeted in early June near stream mouths or lake outlets, where they'll congregate in an attempt to ambush alevins headed for rearing lakes and the out-migrating smolt. Later in the year, the arrival of the first waves of sockeye will push the char upriver, though they'll retreat to holding positions behind the salmon once the eggs start to drop. In the fall, the fish will remain in lower river sections, feasting on the flesh and eggs drifting downstream.

There are a few quality Dolly Varden fisheries in Southcentral Alaska as well, the most popular occuring on the Kenai Peninsula. Quartz Creek, a small pocket fishery that flows alongside the Sterling Highway to where the creek meets Kenai Lake, is a popular stop-off or day trip for peninsula-bound anglers. Better known for numbers rather than the size of its fish, Quartz Creek generally doesn't begin fishing well until July nears a close and significant numbers of sockeye have begun to spawn. The fishery stays strong through September, when the fish duck back into Kenai Lake for the winter. While a few of the other streams of the peninsula harbor good char fishing at times—the Russian, Anchor, and Swanson Rivers among them—none can match the mainstem Kenai for numbers or the size of the fish. While Dollies weighing over 5 pounds aren't at all uncommon on the river, smaller 16- to 20-inch fish can be caught with a scary efficiency.

Throughout a few other areas of coastal Alaska, namely the Alaska Peninsula and Aleutian Islands, Kodiak Island, and along the southeastern panhandle, fly-fishing prospects for sea-run Dolly Varden are even more bountiful than in the other regions. For Kodiak and Southeast, it wouldn't be too much to say that literally every stream that holds a fish population will at one time or another hold Dolly Varden as well. Anglers fishing Kodiak in the autumn will find Dollies everywhere they go—regardless of what they're fishing for. In the small coastal streams of Southeast, the sea-run char will begin to return a little later than much the rest of Alaska, primarily because of the warmer water temperatures. River systems with headwater lakes are the best place to begin the search, as nearly all of them will host overwintering populations. Also in Southeast, the saltwater angler will find plenty of opportunities to cast shrimp and streamer patterns at schools of fish feeding near the surface.

FAR LEFT: *The upper Kenai River is home to a thriving population of Dolly Varden.*

Middle Kenai River Dolly Varden.

Overlooking the
Kukaklek River
rapids.

TONY WEAVER

grayling

FLY-FISHERS TRAVELING to the forty-ninth state
for the first time might be a little dismayed to find the delicate
techniques perfected upon their Lower Forty-eight fishing
grounds so out of place, especially those who are accustomed to
stalking spooky trout with soft, supple leaders and flies that
actually look like something found in the stream. And anyone
with a penchant for picking up emerging bugs and muttering
their Latin names will find that skill more than a little super-
fluous. For only rarely will Alaska anglers find a situation ideal
enough to lure a bright-bodied salmon to the top. Even the rainbow trout, such an eager and aggressive surface feeder in so
much of its range, finds more sustenance than it needs while
holding to the depths of the stream. To many, the Last Frontier
is a land of split shot and weighted flies, with casting that's usually anything but artful. For the dry-fly aficionado, however,
one Alaska game fish will almost never disappoint.

The Arctic grayling, a member of no one's "Big Three," can

nonetheless seem a salvation to fly-fishers wearied of casting sinking lines and flies only slightly less bulky than a full-grown hummingbird. After months of dredging egg and flesh imitations, forced to ignore every insect that isn't intent on sucking a gallon of blood from their arms, a lot of fly-fishers just might look forward to a fish that's looking *up* to feed. And while never to be confused with a bug soup like the Henrys Fork, a lot of Alaska's clean-flowing freestone rivers enjoy quite prolific hatches. Seeing caddis popping off one of the state's remote freestone streams isn't the kind of blockbuster event a salmonfly hatch might be on Montana's Big Hole or Madison, but for many anglers it's just what the good doctor ordered.

Grayling translucence.

The Arctic Grayling
(Thymallus arcticus)

In comparison to the other subfamilies of the family Salmonidae, the subfamily Thymallinae is hardly diverse, containing one genus—*Thymallus*—and four species. One of those species is Alaska's Arctic grayling. Another is widely distributed in Northern Europe, while the remaining two are restricted to Asia.

Much like lake trout, the Arctic grayling has been historically limited in its distribution because of a low tolerance for salt water. The species exists naturally throughout most of Alaska and northwestern Canada, its range stretching east to Hudson Bay. Except for a small population in the Stikine River, however, no grayling occur in coastal drainages of Southeast Alaska and British Columbia. Wild stocks also call the headwaters of the Missouri River in Montana home. After a brief geographic separation, the species' range runs uninterrupted from central Alberta north to the Arctic. In Montana, the grayling lives at the extreme southernmost limits of its natural range.

Without a doubt, the most distinctive characteristic of Arctic grayling is the large, sail-shaped dorsal fin that has come to signify the fish for so many. Otherwise, even the most general scrutiny would reveal that the species' appearance more closely resembles coregonids like whitefish and cisco than any of the trout or salmon. Alaska's Arctic grayling have small mouths, tiny teeth, large scales, and a deeply forked tail. Their body coloration can range from iridescent blue to gunmetal gray, with large, angular spots appearing toward the heads of most fish. The dorsal fins feature irregular rows of light pink or almost white-to-lilac spots and red-to-orange

TYSON O'CONNEL

edges. Occasionally, a population of grayling in Alaska will vary slightly in color; some have no spots on their bodies, while others might show body shades of deeper or lighter hues.

Though an opportunistic feeder like most salmon, trout, and char, the Arctic grayling is chiefly an insectivore, for the most part feeding on aquatic and terrestrial insects on or near the water's surface in both streams and the shallow areas of lakes. Alaska populations sharing watersheds with the state's anadromous salmon species will also eagerly devour both the eggs and the juvenile salmon that eventually wiggle free of the substrate. And grayling eat all the time. Still, even with the most abundant sources of food, they rarely reach anything most would consider great size for a game fish. Studies have shown that a 12-inch fish might already have reached five or six years of age, while a 19-inch trophy grayling is probably ten years old or even older. The world record, taken from the Katseyedie River near Great Bear Lake, Canada, was a 5-pound, 15-ounce specimen. In other northern waters, where grayling frequently live upward of a decade, most reach a maximum size of about 24 inches and 4 pounds.

LIFE HISTORY

Having adapted to survive in the some of the harshest Arctic environments, the grayling presents fairly unusual life history patterns. Stocks hailing from significantly different watersheds will vary from each other, too. For example, some stocks in Alaska use three different streams throughout an average year, one each for spawning, feeding, and overwintering. On the other hand, another population of grayling might not exit a short section of water throughout their entire lives. In general, however, the Arctic grayling in Alaska is a fish that travels a great deal, migrating as far as 100 miles to upstream spawning grounds in the early spring, and then, depending on the water temperature, commencing with reproductive activities sometime in the period between late April and early June.

Much of the research that has been done suggests that grayling return as adults to the locations where they first emerged to spawn. Thus, spawning groups of Arctic grayling are assumed to be somewhat genetically distinct. In Alaska, studies done on the grayling of the glacial Tanana River drainage have shown that approximately 97.5 percent of the fish in different spawning groups (those spawning in the Goodpaster, Caribou, and Volkmar Rivers) were native to that stream. Likewise, recent radio telemetry projects conducted by ADF&G biologists on the grayling stocks of the Jim River (an unsilted, rapid runoff stream near the Dalton Highway) have turned up several separate spawning stocks. During mid-May and early June, spring-spawning populations were found in two places on the Jim River (one a lower reach of the stream and the other upstream near the headwaters), in the South Fork Koyukuk River, in portions of Fish Creek (a tributary to the South Fork Koyukuk), as well as in Prospect Creek. Jim River grayling are also known to have spawned in the outlet of Grayling Lake and in Grayling Creek, both extensions of the greater Jim River watershed.

In water temperatures nearing 50 degrees, grayling develop rapidly, hatching after only eleven to twenty-one

BRIAN O'KEEFE

The grayling's dorsal fin is its most unusual feature.

days. The young usually begin feeding in about three or four days, with all juveniles actively feeding by the eighth day after hatching. This rapid early development is what allows the species to spawn successfully in shallow lakes and small tributary streams that may only flow during the five or six weeks of spring high-water events. However, growth rates subside almost immediately for most populations of grayling.

Interestingly enough, the stocks of the Seward Peninsula, which have produced some of Alaska's largest fish on average, are actually representative of the slow-growing nature of the Arctic grayling, though that wasn't always believed to be the case. For many years, based on the minuscule amounts of evidence available, biologists thought Seward Peninsula grayling populations were structured much the same as interior Alaska stocks. It was believed these fish lived an average of ten to twelve years, and that—because of the great sizes they were known to achieve—they simply grew much faster than the grayling of the Kuskokwim River basin or Interior stocks. Since then, it's been determined that two primary factors account for the proportionately larger sizes attained by Seward Peninsula fish. First, they seem to grow very rapidly up to the age of six or seven, in part due to the presence of large returns of pink salmon to the area, as the eggs, flesh, and fry become a viable food source for the grayling. Also, the aquatic insects of the area benefit greatly from the increase in stream productivity brought by the salmon. This hasty growth slows after the fish reach maturity, for they then spawn annually and channel most of their energy into reproduction. The second factor now known that helps to account for the large size of Seward Peninsula Arctic grayling is their long life span. Populations of grayling in the area have been aged at over twenty years, with the oldest known specimen a thirty-one-year-old fish from the Eldorado River near Nome.

Following spawning, the adult grayling migrate to either upstream areas of the same drainage or to a new watershed completely and take up relatively permanent residence in the pools where they'll feed throughout the summer. Primarily visual feeders, grayling prefer to hold in clear-flowing rivers where they can easily see their prey, which consists primarily of the larval, pupal, and adult forms of midges and caddis, stoneflies, and mayflies. They will feed mostly in mid-depths or on the surface, only seriously directing their attention to a stream's bottom during the fall when benthic drift is much reduced. Within a feeding lane or pool, Arctic grayling will establish a rigid territorial hierarchy, maintained during the season through a series of almost ceremonial challenge displays. The larger fish will occupy the most advantageous feeding positions, generally near the head of the pool, with smaller and weaker grayling relegated to subordinate positions and the weakest fish of all banished to the foot of the lane.

In approximately mid-September, with the onset of falling temperatures, the grayling will leave their smaller tributary feeding positions and head downstream. While

RIGHT: *A pair of Agulowak River grayling.*

FAR RIGHT: *Other than work, grayling are one of the few things float-trip anglers can always count on.*

a few apparently remain in deep pools within the clear-water tributaries, most spawning populations will migrate to either lakes or the lower, deeper reaches of good-sized rivers like the Chena and Gulkana, or to large, glacial streams like the Tanana, Susitna, and the Yukon.

Fly-Fishing for Alaska's Grayling

Grayling will strike dry flies more readily and more consistently than any other fish present in Great Land waters. Even more than the sail fin, this trait makes them special. To be sure, there are occasions when the fish can become selective, and during an especially prolific hatch it might seem impossible to get your fly noticed, but these instances aren't that common. Instead, anglers who've picked a good spot at the right time can realistically expect to be spoiled by the number of fish they'll catch.

This propensity for receptiveness—combined with the grayling's relatively smaller, more manageable sizes—makes them a great fish for the beginning fly-angler. Young or inexperienced hands will be able to learn the basics of fly-fishing, including casting, some streamside entomology, how to make both topwater and subsurface presentations, and how to fight and land a fly-caught fish, before that really becomes a difficult proposition.

Many prize the grayling as a game fish in Alaska for additional reasons, of course. One, they're an undeniably beautiful fish, and in some populations a close look will reveal an entire rainbow of colors present near the gill plates. They're also a species that inhabits some of the state's loneliest and most spectacular destinations, especially those of the Far North. For many, grayling are the perfect excuse to make a float through the still pristine Arctic National Wildlife Refuge or to arrange the arduous

BRIAN O'KEEFE

BRIAN O'KEEFE

RICHARD JOHNSON

Some populations of grayling display exquisite coloring.

logistics for an Arctic coastal plain excursion. And last but certainly not least, a good number of anglers hold a special affection for the Arctic grayling simply because the species has rescued so many trips from the doldrums of bad weather and fishless days. Not a year goes by, in fact, when wilderness floaters don't arrive at the river after twelve months or more of planning only to find the salmon still at sea and the trout dispersed into the farthest reaches of unnavigable tributaries. Luckily, in times like these, it seems the grayling are always around, and always willing to rise to a fly.

Timing

Because they hardly eat during the winter and then spawn almost immediately in the spring, Arctic grayling must feed ravenously throughout the summer and fall to build up substantial fat reserves. Hence, given proper knowledge of the species' migratory habits, excellent angling opportunities exist on almost any day of the year from ice-out until freeze-up.

Although seasonal timing is not as important for the grayling fly-fisher, there are still preferred times of the year, and fishing methods will differ from season to season and area to area. Just after ice-out, fly-fishers targeting spawning congregations can have nonstop action. Even before the ice has completely left a clearwater stream, in fact, grayling will be concentrated near the mouth, awaiting an opportunity to ascend to their spawning grounds. In many areas, there can be thousands of fish in a short section of water. Small size 8 or 10 streamers work well during this early time of the year, especially those that imitate juvenile salmon in watersheds that also contain out-migrating smolt. And even though there usually won't be much insect activity during the early Alaska spring, general attractor patterns like Humpies and Royal Wulffs skated across the surface can bring good results.

Late June through early August present anglers with the most sunlight of the Alaska year. It's also the time of greatest insect activity on the streams of the state. After spawning, grayling will migrate to their summer feeding grounds, usually in small clearwater streams or springs near the headwaters of large river systems. And although Alaska's hatches can be sporadic, depending greatly on relative humidity and temperatures, anglers will encounter the very best dry-fly fishing of the year during these few months, especially in the evenings. Grayling do not, however, take the heat well. They'll generally flee areas where the additional sunlight and the nature of the streams combine to substantially increase water temperatures. Good spots to begin looking for summer congregations of fish are near the outlets and tributary streams of clear alpine lakes and in the inland waters of the Interior, Northwest, and Arctic. In many watersheds of these regions, it can be truly difficult to find any clear-flowing water without at least a few fish present.

Probably the best time to tangle with grayling, though, is the early fall, from September through October in most areas. The fish will be in prime shape, especially in systems where they've had a chance to feed on salmon eggs, and with the falling temperatures they'll be very aggressive toward almost any fly drifted in their vicinity. Nymphs and wet flies will generate fast and furious action, and in the right drainages egg imitations can be deadly. Historically, the week before freeze-up is even better, as grayling become reckless feeders the closer to winter the year moves.

The fish are usually highly concentrated again before freeze-up, as by October they will have begun migrating back toward their overwintering areas, mostly lower stream sections with deep water. There is still some chance of encountering surface activity during the warmer parts of the day, too, but again, nymphs, wet flies, and subsurface streamer presentations will undoubtedly garner the most strikes. In lakes, the areas near shorelines will be most productive during the early

Ugashik: the great trophy-grayling locale.

BRIAN O'KEEFE

morning and evening, as the grayling move in toward the generally greater insect activity that takes place near lake margins during these times of day.

GEAR FOR GRAYLING

Gearing up for grayling is probably as minimalist as it gets for Alaska angling. Knowing that the fish in question aren't apt to snap rod tips with a flick of the head or bust tippets and make fools of knot-tiers can actually be quite comforting. In fact, other than bottom snags, the most frequent break-offs encountered when fly-fishing for grayling will be initiated by anglers who've accidentally hooked a spawning salmon. In fact, a lot of salmon in the stream may predicate using a larger rod. Along those same lines, much of the state's best grayling water can also hold trophy-sized Arctic char, Dolly Varden, and rainbow trout. And no one wants to be fishing a 2-weight rod with 7X tippet when a 30-inch trout decides to strike.

For rods, most fly-anglers will pursue grayling with a 4- or 5-weight outfit, though in the right conditions—perhaps when grayling are the only species present in an area—a 2- or 3-weight rod will more than suffice. The fish are rarely leader-shy, so dry-fly leaders need not be constructed as long as they would be for species of trout. Usually a 7-foot leader with 4X to 7X tippet is fine. If nymphing with sinking tips, 4 to 6 feet of leader is plenty. Most of the time, however, fly-anglers will be fishing for grayling on top, and when that's the case, any weight-forward floating line that matches the rod and conditions will work.

FLIES FOR ALASKA'S GRAYLING

As is the case with Deschutes River redsides and west slope cutts in Idaho's Kelly Creek and the rest of the world's trout, Arctic grayling are usually feeding randomly, not selectively. That is, the fish are looking to take pretty much anything available. The intensity of this feeding will vary throughout the day, depending on changes in light or temperature and the amount of food available. Since mornings and evenings usually coincide with periods of the greatest insect activity, finding randomly feeding fish is also more likely to happen around these times of day. When found, a fly that exhibits the general shape of many types of insects and looks alive in the water will probably produce best. And though most fly-fishers refer to these types of patterns as searching flies, that doesn't mean they look nothing like what's to be found in nature. On the contrary, the most productive and widely used searching patterns at least loosely mimic a natural food form.

Probably the most famous searching dry fly for rough water is the Royal Wulff, which approximates the shape of a mayfly fairly accurately. Likewise, an Adams is always a favorite searching pattern, on any kind of water, rippled or glassy smooth. Originally tied to resemble a caddisfly with its wings whirring, the Adams is the only searching fly a lot of anglers carry; it can also look a lot like a mayfly dun or even a tight group of gray midges. Another versatile pattern to have along is the Humpy, as buggy as a searching fly can get. With a body of simple thread construction, the Humpy can be used to meet a wide variety of circumstances by simply changing the color of the thread.

Selectively feeding fish will often refuse general imitations, however, since they'll be keyed in to and eating only one type food, even though other forms of nourishment may be readily available. These situations occur much less frequently, especially with grayling, but anglers should be prepared with a few more imitative patterns just in case. Because grayling tend to be less discriminating eaters than most western trout, strict imitations like no-hackle duns or Compara-Duns are usually not necessary. A pattern that nails a few of the specific

BRIAN O'KEEFE

Grayling.

traits that selectively feeding fish may clue in on—such as size, color, the action of the material, and the shape of the silhouette—will usually work just fine. Toward that end, the Elk Hair Caddis, which is a famous searching pattern as well, will imitate most hatches of lightly colored caddisflies to near perfection.

With subsurface flies, precise imitation is needed much less frequently than when fishing on top. The Gold-Ribbed Hare's Ear Nymph is a fantastic all-around choice, as it resembles an abundance of natural nymphs, larvae, and pupae. The Pheasant Tail Nymph works equally well in a wide variety of situations in Alaska. Even patterns like the Olive Beadhead Nymph, which closely resembles *Callibaetis* mayfly naturals right before emergence, can be fished with much success for grayling, even when no mayflies appear to be around. If fishing for deep-holding, hopefully larger grayling, dark-colored

Woolly Buggers and sculpin patterns like the Muddler Minnow will also produce well.

Despite the grayling's propensity for feeding on various stages of insect life, any fly-fisher who happens along one of the state's thousands of salmon streams absolutely must have some type of egg or egg-colored pattern available. The grayling certainly isn't the egg-gorger the rainbow trout can be. In Southwest streams particularly, during the summer falling-off period when the rainbows begin to follow the salmon toward their spawning beds, most grayling will actually remain in the feeding lanes they took up after spawning, content to continue with their insects. Not that they'll decline a high-protein salmon egg, though. In most salmon rivers, such as the upper Chena in interior Alaska, grayling will simply feed on a combination of flesh, eggs, biological drift, and emerging insects. For this reason, at least one hybrid

grayling | 225

pattern has been developed and deployed to much success in some streams: the Salcha Pink, a combination egg and traditional hackled fly.

There is typically no need to go to such derivative lengths, however. In truth, trout anglers from the Catskills to the Oregon coast could probably bring their present box of drys and nymphs to Alaska and find the state's grayling willing eaters. While they might show a strong preference for size, these fish rarely feed selectively on a particular insect, probably because the weather in the Last Frontier precludes the type of regular, clock-setting superhatch that gets fly-fishers from the Lower Forty-eight all excited. Consequently, the variety of suggestion afforded by searching patterns is the way to go for the broadest number of watersheds. To simplify matters, an angler can choose a set of flies based on size, form, and color—in that order. Both an array of

nymphs and dry flies should be selected, some of darker hues and a second group more subtly colored, each stocked in sizes from 12 to 20. Don't forget to add a few more fully tied rough-water patterns, as well as some sparse flies for stillwater situations. Throw in some streamers, including smolt imitations up to size 4 if fishing a drainage with salmon returns, and finish the box with egg patterns like the Iliamna Pinkie or Glo-Bug. The resulting collection of flies should cover every base, whether fishing for grayling feeding on midges in the high Arctic or the egg-chomping fall fish of the Ugashik system in Southwest.

ANGLING STRATEGIES

Where Arctic grayling can be found in Alaska, they can found in numbers. And for the well-prepared fly-fisher who totes along an understanding of the species' habits

FAR RIGHT: *Grayling are available in lakes in all seasons.*

BELOW: *Grayling are Alaska's most consistent lake quarry.*

and behavior, especially how those may differ in a range of weather and water conditions, they can be caught with an almost easy efficiency.

Knowing that grayling prefer to see their food well before committing, focus on presenting the fly in a manner that appears as natural as possible. Of course, the most realistic creation, drifted in the most tantalizing manner, won't draw so much as a second glance if there are no grayling around to see it. As with fly-fishing for any species, anglers must be able to find fish before they can catch them. That all starts by knowing where to look.

At the right time of day, of course, anglers' tasks can be made much simpler by spotting and casting to rise-forms during a hatch. However, when no dimpling can be readily observed, fly-fishers can fall back on their water-reading skills to find fish. Arctic grayling will spend most of the open-water season holding within the obvious feeding lanes of a stream—seams between fast and slower current, slicks in the middle of riffles, and behind rocks or other obstructions that will funnel food into narrow chutes of water. The grayling will stack up in these feeding lanes, the largest fish toward the head of the run. If significant surface activity isn't taking place, the larger fish will also tend to hug the bottom, with the smaller grayling more apt to feed in the stream's middle depths. During the summer months, when insect activity is peaking, feeding primarily occurs at or near the surface in pools or runs with moderate to strong flows, preferred for the greater amount of forage contained in the drift. In turbid or muskeg-stained water, most fish will spend their time in deeper and slower flows than usual.

Not all Arctic grayling stick to clearwater rivers during the summer feeding months, either; several noteworthy populations occur in ponds and lakes. In these stillwater situations, which are frequent in the alpine lakes of the Kenai Peninsula and the Swan Lake/Swanson River drainage of the same region, look for fish congre-

gating near outlets and the mouths of tributary streams. Areas with sand and silt bottoms are better for grayling as well, since gravel bottoms tend to be devoid of the species' preferred forage.

In Alaska, that forage tends to comprise insects. Within the state, the four categories of hatches familiar to western U.S. fly-anglers can all be found—mayflies, caddisflies, stoneflies, and midges. Damsels and dragonflies are also common to the state, and in certain areas can become an important component of the grayling's diet. Still, with the exception of the few watersheds with bountiful pink or sockeye salmon populations, like the Ugashik Lake system or the streams of the Seward Peninsula, the heaviest lifting is done by midges, mayflies, and caddisflies.

The most prolific insects in Alaska hail from the order Diptera and occur in just about every lake, stream, river, bog, and swamp in the state. Diptera is the order of the true flies, and despite extreme diversity within the order, most of its species are terrestrial and of no importance to anglers as larvae, only as adults when they end up on the water's surface. Two families in particular, though, are of tremendous importance to Alaska's grayling fly-fishers: Chironomidae and Culicidae, or midges and mosquitoes.

There are over a thousand species of chironomids in North America, and though they're often underestimated because of their small size, midges are an important food source in all of their life stages. In some lakes and streams of the Arctic, in fact, chironomids can make up over 90 percent of the grayling's diet. The larvae (imitated well by the Blood Worm in sizes 14 through 22, Barr's Pure Midge in 18 through 20, and many other segmented tubelike flies) can consistently be found drifting in stream currents or near the bottom of shoreline areas in lakes. When not undulating through open water, the larvae live near the bottom and must be rooted out by the feeding grayling. Anglers fishing lakes in the early spring should target areas near shore with full-sinking lines, sinking tips, or floating lines with 12-foot and longer leaders. The midge larvae are often small, and imitative flies require the use of at least 5X or 6X tippets. A rise-and-fall technique with a hand-twist retrieve will often take fish. Float-tube anglers visiting high alpine lakes can also just cast and let the leader sink, allowing the wave action to impart movement to the fly. In streams, midge larvae imitations should be fished dead-drift, generally in the bottom half of the water column.

After developing on the bottom, either beneath a safety net of assorted debris or inside silk cocoons spun by larvae, the midge pupae swim with a decided wiggling motion toward the surface. During an emergence, this is actually the most important chironomid life stage for grayling anglers to imitate, as fish will often forgo random eating patterns to feed selectively on these rising pupae. Besides during the slow rise itself, midge pupae are also preyed upon by grayling just beneath the surface. Because they're so small, most chironomids can't readily break through the surface film to fly away. On calm days especially, when the surface tension of flat, unbroken waters is at its zenith, anglers can fish their patterns in

The Hatch.

the surface film, where grayling will be eagerly preying on the suspended pupae. Flies that imitate midge pupae include the CDC Midge Emerger in sizes 14 through 20, size 16 through 22 High Lake Midges in both black and olive, the WD-40 in sizes 14 through 20, and Serendipities in sizes 14 through 22. Experimenting with depth is the key for anglers fishing these imitations during an emergence, as grayling can target the midge pupae anywhere in the water column, both while rising and when suspended in the surface film.

Midge adults are not nearly as important to grayling anglers as the pupae. However, the chironomids are available to fish feeding on the surface in two stages. One is the transitional moment when the adults are trying to free themselves from the pupal shuck, and the second is later, when egg-laying swarms form over the lake or stream. Sparse activity is generally better for the angler than fishing during a blanket hatch, when thousands of adults can render the single imitation totally insignificant. Effective techniques include dead-drifting transitional or stillborn midge patterns and skating a full-bodied fly to mimic the chironomid adults taking flight. Foam lines in lakes and seams in flowing waters will often trap the adults in concentrated feeding lanes, where the grayling will gorge. If many adult midges are available, fly-anglers should attempt to discern individual feeding rhythms and then cast to select fish. Popular patterns to use include the Griffith's Gnat in sizes 18 through 22, CDC Midge Adults in 20 through 22, the V-Rib Midge in olive and black in sizes 14 through 20, and Gray Midge Parachutes, White Stillborn Midges, Red Micro-Curved Midges, and Twilight Midges in sizes 16 through 22.

Specimens from the family Culicidae should need little introduction, as Alaska fly-fishers are surely far more familiar with the mosquito than they care to be. The state's ample wetlands are a breeding haven for these pesky biters, and their lifelong proximity to water makes them an insect worth noting when rummaging through a dry-fly box looking for answers. Though there are a few fly patterns that attempt to imitate mosquitoes specifically, grayling very rarely will selectively feed upon the species, making exact replication unnecessary. Thus, general patterns like the Adams can be substituted, as long as a range of sizes and colors is available.

Although prolific at times in Alaska, hatches of caddisflies and mayflies tend not to occur regularly enough for anglers to go out with a mind to fish a particular emergence at a definite time. Nevertheless, caddis hatches at their apex on many of Southwest Alaska's freestone rivers can nearly blacken the sky. The upper Kanektok, Alagnak, Togiak, and upper Nushagak Rivers are all worthy of note. The Alagnak, in fact, has one of the most predictable caddisfly hatches in the area, which occurs during June with enough consistency that Alagnak-bound anglers can realistically plan to put their Elk Hair Caddis to work every year.

Caddisflies pass through four stages of development—egg, larva, pupa, and adult—with the majority of a complete life cycle spent in the larval stage. Fly-fishers wanting to imitate caddis in this stage have a choice to make, as there are two kinds of caddisfly larvae, case-makers and free-living. While getting into the intricacies between the two is probably beyond the grayling angler's required purview, it is

Alaska anglers can always count on one insect—the mosquito.

worth noting that both occur in all types of water, from lake to stream, and that the larger fish prone to feeding at or near the bottom have no problem eating either one.

Even though it doesn't last as long, the pupal stage of the caddisfly is without a doubt the most important to fly-fishers. Caddisfly pupae develop inside their larval cases, and upon emergence they'll drift downstream some before swimming slowly to the surface. Technically called a pharate adult during this stage, they're covered only by the saclike skin of the pupa, which splits open upon reaching the surface. From there, adult caddisflies quickly depart. In fact, they commonly fly away so quickly that most fish concentrate their feeding during a caddis hatch on the rising pupae. When anglers on a Southwest Alaska river see lots of rises but not many insects on the water, the chances are the grayling are coming up to take emergent caddis pupae heading for the surface. The adults are available to feeding fish a second time, however—females in particular, which will return to the water after mating on shore. Again, anglers can choose to fish either on the surface or below during this posthatch activity, as some females will reenter the stream to lay their eggs directly on the bottom, while others never make it past the surface film.

Set for the release.

Although it's worth reiterating the fact that Alaska's Arctic grayling will rarely feed selectively, anglers should be prepared to at least loosely imitate the three stages of the caddisfly hatch. Some patterns that can be employed fairly universally are the Green Rock Worm and Zug Bug, which are used to imitate the free-living caddis larvae, and LaFontaine's Cased Caddis Larva. Cased caddisfly larvae can also be imitated with the Copper Larva, an imitation that incorporates actual river bottom (try using sand or small rock taken from your wading boots after a visit to a favorite river). Two more of Gary LaFontaine's caddis patterns are staples for fishing Alaska's grayling, the Sparkle Pupa and the Emergent Sparkle Pupa (in sizes 12 through 20). The first was designed to be fished deep, along the bottom during the first stage of pupal drift, while the Emergent variation covers the need for a pupa imitation fished just beneath the surface film. Caddisfly adults are most commonly imitated by the ubiquitous Elk Hair Caddis (a size 16 is a good all-around size for most Alaska grayling streams), the Fluttering Caddis, Stimulators, and the X-Caddis, a pattern originally designed for use in Yellowstone Park, in sizes 14 through 18.

Of all the aquatic insects, perhaps none is so closely linked with fly-fishing as the mayfly. Unique with their large front wings, which stand erect when not in use, and their long, diaphanous tails, mayflies can be found in almost every type of water in the West. In Alaska, they're widespread as well, and where present, they'll make up a good portion of the grayling's diet. Mayflies don't undergo the full four-stage metamorphosis like caddisflies; rather they proceed straight from egg to nymph (where the majority of their lives are spent), and then on to adult. There are two forms of mayfly adult, however, commonly called duns and spinners. Mayfly duns are the winged insects that emerge from the nymphs, with the emergence usually taking place in the surface film. After a varying length of time—sometimes an hour, sometimes more than a day—the dun will molt and become a spinner.

Mating swarms form over the water, and the adult mayflies eventually lay their eggs. Spinner falls, much anticipated by western U.S. trout anglers in some watersheds, occur when the spent insects fall back to the water's surface and die. Grayling, like the trout of the

Rockies, will occasionally feed selectively during a mayfly spinner fall, but most of the grayling action during a hatch will take place as the fish feed on the rising nymphs and the duns floating along the surface. This is especially true for pale morning duns, notorious for floating long distances before molting and taking flight.

Sometimes, tough fish will require anglers to come up with a pattern to emulate one of the four basic types of mayfly nymphs: clingers, crawlers like the pale morning dun or trico, burrowers, and swimmer nymphs, which include the *Baetis* and *Callibaetis* mayfly species. But typically for the Arctic grayling angler, matching a mayfly nymph isn't terribly important; the Gold-Ribbed Hare's Ear and Pheasant Tail Nymph are good enough for nearly every occasion. For duns, anything from the Adams family of flies seems to work exceedingly well, and an Alaska grayling angler could realistically go years before running into a situation where a substitute was needed. And lastly, if grayling are encountered feeding selectively on a mayfly spinner fall, anglers can fish the Compara-Spinner or one of the poly-winged flies. In the end, with grayling, presentation will usually be a more critical component to success than the particular dressing chosen.

In line with the need to present flies as realistically as possible, whether it's a mayfly, caddis, or midge imitation, attaining a drag-free drift should be item number one on the grayling angler's agenda for most occasions. *Most*, not all, because heavily feeding specimens have also been known to actually prefer a skittered fly or to attack a presentation just as it begins to speed up at the end of the swing, perhaps much like a caddisfly fluttering at takeoff. Arctic grayling can sometimes also offer one of the most unusual displays in the angling world. In their rush to rise and inhale a particularly enticing dry-fly presentation, the fish will sometimes leap from the water and attempt to take the offering on the way back down, usually missing completely as a result. A duplicate pres-

entation is warranted in this case, as that same fish will often take again, and be much more efficient about it the second time around. They're not always this easy, though. On plenty of occasions, a large school of grayling can be spotted and cast at, only to have no takers appear willing to move to the fly. It's a trait not unique to grayling, but one they've perfected. Persistence will pay off in these situations, though, for as soon as a single fish is lured into a strike, the resulting excitement and agitation seems to trigger an aggressive response in the rest.

Grayling in Alaska

Never the most difficult quarry to hook or land in the first place, Arctic grayling are also plentiful, and they do rise to the dry fly, sometimes so carelessly a fly-fisher could begin to feel shameful about catching them. But there are probably few anglers who would be willing to undertake either the expense or the time needed for an Alaska expedition if the trip was to pivot entirely upon this species. Still, travelers in remote Southwest Alaska can almost always fill the first few days of a headwater float with hundreds of the eager fish, honing their skills for the trout, salmon, and char sure to show later. And in Southcentral or the Interior, the grayling's lack of renown is a blessing, as fly-fishing for the species often means solitude in the kind of settings popular with the people who sell picture postcards.

While no one's ever confused the Arctic grayling with the world's premier game fish, anglers with a taste for adventure can still haul their lightest spring creek rod north and pursue the species without embarrassment, fearlessly administering a size 16 Parachute Adams in a state known for trophy fish that probably couldn't be less interested in aquatic insects. The raison d'être is found in the cool, clear waters coursing through the remaining alcoves of North America's purely wild lands.

Indeed, for many the Arctic grayling represents the regally isolated high Arctic wilderness of Alaska. They're the most reliably encountered sport fish in remote systems lying north of the Brooks Range. They're plentiful in the tundra streams of the Arctic National Wildlife Refuge and in the giant rivers draining into Kotzebue Sound. Seward Peninsula grayling, as large as any on the planet, frequent waters within easy reach of Nome. Other stocks inhabit immaculate alpine lakes and myriad streams only the locals call by name, prospering in areas all but the most enterprising have yet to find.

All told, the Arctic grayling is abundant in clear, inland waters along the entire western coast of the Last Frontier, from the Alaska Peninsula north to the Seward Peninsula and east through the immense Yukon River watershed. They dwell throughout the Interior, especially in tributaries of the Tanana and Copper Rivers. The species exists naturally in several drainages off the Glenn and Parks Highways, and some minor populations even survive in the glacially charged mainland rivers of northern Southeast. Successful stockings have created prolific sport fisheries on the Kenai Peninsula, in the Anchorage area, and on Kodiak Island, providing fly-anglers north of the southern panhandle good chances of finding grayling anywhere a line is wetted.

NORTHWEST AND ARCTIC ALASKA

The northwest corner of Alaska has long been known in fly-fishing circles for the production of Arctic grayling that exceed 3 pounds in size. Most populations reside in separate, often small streams, however, with the numbers of fish present far from prodigious. Only the Niukluk River, which has been estimated to contain about 375 grayling per river mile, hosts a population that rivals those in the Interior portion of the state, where 500 fish per mile is the norm. For other streams in the area, the number of grayling per mile is thought to range

from forty to sixty fish in the Nome and Sinuk Rivers to two hundred grayling per mile in the Fish and Pilgrim. The large size part is correct, though. Since their life spans are extended, Northwest Alaska grayling survive to attain hefty dimensions. In fact, roughly one-quarter of the trophy grayling registered with ADF&G hail from the Seward Peninsula.

The most heavily exploited fisheries on the peninsula definitely occur in the Nome area, which, because of a fairly extensive road system, is unique to rural Alaska. These Arctic grayling have been popular since Alaska statehood (1959), the recognition only growing as the roads have gotten better and the city of Nome has continued to grow. For example, in the mid-1970s a road trip to the Pilgrim River was a considerable undertaking. Today it takes an hour and a half in a two-wheel-drive vehicle. In all, over 200 miles of roads stretch about 70 miles in three directions from Nome and lead to dozens of quality grayling locales. On the southern half of the Seward Peninsula, the Nome–Teller Highway takes anglers past grayling fisheries on the Snake, Sinuk, Feather, and Bluestone Rivers. The Sinuk may not have the number of grayling as some other streams, but the fish are believed to be of above-average size. During sampling in the 1990s, ADF&G personnel documented the average length of the sampled Sinuk River grayling to be almost 19 inches. Nearly half of the trophy grayling taken from the Seward Peninsula have come from this drainage.

If utilizing the Nome–Taylor Highway, fly-fishers can gain access to a number of grayling streams, including the Pilgrim, Kuzitrin, and Kougarok Rivers. All three host good to excellent grayling, though the Pilgrim is by far the most renowned of the triad. The Nome–Council Highway is the third road in the area and leads to another of the more famed rivers in the region, the Niukluk. Two guiding operations with small lodges are located on the Niukluk in the community of Council, and each focuses

on fishing the Niukluk River and its largest tributary, the Fish River. Arctic grayling of trophy potential are taken each year in the clearwater upper stretches of both systems. Beyond the Council operations, a number of local guides operate out of Nome and can assist anglers in reaching the best fishing on the region's other road-accessible streams.

South of Nome, the wild and remote waters draining into eastern Norton Sound offer boundless opportunities for high-quality angling. The Unalakleet and Shaktoolik drainages are the best known of these, but the Golsovia, Egavik, Inglutalik, Ungalik, and Koyuk Rivers contain great grayling potential as well, with the best angling to be had near headwaters. All but the Koyuk drain the Nulato Hills, which separate Norton Sound from the Yukon and Kuskokwim River valleys. Northeast of Nome, some small alpine lakes in the Kigluaik Mountains have good grayling, though access can be difficult. Salmon Lake, the foremost of these, was an important fishing area for gold miners prospecting the area during the first half of the twentieth century. Continuing in a northerly direction, fly-fishers will encounter some of the most pristine and productive river systems to be found anywhere in the world, namely the Noatak and Kobuk Rivers, each of which drains a sizable portion of the western Brooks Range. The third largest drainage in the area is the Selawik River. Others with exceptional fishing potential include the Wulik, Kivalina, and Kukpuk Rivers. For most of these, the little effort that takes place tends to be expended in the pursuit of other species, usually chum salmon, sheefish, or trophy char. Thirteen lakes in the upper Noatak system have native grayling stocks, while several relatively large, oligotrophic lakes in the mountain headwaters of the Kobuk River system also contain healthy populations of the species. Especially noteworthy are Walker, Nutuvukti, and Selby Lakes.

With the exception of the limited network of roads around Nome, the Arctic grayling of Northwest Alaska aren't easily accessible. Most, in fact, require chartering a floatplane. However, fly-anglers looking to access the grayling fisheries of the Arctic can use the Dalton Highway to reach many streams with good to great possibilities. Of these, the Jim River supports the largest regional stock and receives the most attention from anglers. To the north of the Brooks Range on the wide, austere Arctic coastal plain lie several other grayling fisheries, many of which are surprisingly productive, though sizes of individual fish only rarely approach those of the trophies found in Seward Peninsula waters.

The most popular grayling destination for North Slope fly-anglers is probably the Kuparuk River, which can also be reached by the Dalton Highway. With some classic fly-fishing conditions in its shallow, crystal-clear upper stretches, the Kuparuk overshadows its larger neighbor, the Sagavanirktok, when grayling are concerned. Some of the best grayling potential in the swift and sometimes deep Sagavanirktok (which means "swift

For many, grayling has come to signify the streams of the Arctic.

grayling | 233

North of the Brooks Range, grayling anglers are often afforded the rarest of opportunities—the chance to hike in to the fishing in Alaska.

current" in the Inupiat Eskimo language) occurs in the fall. Many of its tributary streams, especially the Wild and Scenic Ivishak River, also offer some exciting fly-fishing possibilities.

With headwaters north of the Arctic Divide in the Philip Smith Mountains, the Ivishak begins in a slender, glacier-carved valley surrounded by tundra-covered peaks stretching to nearly 7,000 feet. The upper river corridor is within the Arctic National Wildlife Refuge and contains excellent grayling possibilities as the largest of the system's summer-feeding fish move toward the clear waters surrounding the Porcupine Lake outlet. A few other ANWR rivers support populations of interest to fly-fishers, most notably the Kongakut and

Canning Rivers. However, most streams on the refuge's coastal plain are less than waist-deep and freeze solid each winter. For grayling to survive, a watershed must contain at least a few deep pools that remain unfrozen throughout the year. Even then, the area's short summers and long winters slow growth to a crawl, most specimens taking up to seven years to reach double digits in length. The best way for anglers to access these systems is by floating, with drop-offs primarily accomplished by floatplane. For instance, floaters can put in near the headwaters of the Ivishak and float down through the river's confluence with the Sagavanirktok, navigating the latter river until they reach a take-out point along the Dalton Highway.

Almost a proverbial redheaded stepchild, the Arctic grayling doesn't stack up very well against its world-famous siblings in Southwest Alaska's family of sport-fishing species. Anglers travel from every corner of the globe to pursue their dreams and a 30-inch Bristol Bay rainbow. Chinook salmon, coho, the world's greatest returns of sockeye, and even chum salmon and Dolly Varden char are all immeasurably bigger draws. Almost no one comes just for the grayling.

Nevertheless, Southwest has some of Alaska's best fishing for the species in terms of abundance and average size, with trophy specimens possible in many watersheds. The best fly-fishing opportunities are generally present near headwater lakes, where many anglers choose to begin their forays into the region in the first place. There are some more concentrated Arctic grayling locations in Southwest, though, primarily those centered on lake systems known to provide consistent trophy potential. Of particular interest is the Ugashik Lake and River system, which has accounted for over two-thirds of the trophy grayling recorded by ADF&G.

Located within the Alaska Peninsula National Wildlife Refuge, the Ugashik Lakes area has long been the site of the state's two best-known trophy-grayling destinations. One is the Narrows that connects Upper and Lower Ugashik Lakes; the other is the outlet, which includes the upper mile of the Ugashik River between Lower Ugashik Lake and a large lagoon. The dual-channeled Ugashik Narrows are barely more than a quarter mile long, while the shallow, braided outlet offers an almost equally concentrated area for anglers to target feeding grayling. During the summer months, particularly in years with significant sockeye runs, Ugashik grayling will turn their attention to salmon eggs and later, flesh, which has much to do with their above-average size. Midseason fly-fishers would do well to come prepared with both egg-imitation patterns and streamers that exhibit the same orange-to-fading-pink coloration.

The Ugashik Lakes area is accessible only by float-plane, usually from the communities of King Salmon or Ugashik. A few lodge operations catering to fly-fishers exist in the area, though fishing pressure is only moderate. The remote nature of the fishery, coupled with the inclement weather of the Alaska Peninsula, probably has much to do with that. The peninsula's climate is under a strong maritime influence, and the Ugashik area rarely sees whole days of sunshine. Anglers who do make the trip can expect a low-hanging layer of clouds, probably some fog, heavy precipitation, high winds, and, of course, big fish.

Also situated along the north Alaska Peninsula, Becharof Lake and its environs promise to become Alaska's "next" famous trophy-grayling destination. The second largest lake in the state, Becharof certainly isn't sliding beneath the radar; it's just that up to the present, it's been too big, too remote, its nasty weather too unforgiving, to have received the visitors and acclaim common for many Southwest fisheries. Like the Ugashik Lakes, Becharof receives staggering returns of sockeye, and its grayling will adjust their menus accordingly.

North of the Alaska Peninsula, the great Arctic grayling fisheries read like a list of the world's best wild rainbow trout rivers. The two species' ranges do in fact overlap throughout most of Southwest Alaska, the primary difference being that the grayling will tend to hold and feed near headwater lakes while the trout disperse throughout a system, seeking the return of their primary food source from the open ocean. Grayling in these Southwest systems will feast on salmon eggs, too, as well as the occasional leech or sculpin, though the better part of their diets comprises the region's aquatic insect life.

In upper reaches of Togiak River tributaries, fly-fishers can find grayling gorging on caddisflies the size of quarters, while a nice pale morning dun hatch on the Agulowak or Agulukpak Rivers of the incomparable Wood-Tikchik system can also bring the surface to life. Grayling are abundant and eager throughout the region, from drainages of the massive Lake Iliamna system north to the headwaters of lower Kuskokwim tributaries like the Kisaralik and Kasigluk Rivers. Hardly ever will a systematic matching of the hatch be necessary, but even if it is, chances are a size 14 or 16 Elk Hair Caddis will come in handy. For instance, the Kanektok River, long a favored float-trip destination, is a classic freestone

stream with long, slightly riffled flats extending for about 10 miles from its lake source. Floaters making their way from Kagati Lake to the river's braids during decent summer weather will likely encounter a caddis hatch that can come off all day long.

Although the caddis is Alaska's most ubiquitous hatch, emerging mayflies or stoneflies will be represented on many rivers as well. The Koktuli River can be one such location. The upper stretches of this clearwater tributary of the Mulchatna River in the Nushagak system (one of Alaska's best river systems for both grayling and float

An angler works to land a big Ugashik Narrows grayling.

BRIAN O'KEEFE

trips in general, with nearly limitless possibilities) will often seem to be completely devoid of fishing throughout the day, and then roar to life when the PMD hatch comes off hard in the evening. In reality, the scenario barely differs across Southwest Alaska. Maybe it's *Baetis* mayflies on one stream or drifting 6mm sockeye eggs on another, but Arctic grayling fly-fishers won't encounter many problems in virtually any of the region's already celebrated fisheries—neither in locating fish nor in finding something they'll eat.

SOUTHCENTRAL ALASKA

The Southcentral region offers some fairly good grayling fishing, but much of the more accessible locations have been well worked over for large fish. For truly exceptional action, the best bet is to hike or fly in to remote headwater tributaries. A great place to start looking is in the upper reaches of Southcentral Alaska's most significant fish producer, the Susitna River drainage.

Issuing from a series of colossal glaciers in the eastern Alaska Range, the silt-laden waters of the mighty Susitna ramble through the region toward a terminus with Cook Inlet. In the upper stretches, and in fact all along its course, grayling abound, usually utilizing the massive waterway for overwintering and then spawning and feeding in the hundreds of clearwater tributaries that branch off to both east and west. The Indian River and Portage Creek are both good possibilities for the fly-fisher looking to escape the summer crowds on the well-known Parks Highway streams, as are west-side Susitna tributaries like the Tyone River and Alexander Creek. The upper reaches of the Chulitna River and its own many tributaries (Coal Creek especially) also host significant populations of summer-feeding grayling. Another significant Susitna tributary, the Talkeetna River, offers excellent fly-fishing for the species in its feeder streams, most notably Clear and Prairie Creeks.

TONY WEAVER

Of course, the streams closer to the Southcentral population centers are popular for more reasons than their proximity to a maintained road. The Deshka River, best known for a resurgent chinook salmon return, hosts a healthy grayling stock in its upper reaches. The river provides an exceptional short float trip, with very few anglers venturing into the upper reaches of the stream where the grayling do their feeding. Sheep Creek, a small clearwater tributary of the middle Susitna, is actually accessible via the well-traveled Parks Highway, and yet it, too, can offer plenty of room to the fly-angler targeting Arctic grayling. A healthy knowledge of the grayling's life history patterns will greatly aid the Sheep Creek angler, as the fish will begin to stage in the stream's mouth section during the fall, waiting for dropping temperatures to induce the final leg of their winter migration. Hundreds of fish will pile into the area in late September and the early part of October, long after most anglers have quit fishing the stream, and fly-fishers can generally time their arrival for a late-afternoon mayfly hatch that sends the fish into a near feeding frenzy.

For fly-out locations, fairly common destinations like

Rafters can often find exceptional grayling fishing at the beginning of headwater floats like those on Southwest Alaska's Kanektok River.

the clearwater Talachulitna River are always good, though high-quality wilderness excursions are available to those willing to try one of the many lakes in the upper Susitna region. Some, like Deadman and Watana Lakes, are known to harbor native populations of grayling.

INTERIOR ALASKA

Grayling are distributed throughout the entire Yukon drainage, from extreme headwaters in Canada to streams that terminate in the Yukon Delta. Sport fishing for the species is likewise widespread. Historically, most of the attention has been focused on the middle section of the Yukon River system, from the mouth of the Porcupine River downstream to the Koyukuk River. Tributaries like the sprawling Melozitna River and the Wild and Scenic Nowitna system offer good opportunities for the species, though access is always a challenge when the Yukon is part of the conversation. Another tributary, the Anvik River in the lower Yukon area, has also been a consistent grayling producer, with much of its fishing accessed via a lodge located on the upper river.

Basically, in the Yukon system, as in most of the rest of interior Alaska, drainages without good Arctic grayling opportunities are more difficult to find than a stream chock-full of eager fish. For much of the region, ADF&G assessments of population densities are significantly higher than those previously discussed for the rivers near Nome in the northwest corner of the state. In fact, many Interior streams contain more than five hundred grayling per mile of water.

One such big producer also happens to support Alaska's second largest grayling sport fishery. The Gulkana River, which originates in the Alaska Range and flows approximately 96 miles to its confluence with the Copper River, provides plentiful bank-, float-, and powerboat-fishing opportunities for anglers. Both the greatest catch and harvest of Arctic grayling from the

river typically occur in the mainstem portion, which flows about 45 miles from the outlet of Paxson Lake to the Sourdough Campground. Generally, adult summer residents of the mainstem Gulkana spawn in tributary creeks, such as Poplar Grove and Sourdough Creeks, and are available to anglers near these tributary mouths and others in the early spring. For the most part, the fish then distribute themselves in the Gulkana River after spawning, according to size. Larger and older fish will take up feeding stations in the upper reaches of the river, while the smaller and younger fish accept banishment to lower reaches near Sourdough.

Another of interior Alaska's most heavily fished grayling populations occurs in tributaries to the glacially occluded Tanana River. The Goodpaster River, a clearwater rapid runoff stream, may offer the most sustained opportunity of these, for Arctic grayling will use the Goodpaster for spawning in the spring and then retreat to other Tanana tributaries for summer feeding. Then again in the fall the grayling migrate back to the Goodpaster for overwintering purposes. The river maintains its own summer stock as well, making the fishery viable from ice-out in May through freeze-up in October. According to ADF&G sampling, the grayling feeding in the Goodpaster River throughout the summer are situated in hierarchal strata much like the grayling in other parts of the state. Juveniles and subadults tend to occupy the lower 33 miles of the Goodpaster, while a mixture of all fish sizes can be found in the middle stretches of the drainage between the confluences with the South Fork Goodpaster River and Central Creek. Typically, the river above Central Creek plays summer pasture for the larger adults only.

Of the streams that Tanana-drainage grayling migrate to for their summer feeding, the Delta Clearwater River is the most significant, and not surprisingly the Goodpaster River contributes the greatest portion of the fish that migrate there after spawning—up to 60 percent of the total summer population. In all, it's believed that Arctic grayling from eight different spawning streams spend their summers in the Delta Clearwater, the largest of several spring-fed tributaries to the Tanana. Good grayling fishing occurs throughout the summer, though low relative humidity can make the insect hatches rather random.

If an interior Alaska grayling fishery rivals the Gulkana for popularity, it occurs in the Tangle Lakes system, an interconnected lake-stream drainage located just west of Paxson on the Denali Highway. Though road accessible, the fact that grayling are the primary sport fish of the area means that only moderate angling pressure occurs even at peak times. Tangle Lakes visitors are also assured they'll encounter a real wilderness character, stunning scenery, and, quite often, excellent fly-fishing potential. Prior to 1953, the Tangle system was inaccessible by road, and predictably the region received little attention. Since then, the most directed effort has been expended on Upper and Round Tangle Lakes and the interconnecting Tangle River, where a pair of Bureau of Land Management campgrounds are located. There are a dozen major lakes in the system, however, and fly-fishers willing to do a little paddling or hiking can easily escape any crowds.

The grayling of the system are highly mobile and migrate throughout the lakes and their interconnected streams to meet their reproductive, feeding, and overwintering needs. Currently, a total of seventeen distinct spawning populations have been documented. For the most part, these concentrations of fish will move together to common summer-feeding locations, though the proportion of the groups as a whole that remain together varies some depending on the spawning population. In the fall before ice-up, the grayling migrate back toward the larger lakes, like Landmark Gap (the largest in the entire system), where they'll overwinter. Open-water season in the Tangle Lakes system is usually from early June through the middle of October, with fly-anglers able to target feeding fish the whole time. Inlets, outlets, and thoroughfares between the lakes provide prime hunting grounds, as do some shallow areas in the lakes' littoral zones where insect activity may peak, typically early in the morning or in the later-evening hours.

An angler works the bank for grayling on Clear Creek in Southcentral Alaska.

Motoring to the
feeding zones.

BRIAN O'KEEFE

alaska's regional and saltwater species

THE SPECIES OF GAME FISH that make up the
first nine chapters of this book are distributed across Alaska and
support steady, if not thriving, fisheries. The ones that follow,
too, can see some directed angling pressure, though for the
most part they're regional targets not available to fly-anglers in
every area of the state. For example, fly-fishers wandering
among the vast, uncharted corridors of the Yukon region might
encounter rapacious groups of marauding pike or intercept a
migrating school of sheefish, the Far North's most exotic and,
in some ways, emblematic fish species.

While neither of those species is available in Southeast Alaska
(except for a single, isolated population of northern pike
found in the Yakutat area), fly-fishers in the region will instead

encounter one of the West's most prized game fish, the cutthroat trout. Alaska's coastal cutts, many of which are sea-run fish, have whittled out a comfortable niche along the southeastern shores of the state, largely unnoticed, except by locals who pretend otherwise. The boreal forests that cloak the jagged coastline of the area—both island and mainland—do much to hide the sometimes tiny creeks that tumble out of nowhere to meet the sea, most of them hosting healthy, genetically pure cutthroat trout populations. Farther inland, basin-bottom lakes also boast thriving stocks of speckled trout, including Alaska's most consistent trophy populations. In the salt, too, fly-anglers can encounter the state's cutthroat cruising the narrows and straits, the bays and back-island estuaries, always in search of a likely looking meal. For fly-fishers who may be frustrated by the bottom-hugging, noneating Pacific salmon species, the cutthroat of Southeast will seem heaven-sent.

All of the species above—the northern pike, the sheefish, and the coastal cutthroat trout—are integral to any discussion of the state's fly-fishing opportunities, despite, and maybe even because of, the fact their distribution and followings are limited. But, to be sure, devotion trumps mere popularity, and while these regional game fish might not garner the acclaim of some of Alaska's more celebrated species, the anglers who do pursue them are quite serious about it.

The saltwater species, found in offshore waters all over Alaska, are included in this chapter for a different reason, primarily because most don't think of halibut, lingcod, or rockfish as quarry for the fly-fisher. Nonetheless, for anglers wishing to spend a day at sea, the bounty of Alaska's salt waters will provide steady and sometimes exhilarating action, enough to change the way many feel about bottomfish. Far away from the madding crowds and in some of the most stunning coastal scenery North America has to offer, fly-fishers wanting to expand their repertoire can cast to fish previously reserved for 2-pound-bait casters with 5-pound weights. In some ways, these saltwater fisheries symbolize the whole of fly-fishing in the Last Frontier, where innovation still means something more than adding a different-colored saddle hackle to an old fly and where much remains undiscovered.

Northern Pike

(Esox lucius)

Layers of gray hang in defiance of the promised sun. What there is of terra firma nearby exists as mere clumps of soggy earth, chaotically arranged between the myriad waters that stretch out like veins, bringing life to the tundra and fifteen different shades of green where none should be. The flat-bottomed riverboat softly sways on water so still, people forget there is any breeze at all. An angler's arm arcs back for a final time, the rod loads in a deliberate forward stroke, and line sails into the crisp spring air, settling lazily on the undisturbed surface. She begins the retrieve with short, quick movements of her hand, fully descending into that realm between feeling and understanding that only anglers share. Her eyes follow the bulky fly, and the world grows dull.

There are other eyes following the streamer creation as well, for beneath the placid, almost table-flat plain of water lurks one of the planet's fiercest ambush predators. The pike stalks these northern waters like a Shakespearean tyrant, its baleful golden eyes searching for that ideal opportunity to spring from the shallows in a lightning-swift strike, much as the Iagos of the world leave most of their dirty dealings to the back rooms and secret chambers of the castles they mean to own.

Suddenly there is a swish of movement. Breathing stops, the water swirls, and the fly disappears in an explosion of sight and sound. The line snaps tight and the rod buckles as the angler and her quarry begin their dance. The fight doesn't match the tug-of-war an angler will encounter when up against a truly adamant chinook; there's none of the speed of the rainbow trout, nor any gravity-defying leaps or extended tail-walking as there is with steelhead and coho. With Alaska's pike, the excitement comes by way of anticipation, as every movement that passes until the fish is finally sighted tends to encourage seriously fantastic dreams. And northern pike do grow quite well in Alaska. Old Eskimo and Athabaskan lore recalls giant specimens, unrepentant predators willing to take on the largest of prey, even humans. The tales coalesce nicely with the waters the species inhabits in the state—slow-moving, unwanted back channels and side sloughs left unarmed and off the page on most maps. It can be almost eerie, fishing for a species in one of these end-of-the-earth locales, never really sure just who is being hunted.

Unfortunately, the northern pike has been much maligned in Alaska, for many of the same reasons it is such a sought-after species in other regions of the world. Old sourdoughs and commercial fishers alike historically disdained the species. Tradition and life itself revolved around the Pacific salmon, and the pike, with its well-earned reputation as a piscivorous glutton, was viewed as a threat. It still is in many Alaska eyes today.

This stealthy predator makes its living by vanishing into bottom structure and submerged weed beds and then simply waiting for its prey to swim by. With a

FAR LEFT: *A sailboat anchors in a protected Southeast cove.*

TONY WEAVER

Fly-anglers can frequently find nonstop action with hammer-handle pike.

powerful thrust of its tail, the pike will rocket from its hiding place to attack. Concentrating on larger forage, pike will often swallow fish a third their own length, sometimes even attempting to eat prey half their size or larger. This insatiable penchant to feed, coupled with the tremendous size mature specimens have been known to achieve, makes the pike an inviting target for sport fishers the world over. It's one case where the nature of the fish and the nature of the fisher combine to form the perfect complement.

Northern pike are opportunistic, voracious feeders programmed to eliminate the weak. Their keen predatory disposition is matched with endowments perfectly suited for the job. Their coloring varies and often depends on the waters where the fish can be found, an evolutionary development that relates to their ability to disappear into a river's bottom. In clear water under a

A Noatak River–drainage northern pike.

THOMAS CAPPIELLO

bright sun, their visual acuity is excellent, especially upward and to either side, which allows them to hold in concealment while scanning their territory for another victim. The inner ear and a long lateral line detect the slightest vibration, another advantage in locating prey. Once located, that prey doesn't have a chance. A single, soft-rayed dorsal fin located far back on the body works in conjunction with ventral and tail fins to provide incredible acceleration, aiding the slender, almost serpentine pike in both open-water pursuit and when attacking quarry from cover. After arriving at its destination, the pike employs the approximately seven hundred backward-slanting canine teeth that adorn its duck-billed jaws, tongue, gill rakers, and the roof of its mouth to grip and devour the overmatched prey.

Fish are the preferred fodder, and it really doesn't matter which kind. Pike will feed on whitefish, suckers, cisco, grayling, trout, juvenile salmon, and even other pike, as well as insects, frogs, mice, shrews, ducklings, and shorebirds. The biggest pike have even been known to make a meal of larger animals such as the beaver and the muskrat, and a single specimen will annually consume three to four times its body weight.

While well documented in the angling literature, the pike is perhaps only recently beginning to gain serious attention as a game fish suitable for fly-rodders in Alaska, and much remains to be learned about this hardy predator and the vast northern watersheds it inhabits. It is known that most Alaska pike overwinter in the deep, slow waters of large rivers and lakes, as their shallower counterparts become depleted of oxygen. With the onset of the thaw, adult northerns migrate en masse from their deep-water winter retreats to take up positions in the shallow margins of lakeshores, slow-moving streams, sloughs, and flooded areas of vegetation, where spawning commences. After completing their reproductive duties, the spent adult pike remain in the shallows for anywhere

BRIAN O'KEEFE

between one and four months and engage in a feeding frenzy. They are extremely vulnerable to fly-anglers both during spawning and immediately afterward.

Pike that inhabit lower latitudes are quite predictable; they usually can be followed in their spring, summer, and fall migrations without much difficulty, especially the lake fish, which are primarily located by minding water temperature: Pike are very sensitive and move to remain within their limited comfort zone. Another key to finding Lower Forty-eight pike is acknowledging their love of a good meal. For example, a typical *Hexagenia* hatch in the summer will bring smaller pelagic fish into the shallows to feed on the insects. The pike in turn follow and target the baitfish. However, the extreme water fluctuations from early snowmelt and the large amounts of forage available can combine to make Alaska's northerns more of a challenge to locate, especially since many populations are known to have expansive river ranges. Plus, the state's relatively stable and cool water temperatures mean that anglers can't count on thermal stratification to narrow the possibilities.

To begin with, the spring angler should focus atten-tion in the shallows around weed beds. Typically, after a long, ice-covered winter season, the pike will migrate toward near-shore heat-gathering basins and bays for spawning. Also, don't discount any oxbow lakes or flooded back channels on streams that host returns of Pacific salmon—in Alaska, small baitfish can often be merely a complement to the stronger, river-bred pike's diet. After the spawning season ends sometime in early to mid-June, the larger fish will linger on the edge of deep water and heavy vegetation until freeze-up. Later in the year, when water temperatures do rise in some areas, particularly those with tannic-stained waters, the bigger fish will again travel to find comfort. Look for a location where cool water flows into an isolated spot that allows it to collect (a lot of current will dissipate the influx of water and negate its effect). Specifically, backwater sloughs and the glacial-green mix where slow-flowing streams empty into silty rivers are good places to begin.

Once a site has been selected, a systematic approach is needed, especially when fishing unknown waters. The method most often utilized is similar to fishing for steel-head in the big rivers of the Pacific Northwest, where an

LEFT: *Having a boat will allow anglers to follow migratory pike.*

BELOW: *Many of Alaska's lakes are ripe for the pike angler.*

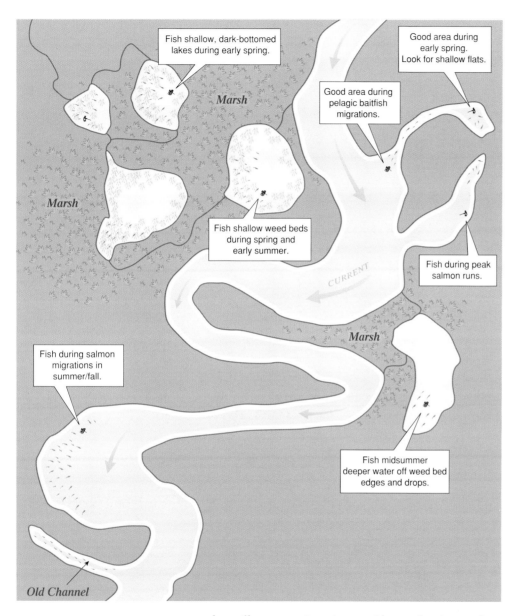

Fish shallow, dark-bottomed lakes during early spring.

Good area during early spring. Look for shallow flats.

Good area during pelagic baitfish migrations.

Marsh

Marsh

Fish shallow weed beds during spring and early summer.

CURRENT

Fish during peak salmon runs.

Marsh

Fish during salmon migrations in summer/fall.

Fish midsummer deeper water off weed bed edges and drops.

Old Channel

angler will create an imaginary grid over the river and cast a searching pattern to each section until the fish are located. Fly selection and presentation can be fine-tuned after the fish have been found, with large baitfish patterns and topwater hybrid flies like the Dahlberg Diver

being most popular. And perhaps it is needless to say, but there is much good northern pike water to seek out in Alaska.

Still virtually untapped, the pike fisheries in the state are as filled with potential as they are immense. Millions of acres of prime habitat make the Last Frontier a prolific pike territory, and though tales of the quantities of fish that can be found might seem less than credible, it's not just a numbers game. As late as the 1950s, there were no pike present in upper Cook Inlet drainages. They're there now, though, in numbers. It's now theorized that the species was able to gain a foothold in the Susitna River system through a series of illegal stockings, and by the 1997–98 fishing seasons, the harvest of northerns from the Matanuska-Susitna Valley had surpassed that from the state's Interior, the region where the largest native pike populations can be found. As a whole, the Susitna drainage covers tens of thousands of square miles and contains innumerable shallow lakes, sloughs, and clear-water tributaries that are prime northern pike spawning and rearing habitat. The drainage is also a hotbed for salmon-chasing sport fishers, who have a legitimate gripe with pike. Currently, the Alaska Department of Fish and Game estimates that as many as thirty thousand fewer adult salmon return to the Susitna drainage each year due to the illegal introduction of pike.

However, the pike is indigenous to much of Alaska and has long been a favorite of the Yup'ik people in Southwest, as well as interior subsistence and sport anglers. Its native range extends from the Alaska Range north to the Arctic Coast, from the Canadian border west to the Seward Peninsula, and from there southwest to the Bristol Bay drainages. Other than a small, isolated population near Yakutat, a remnant of the last ice age, the pike is absent from Southeast. Moving north from the Susitna and into that native range, especially around the bountiful waters of the Tanana River and the sprawling reaches of the state's two largest river systems, the Yukon and the Kuskokwim, logistics for fishing the species become more difficult. The best pike habitats are in low-lying floodplains, lakes, and wetlands and are usually accessible only by plane or riverboat.

The Tanana is a major tributary of the Yukon that originates from meltwater draining off the ice fields and glaciers of the Wrangell Mountains. Since much of its nearly 500 miles is silty from the glacial influence, the bulk of the sport-fishing potential is concentrated in upland tributaries and in the sloughs, lakes, and slower streams of the area's flats. Some of the most prolific pike waters in the region are found in the Minto Flats, an 800-square-mile wetland complex in the Tolvana River drainage west of Fairbanks. Another productive drainage is that of the Kantishna River, which hosts abundant northern populations in East Twin, West Twin, Mucha, and Wein Lakes. Lake Minchumina and many smaller waters, including more than a few within Denali National Park, are also noted producers, as are George Lake near Delta Junction, Fish Creek, and the oxbow lakes and sloughs of the Goodpaster Flats area.

Moving west from where the Tanana empties into the Yukon near Manley Hot Springs, anglers encounter phenomenal pike habitat nearly every step of the way. Fishing such a massive and remote watershed, however, is never easy or cheap. The mainstem Yukon doesn't yield the extensive fly-fishing opportunities of its many clear-water tributary drainages, due to a turbid nature that's especially prevalent in summer months. Throughout much of the drainage, anglers will also find the assistance of a knowledgeable guide indispensable, as potential pike water is more than abundant. The Yukon Flats, an expansive wetland between Circle and Stevens Village, is one such area, noted for its tens of thousands of interconnected lakes and slow-moving backwaters, many of which hold copious populations of pike. Farther down-

There are few flies that a pike won't eat.

BRIAN O'KEEFE

river is the confluence with the Wild and Scenic Nowitna River. The surrounding wetlands within the Nowitna National Wildlife Refuge, which contain more than fourteen thousand lakes and small ponds, are yet another haven for significant numbers of northern pike. Also productive among central Yukon tributaries are the Melozitna and Tozitna River systems, the latter of which contains a profusion of whitefish for the pike to prey upon.

If possible, the Yukon River becomes even more remote and the pike fishing less charted in the next leg. The area between Galena and Holy Cross contains a few hundred miles of what seem to be the wildest portions of the river, with a multitude of tributaries and slow-moving creeks that offers pike possibilities. Near the end of this stretch, anglers can first encounter the Innoko River drainage, perhaps the greatest trophy-pike producer among all of Alaska's world-class habitat. An enormous lowland tributary of the Yukon with plenty of meandering, interconnected sloughs and lakes, the Innoko features a rich environment for northern pike: big, slow water and abundant cisco and whitefish populations. The Innoko's major tributary, the Iditarod River, is itself nearly 350 miles long and is thought to be another phenomenal producer in an area already recognized as one of the world's great pike locales. Pike over 20 pounds (and some much larger) are not irregular for either of these rivers.

Continuing toward the Bering Sea's coast leads to a broad, isolated delta where the two largest rivers in the

Last Frontier spill their waters within 200 miles of each other. It is one of the planet's great wetland habitats, and many of its thousands of small lakes, rivers, and sloughs remain nearly unexplored. But at least two drainages in the area—the Wild and Scenic Andreafsky River north of the village of St. Mary's and the Anvik River—are already known to contain good to great pike-fishing opportunities.

Still, even veteran pike anglers can find themselves grasping for answers when searching for the water wolf on some of Alaska's more remote waterways. Rivers like the Innoko are unique and often demand patience because of the fickle nature of water levels and the huge area they encompass. But that's part of the allure of chasing these sleek predators: the unknown. From the literature of antiquity to legends passed on in the dancing hues of a smoldering campfire, what is fact and what is myth seem to blur when it comes to northern pike. As countless tales from Alaska's fraternity of anglers—ancient and modern—attest, the monster pike are out there, prowling just beneath the surface of waters both known and unknown. For some, to chase them is to forge a living bond with the wild, with the past, and, if justice reigns, with the future as well.

Inevitably, these adventuresome few will find themselves alone one gray Alaska morning, drifting on some secluded waterway a hundred miles from nowhere, hardly daring to breathe as a streamer settles onto the surface, and wondering just for a moment if what they hunt might not also be hunting them.

The Sheefish

(Stenodus leucichthys)

The lands of Alaska's forlorn and rugged Brooks Range, a spine of massive peaks that stretches 600 miles across the northern expanse of the state, are intimidating in their seclusion. And the river systems that wind through the many valleys and rock-walled canyons of the region can be just as isolated and just as mysterious. Within some of them then, it's perhaps fitting that one of the Far North's most exotic game fish makes its home. The sheefish, or inconnu, long an important subsistence species for rural Alaskans, is known to but a few fly-fishers, though that is bound to change as logistics continue to improve and more anglers begin to look north.

Without question, the unique nature of the fish and the pristine environments they inhabit are the primary draws for fly-anglers. Though someone with a sense of humor nicknamed sheefish "the tarpon of the north," they're anything but a considerable challenge to land. They do look something like a tarpon, however, with a silver body, large dime-sized scales, large gill plates, and a bony square jaw, which must be where the moniker came from. Along their backs, the color of the sheefish turns a dark greenish gray or brown. Their eyes are large, befitting their predatory tendencies. An even more pronounced indication of feeding prowess can be seen in the mouth of the sheefish.

A member of the subfamily Coregoninae, the whitefish group, sheefish differ from their much smaller cousins in that they do not display the common tiny mouths geared toward consuming insects and plankton but rather a large, square-shaped box mouth that almost equals the width of its head when fully opened. Unlike the case of pike, there are no rows of teeth for prey to fear. The sheefish instead uses its considerable mouth like a vacuum to consume baitfish whole. The gill plates protrude and serve to expel the excess water while the meal is swallowed.

The sheefish is a long-lived species, taking as long as eight years to reach 30 inches in length and the time of first sexual maturity. Some stocks produce noticeably larger specimens than others, too. For instance, the

sheefish of the Kuskokwim River drainage average between 8 and 15 pounds, with fish up to 37 pounds having been caught. Other stocks, notably the sheefish from northern drainages, can get much bigger, some reaching over 50 pounds. The populations that tend to produce the biggest sheefish are considered semi-sea-run species of game fish, as they spend their winters in the saltwater bays and estuaries where their home rivers terminate. After breakup in the spring, these sheefish will ascend their natal drainages to spawn in the fall in upper reaches.

Technically, biologists refer to the species as estuarine anadromous. In the case of the Selawik River, for example, juvenile sheefish will spend the first summer feeding on plankton and small forage fish. That winter, the young will join all age-classes of sheefish downstream in Kotzebue Sound. With the arrival of spring, typically in late May or June, the fish begin their return to spawning areas in the Selawik or Kobuk Rivers. Reproduction commences in early fall, with females seven years and older leaping out of the water, each scattering as many as four hundred thousand eggs across the surface.

Loading the rods for a dawn takeoff.

BRIAN O'KEEFE

BRIAN O'KEEFE

Breeding males, aged five and older, remain underwater, fertilizing the eggs as they settle to the gravel of the riverbed.

Unlike salmon, the sheefish do not die after spawning. Instead, they return to the Selawik Lakes and the estuary areas of Kotzebue Sound, traveling under the ice to resume their winter feeding. Not all sheefish spawn every year, either, as it's currently believed that individual fish spawn biannually or even less frequently. And though it can take fourteen years to reach 8 pounds, the long life span of the sheefish—often upward of thirty years—accounts for the extremely large size of some specimens.

Because they're such voracious piscivores, the best flies for sheefish are quite often large baitfish patterns, many of the same used for chinook and coho salmon in the salt. Many of the most effective baitfish imitations are tied on size 1 to 3/0 hooks and are between 4 and 6 inches long. The big flies, which not only are more easily seen but also push more water and create more of a disturbance, make good sense in the heavily occluded

waters of many of Alaska's most significant sheefish rivers. For forage, this northern roamer prefers whitefish, cisco, suckers, and sticklebacks, as well as juvenile trout, pike, char, and salmon of all types. Both general patterns like Lefty's Deceiver and the Clouser Minnow and more exact imitations will work for sheefish, as will some of the other baitfish patterns like Dan Blanton's tarpon creations, even during the summer migration period when sheefish feed much less or, in some cases, stop eating altogether. In even rarer circumstances, schooling sheefish will become extremely aggressive and can be successfully lured to the surface with large poppers and other bulky topwater flies that create a great degree of commotion.

Rods are usually in the 7- to 9-weight class, and sinking lines are almost always preferred, as sheefish will hold to rest in the deepest, slowest-moving pockets of their large migratory rivers. The heavier rods are chosen more for their ability to cast the denser sinking lines that may be needed than for any need to control hot fish. Overall, sheefish will occasionally burst from the water for a brief aerial display or two, but again, they're not a line-peeling species, not even the largest specimens. They're certainly not anything remotely like a tarpon. An interchangeable-tip fly line can be carried to cover a variety of situations, or fly-fishers can simply use a combination of lines including a weight-forward floater, a short sinking tip for frog-water situations, and several full-sinking lines up to 400 grains. Sheefish are not leader-shy, consistent with most sinking-line presentations, so nothing more than 4 to 6 feet of leader is needed; 10-pound tippet is sufficient for most circumstances as well.

Exotic, magnificent game fish, sheefish are found only in Arctic areas of Alaska, Canada, and Siberia. The Kuskokwim River is the southernmost system home to the species in the Last Frontier. Extremely wide and flat, it's certainly not a river friendly to fly-anglers, who are limited to working from boats and in areas near tributary mouths for sheefish migrating upstream to spawn. One of the most popular pieces of water is near the Kuskokwim's confluence with the Aniak River, where several lodge operations can put fly-fishers on sheefish from July through mid-August. To the north of the Kuskokwim drainage, the Yukon, Selawik, and Kobuk River systems also host healthy sheefish populations. The Kobuk and its associated watershed may in fact be home to the largest sheefish in terms of both individual size (fish up to 80 pounds have reportedly turned up in nets) and total populations numbers. Fly-fishing for the species on the Kobuk and tributaries like the Wild and Scenic Tagagawik River is generally best between early August and the first week or so of September.

The other great sheefish range in Alaska occurs in the Selawik drainage, which actually means "place of sheefish" in the Inupiat language. The 2-million-acre Selawik National Wildlife Refuge and Wilderness, a vast system of estuaries, brackish coastal lakes, and the corre-

TONY WEAVER

BRIAN O'KEEFE

TONY WEAVER

TONY WEAVER

sponding wetlands, was created primarily to protect the sheefish spawning grounds. The river itself issues from the spruce forests of the Purcell Mountains and slowly winds toward its terminus in the Selawik Lakes. Fly-fishers wanting to experience the largely untouched beauty of the area, and sample the fishing for the Far North's most enigmatic game fish, can gain access by either jet boat or floatplane from the coastal village of Kotzebue.

The Coastal Cutthroat Trout
(Oncorhynchus clarki clarki)

Ironically, fly-fishers in search of the signature trout of the Rockies—in fact, the only trout native to the widely heralded waters of the region—would be better advised to pack their bags for the Lost Coast instead of Colorado,

for Turner or Wilson and not Pyramid Lake, for Petersburg rather than Ennis. While the streams of the Rocky Mountain region are considered among the country's most illustrious blue-ribbon trout waters, it's not because of their cutthroat trout, which has been elbowed out of many of its former strongholds, inadvertently replaced when rainbow and brown trout were long ago introduced to many drainages. But in the small lakes and tumbling creeks that dot and cross the heavily forested southeastern coast of Alaska, the small, speckled, brightly colored trout of the West yet thrives.

For the most part, fisheries scientists recognize fourteen subspecies of cutthroat trout. Two are extinct and a few more—like greenbacks and the Lahontan cutthroat—are on the endangered list. Others still have been proposed for listing. Ever sensitive to changes in water quality and the habitat alterations that seem to accompany most human development, the coastal cutthroat subspecies, too, has seen steady reductions in population from the Eel River in California to the coastal waters of Oregon and Washington. Thankfully, in Alaska the cutthroat's range is vast and primarily occurs along areas of coast unlikely to see any two-legged visitors at all, let alone major development.

The cutthroat, as its scientific name suggests, was named for the captains leading the Corps of Discovery, who first encountered the fish in 1805 while traveling below the falls on the Missouri River. The fish they noted for posterity (the first true trout documented in the United States) was a westslope cutthroat (*Oncorhynchus clarki lewisi*). All of Alaska's cutthroat are of the coastal subspecies (*O. c. clarki*). That doesn't mean the state's cutthroat stocks all look and live similarly, however, as a few distinct life histories are exhibited by Alaska's cutts, sometimes even when residing in the same watershed.

Some coastal cutthroat are considered semi-anadromous, spending their summers feeding in the sea and then returning to fresh water to overwinter and spawn. Others maintain an entirely freshwater existence, either feeding in large river systems and then migrating to small tributary streams to spawn, living in the smaller systems year-round, or spending their lives in landlocked lakes. The great majority of Alaska's cutthroat, existing along the coast from Dixon Entrance at the extreme southern point of the state north to Prince William Sound and Gore Point on the southern side of the Kenai Peninsula, are of two types: lake-resident and sea-run.

Like sheefish, coastal cutthroat trout spend only part of the year in the salt, usually two to three months. During their saltwater existence, the fish never depart the shallow shore zones, generally remaining in bays or along the coastline near their streams of origin. In Alaska, these small sea-run trout depart fresh water after spawning in early spring, with peak movement from mid-May to early June. They return to their natal streams in the late summer through fall, with most having completed their journeys by October. Most overwinter in larger streams or lakes, moving into the smaller tributaries they prefer for spawning in the spring.

Resident cutthroat, on the other hand, spend their entire lives in the many lakes, streams, and small bog ponds of Southeast Alaska. Otherwise, their life histories closely parallel those of the sea-run cutthroat. Resident fish are smaller on average than sea-run cutts, which is not surprising considering the latter's access to the bountiful forage of the sea. Nevertheless, the largest cutthroat trout taken by anglers to date in Alaska have come from landlocked lakes, not areas with sea-run populations. Neither sea-run nor resident cutts overwhelm streams with their numbers, even though the species is considered in good health in the state. A population of more than a few thousand fish is actually a sizable stock.

THOMAS CAPPIELLO

With a close look, it becomes clear that the range of the cutthroat in Southeast Alaska frequently overlaps with that of steelhead. But unlike parts of the Rockies where introduced rainbow and brown trout crowded out cutthroat, the two sea-run species can and have coexisted in many areas. Mostly, this is a function of reproductive isolation: The cutthroat prefer the smallest tributaries for spawning, with steelhead sticking to the main channels. Anglers should never have difficulty telling the different species of trout apart, either, not

Cutthroat trout.

even when they can be found holding in the same stretch of water. First of all, all cutthroat display the two red slash marks beneath the lower jaw that gave the fish their name. They're also smaller than all but the youngest steelhead. While anyone familiar with cutts in other environments won't have trouble recognizing them, the coastal cutthroat trout of Alaska generally aren't as brightly colored as a few of the other cutthroat sub-species. Their more subdued bodies are usually tinted bronze or gold. The spotting pattern also differs, as Alaska's coastal cutts frequently display a profusion of tiny speckles to large black spots similar to those seen on other inland subspecies of cutthroat. Resident cutthroat also tend to be more brightly colored than the sea-run

fish, which, like steelhead and salmon, return from the sea with a bright, nearly total silver coloration.

The growth and maximum attainable size of Alaska's cutthroat are affected by the same limiting factors that the state's other species of game fish experience, namely genetics, life span, food availability and type, and habitat. Water temperature as it relates to metabolism can be especially important. As for feeding habits, coastal cut-throat don't diverge considerably from any other species of trout that resides in a similar environment. Whatever invertebrates are available almost certainly become a source of forage, and in areas with returning salmon, the cutthroat will splurge opportunistically on the seasonal bonanza of eggs and flesh. At other times of year, alevins,

Many of the smallest streams in Southeast Alaska will hold strong populations of sea-run cutthroat trout.

TONY WEAVER

fry, and smolt are the favored prey. As they get older, cutthroat still feed on the insect life traditionally linked to western trout rivers—midges, caddisflies, mayflies, and stoneflies—but they will also look to feed more efficiently, selectively targeting forage fish such as sticklebacks, kokanee, juvenile anadromous salmon, and sculpins.

The overall diet of the cutthroat varies accordingly by region and the time of year, of course. In some areas, leeches will comprise a portion of the cutthroat's diet. In others, insects must make up the bulk of the menu. If there is a single consistency in their diet throughout Alaska, it's that cutts will take advantage of an overlapping range with Pacific salmon wherever possible. This means alevins and fry in the spring, both before and during the out-migration, and eggs and flesh in the late summer and fall, after the cutthroat have returned to their natal streams. At sea, cutthroat feed on small shrimp, juvenile herring, capelins, and salmon smolt. The lake-resident fish that grow so large are very dependent on the significant kokanee populations of their lakes, as well as sticklebacks and any other forage fish they can find.

As with all species displaying some anadromy, finding cutthroat is the first key in successfully fishing for them. The species is notoriously voracious and will hit many different flies at different times of the year, but their dynamic migratory tendencies can make angling difficult. For the most part, cutthroat prefer softer flows than steelhead or Pacific salmon, though they still can often be found near the bottom of the stream or tucked closely to structure. In streams, try the lee edges of sandbars, cutbanks beneath overhanging grass and cover, deep, slow-moving pools, tributary confluences, and behind obstructions like deadfall logs and large boulders. Where they can be found in lakes, cutthroat tend to prefer inlet and outlet stream areas and in general, the shallow shoreline area, especially where they can find some

BRIAN O'KEEFE

structure for cover. However, for the landlocked lakes of Southeast, especially those that carry a heavy tannin influence, stratification during the summer months is a major concern and will send the cutthroat deep.

Most important for Alaska's sea-run cutthroat populations, fly-fishing opportunity depends on the time of the year. While winter cutthroat fishing may be available to anglers in the Pacific Northwest, most of Alaska's cutthroat rivers and streams are either frozen or choked with ice and inaccessible at that time of year. Spring, then, is the time to find cutthroat trout in the Last Frontier, particularly in late March and April, before the fish begin spawning and then depart for their offshore feeding grounds. Access during this time of year is almost entirely dependent on the conditions, as anglers will need to wait for the snow and ice to recede enough to gain access. Flying out to the remote lakes that hold cutthroat is also a possibility, but then, too, anglers must wait on the ice to clear for landings.

In drainages that also host populations of Pacific salmon, spring cutthroat can be targeted with alevin and fry flies and, just prior to their own ocean migrations,

A sea-run cutthroat from one of the many streams slicing through Tongass National Forest.

smolt patterns. Sculpin and leech patterns will also be effective in spots, though spring is also a good time to break out the dry flies for cutthroat. Almost any of the most effective searching patterns will produce trout. Humpies, Elk Hair Caddis, and anything from the Wulff family of flies are good bets. As is usual when fishing with insect imitations, nymphs can be even more productive.

Cutthroat aren't a tremendously popular marine target, partly because of their roaming, unpredictable natures and partly because of their size in relation to the other saltwater species of the areas they inhabit. Saltwater angling can be done, however, as the fish are usually found near their streams of origin in depths not outlandish to saltwater fly-anglers. Sinking tips and full-sinking lines will work for anglers prospecting tidal flats or the rocky shorelines of bays and inlets, and small baitfish patterns can be successful when chasing estuarine cutthroat. Estuaries and stream mouths are also a good place to target schooling cutthroat later in the summer, especially during incoming tides, just before they begin to push upriver. Though navigation and tides can be treacherous, anglers traveling throughout the many straits, narrows, and other inside passages of Southeast can also intercept feeding concentrations near the surface. During these times, the cutthroat have been known to attack dry flies skittered on the surface, particularly patterns like the Humpy, tied full, though what triggers the strike is unknown, as it's doubtful the fish are rising to insects in the salt. Still, for the ultimate in cutthroat trout angling, this scenario's hard to top, and any fly-fisher who's tangled with cuts at sea will have many fine things to say in regard to the species's fight.

An angler finds a frisky cutthroat on a remote Prince William Sound stream.

As the year progresses and the cutthroat begin to reappear in their natal freshwater streams, the dry-fly fishing that peaked in the spring and summer can be hindered: Other than in upper, headwater stretches and small tributary streams, the fish will begin to key in on salmon eggs. *Hindered*, that is, but not obliterated. Cutthroat are notoriously voracious during the fall, when they need to build body fat for the winter. While egg patterns can produce success beyond description in areas, dry flies, nymphs, and streamers will work nearly as well, especially in regions that see little to no angling pressure.

Whether spring or fall, the mobile, cast–two steps–cast scenario common to most western U.S. fly-anglers is often the best tactic for taking on Alaska's cutthroat streams, where fish will usually be found highly concentrated but with distance between the groups. This is particularly true in the short coastal creeks of Southeast, where good holding water is in short supply. Anglers in this region can walk lots of stream before finding a pocket of fish, but once found, there'll tend to be a bunch of cutthroat gathered and willing to eat.

There are so many of these streams that trying to list them all would be a quixotic task. Even the Alaska Department of Fish and Game has yet to catalog them all, only reporting that viable populations of cutthroat exist from Dixon Entrance to Prince William Sound and in almost any drainage, no matter how small, throughout that range. The species is also available in a number of the freshwater lakes of Southeast, including many small bogs or ponds that are as yet unnamed.

A list of just the highlights would have to include the streams and lakes of the Misty Fjords National Monument area on the mainland east of Ketchikan, which is probably home to the highest concentration of directed angling for the species in the state. Only recently free of glaciation, the Misty Fjords region is

characterized by towering walls of granite that majestically lord over the glacier-carved fjords and quiet, undisturbed valleys that lie far below. Vegetation is lush, typical of the temperate rain forest, with the spruce and hemlock only occasionally giving way to alpine meadows and rolling muskeg flats. For cutthroat trout fly-fishers on longer excursions, the U.S. Forest Service cabins of the area can be a major asset, offering clean, dry accommodations ideally located for staging a variety of coastal trout expeditions. There are fourteen cabins in the Misty Fjords monument alone, many of them with small boats available for accessing area watersheds.

While several of the road system lakes and streams near Ketchikan offer good cutthroat prospects, a better bet for fly-fishers would be to visit the Naha River or Ward Creek. Both are relatively large streams and feature several promising pools and deep-water runs that allow traveling cutthroat to hold during their autumn in-migrations. The real draw of the area for trophy trout hunters, though, lies in lakes like Ella and Wilson, where 6-pound-plus cutthroat aren't beyond the realm of possibility. Unsurprisingly, this area around Ketchikan is simply a preview of the sometimes spectacular cutthroat angling to be had in the heart of Southeast Alaska. In fact, anglers would be hard pressed to find an area without a healthy population nearby, whether on Prince of Wales Island or within the environs surrounding Haines, in Turner and Jims Lakes near Juneau or in Lake Eva on Baranof Island, or among the innumerable straits, bays, lakes, and small creeks of the Petersburg and Wrangell region.

The North Gulf Coast, or Lost Coast, probably deserves special mention as a paradise of undiscovered cutthroat trout fishing. The Bering River tributaries present known action, as do the Katalla, Kiklukh, and Kaliakh systems, but of at least equal interest should be

Icy Bay glaciers.

Tony Weaver with a fly-caught halibut.

China rockfish.

Kelp greenling.

Greenling.

the small lakes and even smaller streams with thriving populations that abound along the coast. Many have never been visited by an angler, particularly those in the Icy Bay region. Though it flows to the south of Yakutat, the Akwe River provides a classic example of the nature of the Lost Coast rivers. These wide-open coastal streams lack the old-growth barriers that protect many of the watersheds of Southeast and are thus more exposed to the elements. While a 3-weight rod will suffice for cutthroat throughout much of their Alaska range, it's probably not a good choice here, where anglers will need to cast through the gusting winds common to the region in the fall when the cutthroat action reaches its peak.

Near the northernmost limits of the coastal cutthroat's native range, there are a number of viable options for fly-fishers looking to tread a step or two off the beaten path. The best known of the trout streams are in the vicinity of Cordova, but anglers with access to a boat or floatplane will find that many of the coastal areas in Prince William Sound are home to cutthroat. This includes the creeks that crisscross the region's larger islands, notably Montague and Green. Several landlocked lakes also boast cutthroat stocks, though little is known of their potential. In fact, some quality water in the region, whether creek, bog, pond, or lake, has yet to be named. Just don't be surprised if a quick shore hike in an area not known for its fishing, perhaps just to stretch weary boat legs, instead turns up a small pond with rises dimpling the surface.

Alaska's Saltwater Species

Except when sitting down to lunch or dinner in one of the state's seafood eateries, it's doubtful that many fly-fishers think about the bottomfish prowling Alaska's near-shore saltwater fisheries. While fishing for lingcod, rockfish, and especially halibut remains popular, it's over-

whelmingly accomplished with the heavy weights and heavy tackle of the state's vast charter fleet. Fly-fishing for halibut and other bottomfish isn't only possible, however; it's the logical next step for fly-anglers intent on exploring new fisheries and overcoming new challenges.

The odd-looking but fine-tasting halibut actually makes a superb target for fly-fishers who manage to arrive at the right times, which usually means spring when schools can be found in the shallows with some level of predictability. Most experienced Alaska anglers might think of halibut fishing as usually taking place at depths of 200 feet or more, but as the gigantic schools of salmon smolt leave their home streams each spring—after navigating a gauntlet of hungry lake and rainbow trout—the halibut, actually a voracious fish predator, will move into the shore areas near stream mouths to wait. Timing must be impeccable, but when right, it's not unheard of to find fish in less than 10 feet of water. Another good time to find flatfish near stream mouths is in the fall when tons of salmon flesh will be washing out to sea. These select times aren't the only occasions when fly-fishers are afforded opportunities for halibut. Near rocky coastlines and inshore structure, halibut can sometimes be found in less than 60 feet of water, and anglers can employ large herring patterns and heavy-density sinking lines to great success.

If fly-fishers search out the right conditions and are properly equipped, rockfish, too, can provide exciting and abundant angling action throughout their Alaska range. Yearly timing isn't as much a factor as when searching for shallow halibut, either. Rockfish can be taken year-round in Alaska's waters, only found in deeper water during the winter months. As with halibut, fly-fishing for rockfish has an added benefit: Both can be enjoyed without lengthy, expensive charters or a lot of specialized equipment. Some of the best areas are within reach of major coastal hubs, and good rockfish tackle isn't much different from some of the basic saltwater setups used for other species. Neither is halibut gear, for that matter.

The ideal tackle combination for rockfish will be a fast-action, 9- to 10-weight rod with a 400-grain line. This system is fast sinking, strong enough to handle the big lingcod that are always a possibility when working good rockfish areas, yet still light enough to allow an angler to fully enjoy a good 7- to 8-pound rockfish. A 6-, 7-, or even an 8-weight rod will certainly handle the fish, but the lighter rods create problems when anglers need to go up to lines above 300 grains. The denser fly lines are too cumbersome with the lighter rods, while most lines under 400 grains won't get the fly deep fast enough to effectively fish these species. For halibut, a good tarpon rod for a 12-weight line will suffice.

Reels need to be capable of holding the fly line plus about 150 yards of backing (250 for halibut). Of paramount importance are reels built with a reliable drag system, either sealed graphite or high-quality cork. Salt water is rough on gear, especially reels, so regular maintenance is essential, including liberal rinsing and wiping down after each use and periodic disassembly, cleaning, and lubrication. To meet the challenge of the different conditions encountered on a typical Alaska rockfish or halibut safari, fly-anglers will want an assortment of sinking lines from 200 to 750 grains. There are a variety of companies that manufacture fine sinking lines, from Jim Teeny, Inc., to Scientific Anglers, or anglers can manufacture their own shooting heads, tailoring lines to precise individual tolerances. For leaders, any type of hard monofilament (like Mason Saltwater or Maxima Clear) will work fine. Leaders need not be longer than 5 feet, with a butt section that's about 60 percent of the diameter of the fly line—usually 30- to 40-pound test—tapered to 25-, 20-, and finally 15-pound test.

The number one concern when designing flies for

rockfish and halibut is durability. Epoxy heads can aid in this endeavor. For halibut, almost all of the effective patterns imitate large baitfish, like herring, though in the fall bulky flesh flies can produce well. Rockfish flies should be simple, rugged affairs that will stand up to catching a lot of fish in a day. Most are lightly dressed creations tied tarpon-, jig-, or streamer-style. Keep in mind that colors change drastically with depth; at 20 feet most color is very muted, and at greater depths the only really prominent color is white. Fluorescent and even phosphorescent materials charged with a portable flash can be used to great effect in extreme conditions.

Rockfish in particular can make enticing targets for the fly-angler, as they're abundant in many coastal waters and will often be found in the upper regions of the water column. The Alaska Department of Fish and Game reports that there are currently about thirty-two known species of rockfish to be found in the Gulf of Alaska, though most will never be seen by anglers; just over a dozen can commonly be encountered in near-shore shelf areas less than 100 fathoms deep. And of these, five or six make up the bulk of the rockfish typically caught by Alaska fly-anglers.

Probably the most common target is the black rockfish (*Sebastes melanops*), which is frequently refered to as sea bass or black bass. In fact, it's not uncommon to find schools of black rockfish flopping all over the surface when grouped in active feeding concentrations. Yellowtail, dusky, and blue rockfish can also frequently be found in the top 30 feet of water and make

Lingcod.

Pacific cod.

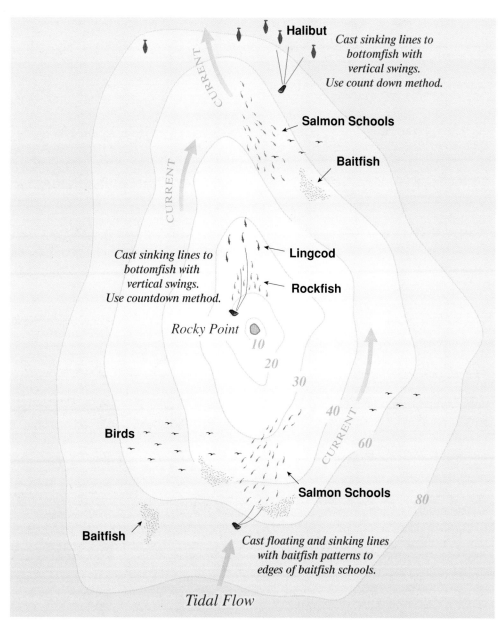

Halibut

Cast sinking lines to bottomfish with vertical swings. Use count down method.

CURRENT

CURRENT

Salmon Schools

Baitfish

Cast sinking lines to bottomfish with vertical swings. Use countdown method.

Lingcod

Rockfish

Rocky Point

10

20

30

40

CURRENT

60

Birds

80

Salmon Schools

Baitfish

Cast floating and sinking lines with baitfish patterns to edges of baitfish schools.

Tidal Flow

coastlines, usually 30 to 60 feet of water, and can thus be targeted by the fly-angler. On rare occasions, or if anglers can get deeper than that, canary, Boccaccio, silvergray, and yelloweye rockfish (or "red snapper") can be targeted.

An NOAA chart can be a major help in selecting potential rockfishing habitat, as will depth finders and portable GPS units. New navigational aids that extrapolate bathymetric data into 3-D representations allow anglers to read the bottom like never before, to pinpoint fish locations and enjoy more productive fishing. Rockfish are not terribly migratory, though, and anglers can follow some simple guidelines to find productive habitat with consistency. First of all, pelagic rockfish tend to gravitate to congregate over rock piles and pinnacles. In the open ocean along the Alaska coast, kelp beds and wash rocks are likely places to begin looking for schools of rockfish. Find a pinnacle that comes up from a couple of hundred feet to 30 or 40 feet below the surface and it's likely home to a rockfish bonanza. Black rockfish in particular will school around these pinnacles. Coppers and quillbacks will be slightly deeper, hugging the bottom structure.

Kelp-bed edges along shorelines are also good prospective sites. The water in these areas will run shallow—15 to 30 feet—and then often fall off steeply to 60 feet or more. This offers ideal habitat, with shallow water for the angler and the appropriate structure to support the sea life that rockfish feed upon. Another good place to search out rockfish is in areas adjacent to a deep-water escape route, as rockfish need to constantly remain wary of predators such as larger fish and seals. Thus, in inland areas of Alaska's coastal waters, populations may vary.

The best situation for taking rockfish on the fly is in depths of 40 feet or less, where they can be reached easily with lines of up to 400 grains. Areas that offer abundant rockfishing at depths of 80 to 100 feet or more

up the rest of the near-surface-feeding pelagic rockfish commonly found in Alaska waters. Copper, quillback, and China rockfish are the most common bottom-dwelling rockfish that stick in the shallower regions near

Sunset on Prince William Sound.

are mostly reserved for all-tackle anglers, as it takes a long time for a fly-angler's line to sink that far and it's hard and often dangerous for a boat operator to anchor on a rock pile. Plus, a physiological feature that allows rockfish to hold in the water column off the bottom creates problems for releasing fish safely—their swim bladders. If a rockfish ascends too quickly, the gas in its system expands. This expansion in the air bladder causes the stomach to be forced out its mouth and, particularly in deep water, the eyes to bulge. Even if released alive after that, the rockfish can never return to the depths and will be easy prey for predators.

The technique for taking rockfish is very similar to that for used for halibut fly-fishing—a vertical sink or swing. After roll-casting the line, saltwater anglers will stack two or three mends on top of the fly to get it down deep. Once the line straightens below, varying retrieve speeds are employed, with the rod tip always pointed at the water. Tides are not as crucial when fly-fishing rockfish as they are with halibut, however. Still, moderate tides will help. Time of day is not critical for either species, with times of direct sunlight producing the best, probably because a good number of contemporary baitfish flies are tied with synthetics that are activated by light. Under the right conditions—crystal-clear water, favorable tide, bright sun—anglers may even be able to coax rockfish to the surface and catch them on floating flies cast off the back of the boat.

Mount Iliamna at
sunset, as seen from
the Kenai Peninsula.

coda

Fly-Fishing the Next Frontier

ANTICIPATING AN EVENING of casts and contemplation, an angler fights through half a mile of tangled undergrowth to emerge alongside the tumbling, boulder-strewn stream. By this time, no doubt, the solstice sunset has turned the peaked horizon a hundred different shades of red and orange, the night as still as it is picturesque. The little creek flows clean and clear, proclaiming its good health in a cascade of little chirps and burbles. It looks and sounds nothing like the played-out waters so often read about.

Ploink! says a small rainbow. A wild trout, too.

There are no other anglers around, not for miles and maybe not for months. The fly-fisher reminds himself that very few have probably ever cast a fly into this tiny tributary rivulet. *Thank goodness for Alaska*, he thinks.

Sometimes, for some of us, only flowing waters—clear, pristine streams and the wild fish that inhabit them—can provide the kind of therapy we really need.

Unfortunately, over the past few years the fly-fishing community has been forced to become increasingly mobilized in defense of the nation's, and indeed the world's fisheries. For decades, they had been at best ignored and at worst disdained in favor of new homes and old jobs, caught between rigid adherence to the traditions of the past and the development said to be necessary for life in a brave new world. As anglers, we've long been force-fed these unintended ironies from those who

would sacrifice the future in the name of progress. Today, when we catalog the forces arrayed against the modern fishery—dams, hatcheries, fugitives from the ever-more-prevalent fish farms, pollution, water for irrigation, overfishing, and the destruction of habitat brought on by industrialization, urban sprawl, mining, logging, and the new corporate face of agriculture—it begins to look like the remaining wild stocks face life impediments enough to make a market-bound steer feel hopeful.

Still, we like to think that sooner or later we'll have to figure it out. Being keen students of history, it's doubtful any American needs to be reminded of what happened when the inhabitants of Easter Island cut down their last tree. The trick to this sort of obliviousness, of course, is to forget that despite strong returns to the Columbia basin in recent years, the wild salmon populations of Washington, Oregon, Idaho, and California have continued on a downward trend that began over 150 years ago. If self-deception proves futile, perhaps taking employment as a gill-netter or sawmill operator will help.

For fly-fishers, it barely needs saying that this sort of

Preserving Alaska's wild stocks.

before the U.S. government took an interest in even half-heartedly managing the region's fisheries, salteries were built near a productive stream or river mouth, and after a cycle of salmon runs, usually four or five years, the salter would move on, after plundering nearly entire runs during that time, not leaving nearly enough escapement to provide for future returns. Subsistence and sport anglers were no better, and the retention limits allowed in the three decades following statehood hardly deserve to be called liberal.

Salmon returns appeared boundless, and that appearance was taken as fact. Eventually, the federal government began regulating Alaska's wild salmon fisheries, but those early attempts at management were either too feeble or rather weakly enforced. And for the longest time, if a game fish wasn't commercially important, then in accordance with regulations in place in Alaska, it wasn't important at all. A bounty was even paid to anglers who didn't mind killing a few Dolly Varden. Not for eating them or for making the species part of their subsistence diets, just for ridding the state's salmon streams of their presence. Even into the late 1970s and early 1980s, restrictions placed on rainbow trout and steelhead fisheries were so loose that entire wild populations were nearly wiped out. Thankfully, much has changed, and just as fortuitously for us, Mother Nature has again proved to be a masterful rebound artist. With some assistance from a much more proactive ADF&G, the trout stocks that were once the worst off are currently showing forty-year highs in abundance. It's not just sport fishing that's changed over the years, either, as commercial fishers are presently in the midst of a period of great transition, with bottomed-out market prices and the infusion of farmed fish, not to mention questions as to the health of some of the most popular fisheries, providing much of the impetus.

Still, it's not an easy tradition to part with; some small

thing is impossible, if not downright detestable. Anglers above, perhaps while working a Little Yellow Stonefly across the small creek's lightly riffled surface, will find some peace in the wine-red fingers of evening light. In that brief harmony, that shuttering against the winds of a world gone mad, a world that no longer knows how to appreciate the beauty of an unaltered stream, they'll inevitably learn to treasure their water even more.

It may be hard to imagine the collapse of the world's ocean fisheries while standing amid a squadron of returning salmon or when a two-hour flight, boat ride, or hike in any direction will land a person smack dab in the middle of some of the planet's most prolific wild trout habitat. But that line of thinking has already led Alaskans to the point where these debates are necessary. Early in the state's history, long before statehood or

FAR RIGHT TOP: *Casting to saltwater silvers in the waning light.*

FAR RIGHT BOTTOM: *Alaska gold.*

villages in Alaska owe their existence to commercial fishing. Alaska's first salmon cannery began operations in the Tlingit village of Klawock on the west coast of Prince of Wales Island in 1878. Statehood didn't come until some eighty-odd years later, and by that time the industry had a stranglehold on many of Alaska's coastal villages. From the writings of Melville and Joseph Conrad to the images of hardy sailors braving Poseidon's most violent storms, fishing the high seas and the men and women who do it have seeped into our national consciousness. They're as embedded in the American myth as much as narrow-eyed, leather-skinned cowboys of the West. It's a mighty tradition, worthy of respect, even from Alaska's sport fishers, who've recently been pitted against the commercial interests in sometimes fierce allocation battles. But it is also ludicrous to prolong the idea that our country's oceans, lakes, rivers, and streams will continue to provide what we need just because we need it.

A fly-fisher's enthusiasm invariably owes its origins to a single location, a piece of water eulogized in memories that only seem to grow more vivid as time marches on. As we age and our passion takes us to new waters, angling takes on the look of a perpetual education. For in fly-fishing, as in life, true wisdom only comes by way of experience, and there is only so much we can learn before nature itself begins giving the lessons. Thus, new rivers are exactly what we seek. As we learn, we suddenly need to learn, and within that transformation a spirit will remain forever restless, becoming still only when surrounded by water. The river becomes Socrates to the angler's Plato, and we're more than happy to simply document what truths we find for those who've yet to come.

Like art, fly-fishing is an endeavor within which perfection is unattainable, where a certain level of expertise may be reached only to reveal another higher, more pro-

BRIAN O'KEEFE

BRIAN O'KEEFE

ficient plateau. Angling is learning, and the better we get at it, the more we know about it, the more that truth reveals itself. Which is what makes it so great. To toil, to practice and study and plan, to risk the ridiculous and have no great guarantee of success other than maybe—a long maybe at that—requires faith. And since having it all pay off, even once, with the disappearance of a fly from the surface and a surge of power at the end of the line is something no angler is assured, it must be faith in something other than the result. The reward must be in the journey, not the destination.

To preserve that journey, not only for ourselves, but also for the others who are bound to come behind us, fly-fishers now know that they must be the stewards of both their tradition and the waters that they've come to love. While that battle has become heated in many parts of the country, where embattled anglers are entrenched around the sole remaining fisheries they can call wild, much is forgiven in the vastness of the Last Frontier. Sheer space allows for encroachments on wild fisheries that would never be tolerated by residents of the Lower Forty-eight. It's exactly that space, however, in exactly the multitude of still-wild and remote fisheries, that makes Alaska important to preserve.

The fly-fisher takes in the crimson sky, the sounds of the rushing water, the look of the slick that spreads behind a large, midstream boulder, and he makes one last cast. Halfway upon the drift, the fly goes under, and he lifts his rod to feel the weight of a nice fish, which is soon in hand. Releasing the trout back into the water where it belongs feels good, and the angler thinks that all selfishness isn't necessarily to be avoided.

There is suddenly no need to cast again. A seat is taken on a nearby rock and, perhaps, a cigar is lit. For those who don't know, this, too, is fly-fishing, this watching without waiting, this being without being busy.

Trying to postpone the inevitable, most people will never come to experience, to know this feeling, instead spending their time warding off thoughts of the Reaper by purchasing another car, building a bigger house, climbing a rung higher on the corporate ladder. Perhaps the fly-fisher's calm comes not from accepting the fact that he'll one day die, but from knowing that doesn't mean his rivers will, too.

Ploink! says the little trout. Wild, no doubt. Thank goodness.

One last cast.

FAR LEFT: *Summer bloom along the banks of the Alagnak River braids.*

appendix

Fly Patterns for Alaska's Game Fish

AS ANY FLY-FISHER who has managed to avoid the ensnaring tentacles of dogma for even a week or two well knows, there's no end to the number of specific fly patterns that can be used to success by a skilled and persistent angler. In fishing for Pacific salmon, especially, the numbers of productive patterns reach into the thousands, and since most freshwater salmon flies are of the attractor class, there's also a virtually never-ending array of color combinations to known productive patterns that can and do catch fish.

Many fly-fishing books have recently succumbed to the habit of including numerous personal or entirely esoteric patterns that are unavailable to anglers who may not be proficient tiers. There is a place for intricate, specialized fly patterns, of course, but this book isn't one of them. A general work on fly-fishing in Alaska, we believe, should include general fly patterns for the state,

not a list of flies encumbered with personal touches or variances.

In deciding on the flies for this book, then, we chose not only patterns that we know have their place in Alaska's fly-fishing environment, but also flies that are available commercially. Nearly any one of these flies, or something quite similar, can be found in the bins of any fly shop in the state, or from the two companies mentioned in the acknowledgments, Doug's Bugs and Umpqua Feather Merchants.

To condense these pages, and since many of the patterns within can be used with success on a variety of Alaska's game fish species, the flies are broken into four very general and sometimes quite arbitrary categories: attractors, eggs to flesh, insects, and baitfish patterns, which includes both freshwater smolt and fry imitations as well as the saltwater forage-fish patterns.

insects

DRY FLIES

Elk Hair Caddis, black
(rainbow trout, Dolly Varden, grayling)

Elk Hair Caddis, brown
(rainbow trout, Dolly Varden, grayling)

Elk Hair Caddis, olive
(rainbow trout, Dolly Varden, grayling)

Elk Hair Caddis, olive
(rainbow trout, Dolly Varden, grayling)

Elk Hair Caddis, orange
(rainbow trout, Dolly Varden, grayling)

Fluttering Mayfly Cripple, mahogany
(rainbow trout)

Fluttering Mayfly Cripple, trico
(rainbow trout, Dolly Varden, Arctic char, grayling)

Hackle Stacker Sparkle Dun
(grayling)

HS Mayfly Dun, *Callibaetis*
(grayling, Dolly Varden)

Nasty Sally, yellow
(rainbow trout)

Parachute Twilight PMD, chartreuse
(rainbow trout, Dolly Varden, grayling)

Parachute Twilight PMD, pink
(rainbow trout, Dolly Varden, grayling)

Peacock Caddis
(rainbow trout)

Renegade
(grayling, rainbow trout, Dolly Varden)

Royal Wulff
(steelhead, rainbow trout, cutthroat trout)

Rubber Legs Hopper/Stone, Madame X
(rainbow trout)

Ruling Stone, black
(rainbow trout)

Steelhead Caddis
(rainbow trout)

Stimulator, olive
(rainbow trout)

Twilight Elk Hair Caddis, black
(rainbow trout, Dolly Varden, cutthroat trout)

Twilight Elk Hair Caddis, bright green
(rainbow trout, Dolly Varden, cutthroat trout)

Twilight Elk Hair Caddis, cream
(rainbow trout, Dolly Varden, cutthroat trout)

Twilight Elk Hair Caddis, dun
(rainbow trout, Dolly Varden, cutthroat trout)

Twilight Elk Hair Caddis, tan
(rainbow trout, Dolly Varden, cutthroat trout)

Twilight Hairwing Dun
(rainbow trout, Dolly Varden, grayling)

Wally Waker Moth
(steelhead)

X-Caddis, black
(rainbow trout, Dolly Varden, Arctic char, grayling)

X-Stone, tan/orange
(rainbow trout)

insects

WET FLIES
AND NYMPHS

Beadhead Stone, brown
(rainbow trout, Dolly Varden)

BH Flashbody Larva, green
(grayling)

Brassie, copper
(rainbow trout, Dolly Varden, grayling)

Caddis Larva, tan
(rainbow trout, Dolly Varden, grayling)

CDC Red Brassie
(rainbow trout, Dolly Varden, grayling)

Micro-Curved Midge, red
(grayling, Dolly Varden, Arctic char, cutthroat)

Foam Suspender Midge
(grayling)

Hare's Ear Nymph, black (rainbow trout,
Dolly Varden, Arctic char, grayling, cutthroat)

Hare's Ear Nymph, olive (rainbow trout,
Dolly Varden, Arctic char, grayling, cutthroat)

Kenny's Sparkle Humpy, green
(rainbow trout, Dolly Varden, grayling)

King Stone Nymph, black
(rainbow trout, Dolly Varden)

Midge, group of six
(grayling)

Mosquito Larva
(rainbow trout)

Vitamin D
(rainbow trout)

Shaggy Beadhead Midge, olive
(grayling, Dolly Varden)

Shaggy Beadhead Midge, red
(grayling, Dolly Varden)

Soft Hackle, partridge/yellow
(rainbow trout, Dolly Varden)

V-Rib Midge, black
(rainbow trout, Dolly Varden, Arctic char, grayling)

Winged Midge Emerger, olive
(grayling)

Winged Midge Emerger, red
(grayling)

Zebra Midge, silver
(grayling)

attractors

Agitator, black
(coho salmon, chum salmon)

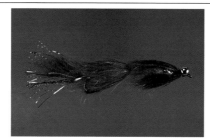

Articulated Hairball Leech, blue
(chinook salmon, coho salmon)

Big Boss Diver, black
(northern pike)

Big-Eyed Bunny Leech, black
(chinook salmon, coho salmon)

Borden Special
(cutthroat trout)

Boss, black/orange
(steelhead)

Bunny Death, black/red
(chinook salmon, coho salmon)

Bunny Diver, red/white
(northern pike)

Cabollera
(cutthroat trout, steelhead)

Chinook Chaser, pink
(chinook salmon)

Comet, silver/orange
(sockeye salmon)

Conehead Western Bunny
(rainbow trout, Dolly Varden, Arctic char)

Conehead Western Bunny, brown/tan
(rainbow trout, Dolly Varden, Arctic char)

Conehead Western Bunny, red/brown
(rainbow trout, Dolly Varden, Arctic char)

Conrad
(sockeye salmon)

Dahlberg Mega Diver, white
(northern pike)

Dan's Favorite, silver/blue
(sockeye salmon)

Davis Spanker, pink
(coho salmon)

Davis Spanker, chartreuse/pink
(coho salmon)

Davis Spanker, chartreuse/white
(coho salmon)

Deep Eyed 'Wog
(coho salmon)

Diamond-Head Snake, chartreuse/olive
(northern pike, rockfish)

Diamond-Head Snake, yellow/red
(northern pike)

Eel Diver, black
(northern pike)

Eel Diver, olive
(northern pike)

Ferry Canyon
(steelhead)

Fireball Leech, black
(rainbow trout, coho salmon)

Flash-a-Bugger, white (rainbow trout,
lake trout, cutthroat trout, Dolly Varden)

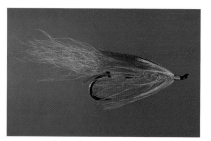

General Practitioner, orange
(steelhead)

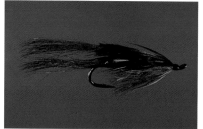

General Practitioner, purple
(steelhead)

Motion Prawn, hot pink
(chinook salmon, steelhead)

Motion Prawn, orange
(chinook salmon, steelhead)

GP Prawn, purple
(chinook salmon, steelhead)

Grease Liner
(coho salmon)

Green Butt Skunk
(steelhead)

Green Lantern
(sockeye salmon, saltwater coho, steelhead)

Kenai Special, chartreuse/silver (chinook salmon,
coho salmon, chum and pink salmon)

Kenai Special, pink/silver (chinook salmon,
coho salmon, chum salmon, pink salmon)

King Tooka, black
(chinook salmon)

Kinney's Skagit Minnow, black
(chinook salmon)

Kinney's Skagit Minnow, chartreuse
(chinook salmon)

Kinney's Skagit Minnow, orange/purple
(chinook salmon)

Kinney's Skagit Minnow, purple
(chinook salmon)

Midnight Express Summer Spey
(steelhead)

Muddler After Dinner Mint, purple
(steelhead, coho salmon)

Muddler After Dinner Mint, red
(steelhead, coho salmon)

Nucleic Bunny, black
(chinook salmon, coho salmon)

Pinwheel Marabou Spey, black
(chinook salmon, coho salmon)

Pinwheel Marabou Spey, cerise (chinook salmon,
coho salmon, steelhead, chum salmon)

Pinwheel Marabou Spey, orange (chinook salmon,
coho and chum, salmon, steelhead)

Pinwheel Marabou Spey, purple (chinook salmon,
coho and chum salmon, steelhead)

Polar Shrimp, hot orange
(steelhead, Arctic char, Dolly Varden, cutthroat)

R. J. Woolly
(rainbow trout, Dolly Varden)

Rajah
(steelhead)

Rattlebugger, black
(chinook salmon, coho salmon)

Rattlebugger, black/olive
(chinook salmon, coho salmon)

Rattlebugger, orange
(chinook salmon, coho salmon)

Rattlebugger, pink
(chinook salmon, coho salmon)

Rattlebugger, purple
(chinook salmon, coho salmon)

Rattlebugger, shell pink/white
(chinook salmon, coho salmon)

Skykomish Sunrise
(steelhead)

Steel Tooka, black
(chinook salmon)

Steel Tooka, black/chartreuse
(chinook salmon)

Steel Tooka, orange
(chinook salmon)

Steel Tooka, purple
(chinook salmon)

Summer Deep Purple Spey
(steelhead)

113Super S Prawn, purple
(steelhead)

Tim's Hot Shot Comet, chartreuse
(coho salmon)

Undertaker
(steelhead)

Whiz Banger Leech, black/chartreuse
(chinook salmon, coho salmon, chum salmon)

Whiz Banger Leech, black/fluorescent pink
(chinook salmon, coho salmon, chum salmon)

Whiz Banger Leech, chartreuse/fluorescent red
(chinook salmon, coho salmon, chum salmon)

Winter Expression Spey, purple
(steelhead)

Winter Punch Spey
(steelhead)

Winter's Hope
(steelhead, pink salmon)

Ames' Hot Lips
(coho salmon)

Apex Skater, purple
(steelhead)

Bunny Slider, gray
(rainbow trout, northern pike)

H_2O 'Wog, pink
(coho salmon)

Hammerhead 'Wog, chartreuse
(coho salmon)

LMP Popper, pink
(chinook salmon, coho salmon)

LMP Popper, green
(chinook salmon)

Puget Slider, blue
(saltwater coho)

Puget Slider, chartreuse
(saltwater coho)

Techno 'Wog, pink
(coho salmon)

Ultimate 'Wog, pink
(coho salmon, chum salmon)

eggs to flesh

Battle Creek (rainbow trout, cutthroat trout,
Dolly Varden, Arctic char)

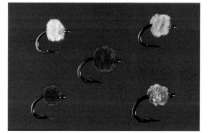

Chenille Eggs
(rainbow trout, Dolly Varden, cutthroat trout)

Flesh Flies
(rainbow trout, Dolly Varden, Arctic char)

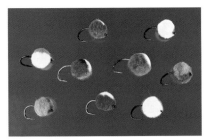

Jerry Garcia Glo-Bugs
(steelhead)

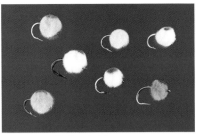

Glo-Bugs (rainbow trout,
Dolly Varden, Arctic char, grayling, cutthroat trout)

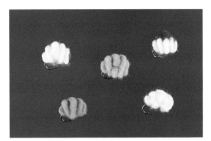

Micro Spawn
(steelhead)

forage fish and baitfish

Alaskan Fry
(rainbow trout, lake trout)

Alevins
(rainbow trout, lake trout, Dolly Varden)

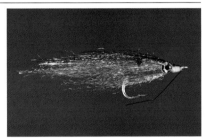

ALF Minnow, gray/olive
(northern pike)

ALF Nursery Schooler, pinhead anchovy
(saltwater chinook, saltwater coho, lake trout)

ALF Stir Fly, anchovy
(saltwater chinook, saltwater coho, lake trout)

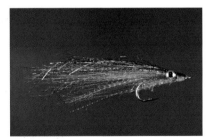

ALF Stir Fly, green
(saltwater chinook, saltwater coho, lake trout)

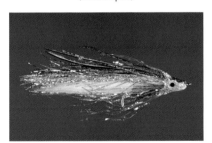

Anchovy
(saltwater chinook, saltwater coho, lake trout)

Articulated Leech, black
(rainbow trout)

Articulated Water Rat, natural brown
(northern pike, rainbow trout)

Baitfish, brown
(lake trout)

Bay Striper Fly, blue/grizzly
(saltwater coho)

Conehead Rabbit String Leech, black
(rainbow trout, lake trout)

Conehead Rabbit String Leech, olive
(rainbow trout, lake trout)

Crafty Shrimp, shrimp orange
(saltwater sockeye salmon)

Crazy Charlie, pink
(sockeye salmon, cutthroat trout)

Dead Coral Charley, tan
(sockeye salmon)

Deceiver, blue/white
(lingcod)

Deep-Eyed Bait Fish, anchovy
(saltwater chinook, saltwater coho)

Deep-Eyed Minnow, olive
(rainbow trout, lake trout)

Del Mar Squid, pink/white
(saltwater chinook, rockfish)

Euphausiid, pearlescent
(saltwater Dolly Varden, saltwater sockeye salmon)

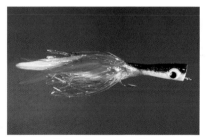

Flashy Fish Salt Popper, blue
(saltwater coho, sheefish)

Flashy Fish Salt Popper, green
(saltwater coho, sheefish)

Flashy Fish Salt Popper, hot pink
(saltwater coho, sheefish)

Furry Crab, tan
(saltwater Dolly Varden, rockfish)

Fuzzy Mullet, gray/white
(lake trout, sheefish)

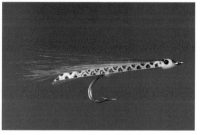

Glass Minnow, blue back (saltwater
Dolly Varden and coho; rainbow and lake trout)

Glass Minnow, blue/green back (saltwater
Dolly Varden and coho, rainbow and lake trout)

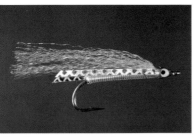

Glass Minnow, green back (saltwater Dolly Varden
and coho, rainbow and lake trout)

Glasschovy, olive/silver
(saltwater coho)

Golf Ball Darter, olive
(rainbow trout, lake trout)

Gotcha, pink
(sockeye salmon, saltwater sockeye)

Gotcha, tan/pearl
(sockeye salmon, saltwater sockeye)

Gummy Minnow (rainbow trout,
saltwater coho, saltwater pink salmon)

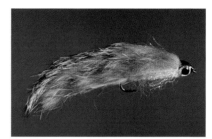

Lake Chubb, white belly
(lake trout)

Lake Chubb, yellow belly
(lake trout)

Livin' Helgrammite, brown
(lake trout, rainbow trout)

Mini Crystal Shrimp (sockeye salmon,
saltwater sockeye, saltwater chum salmon)

Mudpuppy Sculpin, olive
(rainbow trout, lake trout)

Mudpuppy Sculpin, black
(rainbow trout, lake trout)

Pencil Popper, blue holographic
(saltwater coho, saltwater chinook, sheefish)

Ramsey Deceiver, peacock/white
(lingcod, lake trout, chinook, saltwater chinook)

Rattlefish, green/gold
(lake trout, sheefish)

Sand Eel, olive/white (saltwater chum and Dolly Varden, saltwater sockeye salmon)

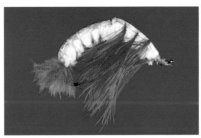

Sand Shrimp, multi (pink salmon, cutthroat trout, saltwater pink, chum, and coho salmon)

Seaducer, brown (lingcod, lake trout, northern pike, sheefish)

Seaducer, orange/grizzly (lingcod, lake trout, northern pike, sheefish)

Serpent Dart, black/chartreuse (rockfish)

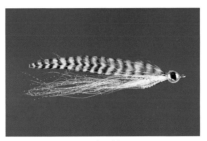

Snooker, blue (rainbow trout, lake trout, sheefish)

Snooker, olive (rainbow trout, lake trout, sheefish)

Streaker Deceiver (lake trout, chinook salmon, saltwater chinook)

The Hoover, chartreuse (rainbow trout, Dolly Varden, lake trout)

The Hoover, pink (rainbow trout, Dolly Varden, lake trout)

Whitlock Hare Sculpin, natural brown (rainbow trout, lake trout)

Whitlock Hare Sculpin, olive (rainbow trout, lake trout)

Wild Bill Deceiver, multi (lingcod, lake trout, saltwater chinook, saltwater coho)

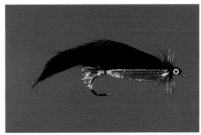

Zonker, black (rainbow trout, lake trout, Dolly Varden)

Polar Fibre Baitfish (rainbow and lake trout, saltwater chinook and coho, sheefish)

Polar Fibre Baitfish (rainbow and lake trout, saltwater chinook and coho, sheefish)

selected bibliography

DUE TO THE BREADTH of this work and the nature of the sources used—virtual mountains of data stretching over decades—only a partial accounting of sources can be offered here. The books and scientific reports listed are those that were most essential for the research that went into writing *Top Water*, though innumerable personal conversations with fly-fishers, guides, ADF&G management biologists, U.S. Fish & Wildlife biologists, and the authors' many friends, acquaintances, and fly-fishing mentors were of incalculable value. Only space precludes listing them here.

Arvey, William D. "Stock Status of Anadromous Dolly Varden in Waters of Alaska's North Slope." Alaska Department of Fish and Game Sport Fish Publications, Fishery Manuscript No. 91-3 (May 1991).

Arvey, William D., and Michael J. Mills. "Sport Harvest of Anadromous Salmon in the Yukon River Drainage, 1977–1991." Alaska Department of Fish and Game Sport Fish Publications, Fishery Data Series No. 93-3 (February 1993).

Atcheson, Dave. *Fishing Alaska's Kenai Peninsula*. Woodstock, VT: The Countryman Press, 2002.

Bates, Joseph D. Jr. *The Art of the Atlantic Salmon Fly*. Boston: David R. Godine, 1987.

Begich, Robert N. "Deep Creek Chinook and Coho Salmon Escapement Studies, 1999." Alaska Department of Fish and Game Sport Fish Publications, Fishery Data Series No. 02-13 (July 2002).

———. "Assessment of the 1995 Return of Steelhead to the Karluk River, Alaska." Alaska Department of Fish and Game Sport Fish Publications, Fishery Data Series No. 97-6 (February 1997).

Begich, Robert N., Leonard J. Schwartz, and Tim Motis. "Sport Effort, Harvest, and Escapement of Coho Salmon in Selected Kodiak Management Area Streams, 1997 and 1998." Alaska Department of Fish and Game Sport Fish Publications, Fishery Data Series No. 00-9 (July 2000).

Behnke, Robert J. *Trout and Salmon of North America*. New York: The Free Press, 2002.

Bendock, Terry, and Marianna Alexandersdottir. "Mortality and Movement Behavior of Hooked-and-Released Chinook Salmon in the Kenai River Recreational Fishery, 1989–1991." Alaska Department of Fish and Game Sport Fish Publications, Fishery Manuscript No. 92-2 (May 1992).

Bernard, David R., and A. L. DeCicco. "Stock Assessment of the Dolly Varden Char of Kotzebue Sound." Alaska Department of Fish and Game Sport Fish Publications, Fishery Data Series No. 19 (December 1987).

Bethe, Michael L., Larry E. Marsh, Patricia Berkhahn, and Sandra Sonnichsen. "Area Management Report for the Recreational Fisheries of the Northern Kenai Peninsula, 1998–1999." Alaska Department of Fish and Game Sport Fish Publications, Fishery Management Report No. 02-01 (March 2002).

Bosch, Daniel, and Debby Burwen. "Estimates of Chinook Salmon Abundance in the Kenai River Using Split-Beam Sonar, 1998." Alaska Department of Fish and Game Sport Fish Publications, Fishery Data Series No. 00-12 (August 2000).

Bosch, Daniel, Lewis Coggins, and R. Eric Minard. "Evaluation of the Thermal Habitat Volume for Lake Trout in Selected Lakes of Southwest Alaska, 1994." Alaska Department of Fish and Game Sport Fish Publications, Fishery Data Series No. 95-26 (November 1995).

Brown, Tricia, rev. *Wild Alaska: The Complete Guide to Parks, Preserves, Wildlife Refuges, and Other Public Lands*. Seattle: The Mountaineers, 1999.

Burr, John. "Fishery Management Report for Sport Fisheries in the Arctic-Yukon-Kuskokwim Management Area, 2000–2001." Alaska Department of Fish and Game Sport Fish Publications, Fishery Management Report No. 02-08 (December 2002).

———. "Middle Kuskokwim Chinook Salmon Angler Survey, 2000." Alaska Department of Fish and Game Sport Fish Publications, Fishery Data Series No. 02-15 (July 2002).

———. "Synopsis and Bibliography of Lake Trout (*Salvelinus namaycush*) in Alaska." Alaska Department of Fish and Game Sport Fish Publications, Fishery Manuscript No. 5 (January 1987).

Clapsadl, Mark. "Age Composition and Spawning Escapement of Chinook Salmon in the Karluk, Ayakulik, and Chignik Rivers, Alaska, 1997 and 1998." Alaska Department of Fish and Game Sport Fish Publications, Fishery Data Series No. 02-02 (March 2002).

Clark, John H., Gordon F. Woods, and Steve Fleischman. "Revised Biological Escapement Goal for the Sockeye Salmon Stock Returning to the East Alsek–Doame River System of Yakutat, Alaska." Alaska Department of Fish and Game Sport Fish Publications, Special Publication No. 03-04 (June 2003).

Coggins, Lewis G. "Compilation of Age, Weight, and Length Statistics for Arctic Grayling Samples Collected in Southwest Alaska, 1964 through 1989." Alaska Department of Fish and Game Sport Fish Publications, Fishery Data Series No. 92-52 (November 1992).

Combs, Trey. *Bluewater Flyfishing*. New York: Lyons & Burford, 1995.

————. *Steelhead Fly Fishing*. New York: The Lyons Press, 1999.

Crawford, Jim. *Salmon to a Fly*. Portland, OR: Frank Amato Publications, 1995.

DeCicco, Alfred L. "Abundance of Dolly Varden Overwintering in the Wulik River, Northwestern Alaska, During 1994/1995." Alaska Department of Fish and Game Sport Fish Publications, Fishery Data Series No. 96-3 (March 1996).

————. "Assessment of Dolly Varden Overwintering in Selected Streams of the Seward Peninsula, Alaska, During 1992." Alaska Department of Fish and Game Sport Fish Publications, Fishery Data Series No. 93-20 (August 1993).

DeCicco, Fred. "Fishery Management Plan for Arctic Grayling Sport Fisheries Along the Nome Road System, 2001–2004." Alaska Department of Fish and Game Sport Fish Publications, Fishery Management Report No. 02-03 (April 2002).

————. "Fishery Management Report for Sport Fisheries in the Northwest Alaska Management Area, 1995–1997." Alaska Department of Fish and Game Sport Fish Publications, Fishery Management Report No. 00-5 (June 2000).

Dunaway, Dan O. "Monitoring the Sport Fisheries of the Aniak River, Alaska, 1996." Alaska Department of Fish and Game Sport Fish Publications, Fishery Management Report No. 97-4 (December 1997).

————. "Surveys of the Chinook and Coho Salmon Sport Fisheries in the Alagnak River, Alaska, 1993." Alaska Department of Fish and Game Sport Fish Publications, Fishery Data Series No. 94-24 (September 1994).

Dunaway, Dan O., and Allen E. Bingham. "Creel Surveys on the Chinook Salmon Sport Fishery on the Lower Nushagak River and Mid-Mulchatna River, Alaska, 1991." Alaska Department of Fish and Game Sport Fish Publications, Fishery Data Series No. 92-16 (June 1992).

————. "Effort, Catch, Harvest, and Escapement Statistics for the Chinook Salmon Sport Fishery in the Lower Togiak River, Alaska, During 1990." Alaska Department of Fish and Game Sport Fish Publications, Fishery Data Series No. 91-10 (June 1991).

Dunaway, Dan O., and Steve J. Fleischman. "Surveys of the Sockeye Salmon Sport Fishery in the Upper Kvichak River, Alaska, 1995." Alaska Department of Fish and Game Sport Fish Publications, Fishery Data Series No. 96-18 (July 1996).

————. "Surveys of the Chinook and Coho Salmon Sport Fisheries in the Kanektok River, Alaska 1994." Alaska Department of Fish and Game Sport Fish Publications, Fishery Data Series No. 95-22 (September 1995).

Dye, Jason. "Surveys of the Chinook Salmon Sport Fisheries of the Muklung and Upper Wood Rivers, Alaska, 2000." Alaska Department of Fish and Game Sport Fish Publications, Fishery Data Series No. 02-27 (December 2002).

Earnhardt, Tom. *Fly Fishing the Tidewaters*. New York: The Lyons Press, 1995.

Ericksen, Randolph P. "Smolt Production and Harvest of Coho Salmon from the Chilkat River, 2000–2001." Alaska Department of Fish and Game Sport Fish Publications, Fishery Data Series No. 02-18 (September 2002).

Evenson, Matthew J., and James W. Savereide. "A Historical Summary of Harvest, Age Composition, and Escapement Data for Copper River Chinook Salmon, 1969–1998." Alaska Department of Fish and Game Sport Fish Publications, Fishery Data Series No. 99-27 (October 1999).

Evenson, Matthew J., and Klaus G. Wuttig. "Inriver Abundance, Spawning Distribution, and Migratory Timing of Copper River Chinook Salmon in 1999." Alaska Department of Fish and Game Sport Fish Publications, Fishery Data Series No. 00-32 (November 2000).

Falkus, Hugh. *Salmon Fishing*. London: H. F. & G. Witherby Ltd., 1986.

Fish, James T. "Radio-Telemetry Studies of Arctic Grayling in the Jim River (Dalton Highway) During 1997–1998." Alaska Department of Fish and Game Sport Fish Publications, Fishery Manuscript Report No. 98-4 (December 1998).

Fish, James T., and Stafford M. Roach. "Evaluation of the Arctic Grayling Stock in the Gulkana River, 1998." Alaska Department of Fish and Game Sport Fish Publications, Fishery Data Series No. 99-28 (October 1999).

Freeman, Glenn M. "Smolt Production and Adult Harvest of Coho Salmon from the Naha River, 1998–2000." Alaska Department of Fish and Game Sport Fish Publications, Fishery Data Series No. 03-07 (May 2003).

Hafele, Rick, and Scott Roederer, rev. *An Angler's Guide to Aquatic Insects and Their Imitations for All North America*. Boulder, CO: Johnson Printing, 1995.

Hubartt, Dennis J., and Paul D. Kissner. "A Study of Chinook Salmon in Southeast Alaska." Alaska Department of Fish and Game Sport Fish Publications, Fishery Data Series No. 32 (June 1987).

Hughes, Dave. *Reading the Water*. Mechanicsburg, PA: Stackpole Books, 1988.

————. *Trout Flies: A Tier's Reference*. Mechanicsburg, PA: Stackpole Books, 1999.

Jaenicke, Michael J., and Ronald C. Squibb. "Survey of the Sport Fishery at Ugashik Narrows, 1998." Alaska Department of Fish and Game Sport Fish Publications, Fishery Data Series No. 00-11 (August 2000).

Jettmar, Karen, rev. *The Alaska River Guide*. Portland, OR: Alaska Northwest Books, 2002.

Kaufmann, Randall. *Lake Fishing with a Fly*. Portland, OR: Frank Amato Publications, 1984.

Lafferty, Robert. "Summary of Escapement Index Counts of Chinook Salmon in the Northern Cook Inlet Management Area, 1958–1996." Alaska Department of Fish and Game Sport Fish Publications, Fishery Data Series No. 97-8 (March 1997).

Larson, Larry L. "Lower Kenai Peninsula Dolly Varden Studies During 1995." Alaska Department of Fish and Game Sport Fish Publications, Fishery Data Series No. 97-2 (February 1997).

Limeres, René, and Gunnar Pedersen. *Alaska Fishing*. Petaluma, CA: Foghorn Press, 1997.

Linsenman, Bob, and Kelly Galloup. *Modern Streamers for Trophy Trout*. Woodstock, VT: The Countryman Press, 1999.

McMillan, Bill. *Dry Line Steelhead*. Portland, OR: Frank Amato Publications, 1984.

McPherson, Scott A., David R. Bernard, and John H. Clark. "Optimal Production of Chinook Salmon from the Taku River." Alaska Department of Fish and Game Sport Fish Publications, Fishery Manuscript No. 00-2 (May 2000).

McPherson, Scott, David Bernard, John H. Clark, Keith Pahlke, Edgar Jones, John Der Hovanisian, Jan Weller, and Randy Ericksen. "Stock Status and Escapement Goals for Chinook Salmon Stocks in Southeast Alaska." Alaska Department of Fish and Game Sport Fish Publications, Special Publication 03-01 (February 2003).

Meyer, Deke. *Advanced Fly Fishing for Steelhead*. Portland, OR: Frank Amato Publications, 1992.

Minard, R. Eric, and Dan O. Dunaway. "Compilation of Age, Weight, and Length Statistics for Rainbow Trout Samples Collected in Southwest Alaska, 1954 through 1989." Alaska Department of Fish and Game Sport Fish Publications, Fishery Data Series No. 91-62 (November 1991).

Morrow, James E. *The Freshwater Fishes of Alaska*. Anchorage: Alaska Northwest Publishing Company, 1980.

Naughton, George P., and Andrew D. Gryska. "Surveys of the 1998 Coho Salmon and 1999 Chinook Salmon Sport Fisheries in the Lower Kanektok River, Alaska." Alaska Department of Fish and Game Sport Fish Publications, Fishery Data Series No. 00-35 (December 2000).

Newman, Bob. *Flyfishing Structure: The Flyfisher's Guide to Reading and Understanding the Water*. Boulder, CO: Sycamore Islands Books, 1998.

Parker, James F. "Fishery Management Plan for Arctic Grayling in the Delta Clearwater River, 2001–2004." Alaska Department of Fish and Game Sport Fish Publications, Fishery Management Report No. 03-02 (February 2003).

———. "Fishery Management Plan for Arctic Grayling in the Goodpaster River, 2001–2004." Alaska Department of Fish and Game Sport Fish Publications, Fishery Management Report No. 03-03 (February 2003).

Repine, Jim. *Pacific Rim Fly Fishing: The Unrepentant Predator*. Portland, OR: Frank Amato Publications, 1995.

Reynolds, Barry, and John Berryman. *Pike on the Fly*. Boulder, CO: Johnson Printing, 1993.

Ridder, William P. "Abundance, Composition, and Exploitation of Selected Arctic Grayling Spawning Stocks in the Tangle Lakes System, 1991." Alaska Department of Fish and Game Sport Fish Publications, Fishery Data Series No. 92-6 (March 1992).

Route, Anthony, J. *Flies for Alaska*. Boulder, CO: Johnson Printing, 1995.

Schwanke, Craig J. "Abundance and Movement of the Rainbow Trout Spawning Stock in the Upper Naknek River, Alaska." University of Wyoming, Laramie, Department of Zoology and Physiology Master's Thesis (May 2002).

Schwarz, Len, Donn Tracy, and Suzanne Schmidt. "Area Management Report for the Recreational Fisheries of the Kodiak and Alaska Peninsula/Aleutian Islands Regulatory Areas, 1999 and 2000." Alaska Department of Fish and Game Sport Fish Publications, Fishery Management Report No. 02-02 (April 2002).

Scott, Jock. *Greased Line Fishing for Salmon and Steelhead*. Portland, OR: Frank Amato Publishing, 1982.

Shaul, Leon, Scott McPherson, Edgar Jones, and Kent Crabtree. "Stock Status and Escapement Goals for Coho Salmon Stocks in Southeast Alaska." Alaska Department of Fish and Game Sport Fish Publications, Special Publication No. 03-02 (February 2003).

Sweet, Dana E. "Performance of the Chinook Salmon Enhancement Program in Willow Creek, Alaska, Through 1996." Alaska Department of Fish and Game Sport Fish Publications, Fishery Manuscript No. 99-2 (May 1999).

Szarzi, Nicole J., and David R. Bernard. "Evaluation of Lake Trout Stock Status and Abundance in Selected Lakes in the Upper Copper and Upper Susitna Drainages, 1995." Alaska Department of Fish and Game Sport Fish Publications, Fishery Data Series No. 97-5 (February 1997).

Taube, Tom. "Area Management Report for the Recreational Fisheries of the Upper Copper/Upper Susitna River Management Area, 2000–2001." Alaska Department of Fish and Game Sport Fish Publications, Fishery Management Report No. 02-07 (December 2002).

Walker, Robert J., Cynthia Olnes, Kathrin Sundet, Allen L. Howe, and Allen E. Bingham. "Participation, Catch, and Harvest in Alaska Sport Fisheries During 2000." Alaska Department of Fish and Game Sport Fish Publications, Fishery Data Series No. 03-05 (April 2003).

Wulff, Lee. *Trout on a Fly*. New York: Nick Lyons Books, 1986.

Wuttig, Klaus G. "Escapement of Chinook Salmon in the Unalakleet River in 1998." Alaska Department of Fish and Game Sport Fish Publications, Fishery Data Series No. 99-10 (June 1999).

index

a

Adams, 224, 229
Admiralty Island, 25, 89
Afognak Archipelago, 21, 29, 30
Afognak Island, 30, 92, 120, 121
Afognak Lake, 92
Afognak River, 92, 121
Agitator, 272
Agulowak River, 78, 156, 168, 236
Agulukpak River, 168, 236
Akalura Creek, 121
Ahklun Mountains, 63, 194
Akwe River, 54, 116, 258
Alaganik Slough, 90, 115
Alagnak River, 35, 53, 64, 65, 75,
    80, 84, 88, 95, 114, 121, 132,
    133, 134, 139, 147, 156, 191,
    229
    rainbow trout fishing locations,
    169–170
Alaska
    fisheries history, 264–265
    grandeur and magnificence of, 1
    guidebooks, 2
    supply of water and fish, 2
Alaska Mary Ann, 185
Alaska Peninsula, 2, 7, 11, 16, 20, 21,
    53, 59, 65, 68, 79, 87, 88, 95,
    110, 113, 114, 123, 178, 190,
    202, 203, 212, 215, 232, 235
    steelhead trout fishing locations,
    30–31
Alaska Peninsula National Wildlife
    Refuge, 95, 235

Alaska Range, 1, 31, 58, 71, 91, 113,
    117, 170, 172, 180, 189, 237,
    238, 246
Alaskan Fry, 278
Aleutian Islands, 35, 79, 103, 123,
    128, 129, 202, 215
Aleutian Range, 1, 95
Alevin, 278
Alexander Creek, 47, 58, 237
ALF, 40, 106, 185
ALF Minnow, 278
ALF Nursery Schooler, 278
ALF Stir Fly, 278
Alsek River, 53, 54, 79, 80, 116
American Creek, 95, 147, 162
American River, 114, 119, 205
Ames' Hot Lips, 277
Amiloyak Lake, 197
Anaktuvuk Pass, 197
Anaktuvuk River, 179, 197
Anan Creek, 24
Anchor Angler, 26
Anchor Point, 26, 29, 51
Anchor River, 7, 9, 20, 26, 29, 55,
    118, 203, 205, 215
Anchor River Inn, 26
Anchorage, 25, 26, 57, 118, 161, 164,
    167, 170, 171, 172, 192, 195
Anchorage Bowl, 154
Anchovy, 278
Andersen Island, 115
Andreafsky River, 71, 122, 248
Andrew Creek, 24, 53, 54
Angayukaksurak char, 202, 204
Aniak, 62, 170

Aniak Lake, 62
Aniak River, 44, 62, 112, 121, 136,
    170, 212, 251
Aniakchak National Monument and
    Preserve, 95
Anvik River, 238, 248
Apex Skater, 277
Arctic Alaska, 180, 189, 190, 222
Arctic Alaska fishing locations
    Arctic grayling, 232–234
    chinook salmon, 66–67, 68, 70
    lake trout, 196–197
Arctic char (*Salvelinus alpinus*) and
    Dolly Varden (*Salvelinus malva*)
    best locations for, 212–215
    confusion over, 200–201
    fly-fishing for
        in autumn, 206–207
        flies, 206–207, 209
        leaders, 209
        lines, 208–209
        monitoring the hatches, 211
        prospecting, 211–212
        rods, 208
        timing, 207–208
        using rainbow trout techniques,
        209–210
    life histories, 203–206
Arctic char
    complexity and controversial
        nature, 201
    physical characteristics, 201
    size, 204
Dolly Varden
    as an enemy to salmon, 199–200

diet, 206
    northern and southern forms, 202
    physical characteristics, 202–203
    preference for cold waters, 203
    recognized Arctic char subspecies,
        201–202
    size, 205–206
Arctic Coast, 35
Arctic Divide, 197
Arctic grayling (*Thymallus arcticus*)
    best locations for
        Interior Alaska, 238–239
        Northwest and Arctic Alaska,
            232–234
        overview of, 231–232
        Southcentral Alaska, 237–238
        Southwest Alaska, 235–237
    diet, 219
    fly-fishing for
        in autumn, 223
        casting tips, 231
        flies, 224–226, 228–231
        before freeze-up, 223–224
        after ice-out, 222
        after ice-out, 222
        imitating caddisflies, 229–230
        imitating mayflies, 230–231
        imitating midges and mosquitoes,
            228–229
    life expectancy, 220
    life history, 219–221
    physical characteristics, 218–219
    range, 218
    size, 219
    as sport fish, 217–218, 221–222